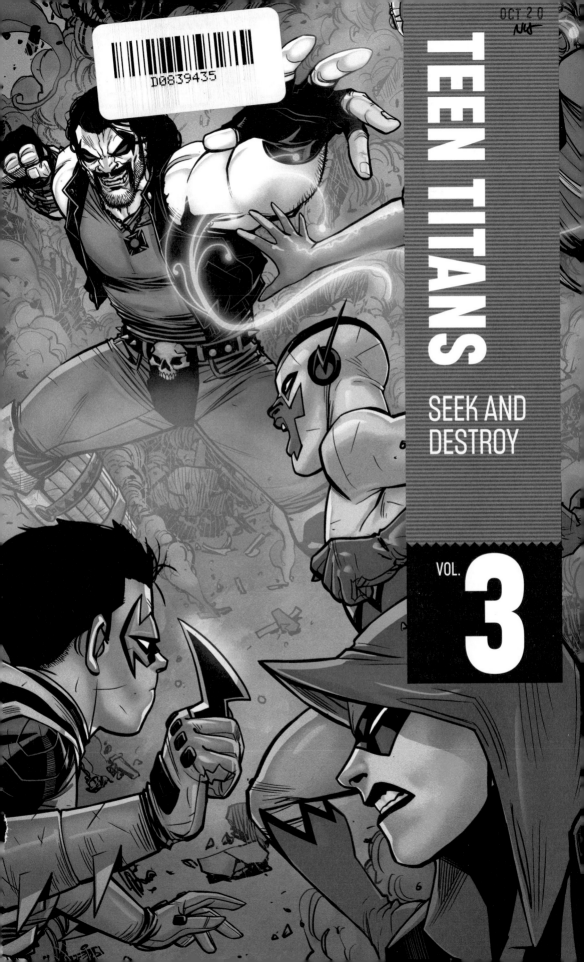

TEEN TITANS

SEEK AND
DESTROY

VOL. 3

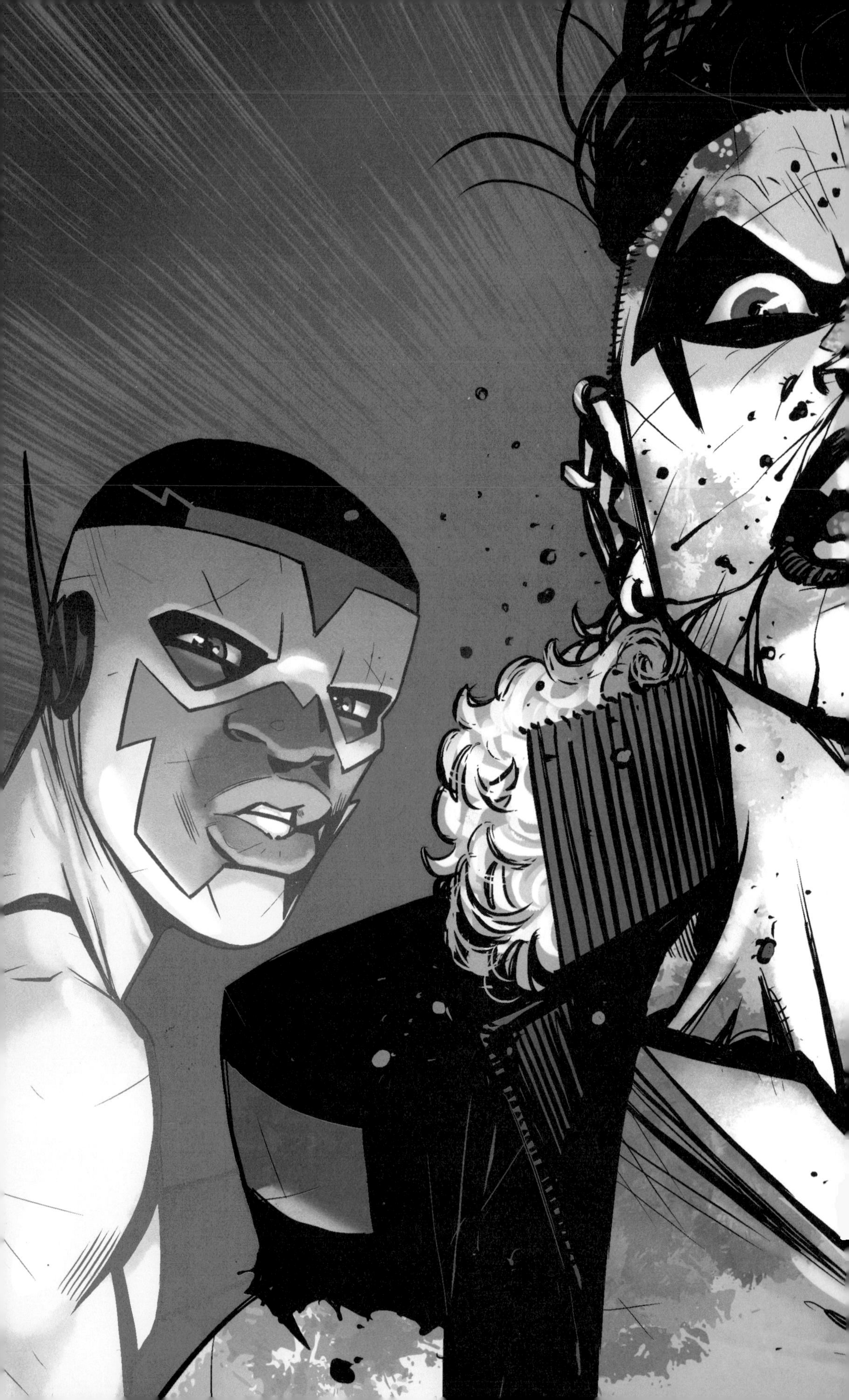

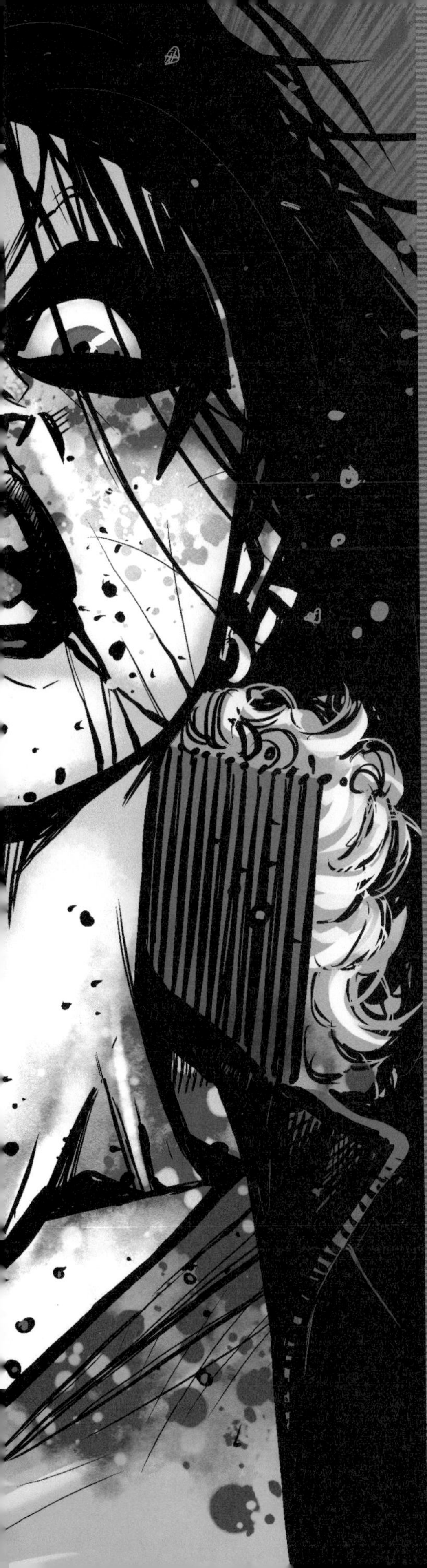

TEEN TITANS

SEEK AND DESTROY

writers

ADAM GLASS

BERNARD CHANG

pencillers

BERNARD CHANG

SEAN CHEN

inkers

BERNARD CHANG

SCOTT HANNA

NORM RAPMUND

colorists

MARCELO MAIOLO

IVAN PLASCENCIA

HI-FI

letterer

ROB LEIGH

collection cover artist

FRANCIS MANAPUL

VOL. 3

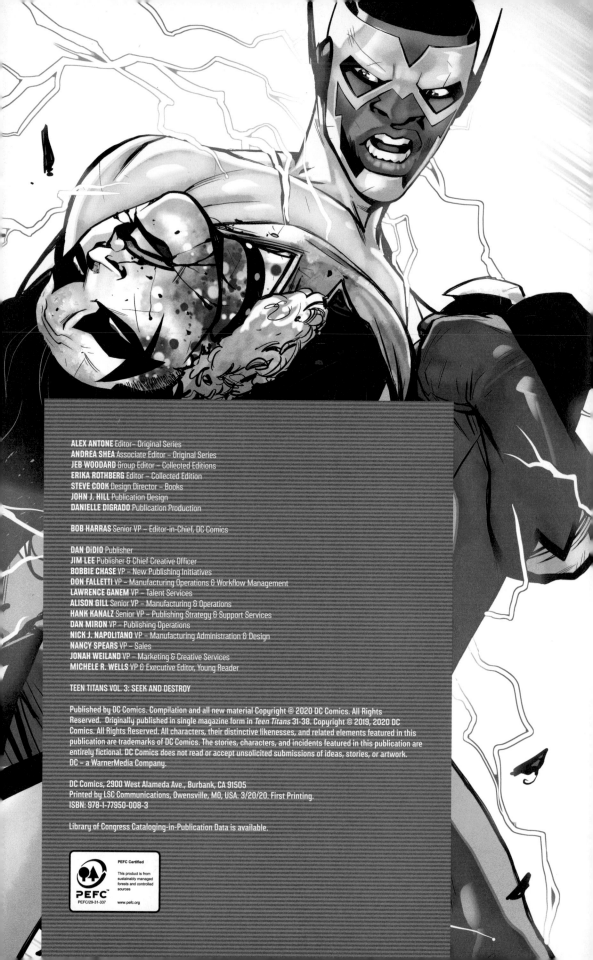

ALEX ANTONE Editor– Original Series
ANDREA SHEA Associate Editor – Original Series
JEB WOODARD Group Editor – Collected Editions
ERIKA ROTHBERG Editor – Collected Edition
STEVE COOK Design Director – Books
JOHN J. HILL Publication Design
DANIELLE DIGRADO Publication Production

BOB HARRAS Senior VP – Editor-in-Chief, DC Comics

DAN DiDIO Publisher
JIM LEE Publisher & Chief Creative Officer
BOBBIE CHASE VP – New Publishing Initiatives
DON FALLETTI VP – Manufacturing Operations & Workflow Management
LAWRENCE GANEM VP – Talent Services
ALISON GILL Senior VP – Manufacturing & Operations
HANK KANALZ Senior VP – Publishing Strategy & Support Services
DAN MIRON VP – Publishing Operations
NICK J. NAPOLITANO VP – Manufacturing Administration & Design
NANCY SPEARS VP – Sales
JONAH WEILAND VP – Marketing & Creative Services
MICHELE R. WELLS VP & Executive Editor, Young Reader

TEEN TITANS VOL. 3: SEEK AND DESTROY

DC Comics, 2900 West Alameda Ave., Burbank, CA 91505
Printed by LSC Communications, Owensville, MO, USA. 3/20/20. First Printing.
ISBN: 978-1-77950-008-3

Library of Congress Cataloging-in-Publication Data is available.

PEFC Certified
This product is from sustainably managed forests and controlled sources
PEFC
PEFC/29-31-337
www.pefc.org

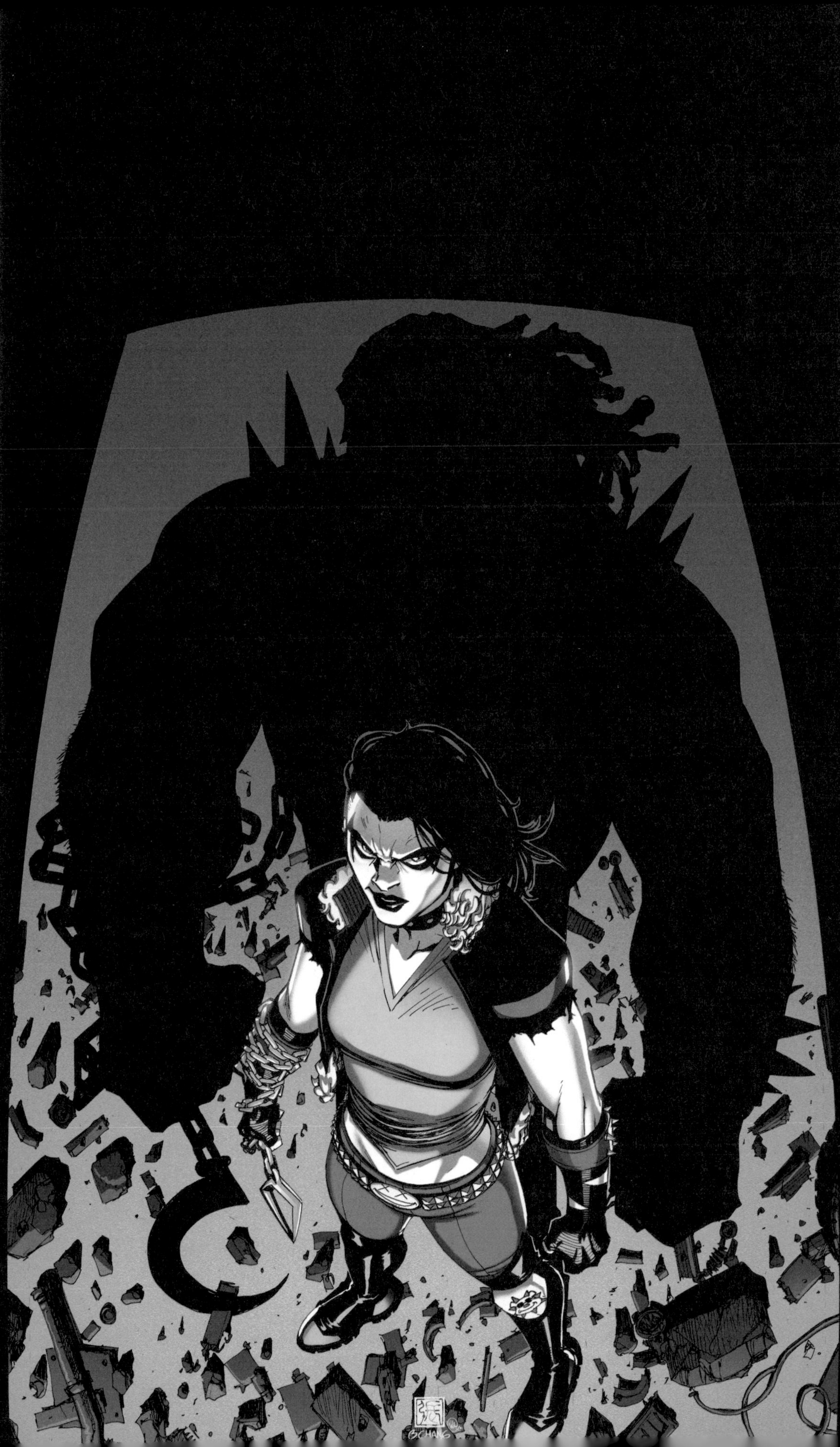

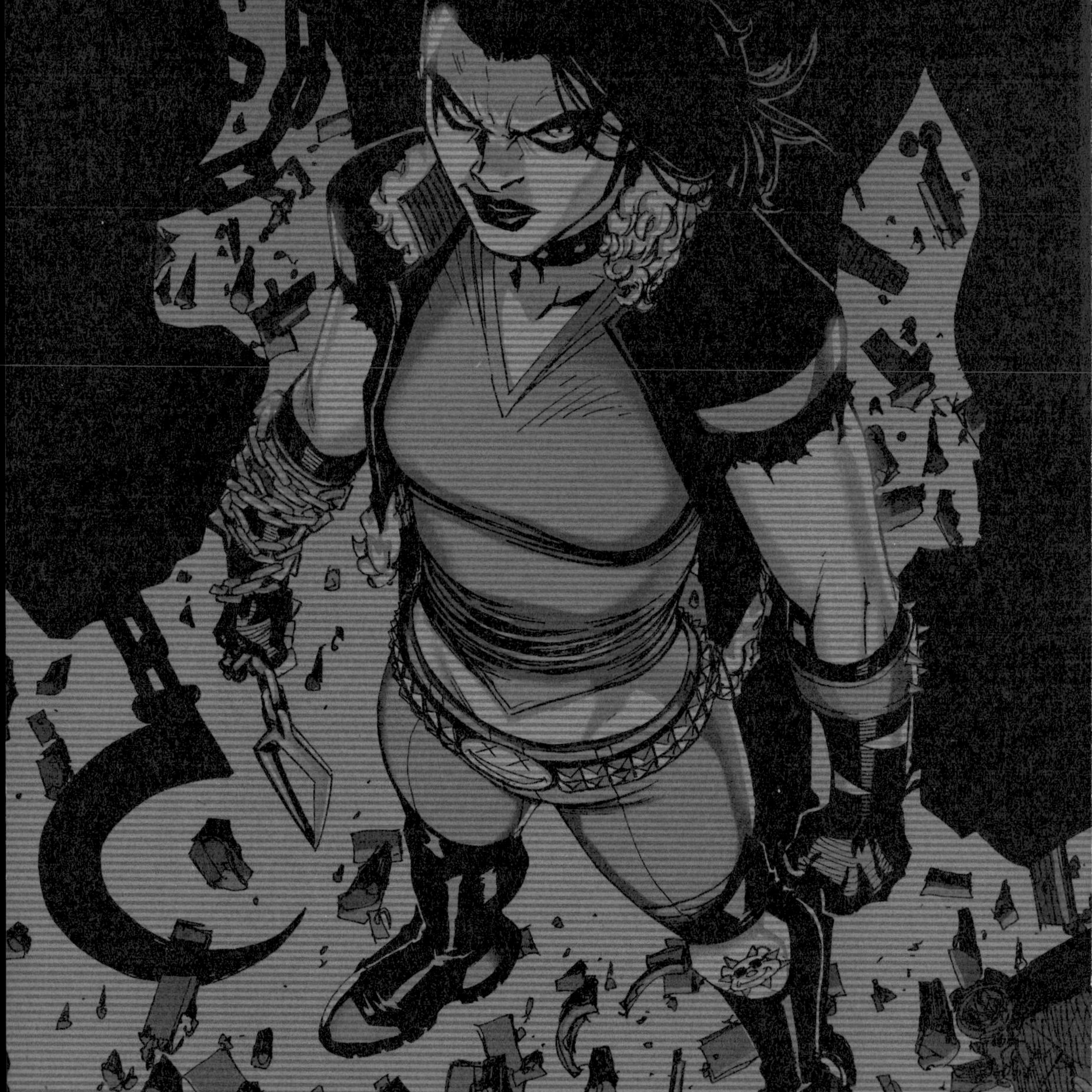

TEEN TITANS
#31

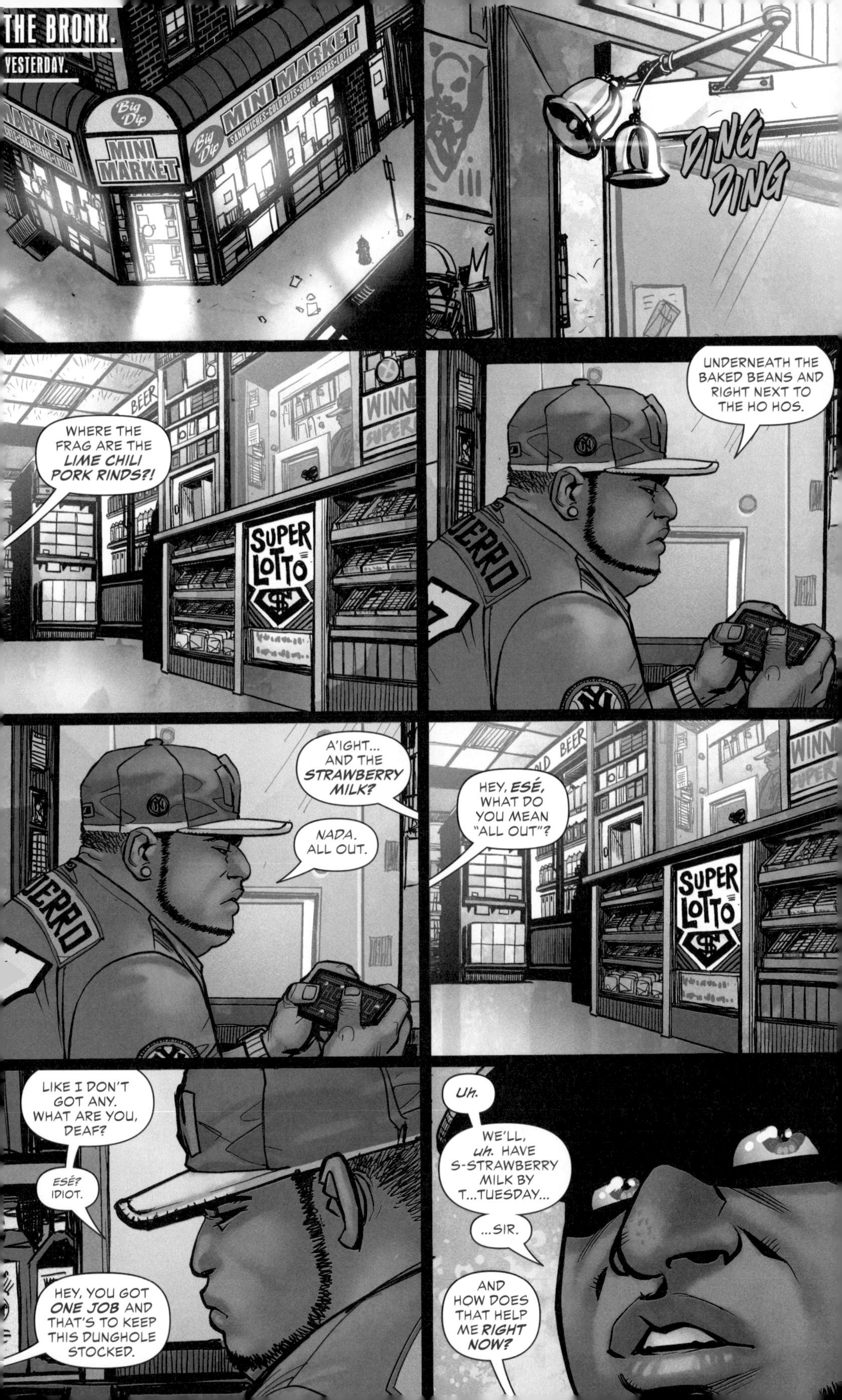
THE BRONX.
YESTERDAY.
BIG DIP MINI MARKET
SANDWICHES • COLD CUTS • SODA • CIGARS • LOTTERY
DING DING
WHERE THE FRAG ARE THE *LIME CHILI PORK RINDS?!*
UNDERNEATH THE BAKED BEANS AND RIGHT NEXT TO THE HO HOS.
SUPER LOTTO
A'IGHT... AND THE *STRAWBERRY MILK?*
NADA. ALL OUT.
HEY, *ESÉ,* WHAT DO YOU MEAN "ALL OUT"?
SUPER LOTTO
LIKE I DON'T GOT ANY. WHAT ARE YOU, DEAF?
ESÉ? IDIOT.
HEY, YOU GOT *ONE JOB* AND THAT'S TO KEEP THIS DUNGHOLE STOCKED.
Uh.
WE'LL, *uh.* HAVE S-STRAWBERRY MILK BY T...TUESDAY...
...SIR.
AND HOW DOES THAT HELP ME *RIGHT NOW?*

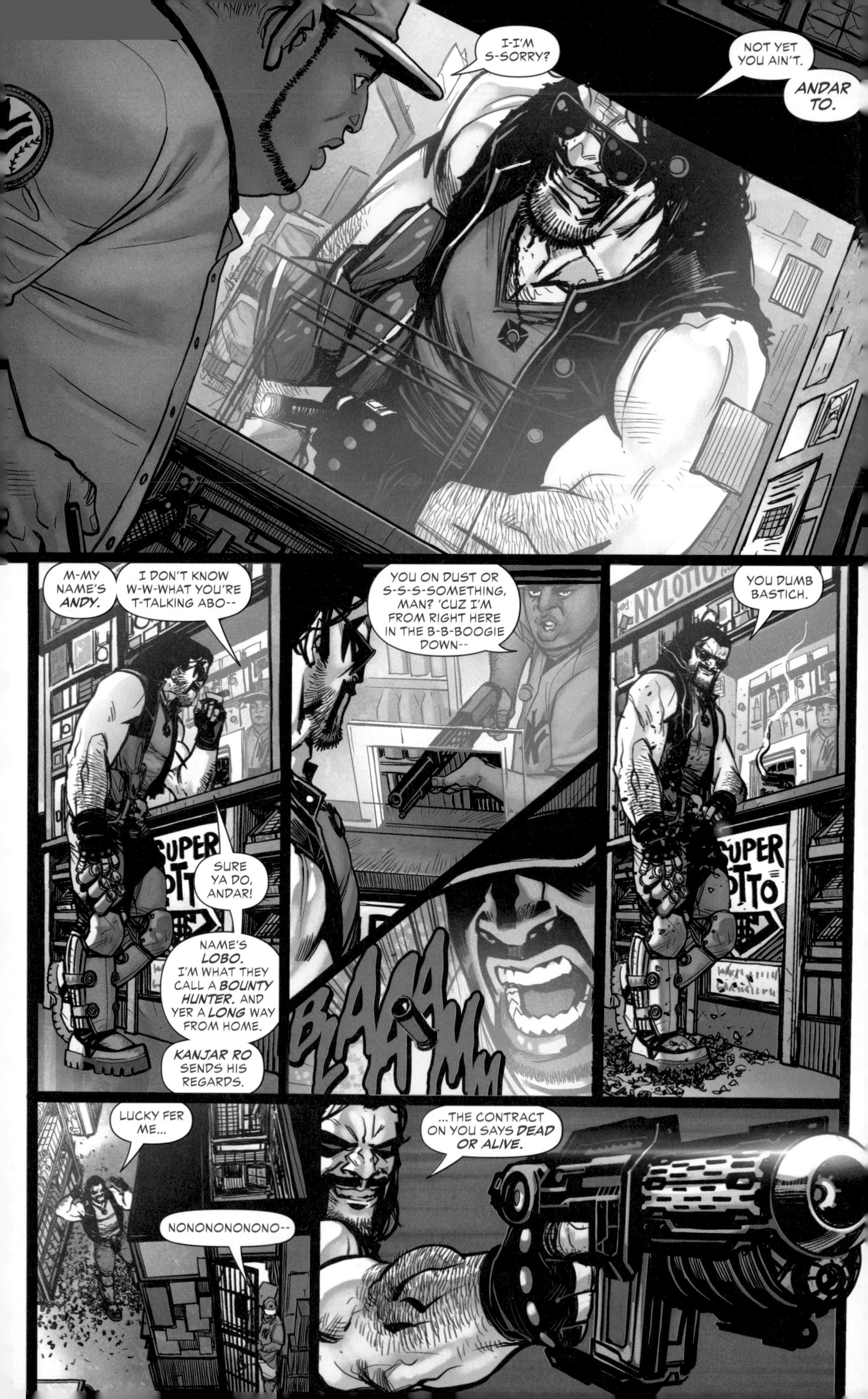
I-I'M S-SORRY?
NOT YET YOU AIN'T.
ANDAR TO.
M-MY NAME'S ANDY.
I DON'T KNOW W-W-WHAT YOU'RE T-TALKING ABO--
SURE YA DO, ANDAR!
NAME'S LOBO. I'M WHAT THEY CALL A BOUNTY HUNTER. AND YER A LONG WAY FROM HOME.
KANJAR RO SENDS HIS REGARDS.
YOU ON DUST OR S-S-S-SOMETHING, MAN? 'CUZ I'M FROM RIGHT HERE IN THE B-B-BOOGIE DOWN--
BLAAAM
YOU DUMB BASTICH.
SUPER LOTTO
LUCKY FER ME...
NONONONONONO--
...THE CONTRACT ON YOU SAYS DEAD OR ALIVE.

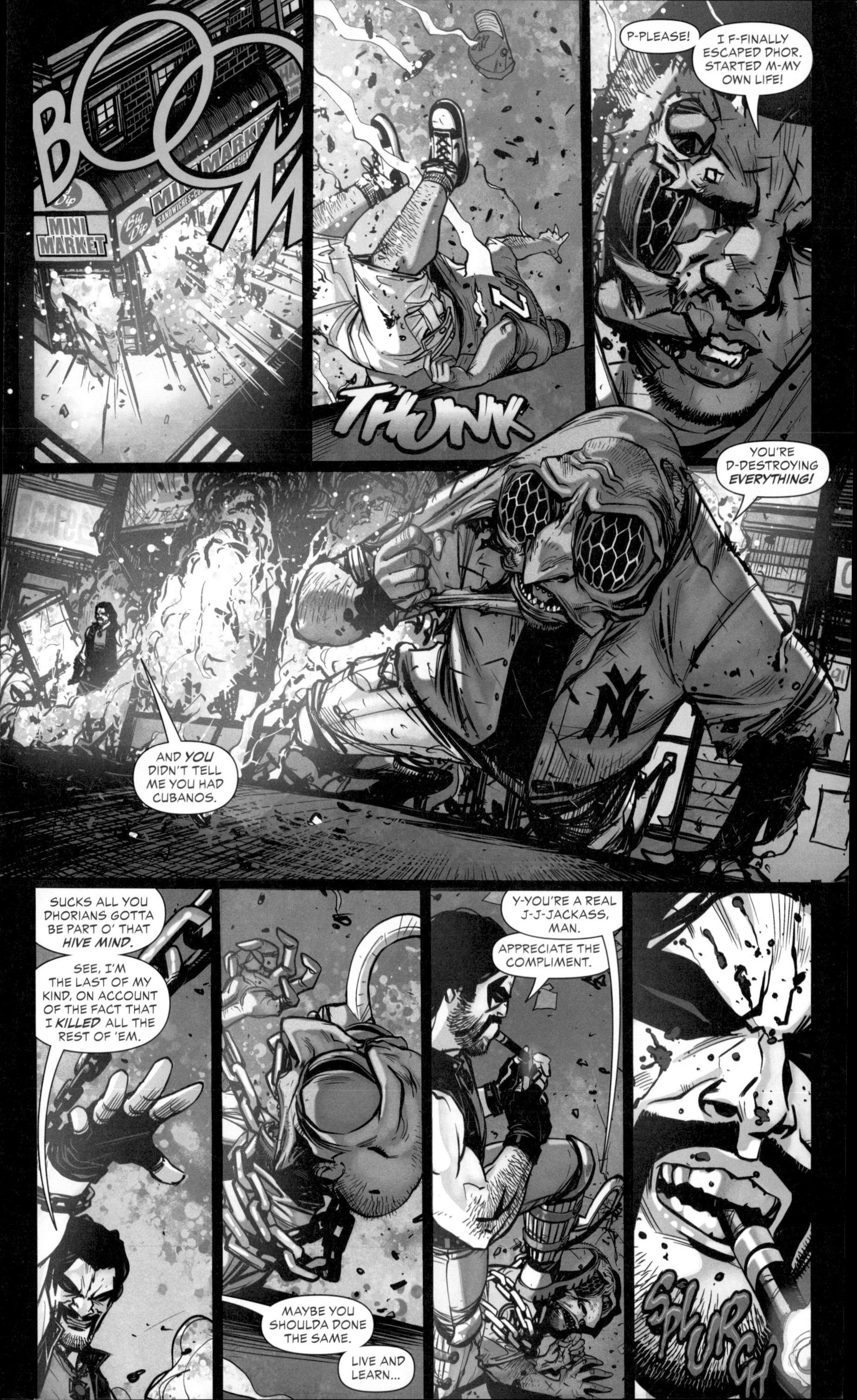
BOOM
MINI MARKET
THUNK
P-PLEASE!
I F-FINALLY ESCAPED DHOR. STARTED M-MY OWN LIFE!
YOU'RE D-DESTROYING *EVERYTHING!*
AND *YOU* DIDN'T TELL ME YOU HAD CUBANOS.
SUCKS ALL YOU DHORIANS GOTTA BE PART O' THAT *HIVE MIND.*
SEE, I'M THE LAST OF MY KIND, ON ACCOUNT OF THE FACT THAT I *KILLED* ALL THE REST OF 'EM.
MAYBE YOU SHOULDA DONE THE SAME.
LIVE AND LEARN...
Y-YOU'RE A REAL J-J-JACKASS, MAN.
APPRECIATE THE COMPLIMENT.
SPLURCH

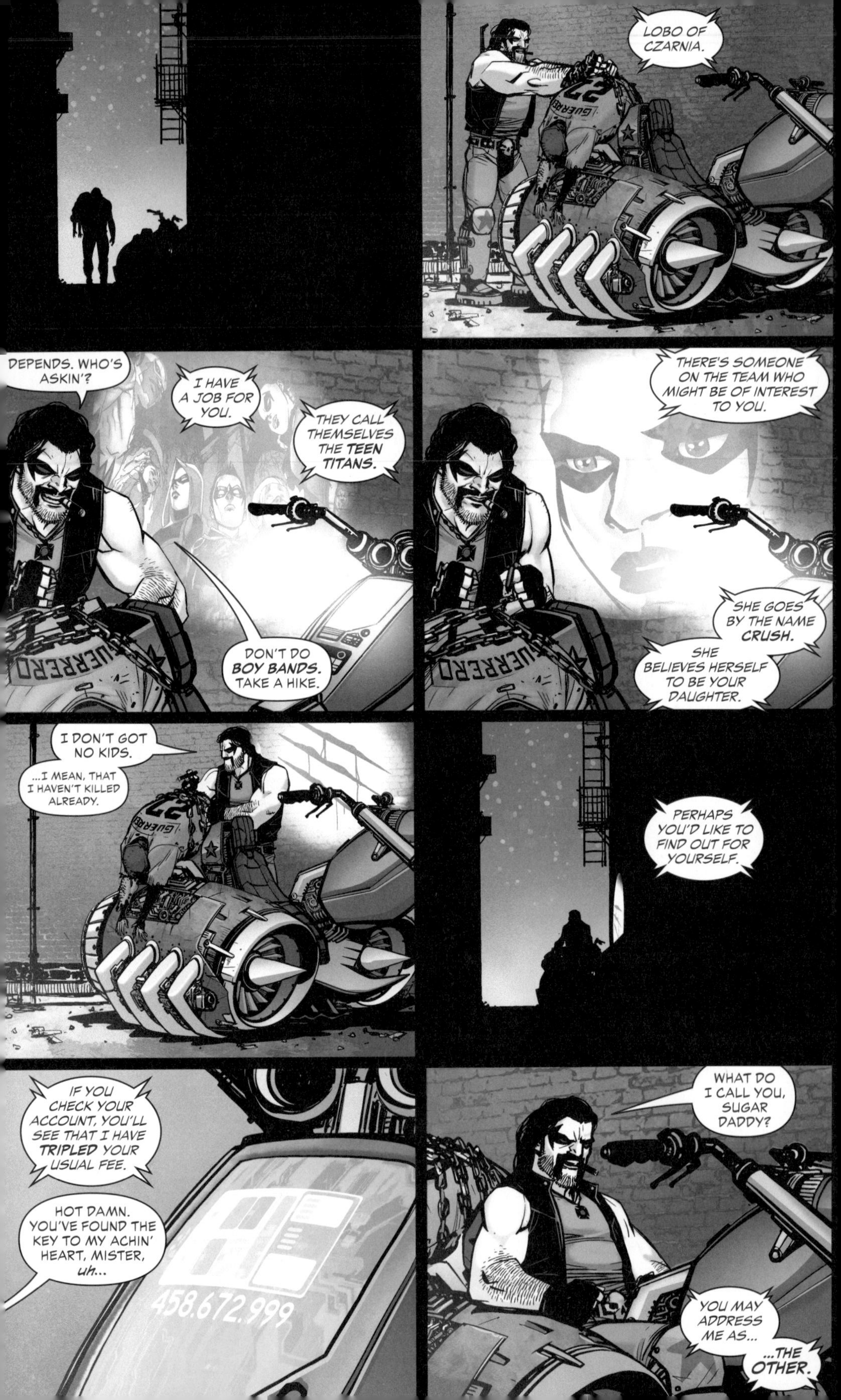

LOBO OF CZARNIA.
DEPENDS. WHO'S ASKIN'?
I HAVE A JOB FOR YOU.
THEY CALL THEMSELVES THE TEEN TITANS.
DON'T DO BOY BANDS. TAKE A HIKE.
GUERRERO
THERE'S SOMEONE ON THE TEAM WHO MIGHT BE OF INTEREST TO YOU.
SHE GOES BY THE NAME CRUSH.
SHE BELIEVES HERSELF TO BE YOUR DAUGHTER.
I DON'T GOT NO KIDS.
...I MEAN, THAT I HAVEN'T KILLED ALREADY.
PERHAPS YOU'D LIKE TO FIND OUT FOR YOURSELF.
IF YOU CHECK YOUR ACCOUNT, YOU'LL SEE THAT I HAVE TRIPLED YOUR USUAL FEE.
HOT DAMN. YOU'VE FOUND THE KEY TO MY ACHIN' HEART, MISTER, uh...
458.672.999
WHAT DO I CALL YOU, SUGAR DADDY?
YOU MAY ADDRESS ME AS...
...THE OTHER.

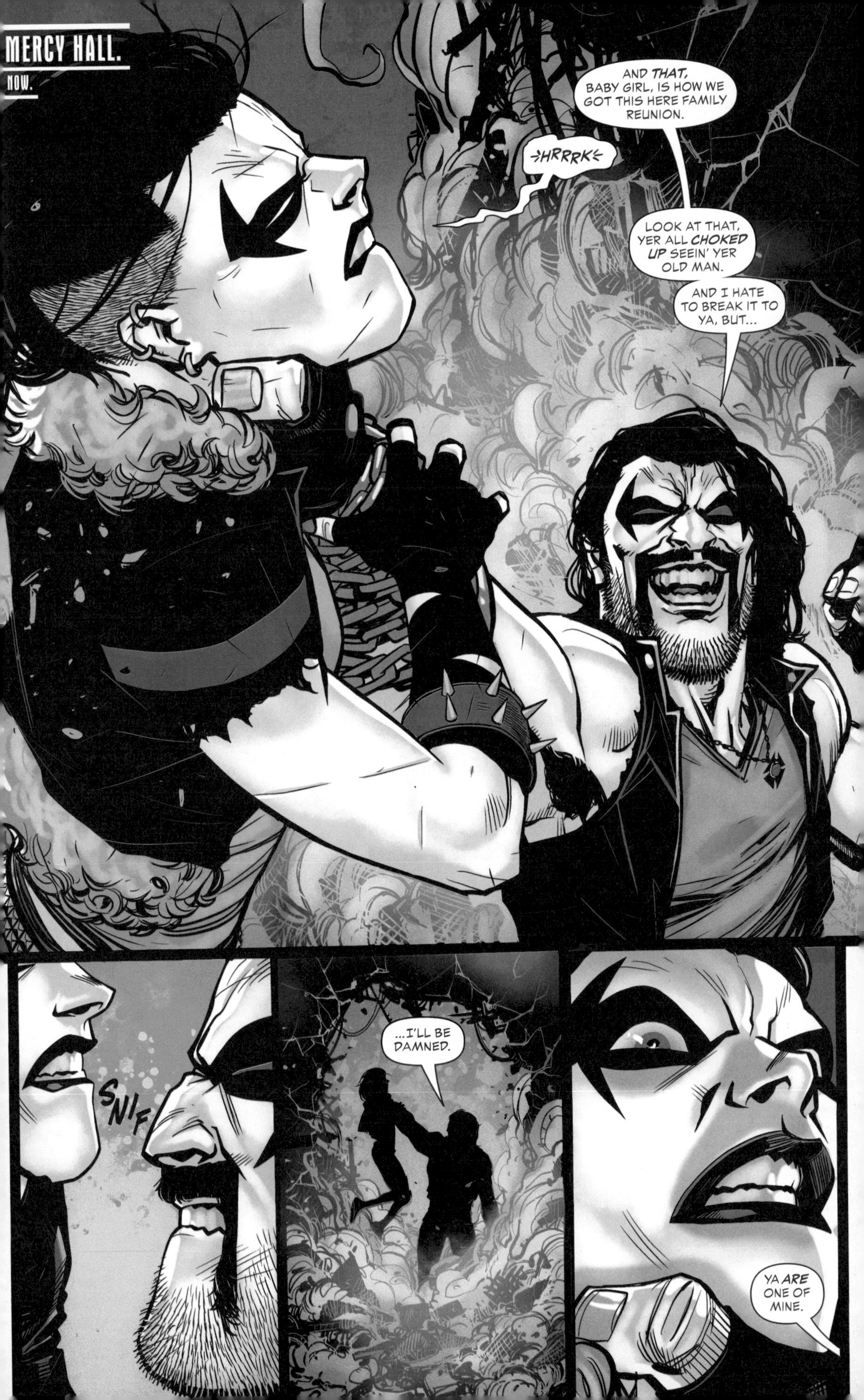
MERCY HALL.
NOW.
AND THAT, BABY GIRL, IS HOW WE GOT THIS HERE FAMILY REUNION.
HRRRK
LOOK AT THAT, YER ALL CHOKED UP SEEIN' YER OLD MAN.
AND I HATE TO BREAK IT TO YA, BUT...
SNIF
...I'LL BE DAMNED.
YA ARE ONE OF MINE.

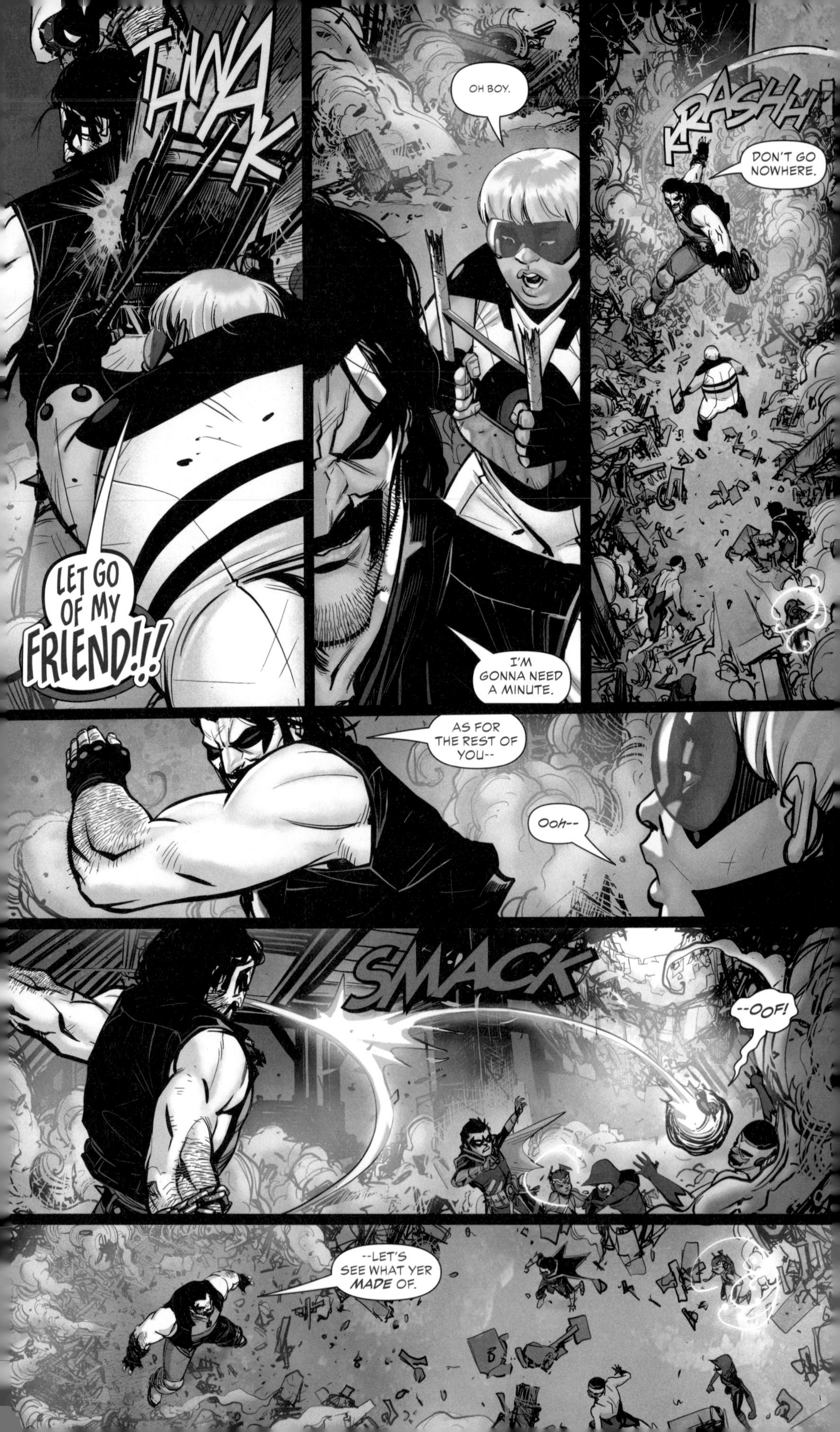
THWAK
LET GO OF MY FRIEND!!!
OH BOY.
I'M GONNA NEED A MINUTE.
KRASHH
DON'T GO NOWHERE.
AS FOR THE REST OF YOU--
Ooh--
SMACK
--OOF!
--LET'S SEE WHAT YER MADE OF.

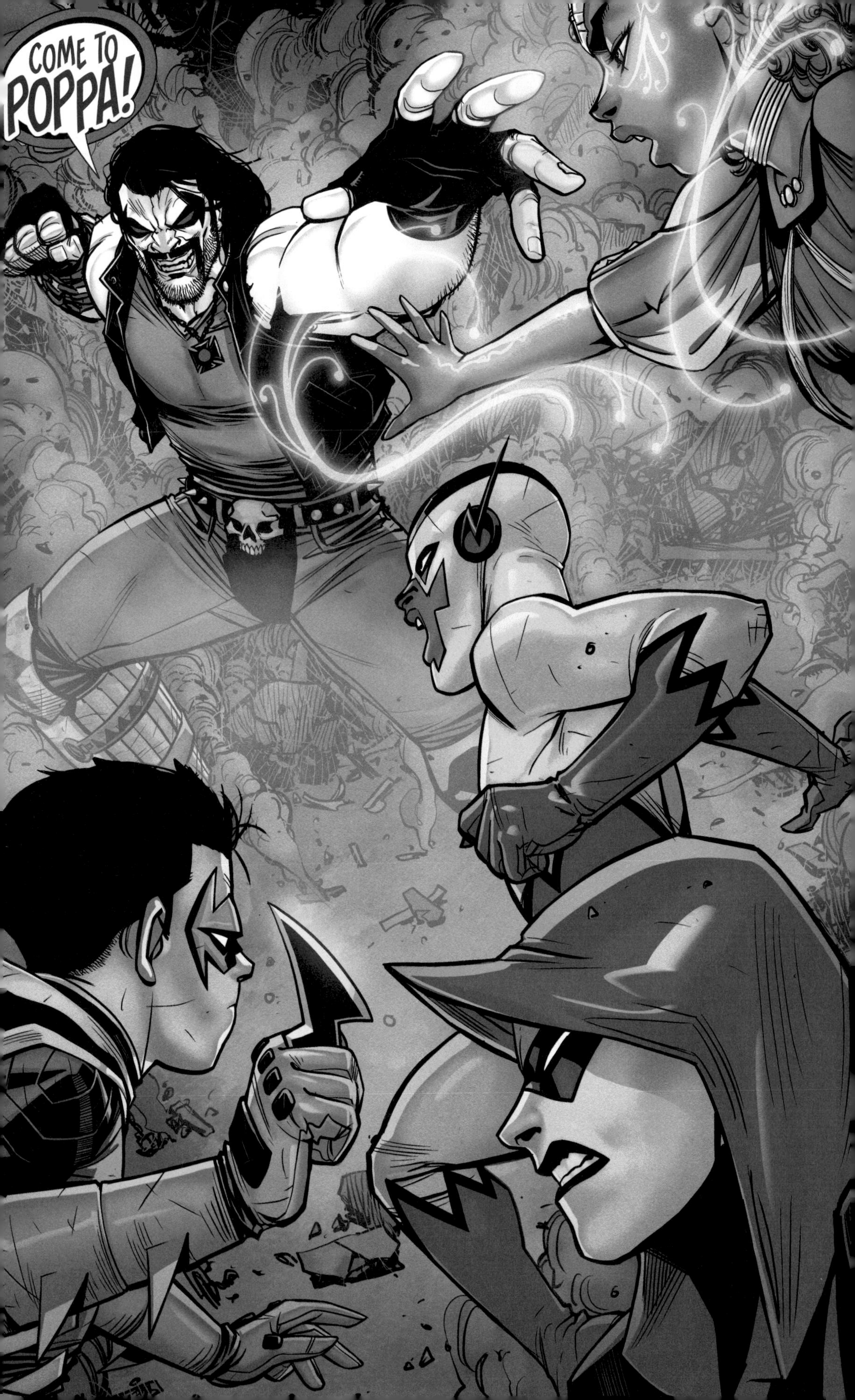
COME TO POPPA!

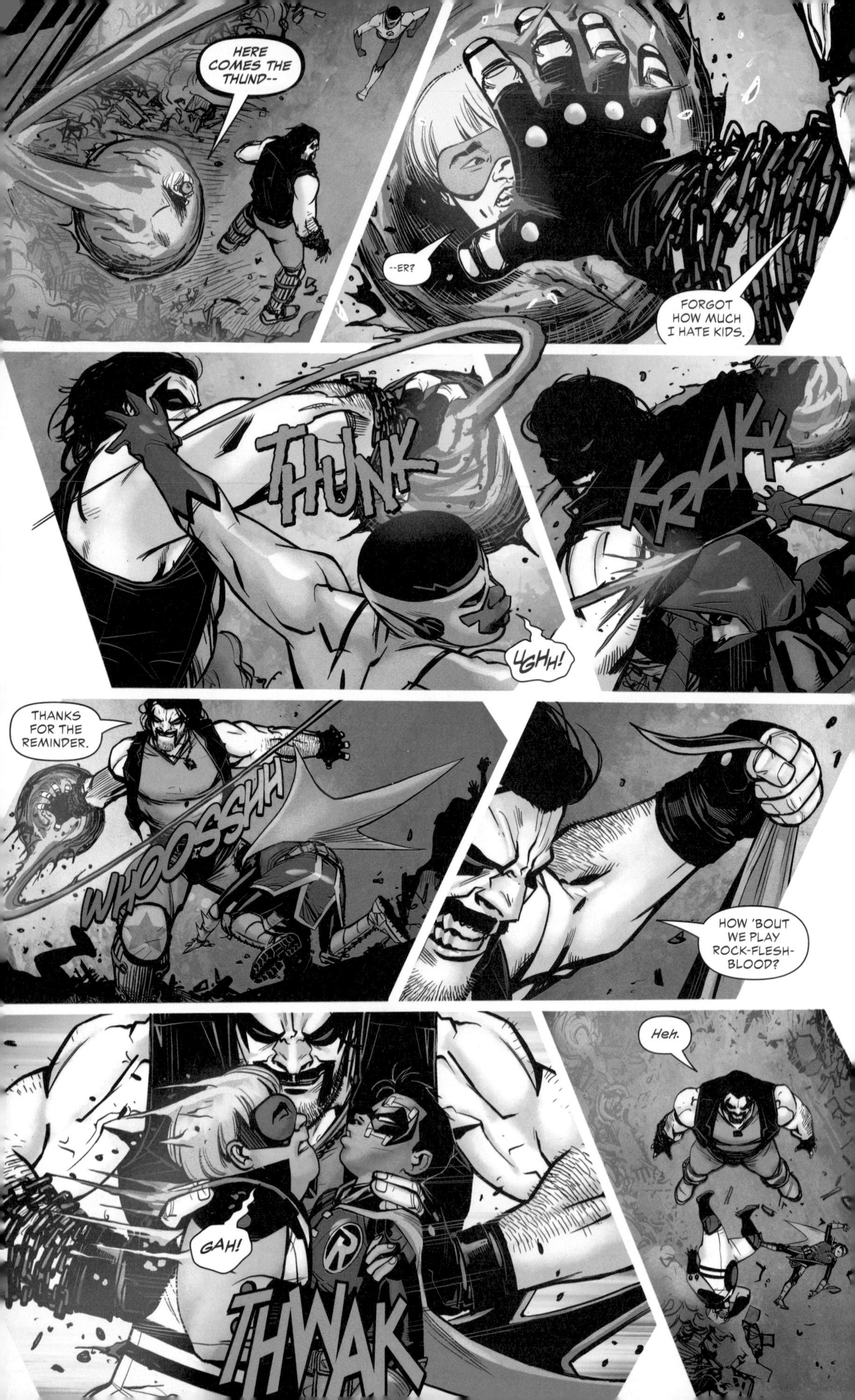
HERE COMES THE THUND--
--ER?
FORGOT HOW MUCH I HATE KIDS.
THUNK
UGHH!
KRAKK
THANKS FOR THE REMINDER.
WHOOSSHH
HOW 'BOUT WE PLAY ROCK-FLESH-BLOOD?
GAH!
THWAK
Heh.

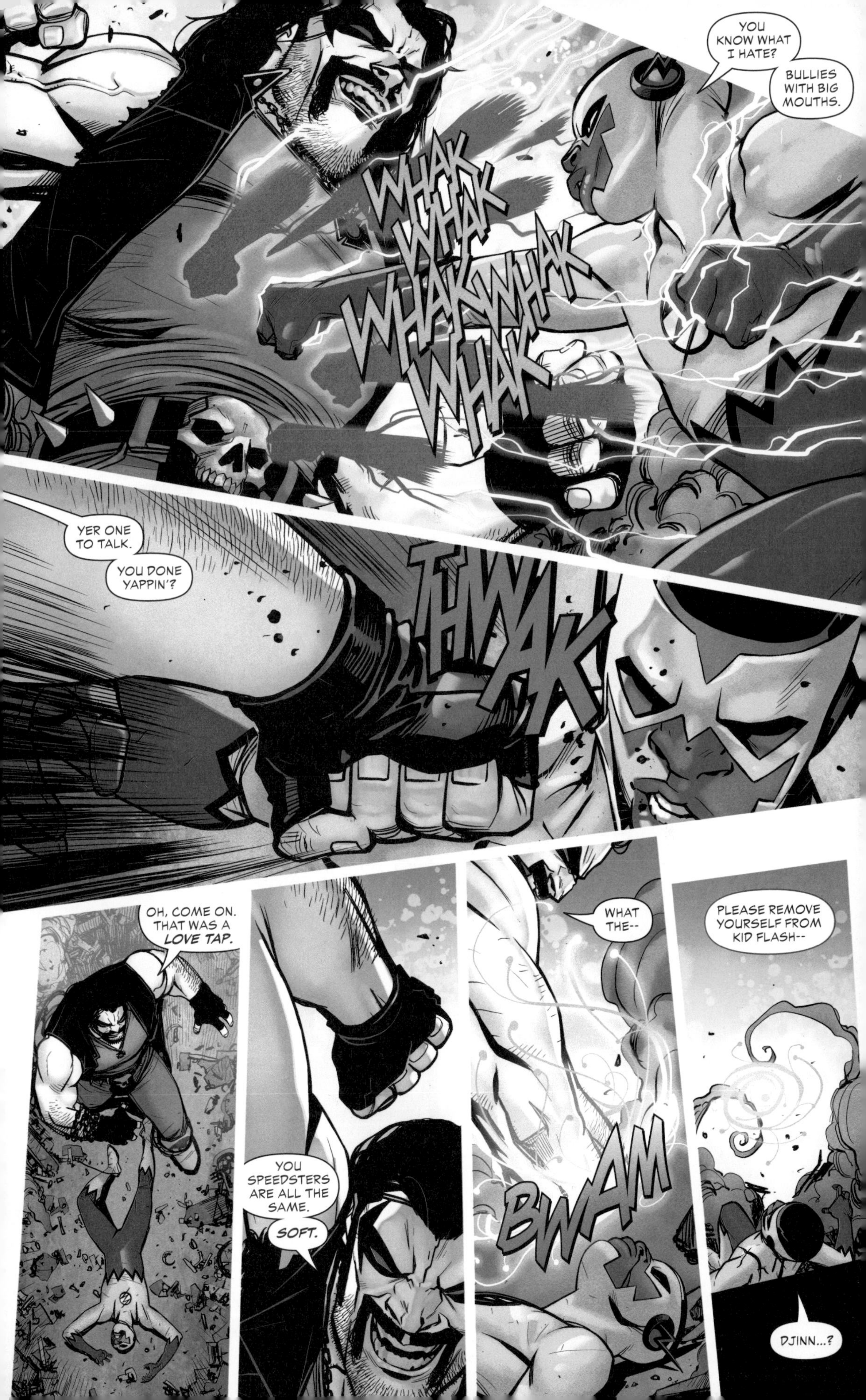
YOU KNOW WHAT I HATE?
BULLIES WITH BIG MOUTHS.
WHAK WHAK WHAK WHAKWHAK WHAK
YER ONE TO TALK.
YOU DONE YAPPIN'?
THWAK
OH, COME ON. THAT WAS A LOVE TAP.
YOU SPEEDSTERS ARE ALL THE SAME.
SOFT.
WHAT THE--
BWAM
PLEASE REMOVE YOURSELF FROM KID FLASH--
DJINN...?

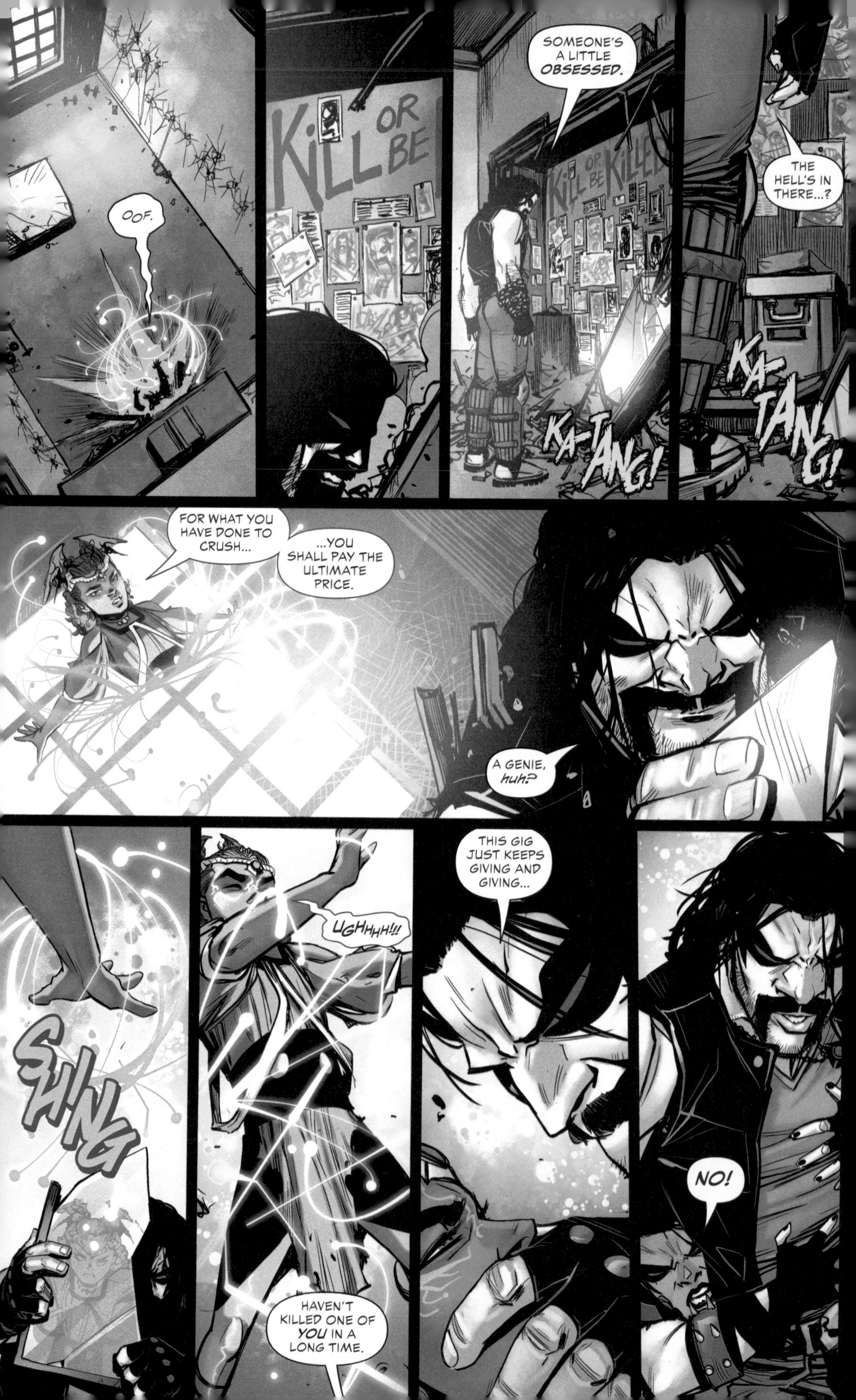

OOF.
KILL OR BE
SOMEONE'S A LITTLE *OBSESSED*.
KILL OR BE KILLED
THE HELL'S IN THERE...?
KA-TANG!
KA-TANG!
FOR WHAT YOU HAVE DONE TO CRUSH...
...YOU SHALL PAY THE ULTIMATE PRICE.
A GENIE, *huh?*
SHING
UGHHHH!!!
HAVEN'T KILLED ONE OF *YOU* IN A LONG TIME.
THIS GIG JUST KEEPS GIVING AND GIVING...
NO!

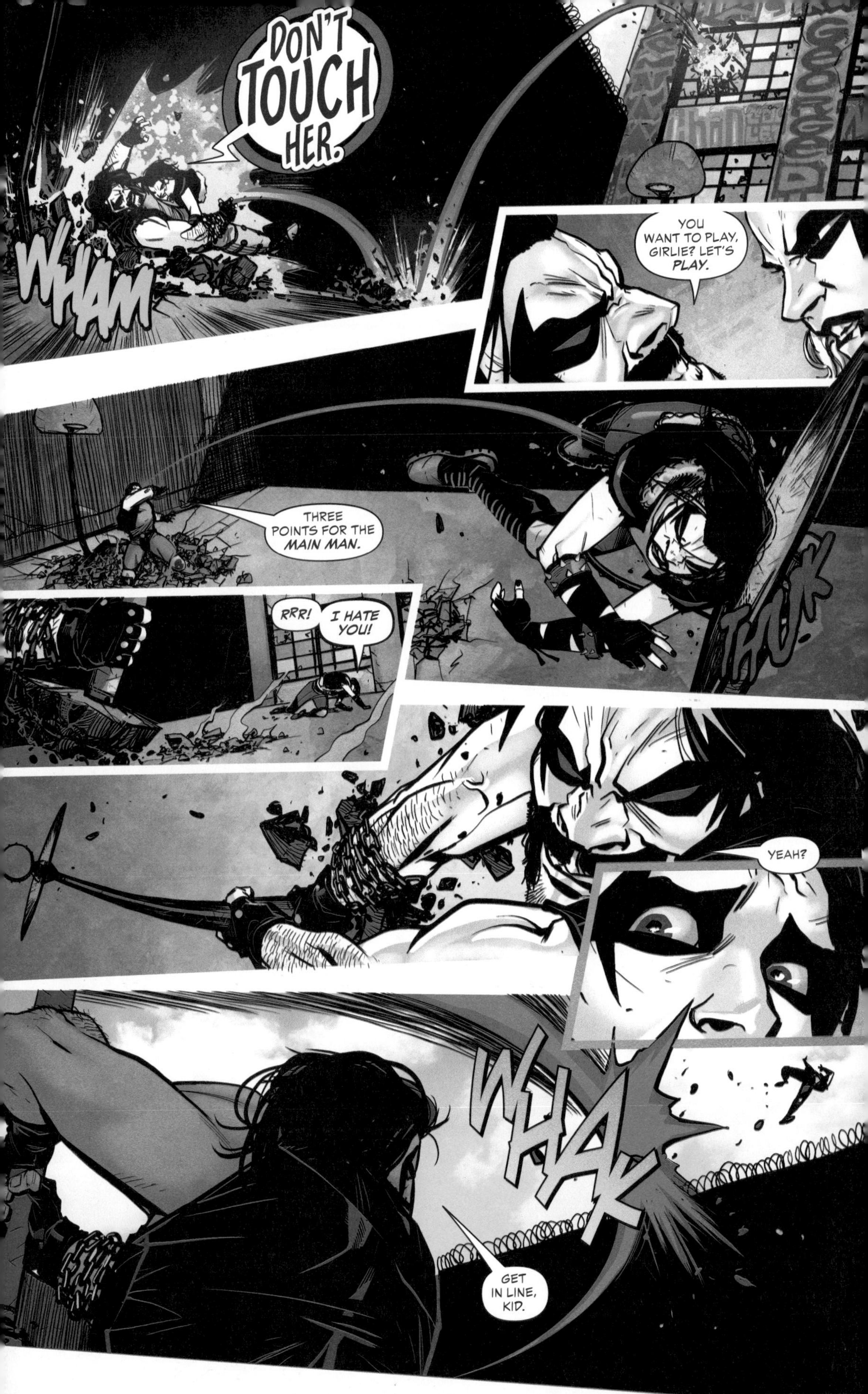
DON'T TOUCH HER.
WHAM
YOU WANT TO PLAY, GIRLIE? LET'S PLAY.
THREE POINTS FOR THE MAIN MAN.
THUK
RRR!
I HATE YOU!
YEAH?
WHAK
GET IN LINE, KID.

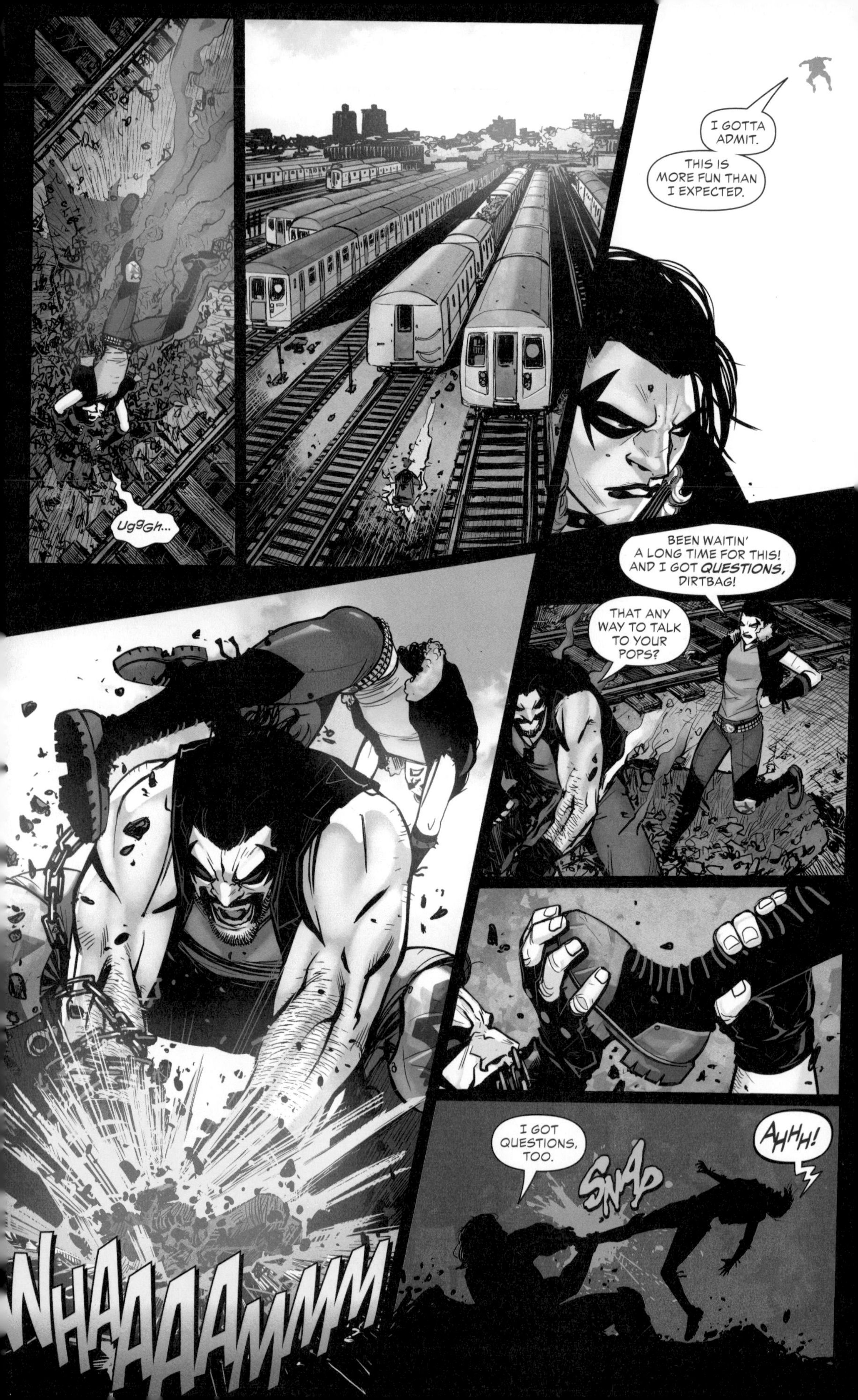
UggGh...
I GOTTA ADMIT.
THIS IS MORE FUN THAN I EXPECTED.
BEEN WAITIN' A LONG TIME FOR THIS! AND I GOT QUESTIONS, DIRTBAG!
THAT ANY WAY TO TALK TO YOUR POPS?
WHAAAAMMM
I GOT QUESTIONS, TOO.
SNAP
AHHH!

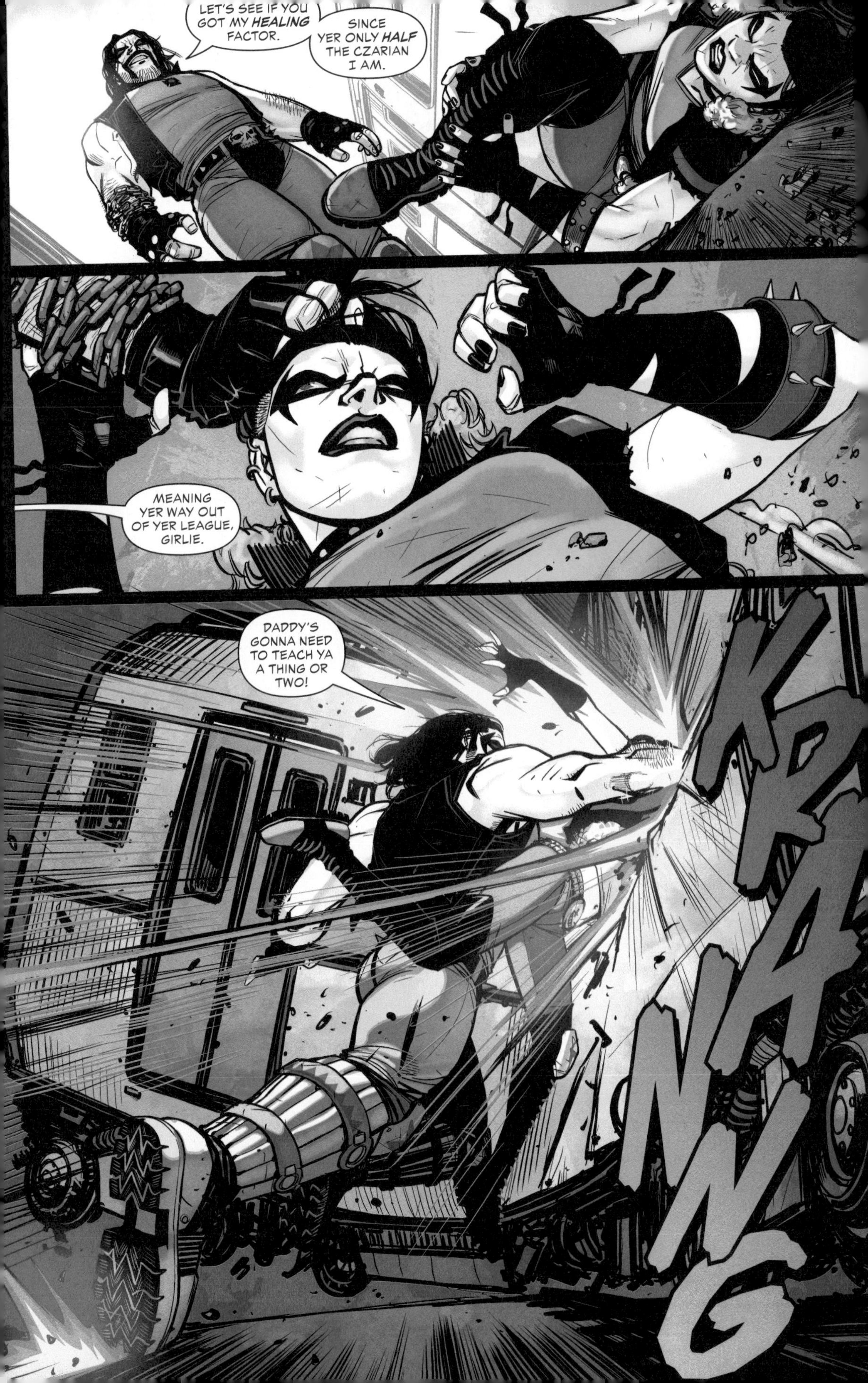
LET'S SEE IF YOU GOT MY HEALING FACTOR.
SINCE YER ONLY HALF THE CZARIAN I AM.
MEANING YER WAY OUT OF YER LEAGUE, GIRLIE.
DADDY'S GONNA NEED TO TEACH YA A THING OR TWO!
KRANNG

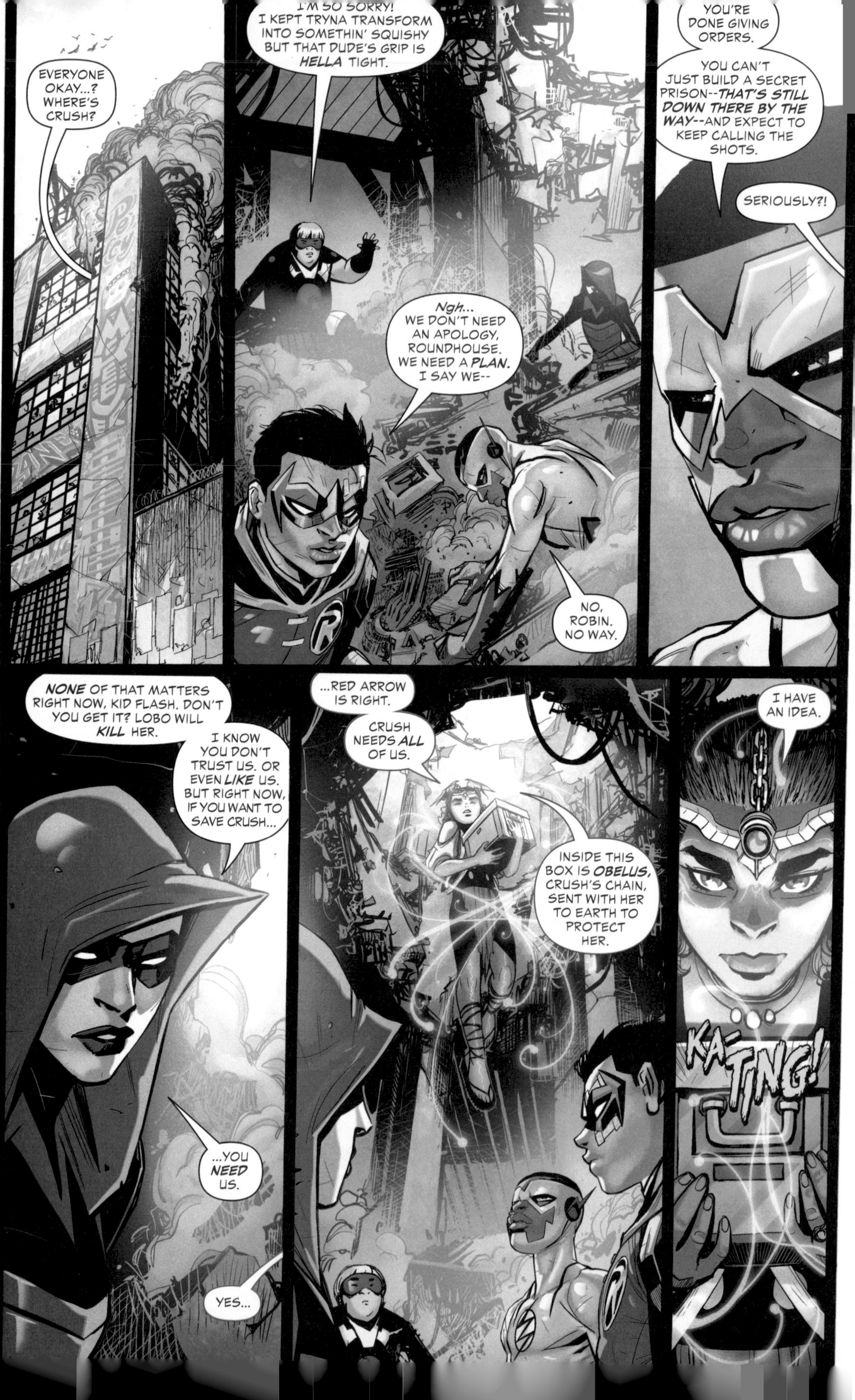
EVERYONE OKAY...? WHERE'S CRUSH?
I'M SO SORRY! I KEPT TRYNA TRANSFORM INTO SOMETHIN' SQUISHY BUT THAT DUDE'S GRIP IS *HELLA* TIGHT.
Ngh... WE DON'T NEED AN APOLOGY, ROUNDHOUSE. WE NEED A *PLAN.* I SAY WE--
NO, ROBIN. NO WAY.
YOU'RE DONE GIVING ORDERS.
YOU CAN'T JUST BUILD A SECRET PRISON--*THAT'S STILL DOWN THERE BY THE WAY*--AND EXPECT TO KEEP CALLING THE SHOTS.
SERIOUSLY?!
NONE OF THAT MATTERS RIGHT NOW, KID FLASH. DON'T YOU GET IT? LOBO WILL *KILL* HER.
I KNOW YOU DON'T TRUST US. OR EVEN *LIKE* US. BUT RIGHT NOW, IF YOU WANT TO SAVE CRUSH...
...YOU *NEED* US.
YES...
...RED ARROW IS RIGHT.
CRUSH NEEDS *ALL* OF US.
INSIDE THIS BOX IS *OBELUS,* CRUSH'S CHAIN, SENT WITH HER TO EARTH TO PROTECT HER.
I HAVE AN IDEA.
KA-TING!

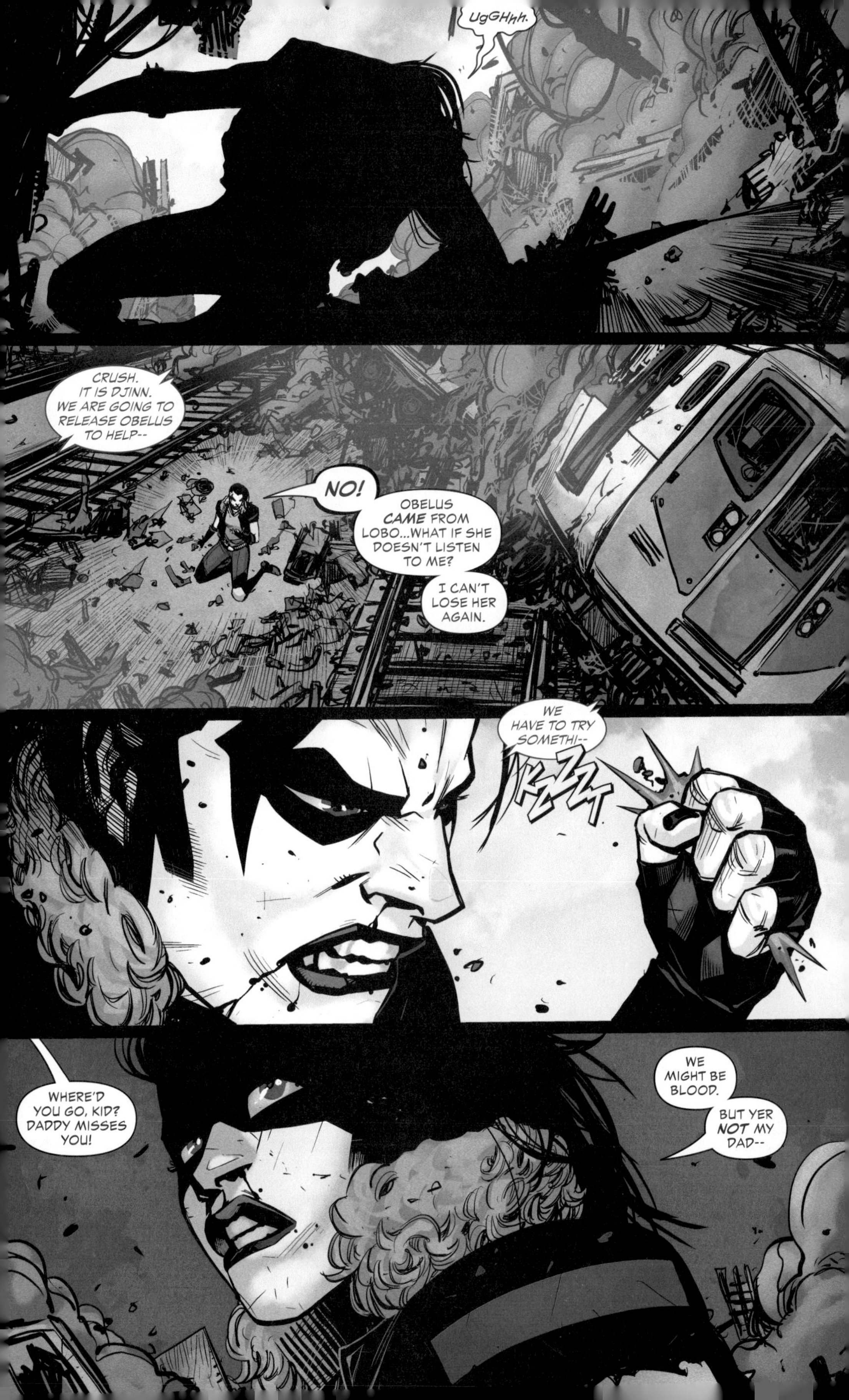
UgGHhh.
CRUSH. IT IS DJINN. WE ARE GOING TO RELEASE OBELUS TO HELP--
NO!
OBELUS CAME FROM LOBO...WHAT IF SHE DOESN'T LISTEN TO ME?
I CAN'T LOSE HER AGAIN.
WE HAVE TO TRY SOMETHI--
KZZZT
WHERE'D YOU GO, KID? DADDY MISSES YOU!
WE MIGHT BE BLOOD.
BUT YER NOT MY DAD--

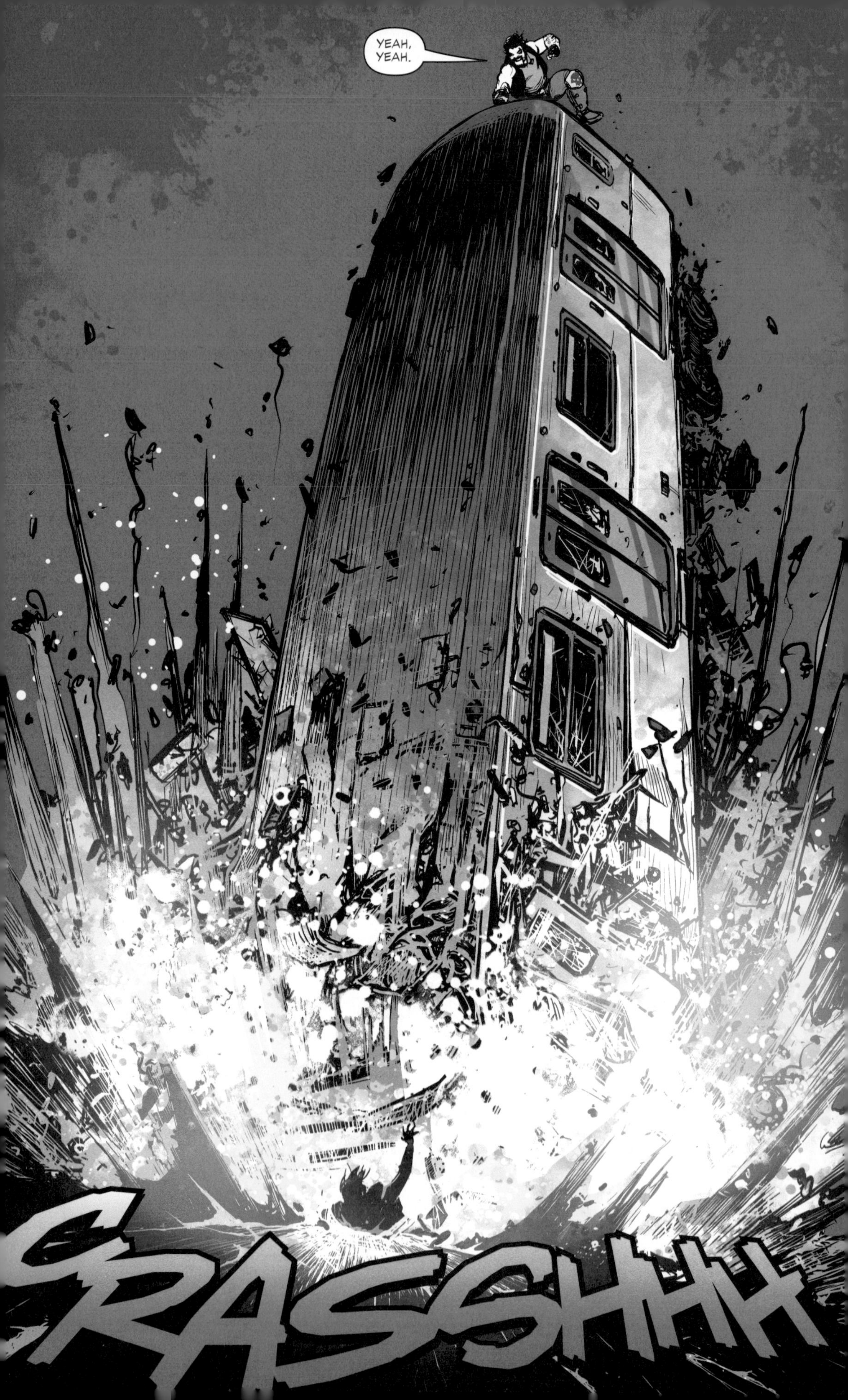
YEAH, YEAH.
CRASSHHK

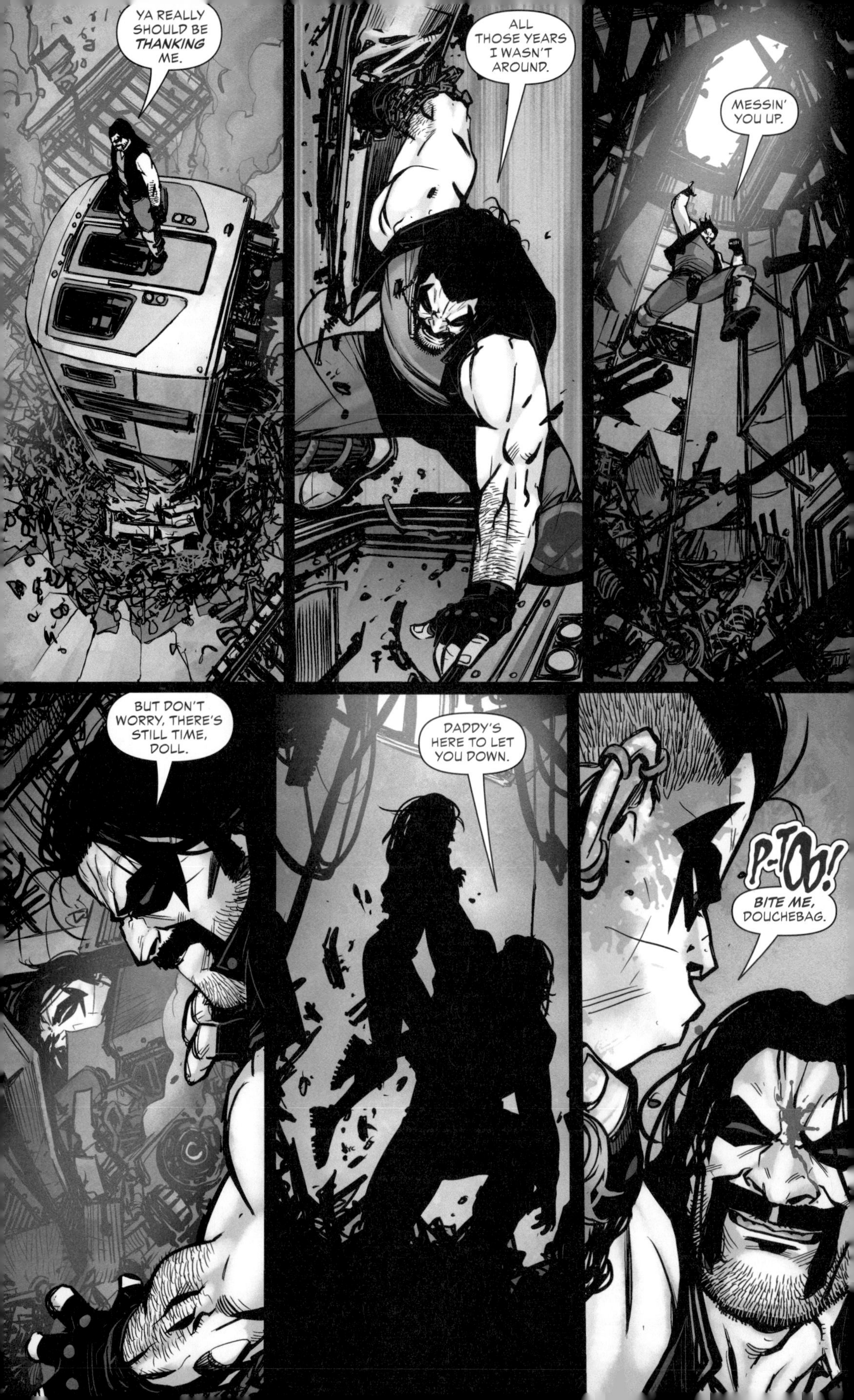
YA REALLY SHOULD BE *THANKING* ME.
ALL THOSE YEARS I WASN'T AROUND.
MESSIN' YOU UP.
BUT DON'T WORRY, THERE'S STILL TIME, DOLL.
DADDY'S HERE TO LET YOU DOWN.
P-TOO!
BITE ME, DOUCHEBAG.

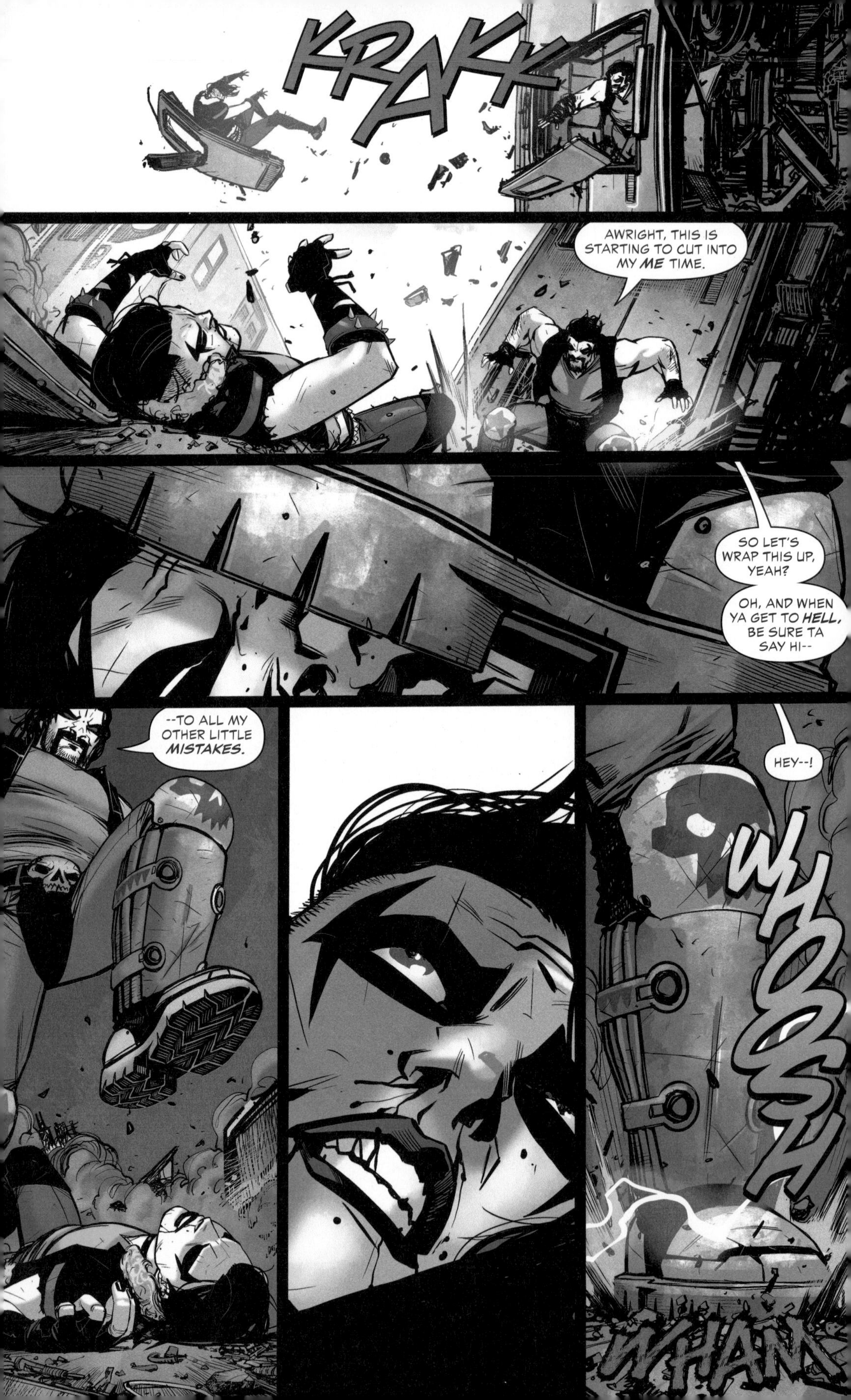
KRAKK
AWRIGHT, THIS IS STARTING TO CUT INTO MY ME TIME.
SO LET'S WRAP THIS UP, YEAH?
OH, AND WHEN YA GET TO HELL, BE SURE TA SAY HI--
--TO ALL MY OTHER LITTLE MISTAKES.
HEY--!
WHOOSH
WHAM

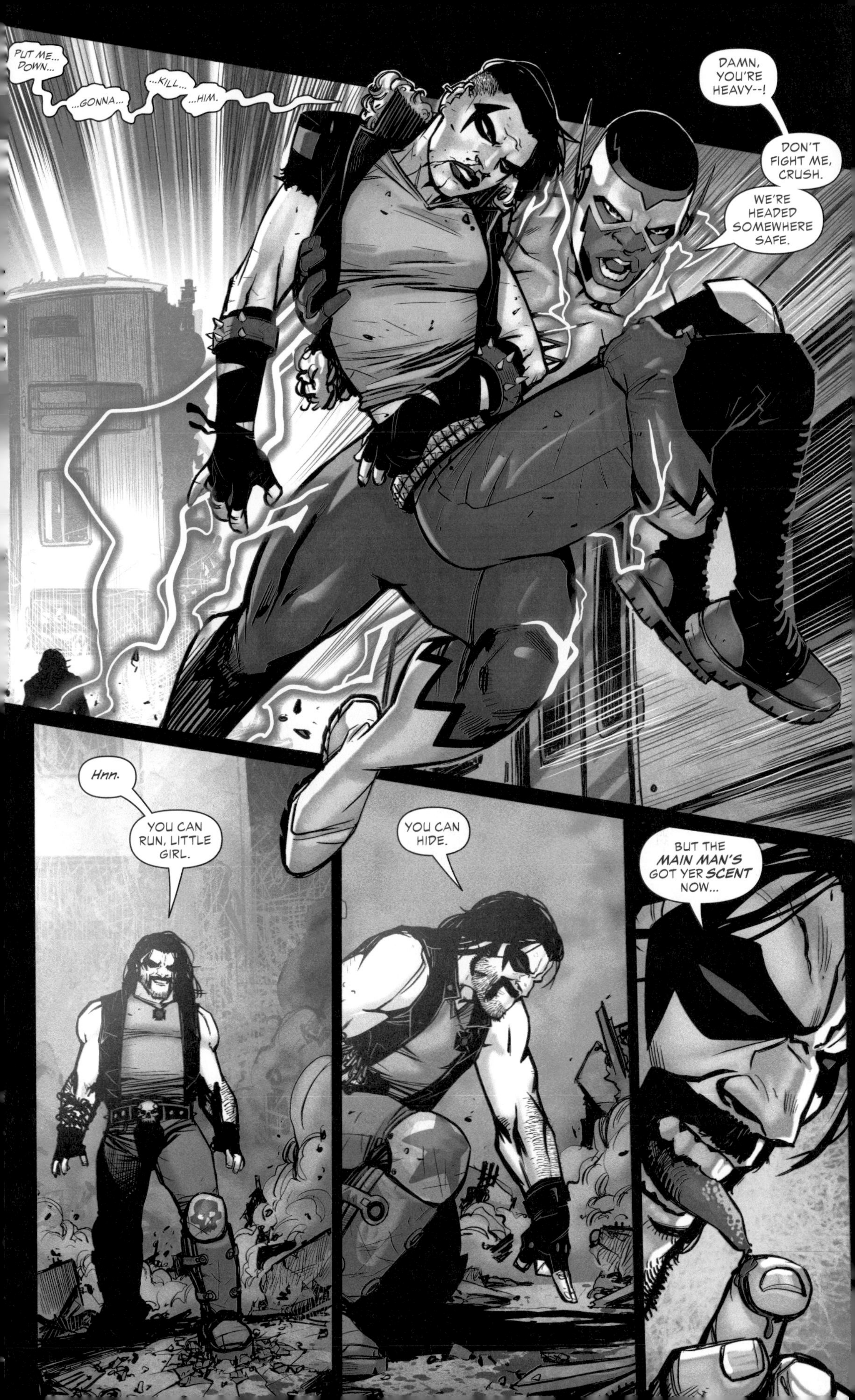
PUT ME... DOWN...
...GONNA...
...KILL...
...HIM.
DAMN, YOU'RE HEAVY--!
DON'T FIGHT ME, CRUSH.
WE'RE HEADED SOMEWHERE SAFE.
Hnn.
YOU CAN RUN, LITTLE GIRL.
YOU CAN HIDE.
BUT THE MAIN MAN'S GOT YER SCENT NOW...

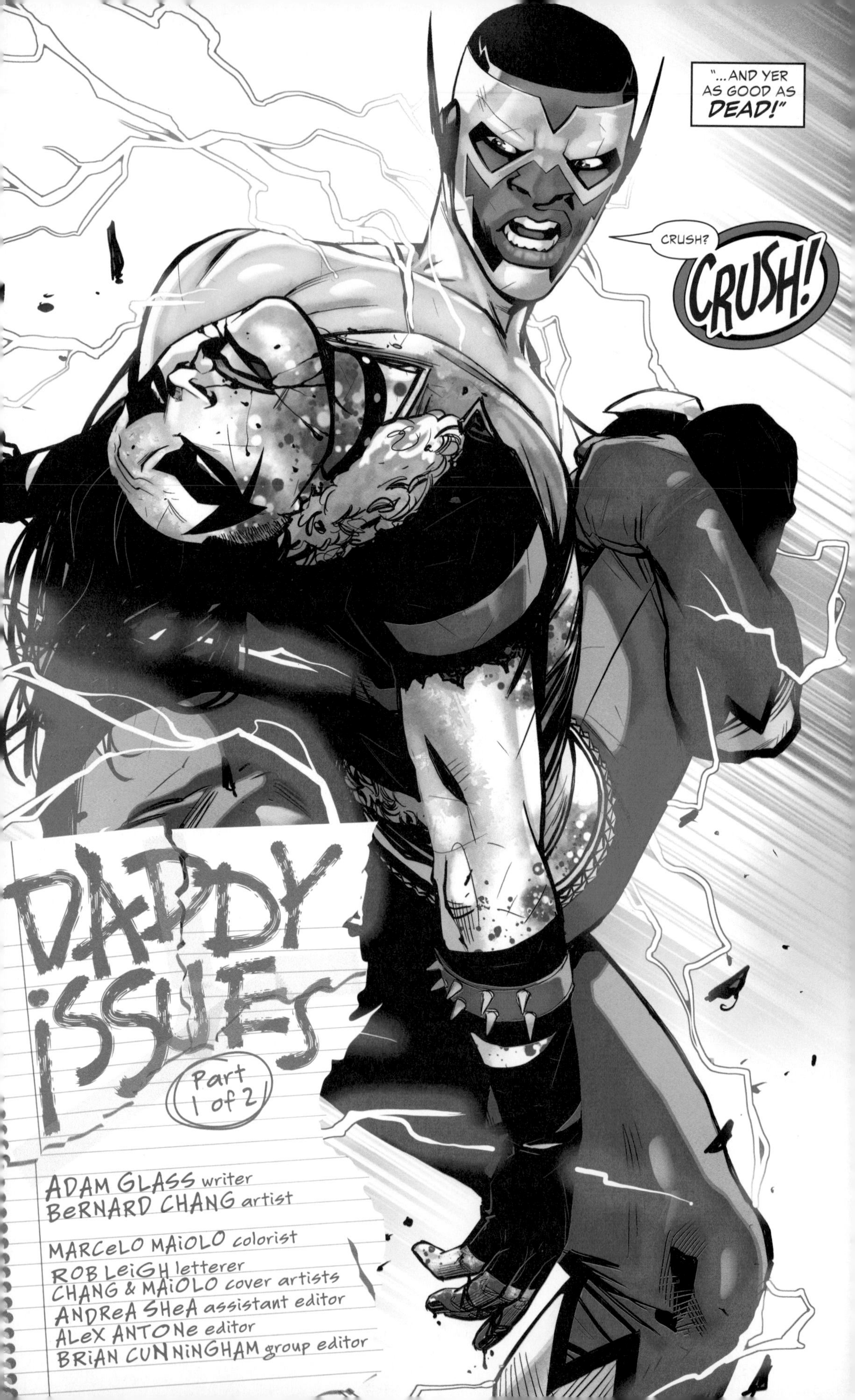
"...AND YER AS GOOD AS DEAD!"
CRUSH?
CRUSH!
DADDY ISSUES
Part 1 of 2
ADAM GLASS writer
BERNARD CHANG artist
MARCELO MAIOLO colorist
ROB LEIGH letterer
CHANG & MAIOLO cover artists
ANDREA SHEA assistant editor
ALEX ANTONE editor
BRIAN CUNNINGHAM group editor

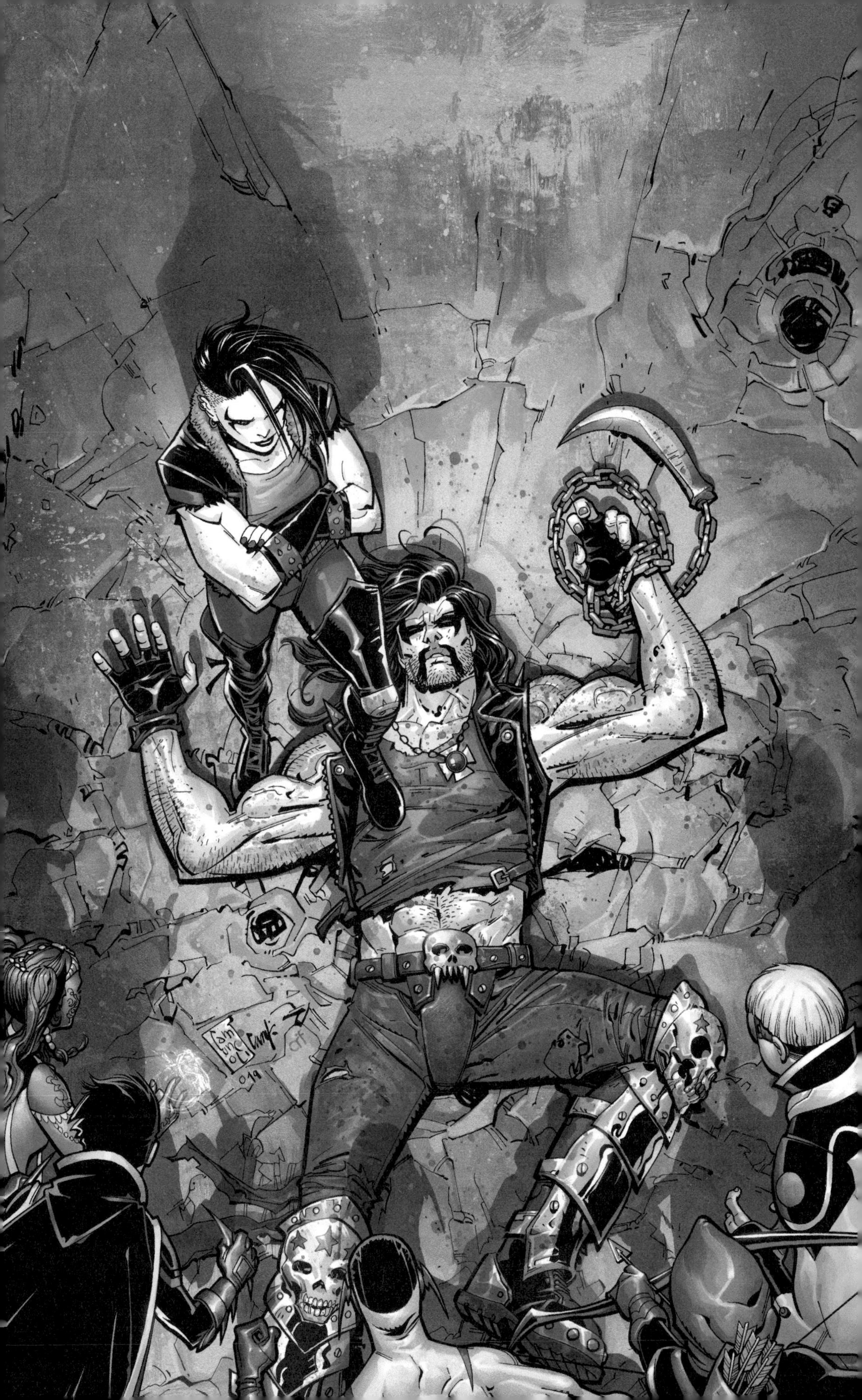

TEEN TITANS
#32

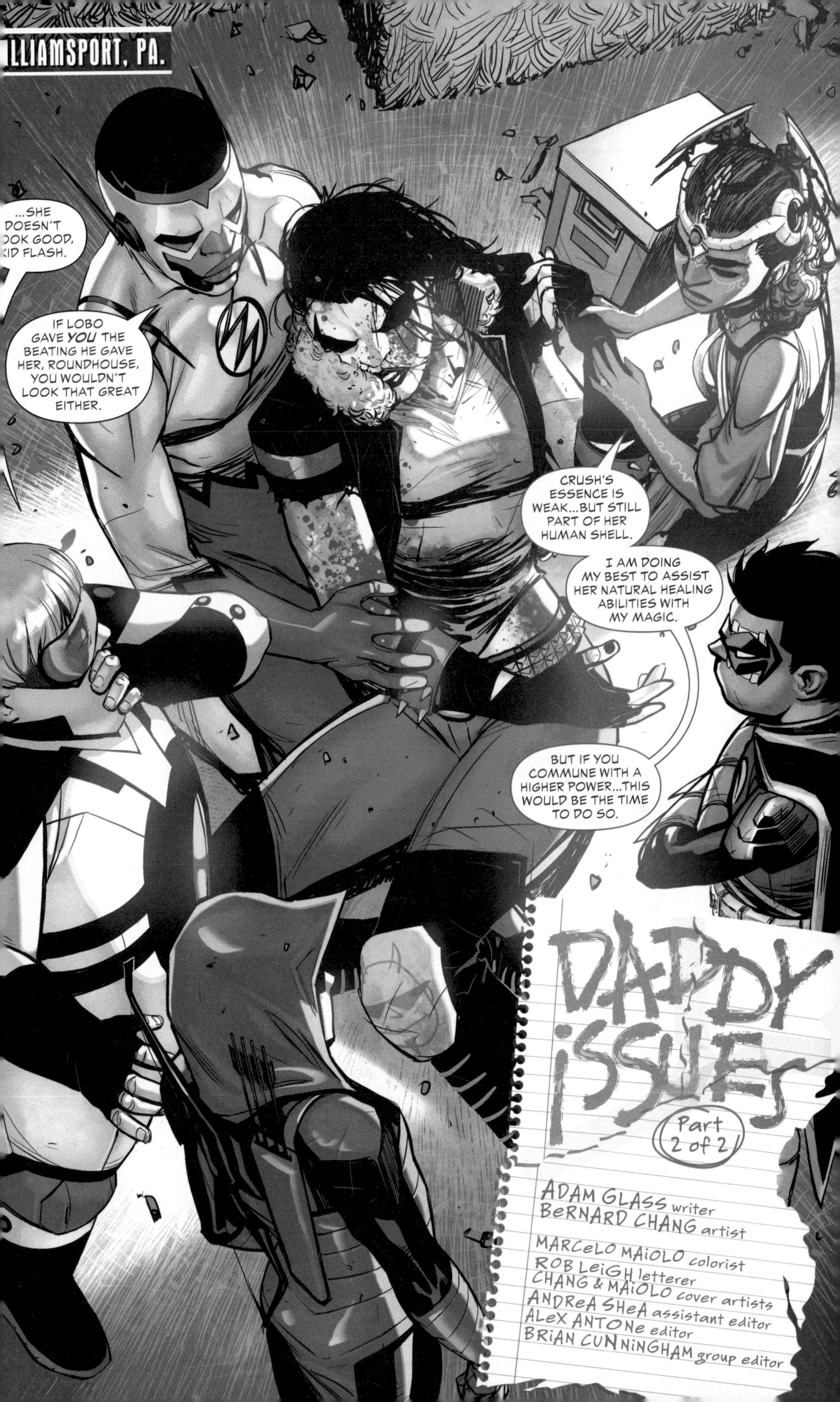

LLIAMSPORT, PA.
...SHE DOESN'T OOK GOOD, KID FLASH.
IF LOBO GAVE YOU THE BEATING HE GAVE HER, ROUNDHOUSE, YOU WOULDN'T LOOK THAT GREAT EITHER.
CRUSH'S ESSENCE IS WEAK...BUT STILL PART OF HER HUMAN SHELL.
I AM DOING MY BEST TO ASSIST HER NATURAL HEALING ABILITIES WITH MY MAGIC.
BUT IF YOU COMMUNE WITH A HIGHER POWER...THIS WOULD BE THE TIME TO DO SO.
DADDY ISSUES
Part 2 of 2
ADAM GLASS writer
BERNARD CHANG artist
MARCELO MAIOLO colorist
ROB LEIGH letterer
CHANG & MAIOLO cover artists
ANDREA SHEA assistant editor
ALEX ANTONE editor
BRIAN CUNNINGHAM group editor

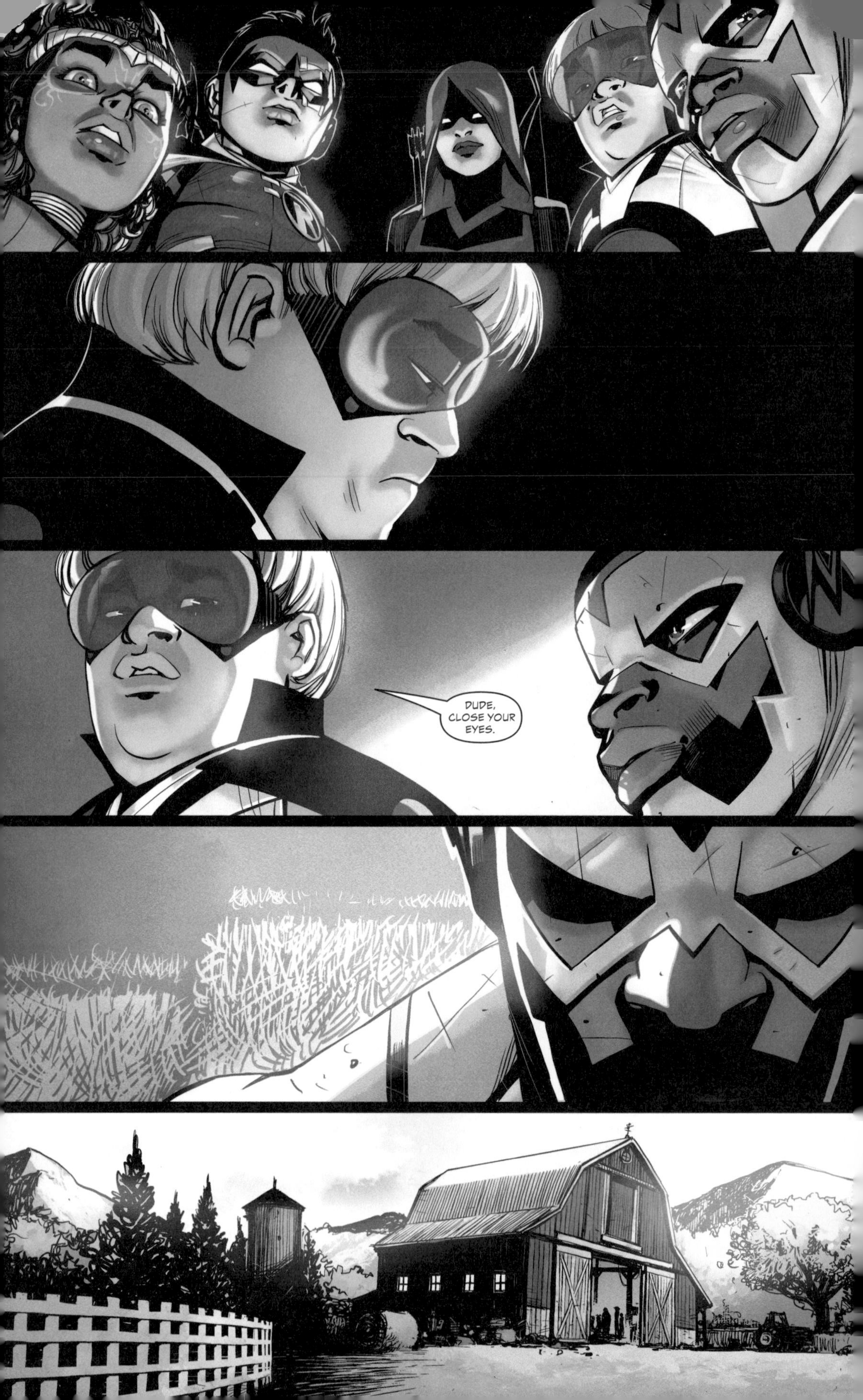
DUDE, CLOSE YOUR EYES.

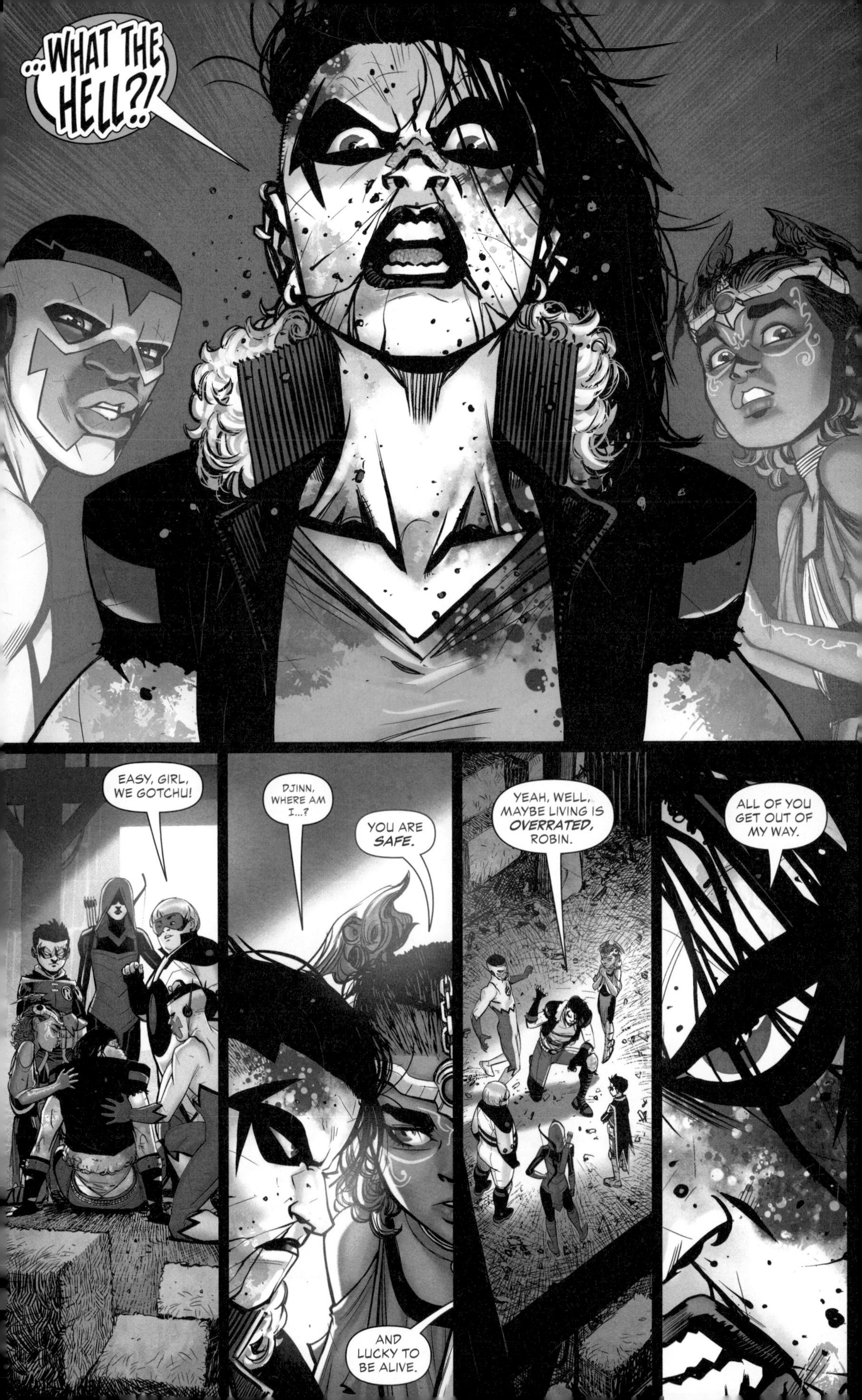
...WHAT THE HELL?!
EASY, GIRL, WE GOTCHU!
DJINN, WHERE AM I...?
YOU ARE SAFE.
AND LUCKY TO BE ALIVE.
YEAH, WELL, MAYBE LIVING IS OVERRATED, ROBIN.
ALL OF YOU GET OUT OF MY WAY.

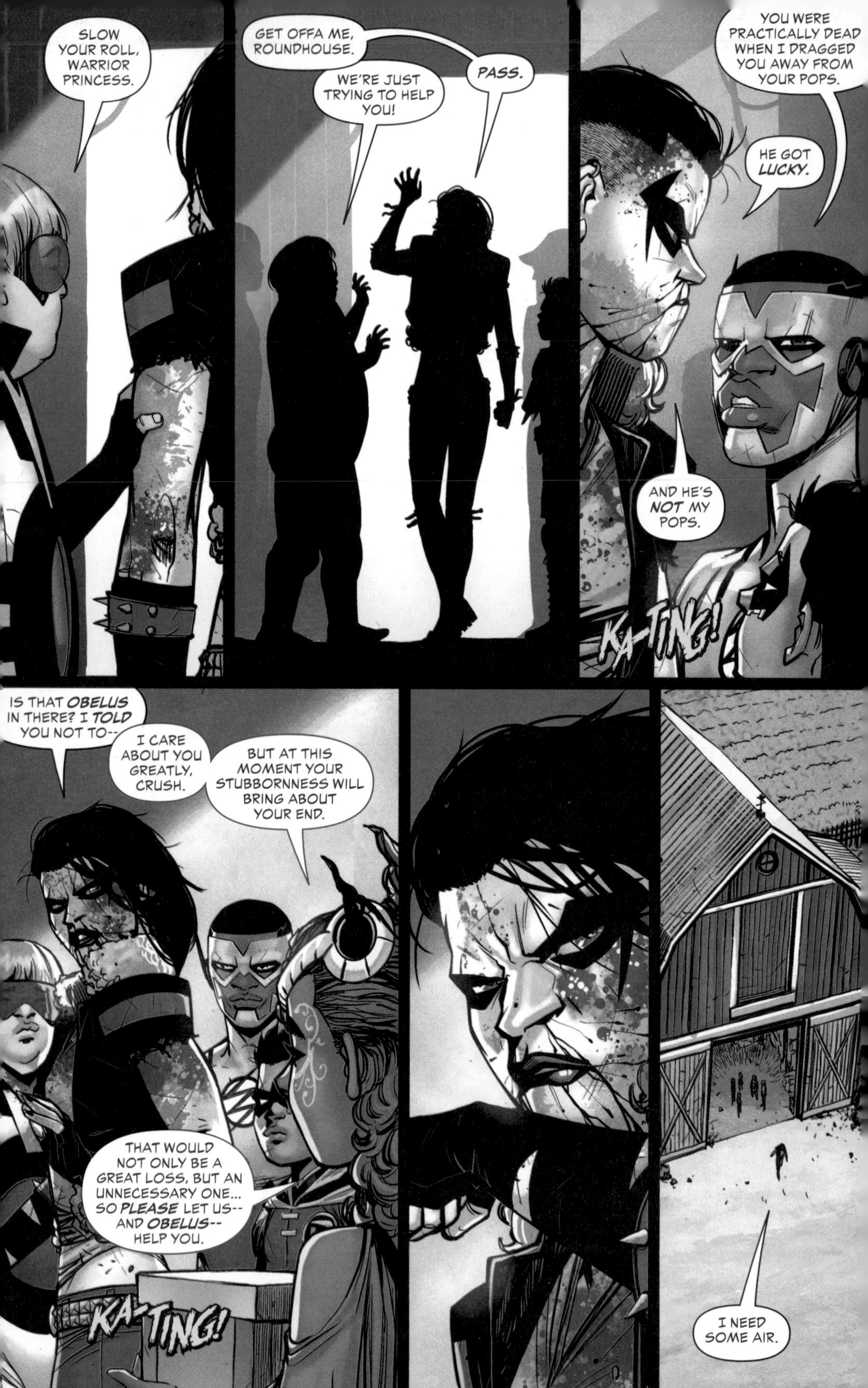
SLOW YOUR ROLL, WARRIOR PRINCESS.
GET OFFA ME, ROUNDHOUSE.
WE'RE JUST TRYING TO HELP YOU!
PASS.
YOU WERE PRACTICALLY DEAD WHEN I DRAGGED YOU AWAY FROM YOUR POPS.
HE GOT LUCKY.
AND HE'S NOT MY POPS.
KA-TING!
IS THAT OBELUS IN THERE? I TOLD YOU NOT TO--
I CARE ABOUT YOU GREATLY, CRUSH.
BUT AT THIS MOMENT YOUR STUBBORNNESS WILL BRING ABOUT YOUR END.
THAT WOULD NOT ONLY BE A GREAT LOSS, BUT AN UNNECESSARY ONE... SO PLEASE LET US-- AND OBELUS-- HELP YOU.
KA-TING!
I NEED SOME AIR.

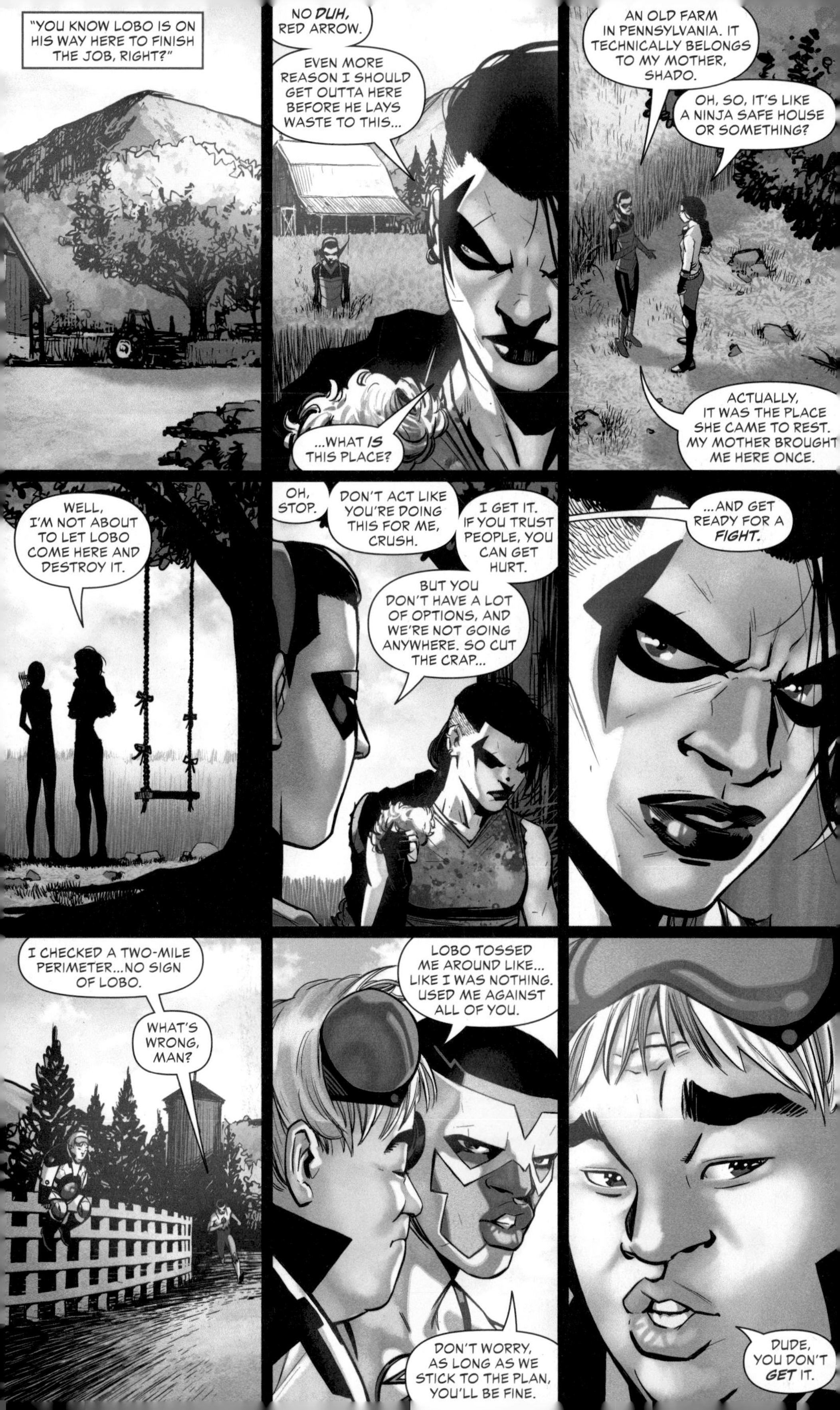
"YOU KNOW LOBO IS ON HIS WAY HERE TO FINISH THE JOB, RIGHT?"
NO DUH, RED ARROW.
EVEN MORE REASON I SHOULD GET OUTTA HERE BEFORE HE LAYS WASTE TO THIS...
...WHAT IS THIS PLACE?
AN OLD FARM IN PENNSYLVANIA. IT TECHNICALLY BELONGS TO MY MOTHER, SHADO.
OH, SO, IT'S LIKE A NINJA SAFE HOUSE OR SOMETHING?
ACTUALLY, IT WAS THE PLACE SHE CAME TO REST. MY MOTHER BROUGHT ME HERE ONCE.
WELL, I'M NOT ABOUT TO LET LOBO COME HERE AND DESTROY IT.
OH, STOP.
DON'T ACT LIKE YOU'RE DOING THIS FOR ME, CRUSH.
I GET IT. IF YOU TRUST PEOPLE, YOU CAN GET HURT.
BUT YOU DON'T HAVE A LOT OF OPTIONS, AND WE'RE NOT GOING ANYWHERE. SO CUT THE CRAP...
...AND GET READY FOR A FIGHT.
I CHECKED A TWO-MILE PERIMETER...NO SIGN OF LOBO.
WHAT'S WRONG, MAN?
LOBO TOSSED ME AROUND LIKE... LIKE I WAS NOTHING. USED ME AGAINST ALL OF YOU.
DON'T WORRY, AS LONG AS WE STICK TO THE PLAN, YOU'LL BE FINE.
DUDE, YOU DON'T GET IT.

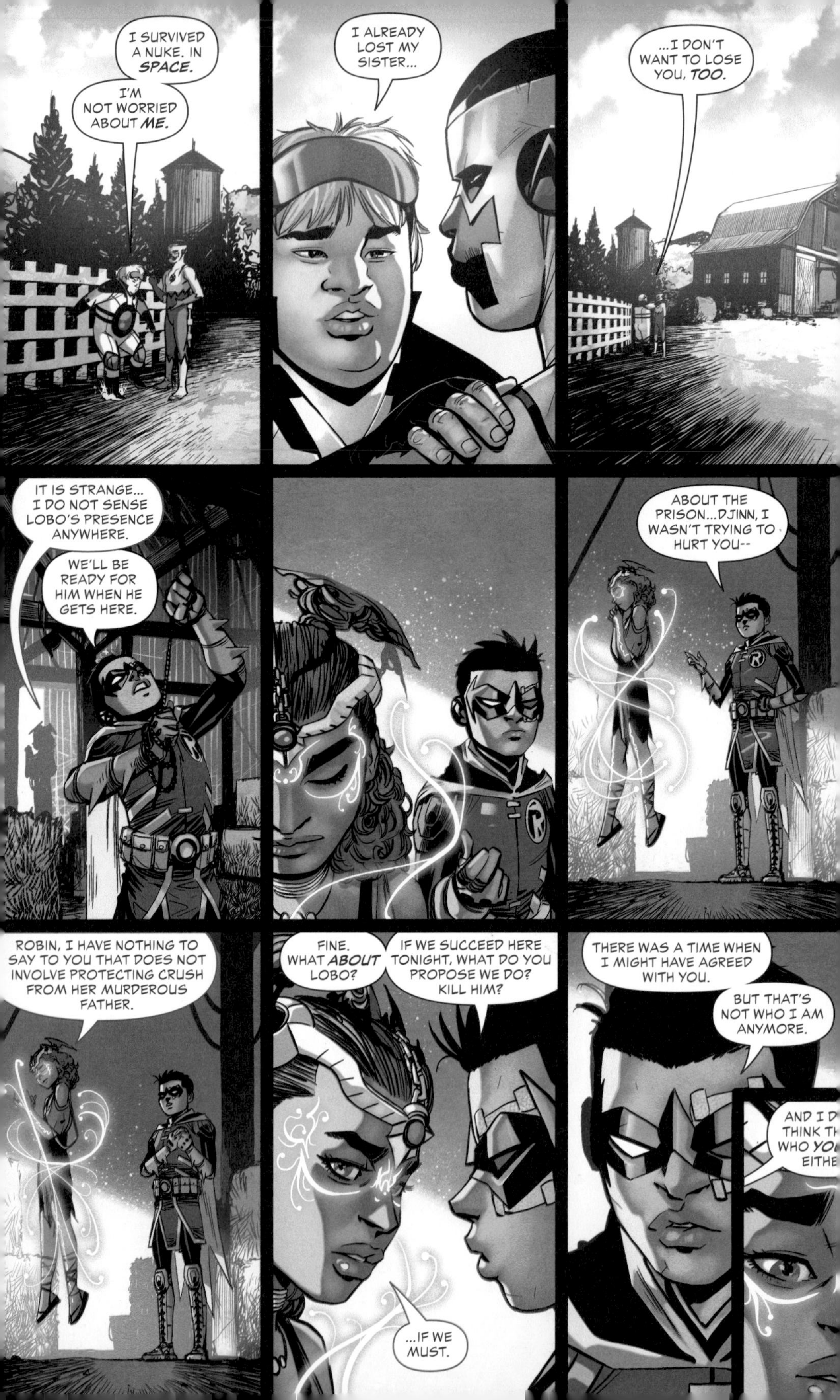

I SURVIVED A NUKE. IN SPACE.
I'M NOT WORRIED ABOUT ME.
I ALREADY LOST MY SISTER...
...I DON'T WANT TO LOSE YOU, TOO.
IT IS STRANGE... I DO NOT SENSE LOBO'S PRESENCE ANYWHERE.
WE'LL BE READY FOR HIM WHEN HE GETS HERE.
ABOUT THE PRISON...DJINN, I WASN'T TRYING TO HURT YOU--
ROBIN, I HAVE NOTHING TO SAY TO YOU THAT DOES NOT INVOLVE PROTECTING CRUSH FROM HER MURDEROUS FATHER.
FINE. WHAT ABOUT LOBO?
IF WE SUCCEED HERE TONIGHT, WHAT DO YOU PROPOSE WE DO? KILL HIM?
...IF WE MUST.
THERE WAS A TIME WHEN I MIGHT HAVE AGREED WITH YOU.
BUT THAT'S NOT WHO I AM ANYMORE.

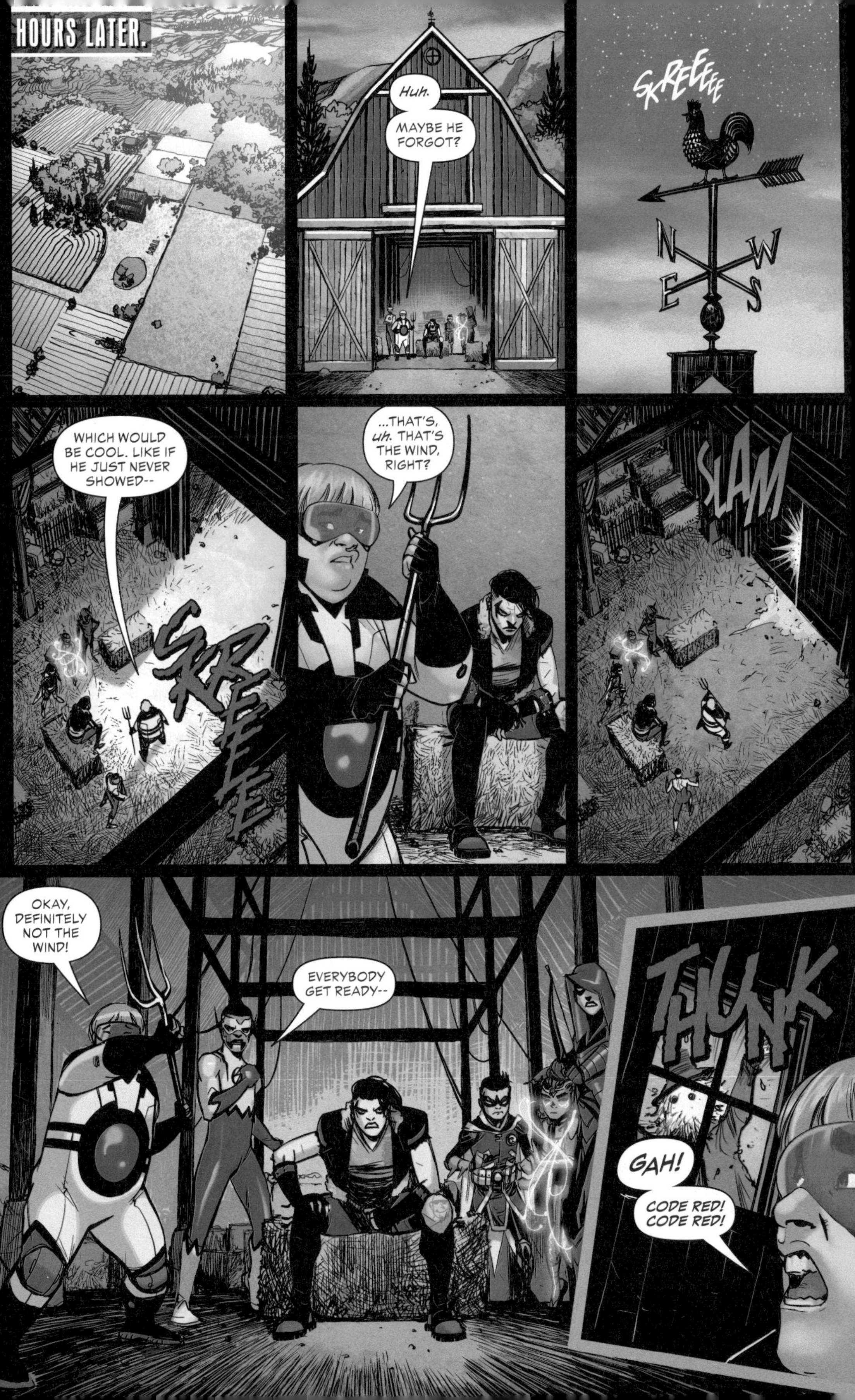
HOURS LATER.
Huh.
MAYBE HE FORGOT?
SKREEEEE
WHICH WOULD BE COOL. LIKE IF HE JUST NEVER SHOWED--
SKREEEE
...THAT'S, uh. THAT'S THE WIND, RIGHT?
SLAM
OKAY, DEFINITELY NOT THE WIND!
EVERYBODY GET READY--
THUNK
GAH!
CODE RED! CODE RED!

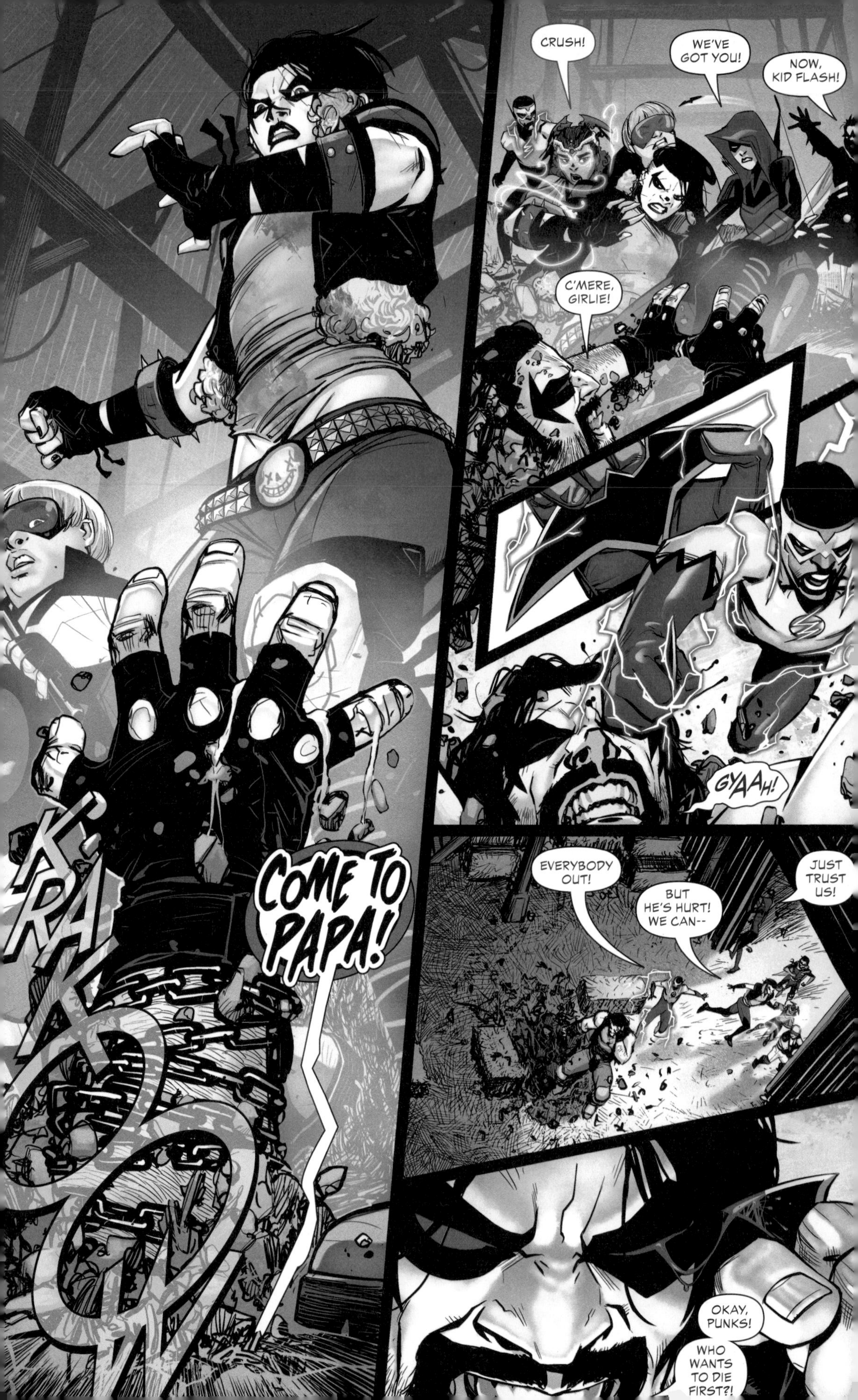
KRAKOOW
COME TO PAPA!
CRUSH!
WE'VE GOT YOU!
NOW, KID FLASH!
C'MERE, GIRLIE!
GYAAH!
EVERYBODY OUT!
BUT HE'S HURT! WE CAN--
JUST TRUST US!
OKAY, PUNKS!
WHO WANTS TO DIE FIRST?!

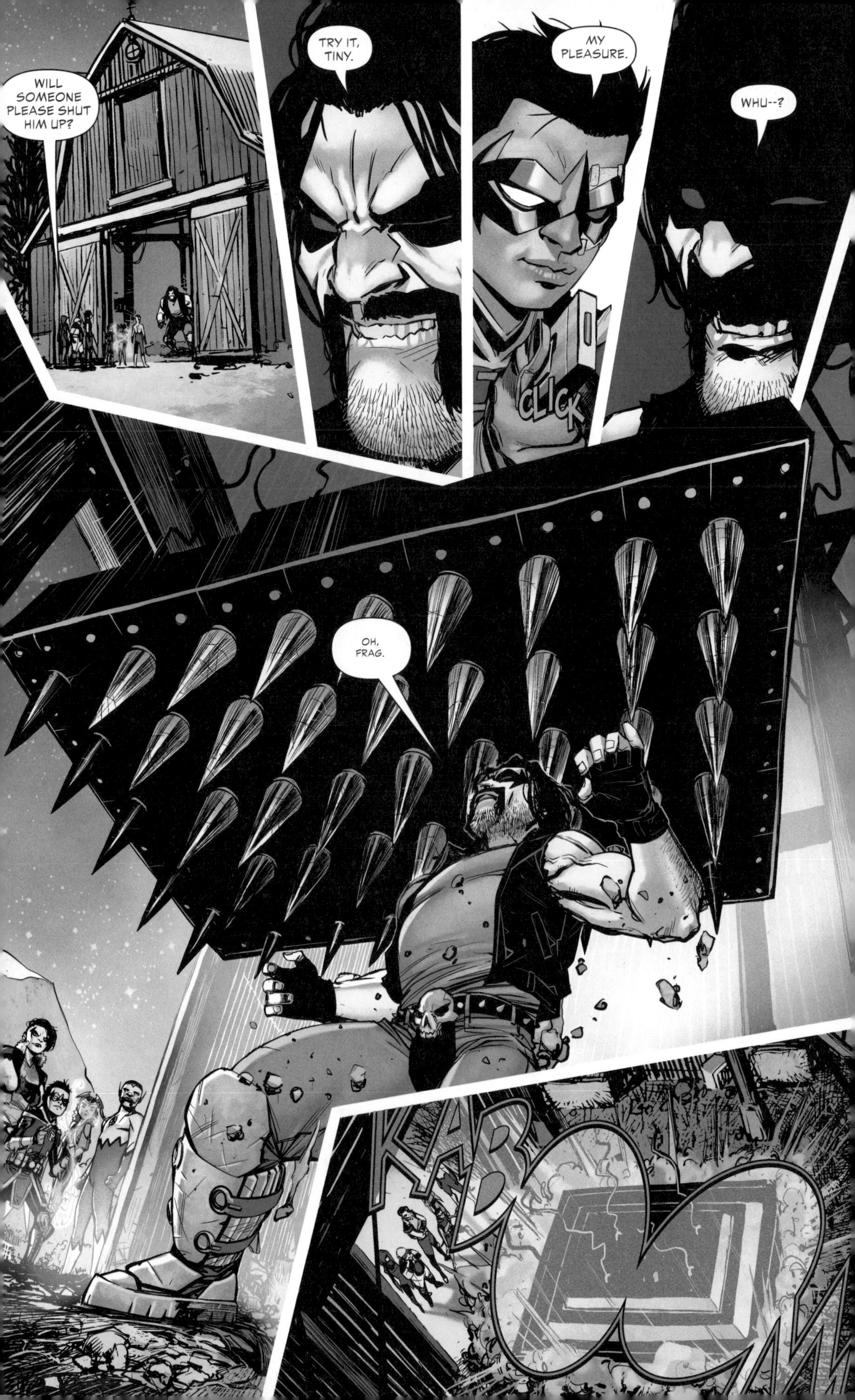
WILL SOMEONE PLEASE SHUT HIM UP?
TRY IT, TINY.
MY PLEASURE.
CLICK
WHU--?
OH, FRAG.

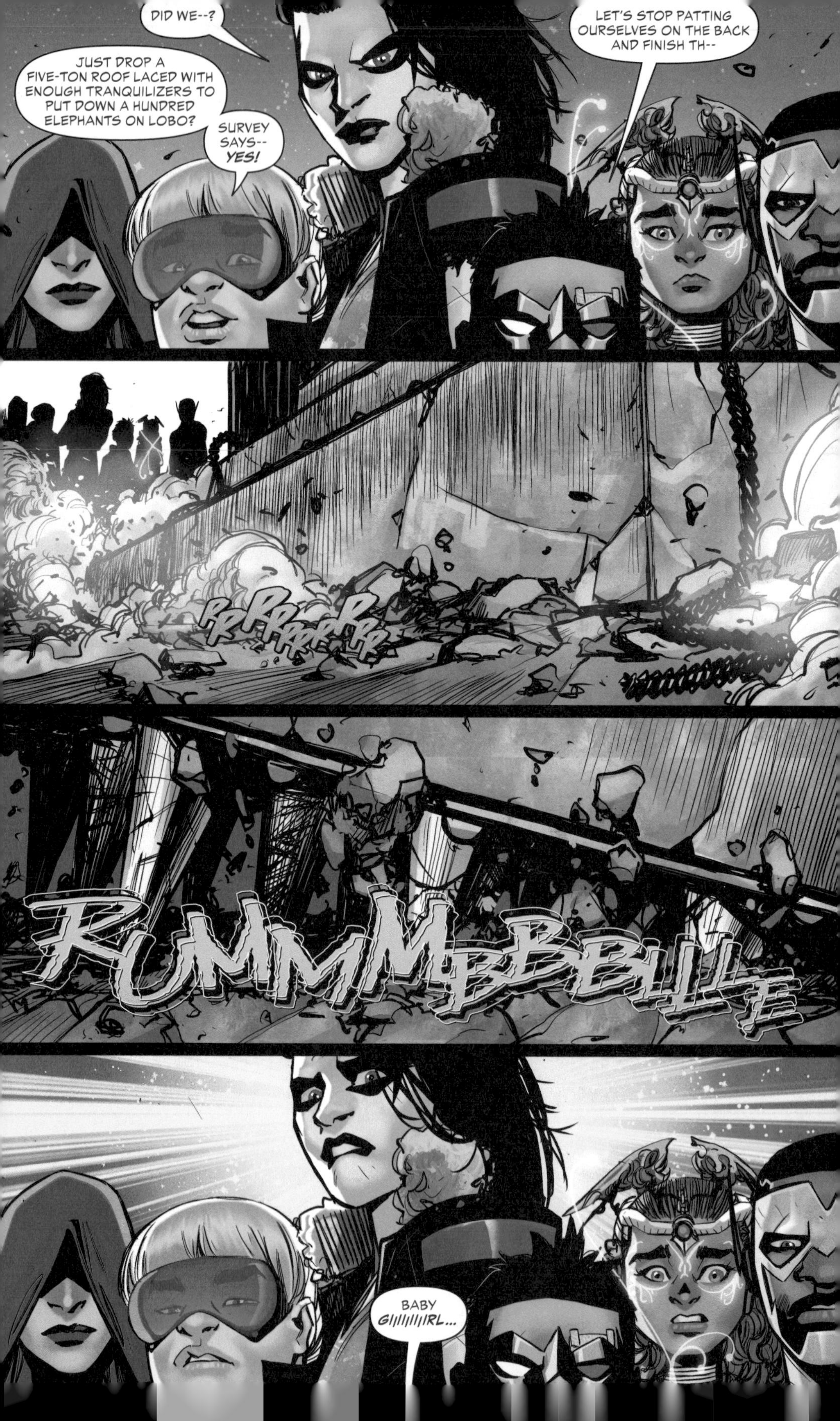
DID WE--?
JUST DROP A FIVE-TON ROOF LACED WITH ENOUGH TRANQUILIZERS TO PUT DOWN A HUNDRED ELEPHANTS ON LOBO?
SURVEY SAYS-- *YES!*
LET'S STOP PATTING OURSELVES ON THE BACK AND FINISH TH--
RUMMMBBBLLLE
BABY GI////////RL...

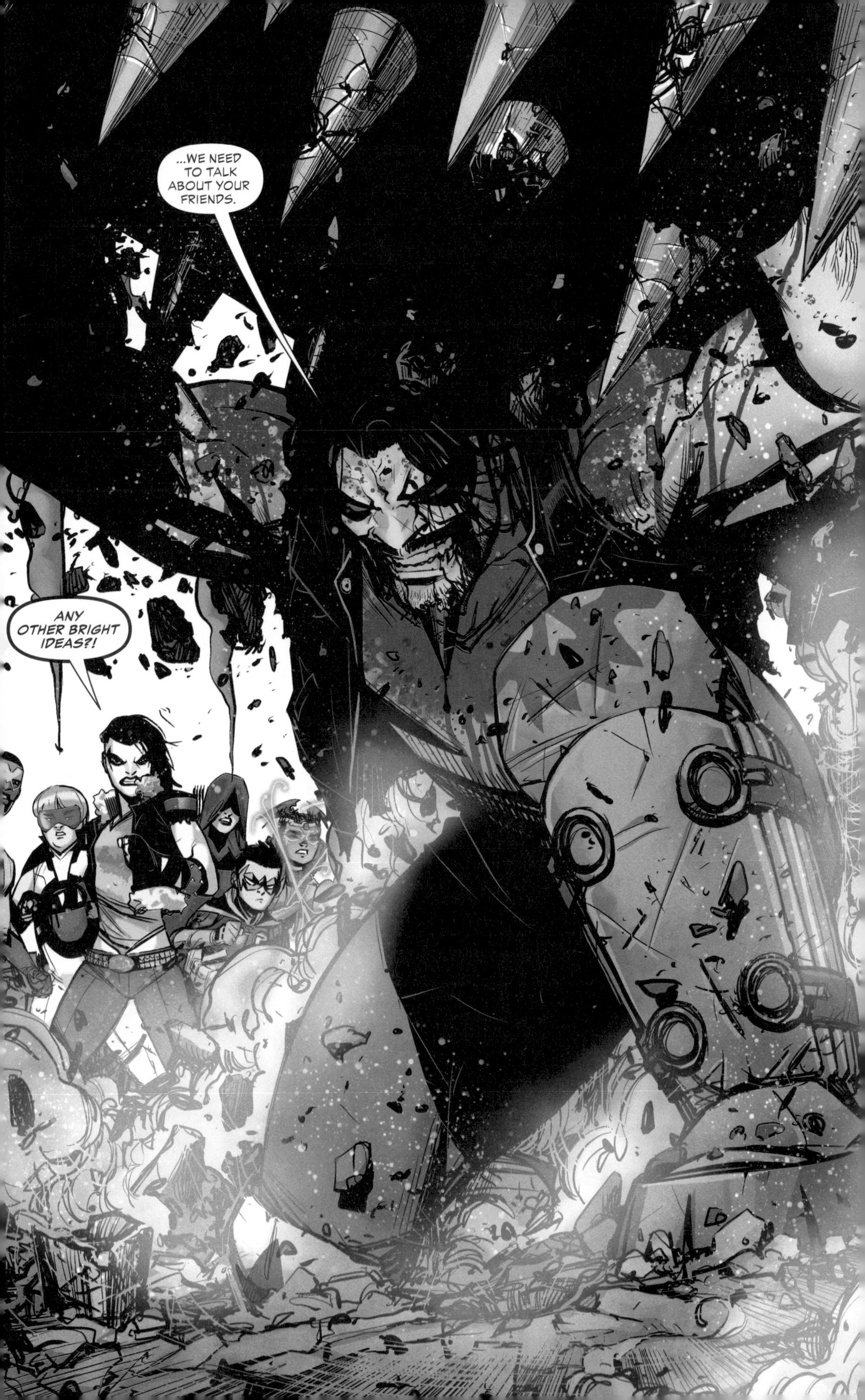
...WE NEED TO TALK ABOUT YOUR FRIENDS.
ANY OTHER BRIGHT IDEAS?!

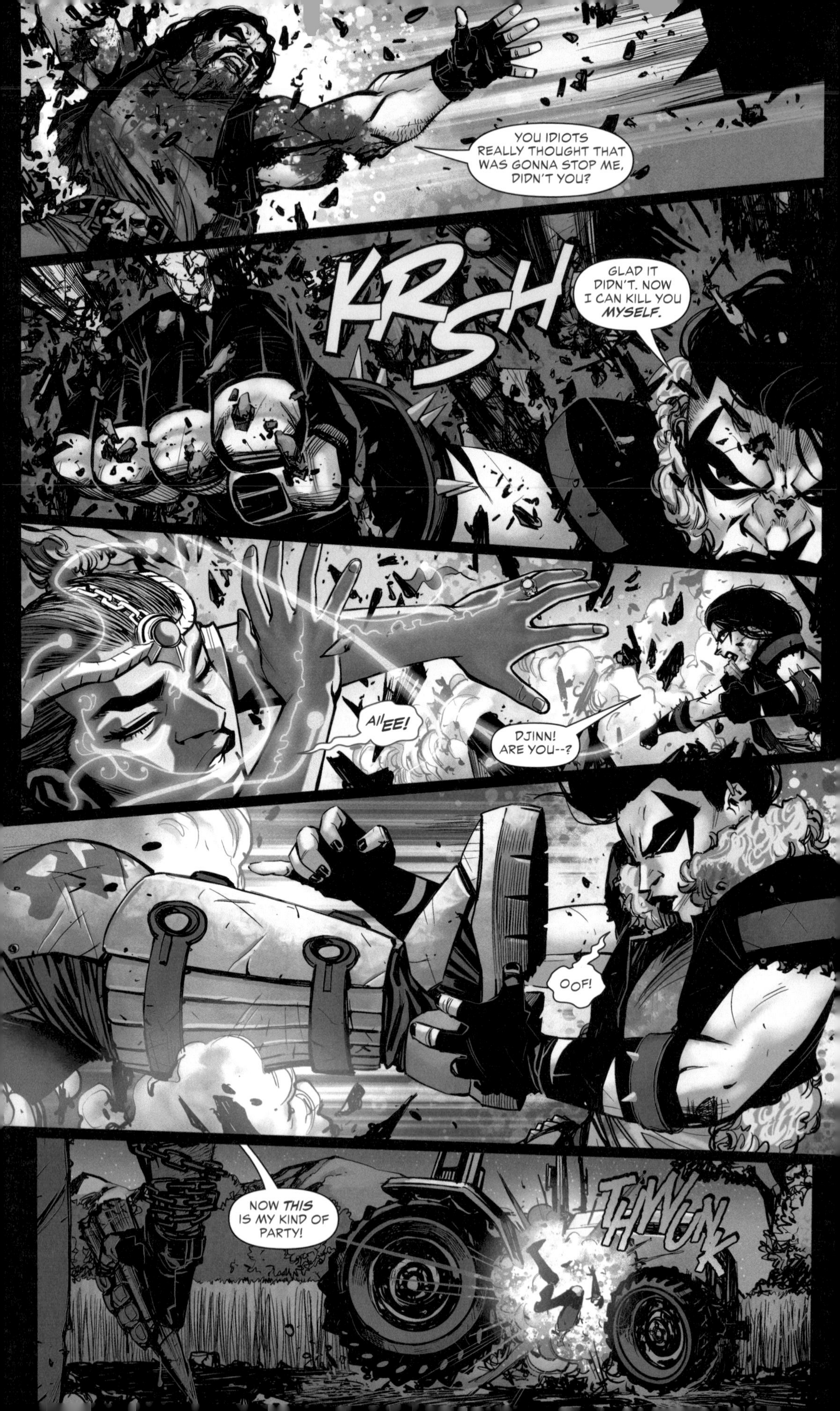

YOU IDIOTS REALLY THOUGHT THAT WAS GONNA STOP ME, DIDN'T YOU?
KRSH
GLAD IT DIDN'T. NOW I CAN KILL YOU MYSELF.
AIIEE!
DJINN! ARE YOU--?
OOF!
NOW THIS IS MY KIND OF PARTY!
THWUNK

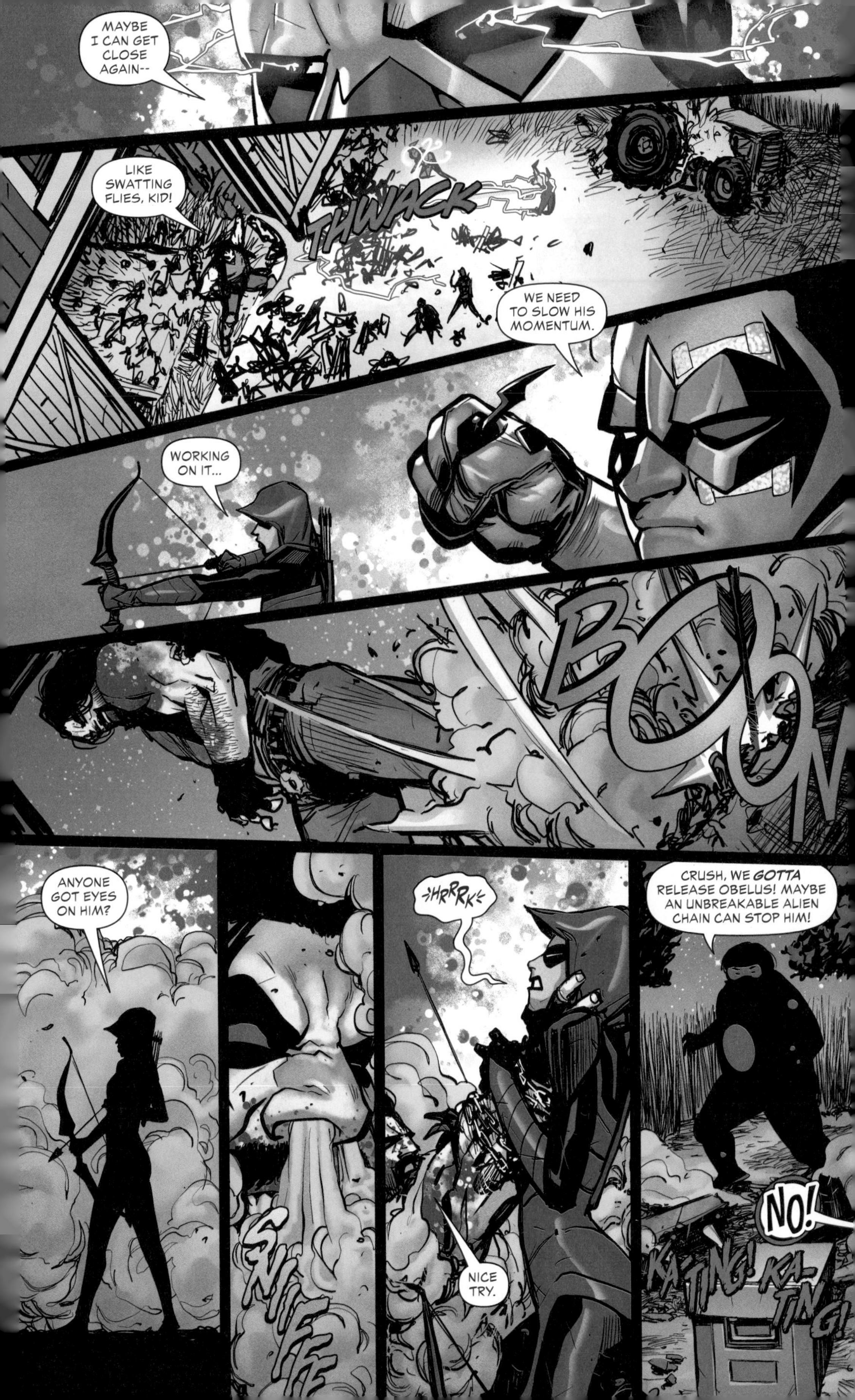

MAYBE I CAN GET CLOSE AGAIN--
LIKE SWATTING FLIES, KID!
THWACK
WE NEED TO SLOW HIS MOMENTUM.
WORKING ON IT...
BOOM
ANYONE GOT EYES ON HIM?
SNIFF
HRRRK
NICE TRY.
CRUSH, WE GOTTA RELEASE OBELUS! MAYBE AN UNBREAKABLE ALIEN CHAIN CAN STOP HIM!
NO!
KA-TING! KA-TING!

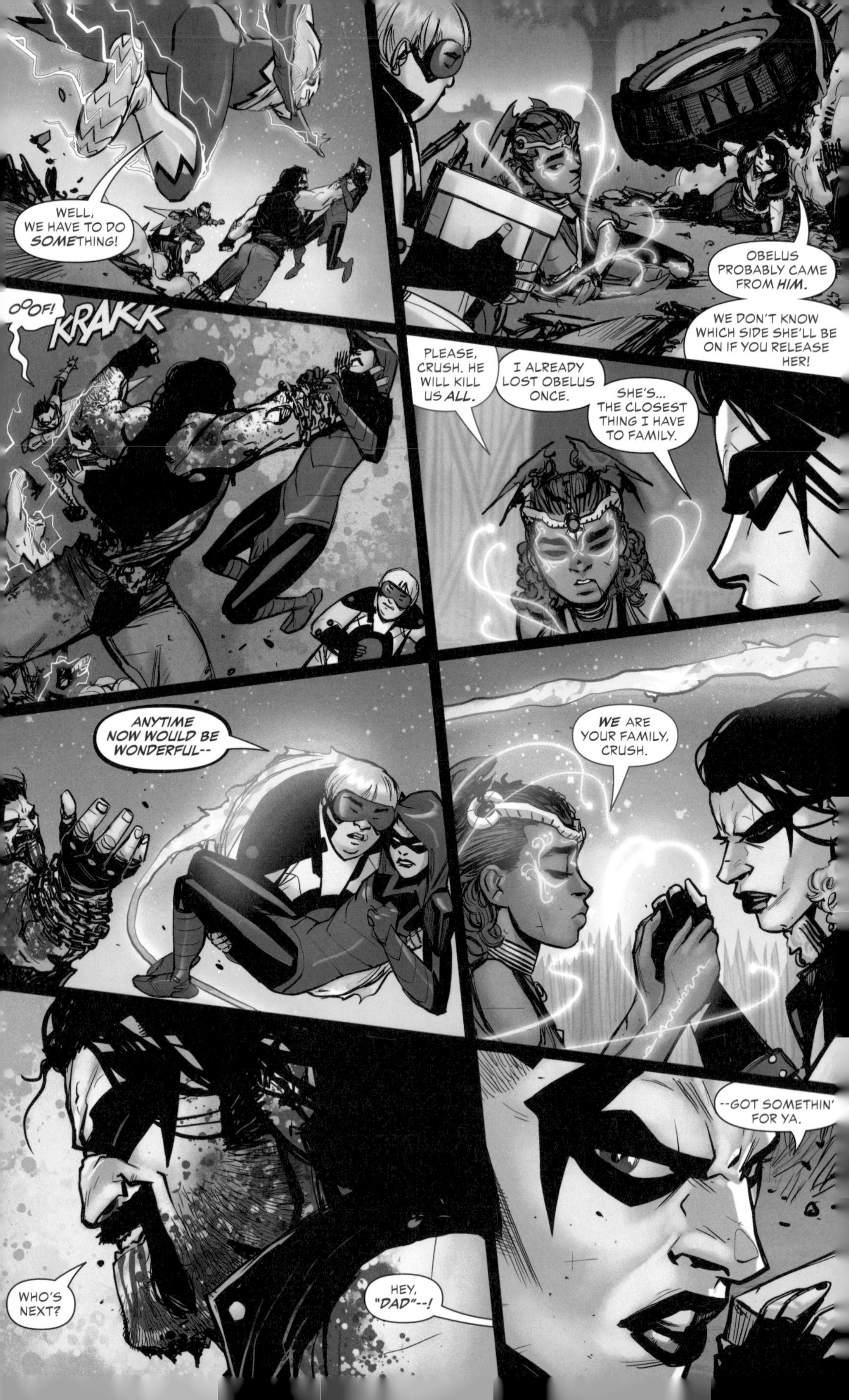
WELL, WE HAVE TO DO SOMETHING!
OBELUS PROBABLY CAME FROM HIM.
WE DON'T KNOW WHICH SIDE SHE'LL BE ON IF YOU RELEASE HER!
OOOF!
KRAKK
PLEASE, CRUSH. HE WILL KILL US ALL.
I ALREADY LOST OBELUS ONCE.
SHE'S... THE CLOSEST THING I HAVE TO FAMILY.
ANYTIME NOW WOULD BE WONDERFUL--
WE ARE YOUR FAMILY, CRUSH.
WHO'S NEXT?
HEY, "DAD"--!
--GOT SOMETHIN' FOR YA.

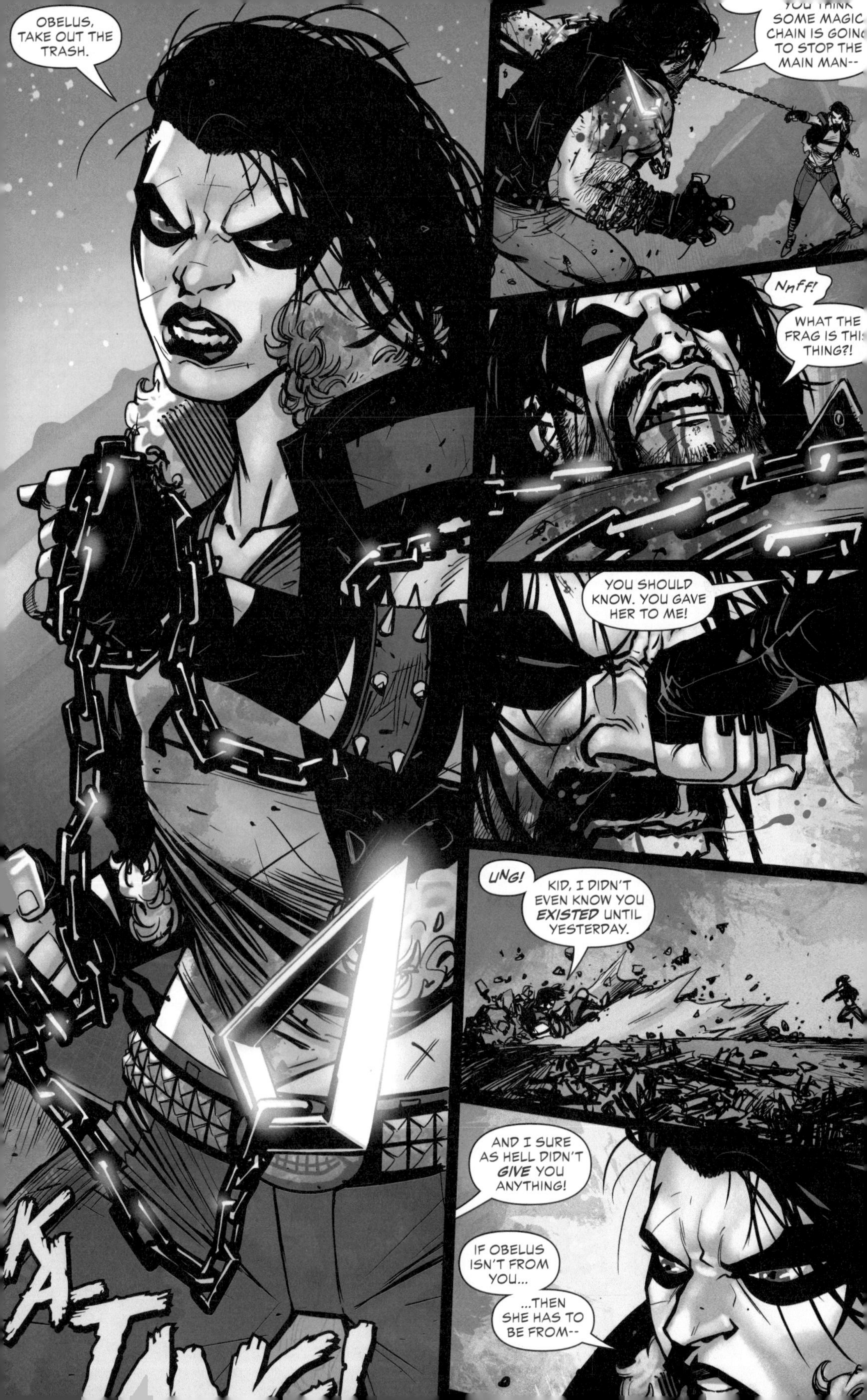
OBELUS, TAKE OUT THE TRASH.
KA-TANG!
SOME MAGIC CHAIN IS GOING TO STOP THE MAIN MAN--
Nnff!
WHAT THE FRAG IS THIS THING?!
YOU SHOULD KNOW. YOU GAVE HER TO ME!
UNG!
KID, I DIDN'T EVEN KNOW YOU EXISTED UNTIL YESTERDAY.
AND I SURE AS HELL DIDN'T GIVE YOU ANYTHING!
IF OBELUS ISN'T FROM YOU...
...THEN SHE HAS TO BE FROM--

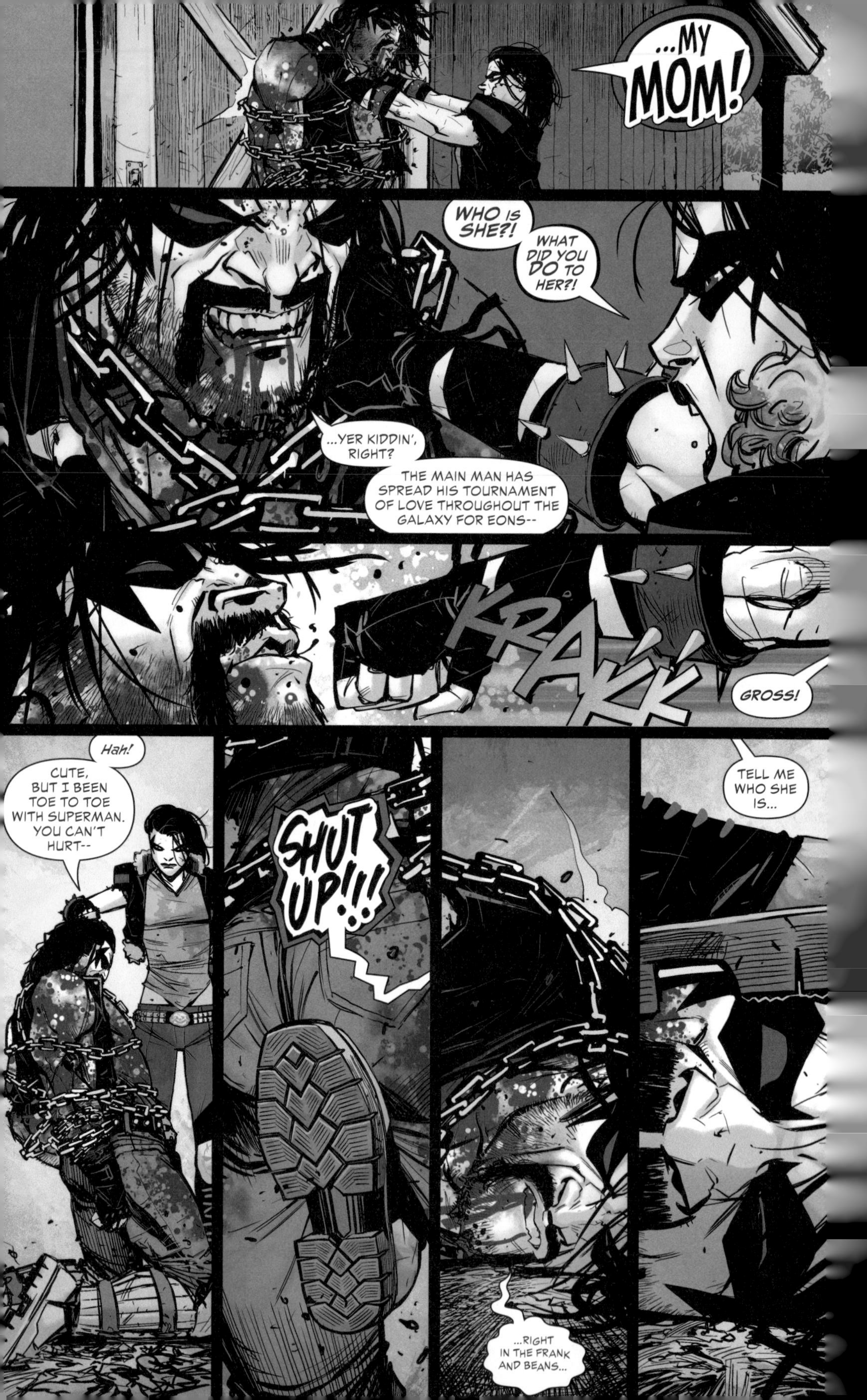
...MY MOM!
WHO IS SHE?!
WHAT DID YOU DO TO HER?!
...YER KIDDIN', RIGHT?
THE MAIN MAN HAS SPREAD HIS TOURNAMENT OF LOVE THROUGHOUT THE GALAXY FOR EONS--
KRAKK
GROSS!
Hah!
CUTE, BUT I BEEN TOE TO TOE WITH SUPERMAN. YOU CAN'T HURT--
SHUT UP!!!
TELL ME WHO SHE IS...
...RIGHT IN THE FRANK AND BEANS...

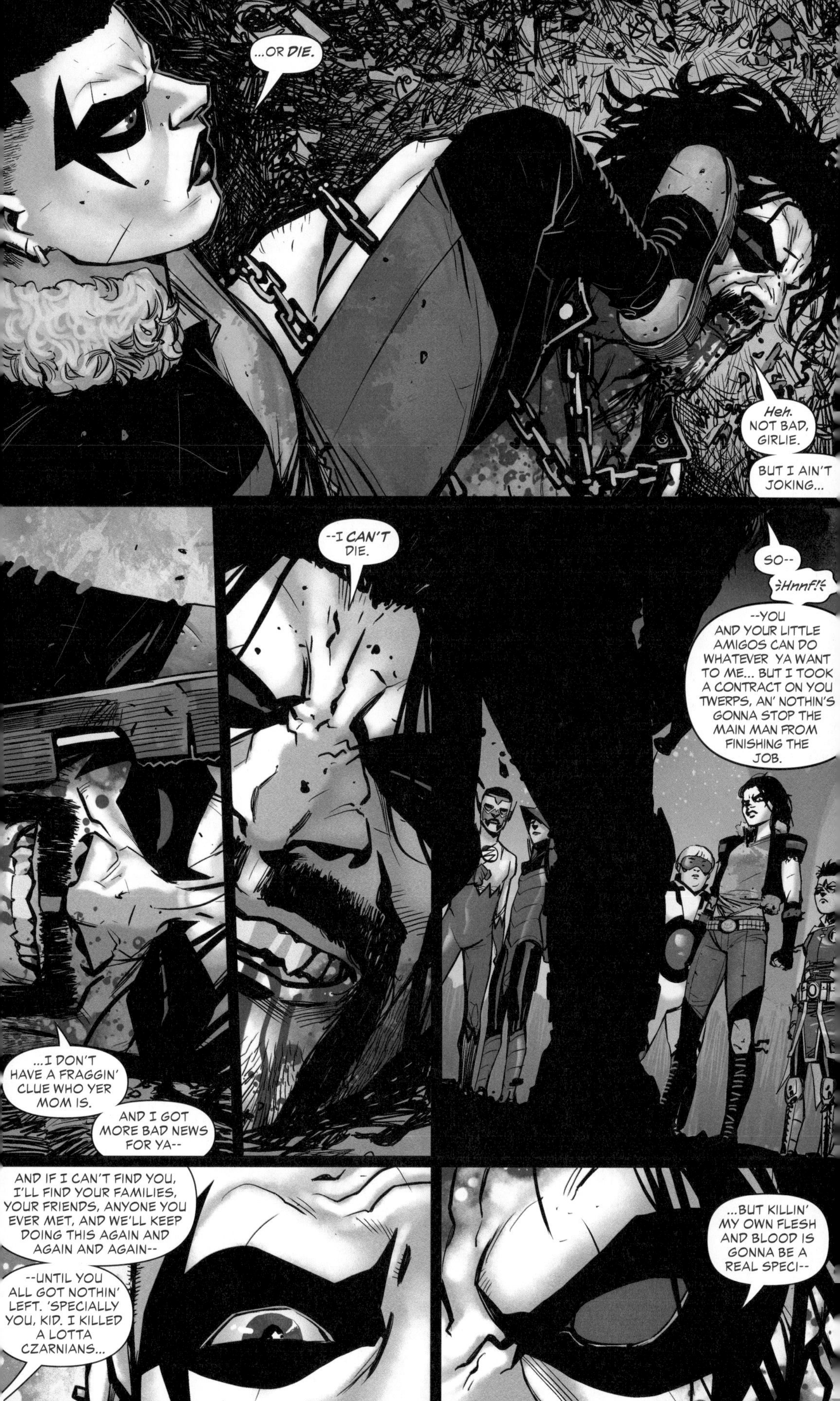
...OR DIE.
Heh. NOT BAD, GIRLIE.
BUT I AIN'T JOKING...
--I CAN'T DIE.
...I DON'T HAVE A FRAGGIN' CLUE WHO YER MOM IS.
AND I GOT MORE BAD NEWS FOR YA--
SO--
Hnnf!
--YOU AND YOUR LITTLE AMIGOS CAN DO WHATEVER YA WANT TO ME... BUT I TOOK A CONTRACT ON YOU TWERPS, AN' NOTHIN'S GONNA STOP THE MAIN MAN FROM FINISHING THE JOB.
AND IF I CAN'T FIND YOU, I'LL FIND YOUR FAMILIES, YOUR FRIENDS, ANYONE YOU EVER MET, AND WE'LL KEEP DOING THIS AGAIN AND AGAIN AND AGAIN--
--UNTIL YOU ALL GOT NOTHIN' LEFT. 'SPECIALLY YOU, KID. I KILLED A LOTTA CZARNIANS...
...BUT KILLIN' MY OWN FLESH AND BLOOD IS GONNA BE A REAL SPECI--

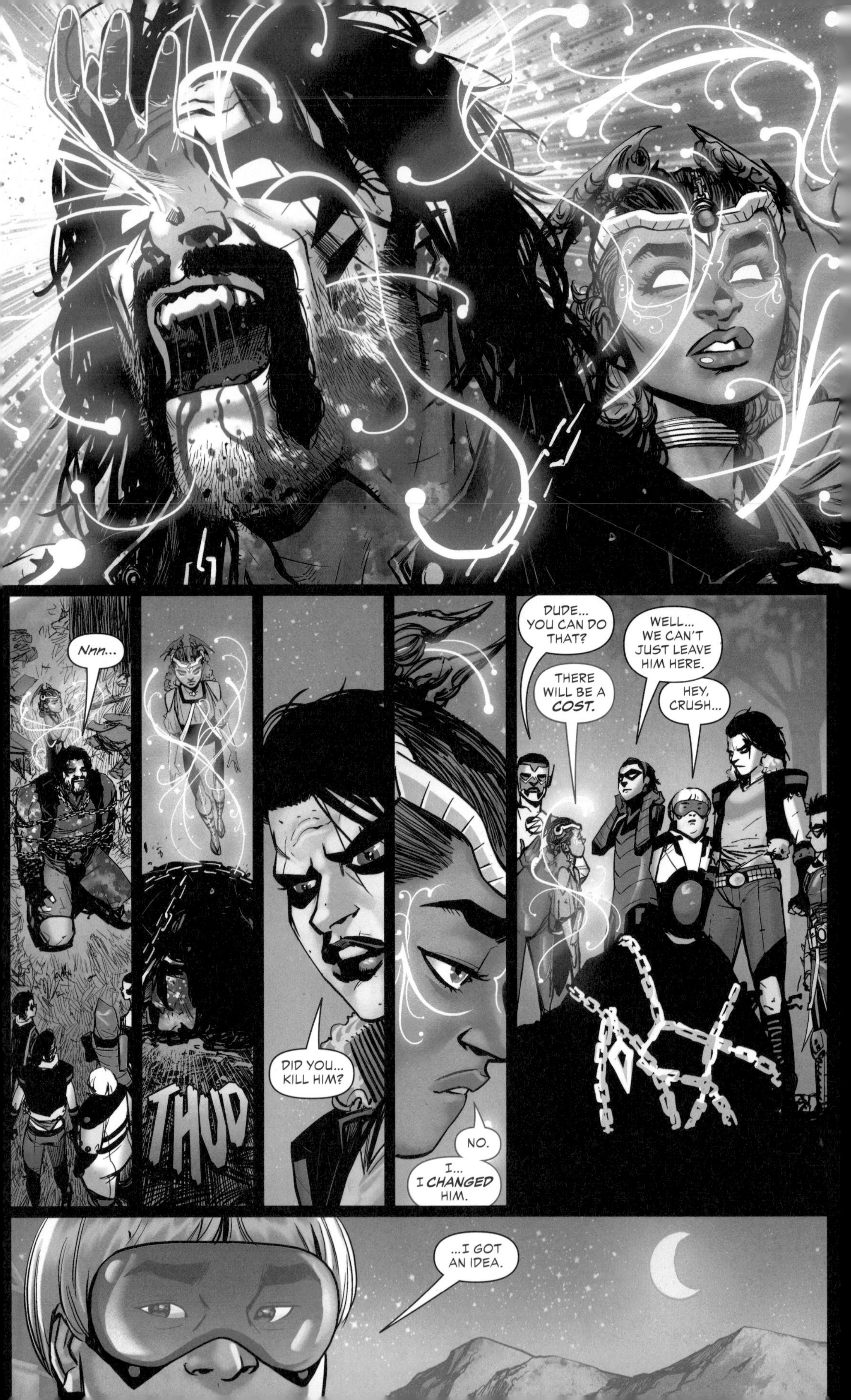
Nnn...
THUD
DID YOU... KILL HIM?
NO.
I... I CHANGED HIM.
DUDE... YOU CAN DO THAT?
THERE WILL BE A COST.
WELL... WE CAN'T JUST LEAVE HIM HERE.
HEY, CRUSH...
...I GOT AN IDEA.

"I'VE COME QUITE A WAYS TO FIND YOU.

"BUT IF THERE'S ANYTHING I'VE LEARNED OVER THE YEARS...

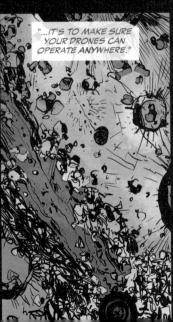

"...IT'S TO MAKE SURE YOUR DRONES CAN OPERATE ANYWHERE."

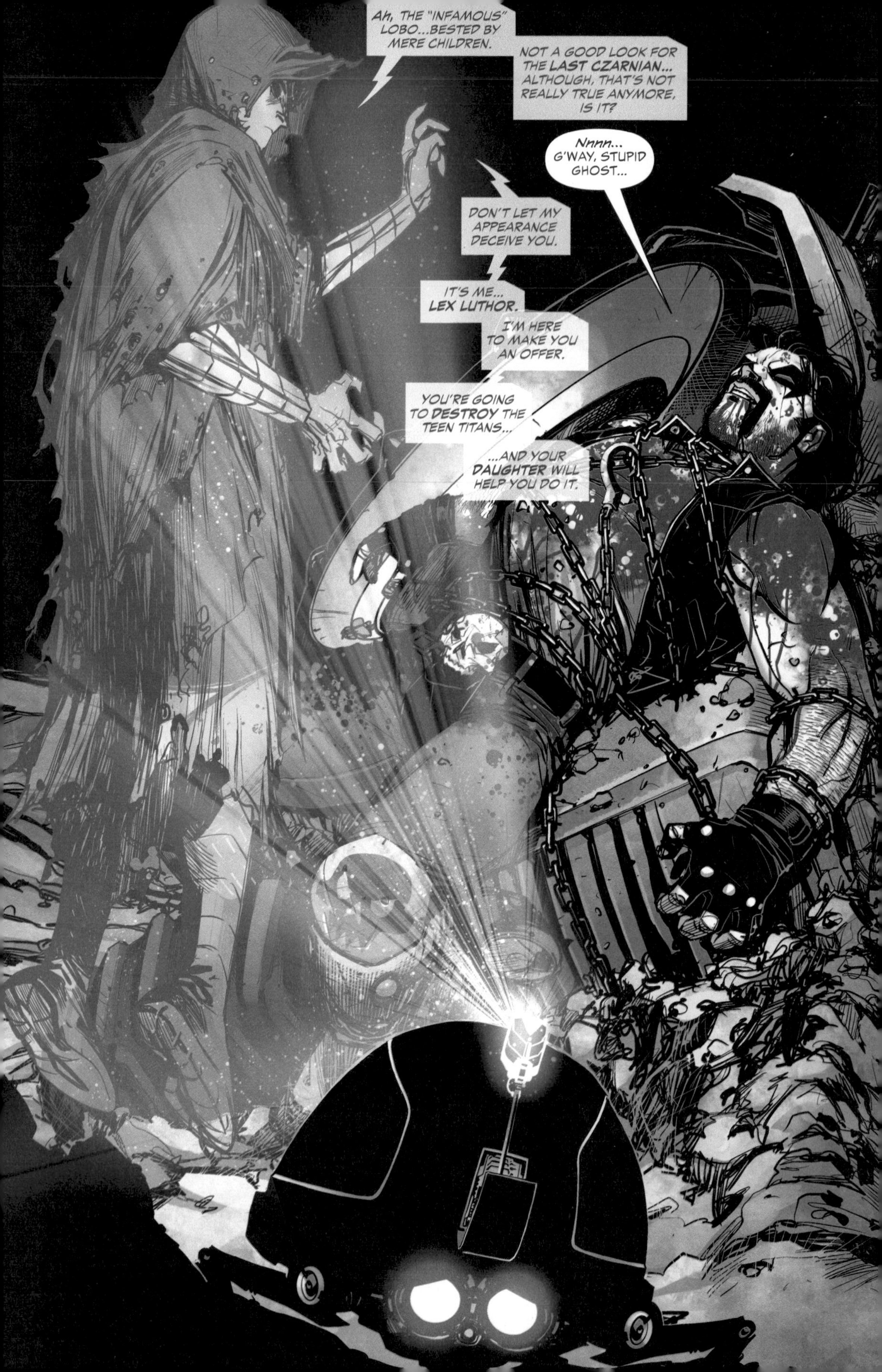

AH, THE "INFAMOUS" LOBO...BESTED BY MERE CHILDREN.
NOT A GOOD LOOK FOR THE LAST CZARNIAN... ALTHOUGH, THAT'S NOT REALLY TRUE ANYMORE, IS IT?
NNNN... G'WAY, STUPID GHOST...
DON'T LET MY APPEARANCE DECEIVE YOU.
IT'S ME... LEX LUTHOR.
I'M HERE TO MAKE YOU AN OFFER.
YOU'RE GOING TO DESTROY THE TEEN TITANS...
...AND YOUR DAUGHTER WILL HELP YOU DO IT.

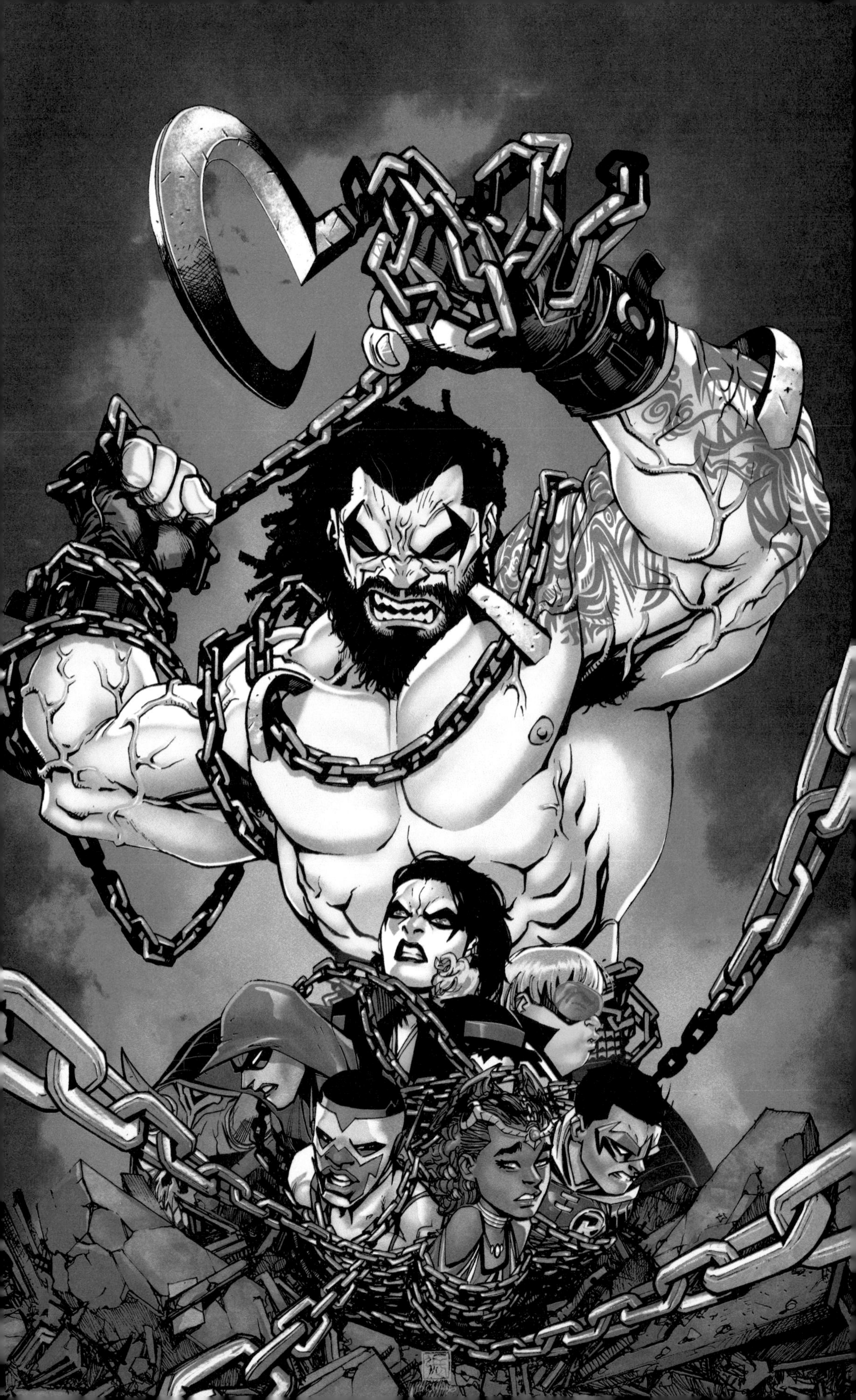

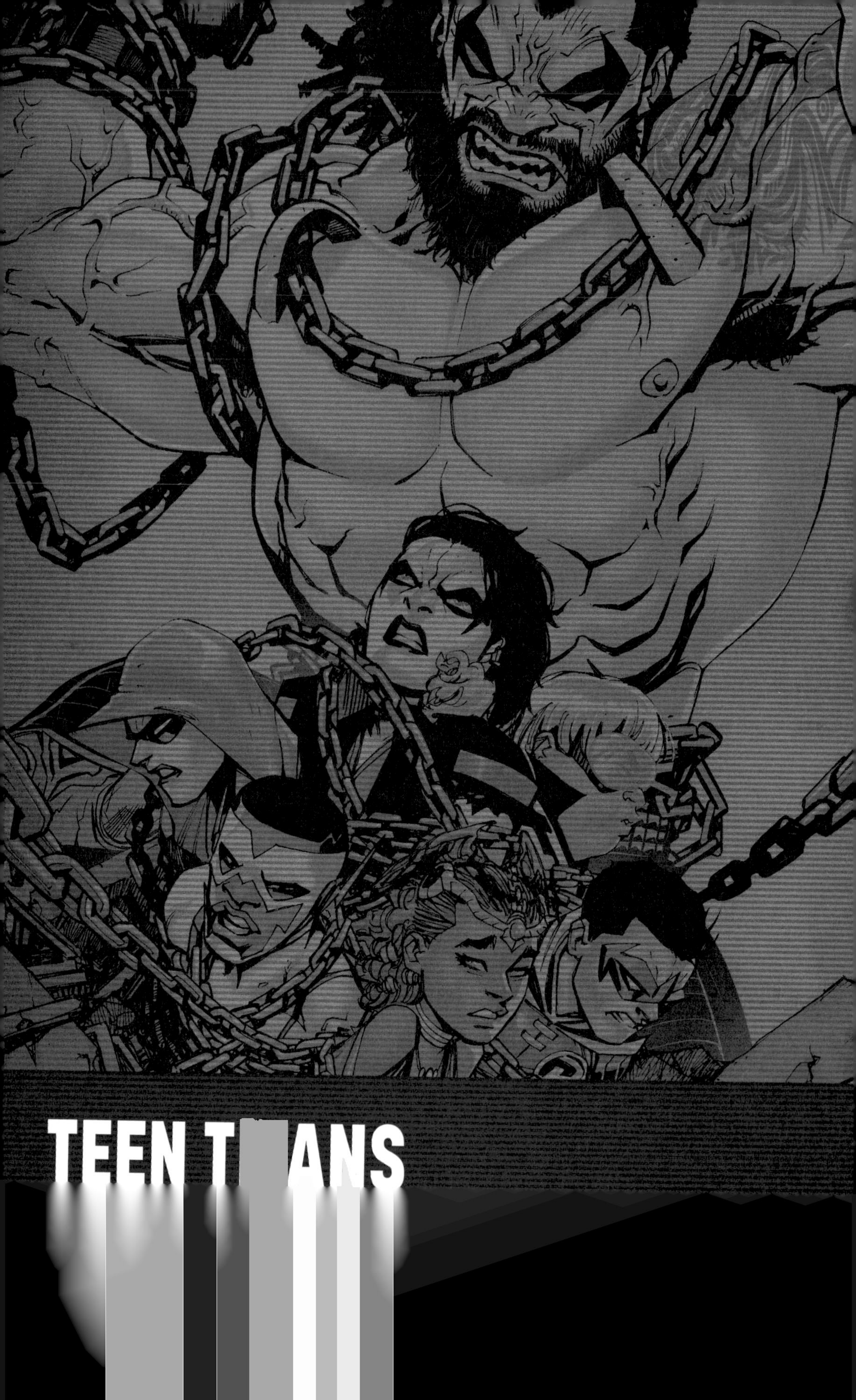

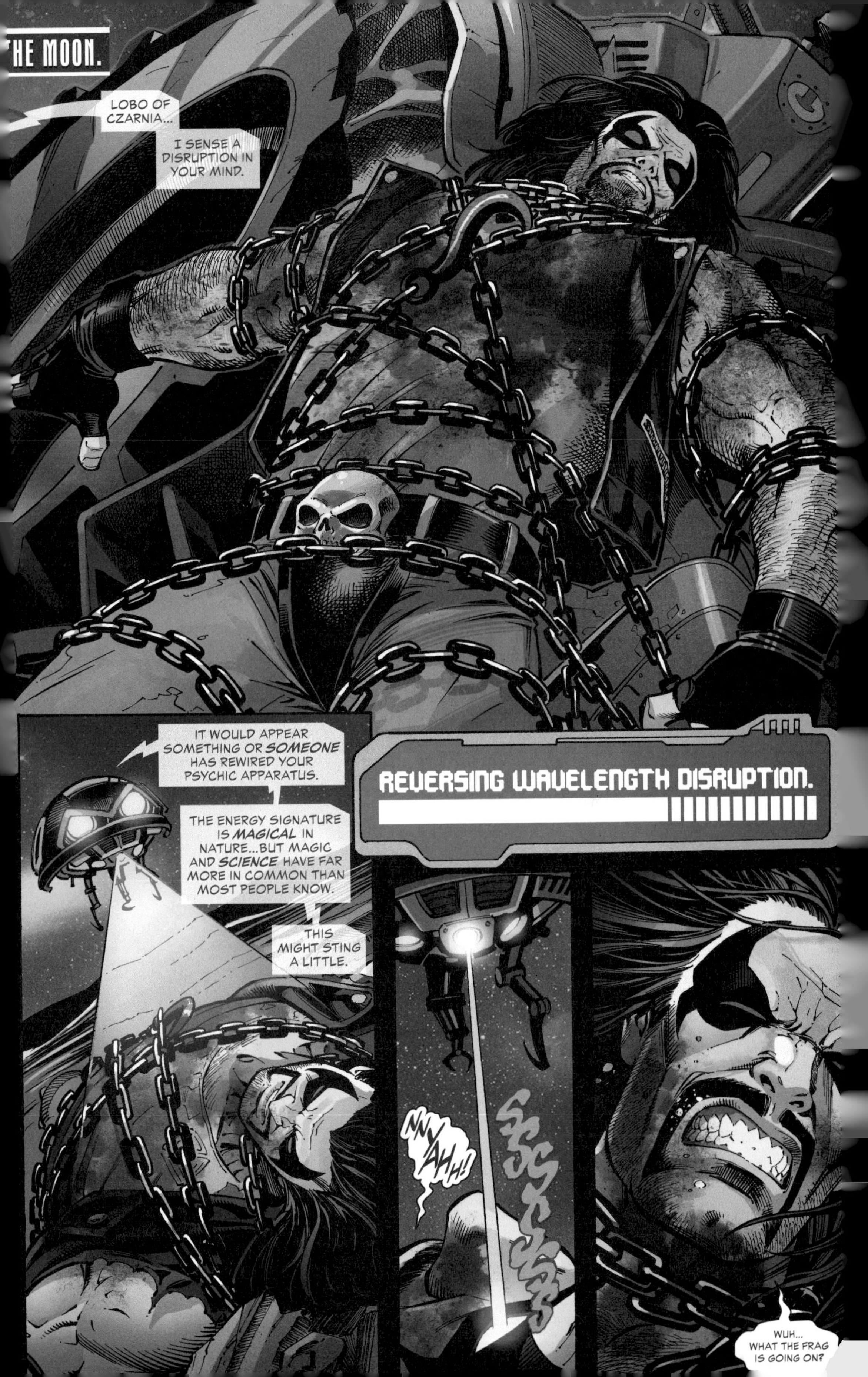
THE MOON.
LOBO OF CZARNIA...
I SENSE A DISRUPTION IN YOUR MIND.
IT WOULD APPEAR SOMETHING OR SOMEONE HAS REWIRED YOUR PSYCHIC APPARATUS.
THE ENERGY SIGNATURE IS MAGICAL IN NATURE...BUT MAGIC AND SCIENCE HAVE FAR MORE IN COMMON THAN MOST PEOPLE KNOW.
THIS MIGHT STING A LITTLE.
REVERSING WAVELENGTH DISRUPTION.
NNYAHH!
SSSSSSSS
WUH... WHAT THE FRAG IS GOING ON?

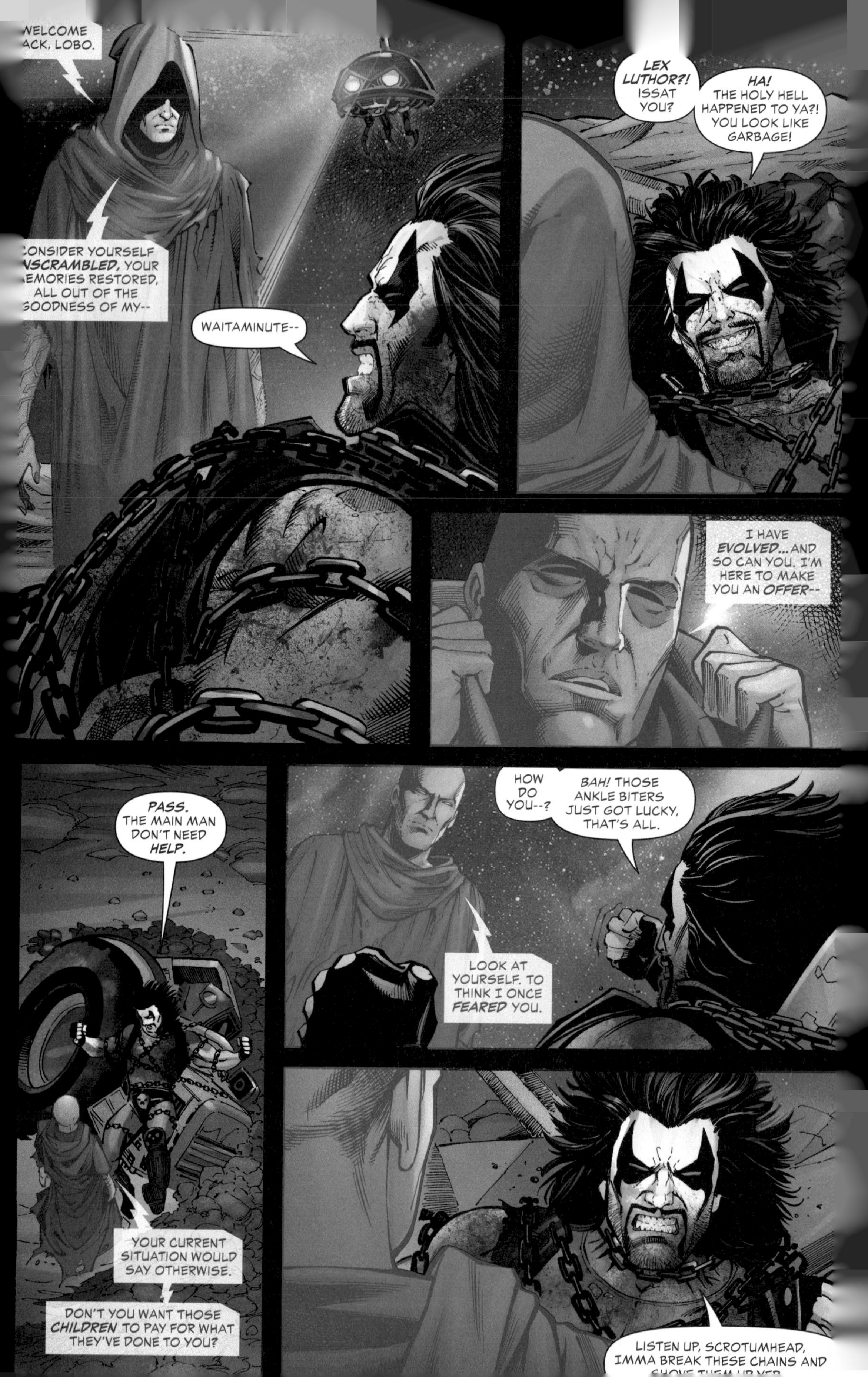
WELCOME BACK, LOBO.
CONSIDER YOURSELF UNSCRAMBLED, YOUR MEMORIES RESTORED, ALL OUT OF THE GOODNESS OF MY--
WAITAMINUTE--
LEX LUTHOR?! ISSAT YOU?
HA! THE HOLY HELL HAPPENED TO YA?! YOU LOOK LIKE GARBAGE!
I HAVE EVOLVED...AND SO CAN YOU. I'M HERE TO MAKE YOU AN OFFER--
PASS. THE MAIN MAN DON'T NEED HELP.
YOUR CURRENT SITUATION WOULD SAY OTHERWISE.
DON'T YOU WANT THOSE CHILDREN TO PAY FOR WHAT THEY'VE DONE TO YOU?
HOW DO YOU--?
BAH! THOSE ANKLE BITERS JUST GOT LUCKY, THAT'S ALL.
LOOK AT YOURSELF. TO THINK I ONCE FEARED YOU.
LISTEN UP, SCROTUMHEAD, IMMA BREAK THESE CHAINS AND

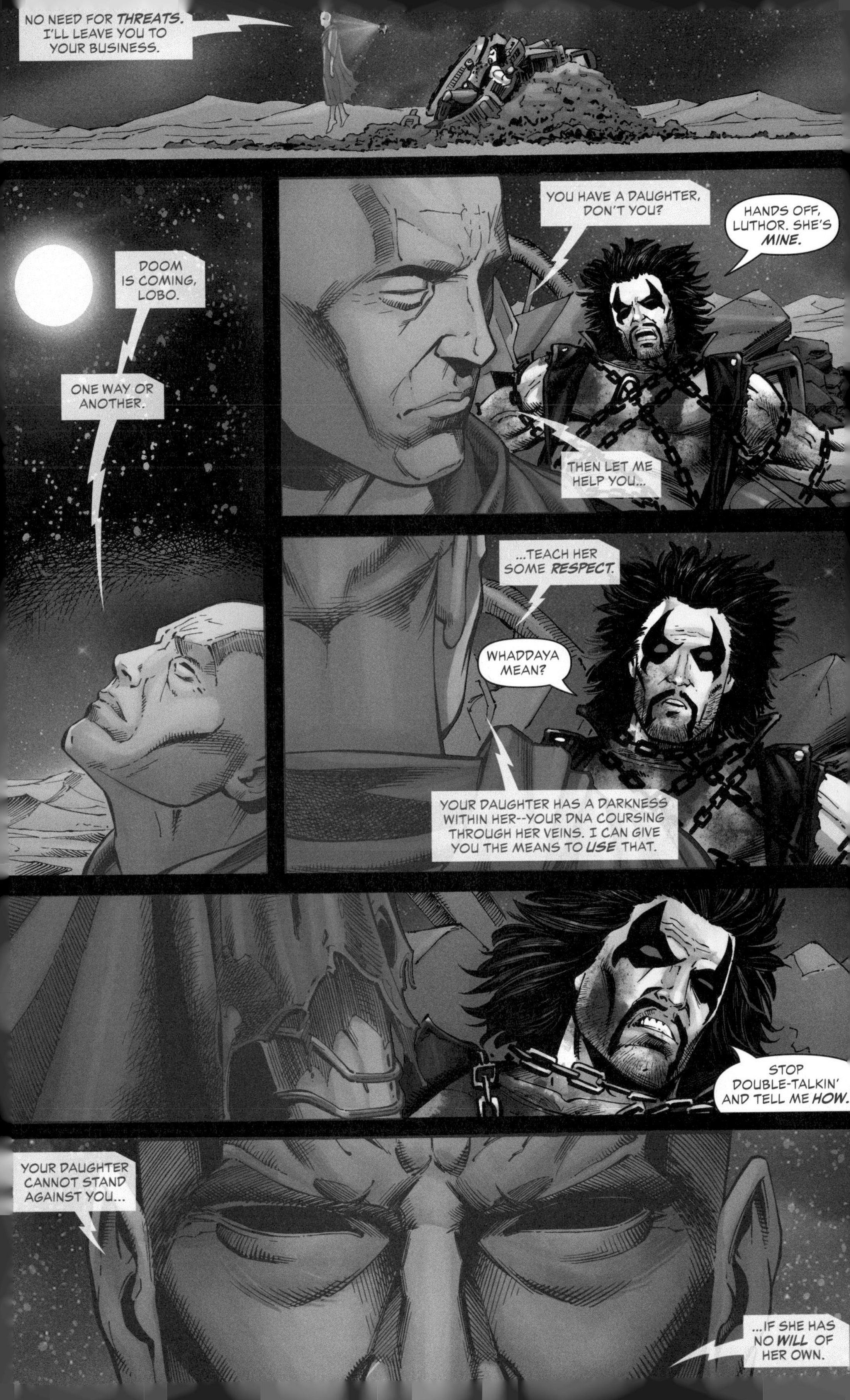
NO NEED FOR THREATS. I'LL LEAVE YOU TO YOUR BUSINESS.
DOOM IS COMING, LOBO.
ONE WAY OR ANOTHER.
YOU HAVE A DAUGHTER, DON'T YOU?
HANDS OFF, LUTHOR. SHE'S MINE.
THEN LET ME HELP YOU...
...TEACH HER SOME RESPECT.
WHADDAYA MEAN?
YOUR DAUGHTER HAS A DARKNESS WITHIN HER--YOUR DNA COURSING THROUGH HER VEINS. I CAN GIVE YOU THE MEANS TO USE THAT.
STOP DOUBLE-TALKIN' AND TELL ME HOW.
YOUR DAUGHTER CANNOT STAND AGAINST YOU...
...IF SHE HAS NO WILL OF HER OWN.

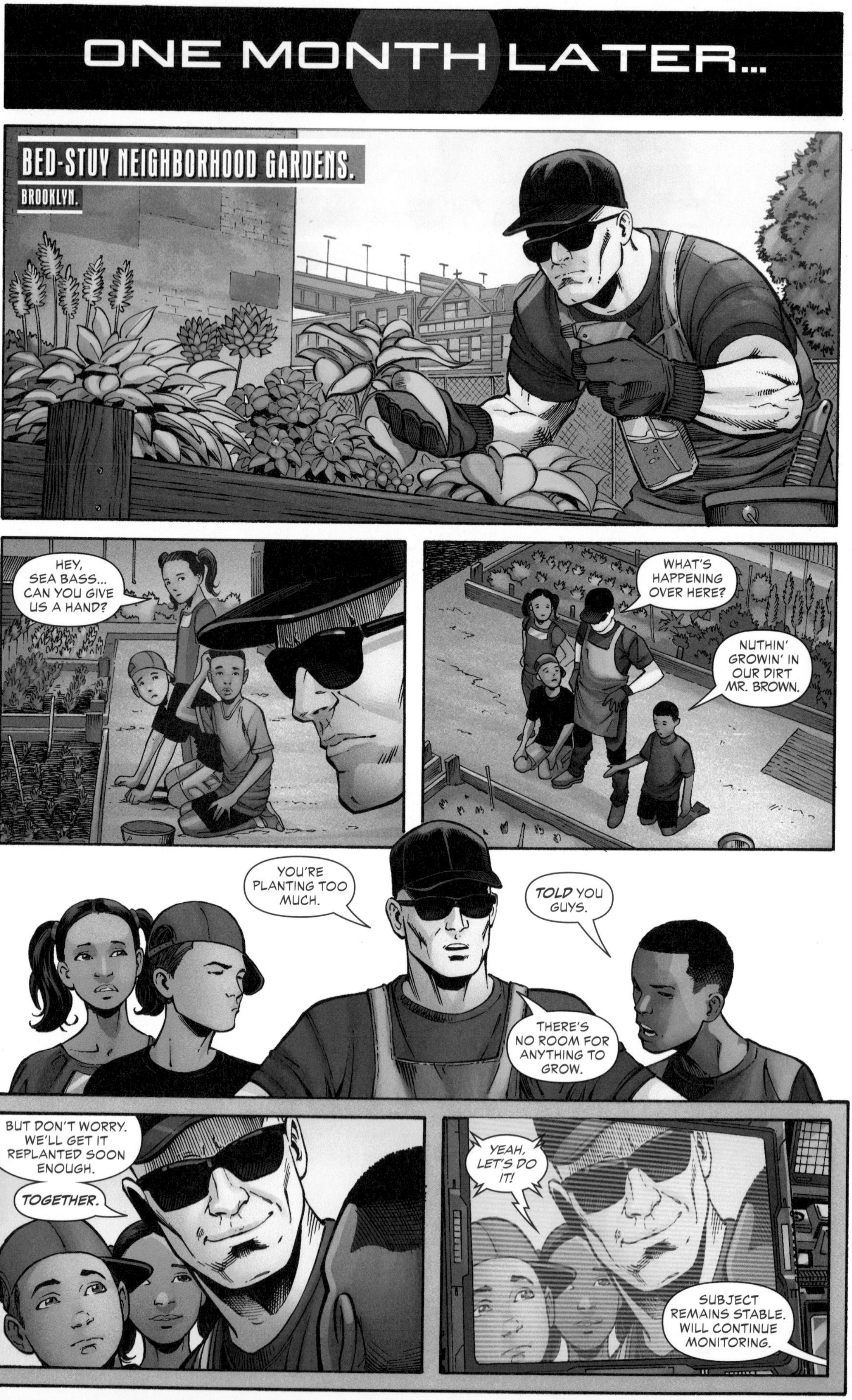
ONE MONTH LATER...
BED-STUY NEIGHBORHOOD GARDENS.
BROOKLYN.
HEY, SEA BASS... CAN YOU GIVE US A HAND?
WHAT'S HAPPENING OVER HERE?
NUTHIN' GROWIN' IN OUR DIRT MR. BROWN.
YOU'RE PLANTING TOO MUCH.
TOLD YOU GUYS.
THERE'S NO ROOM FOR ANYTHING TO GROW.
BUT DON'T WORRY. WE'LL GET IT REPLANTED SOON ENOUGH.
TOGETHER.
YEAH, LET'S DO IT!
SUBJECT REMAINS STABLE. WILL CONTINUE MONITORING.

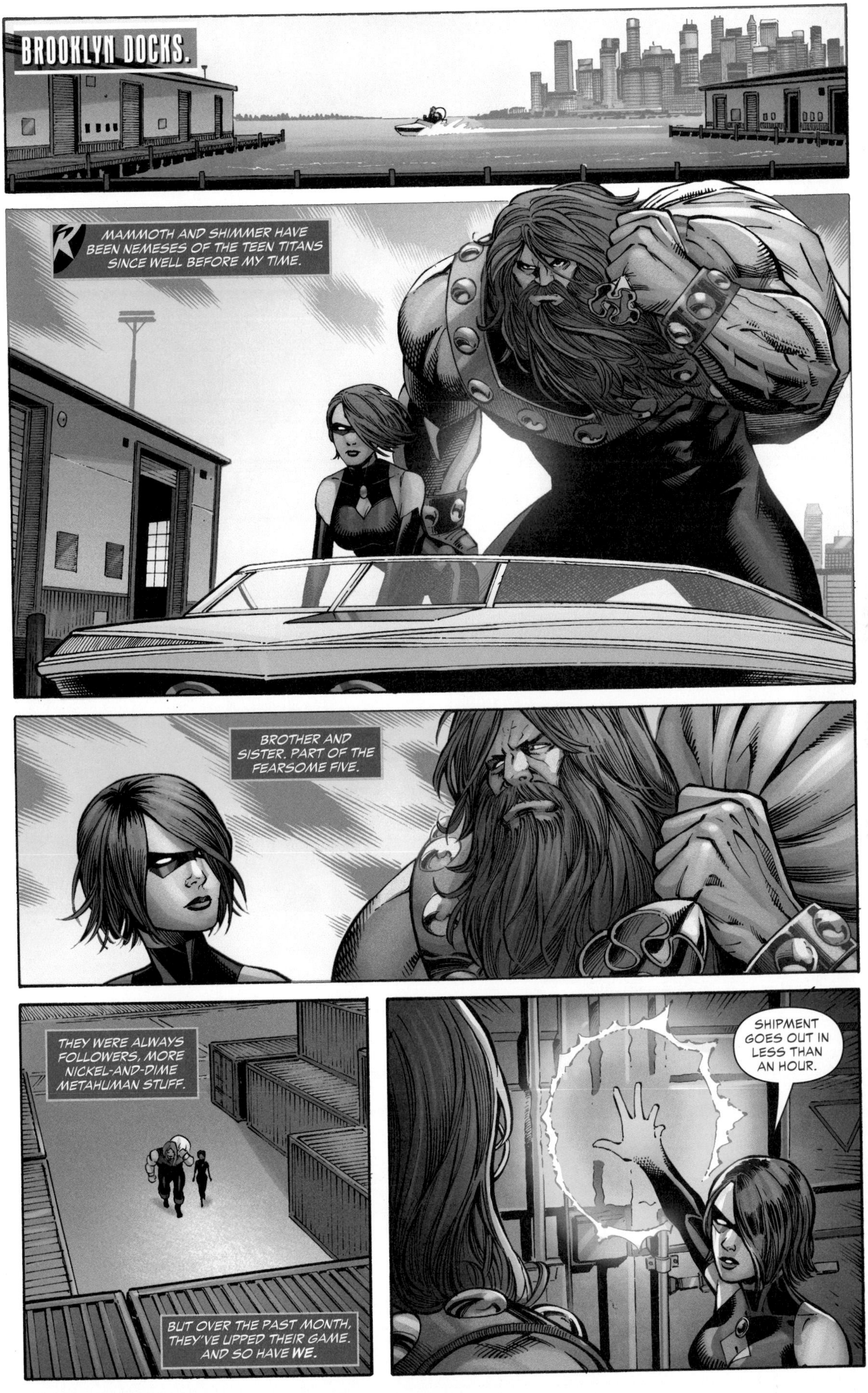
BROOKLYN DOCKS.
MAMMOTH AND SHIMMER HAVE BEEN NEMESES OF THE TEEN TITANS SINCE WELL BEFORE MY TIME.
BROTHER AND SISTER. PART OF THE FEARSOME FIVE.
THEY WERE ALWAYS FOLLOWERS, MORE NICKEL-AND-DIME METAHUMAN STUFF.
BUT OVER THE PAST MONTH, THEY'VE UPPED THEIR GAME. AND SO HAVE WE.
SHIPMENT GOES OUT IN LESS THAN AN HOUR.

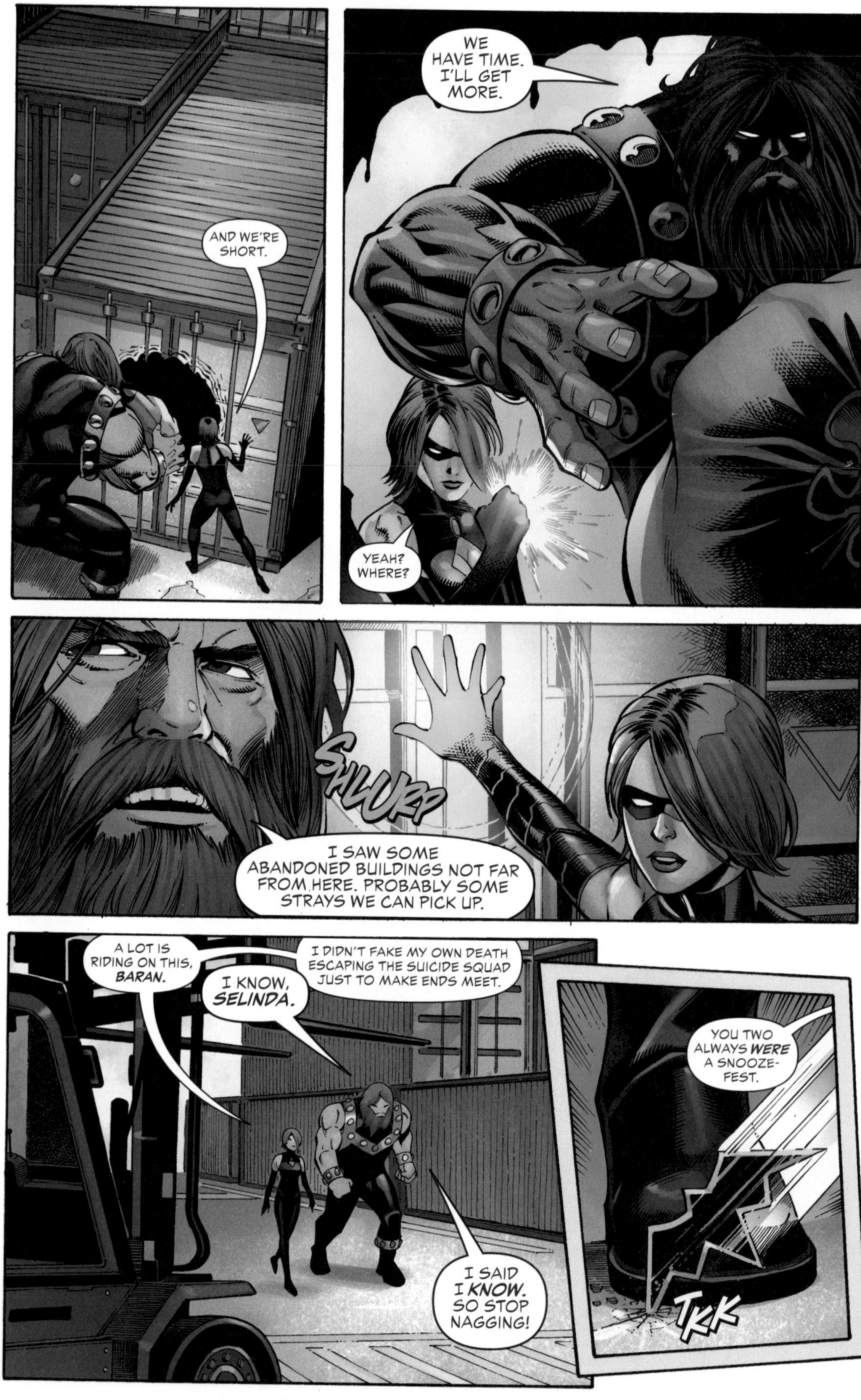
AND WE'RE SHORT.
WE HAVE TIME. I'LL GET MORE.
YEAH? WHERE?
SHLURP
I SAW SOME ABANDONED BUILDINGS NOT FAR FROM HERE. PROBABLY SOME STRAYS WE CAN PICK UP.
A LOT IS RIDING ON THIS, *BARAN.*
I DIDN'T FAKE MY OWN DEATH ESCAPING THE SUICIDE SQUAD JUST TO MAKE ENDS MEET.
I KNOW, *SELINDA.*
I SAID I *KNOW.* SO STOP NAGGING!
YOU TWO ALWAYS *WERE* A SNOOZE-FEST.
TKK

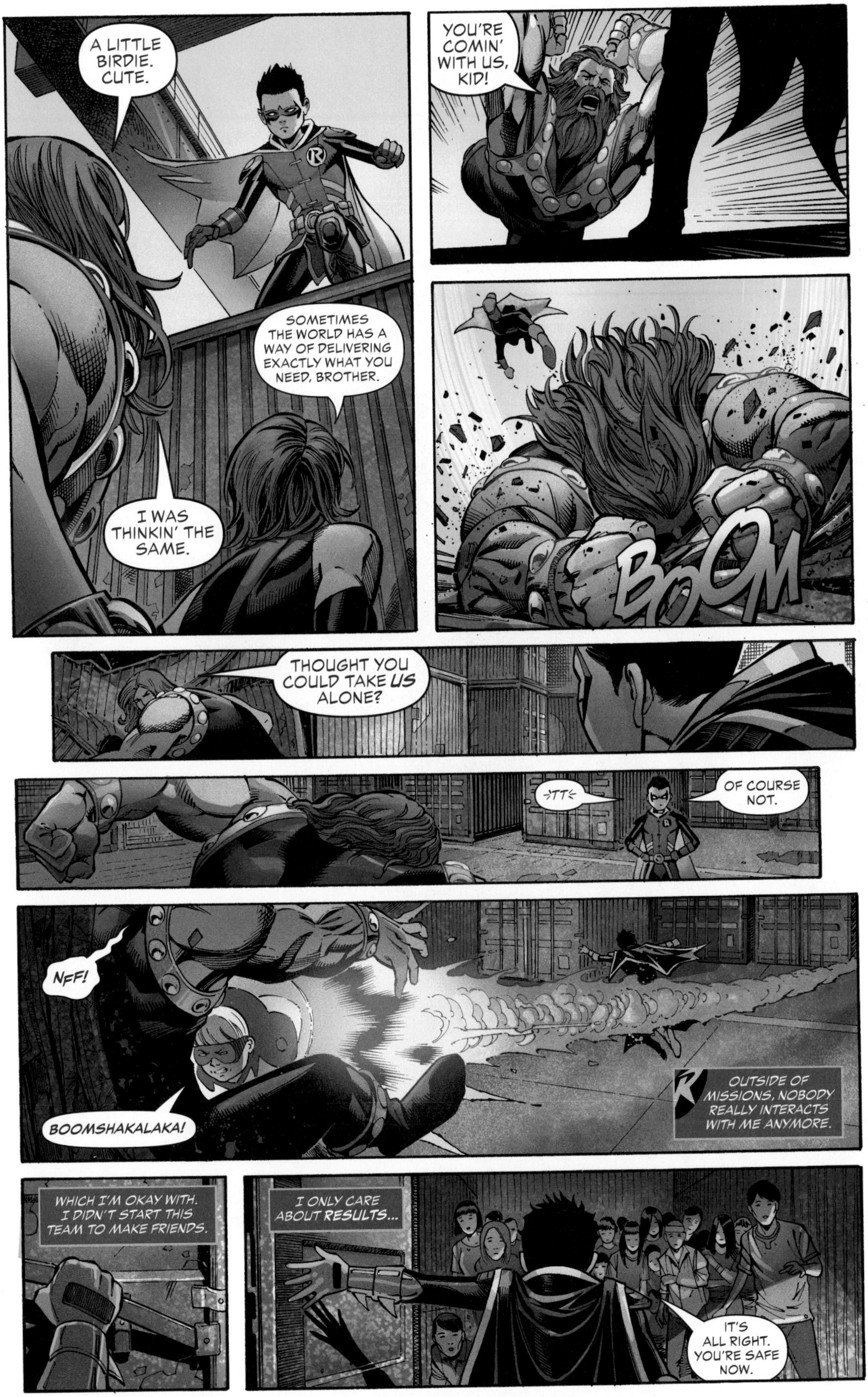
A LITTLE BIRDIE. CUTE.
SOMETIMES THE WORLD HAS A WAY OF DELIVERING EXACTLY WHAT YOU NEED, BROTHER.
I WAS THINKIN' THE SAME.
YOU'RE COMIN' WITH US, KID!
BOOM
THOUGHT YOU COULD TAKE US ALONE?
TT
OF COURSE NOT.
NFF!
BOOMSHAKALAKA!
OUTSIDE OF MISSIONS, NOBODY REALLY INTERACTS WITH ME ANYMORE.
WHICH I'M OKAY WITH. I DIDN'T START THIS TEAM TO MAKE FRIENDS.
I ONLY CARE ABOUT RESULTS...
IT'S ALL RIGHT. YOU'RE SAFE NOW.

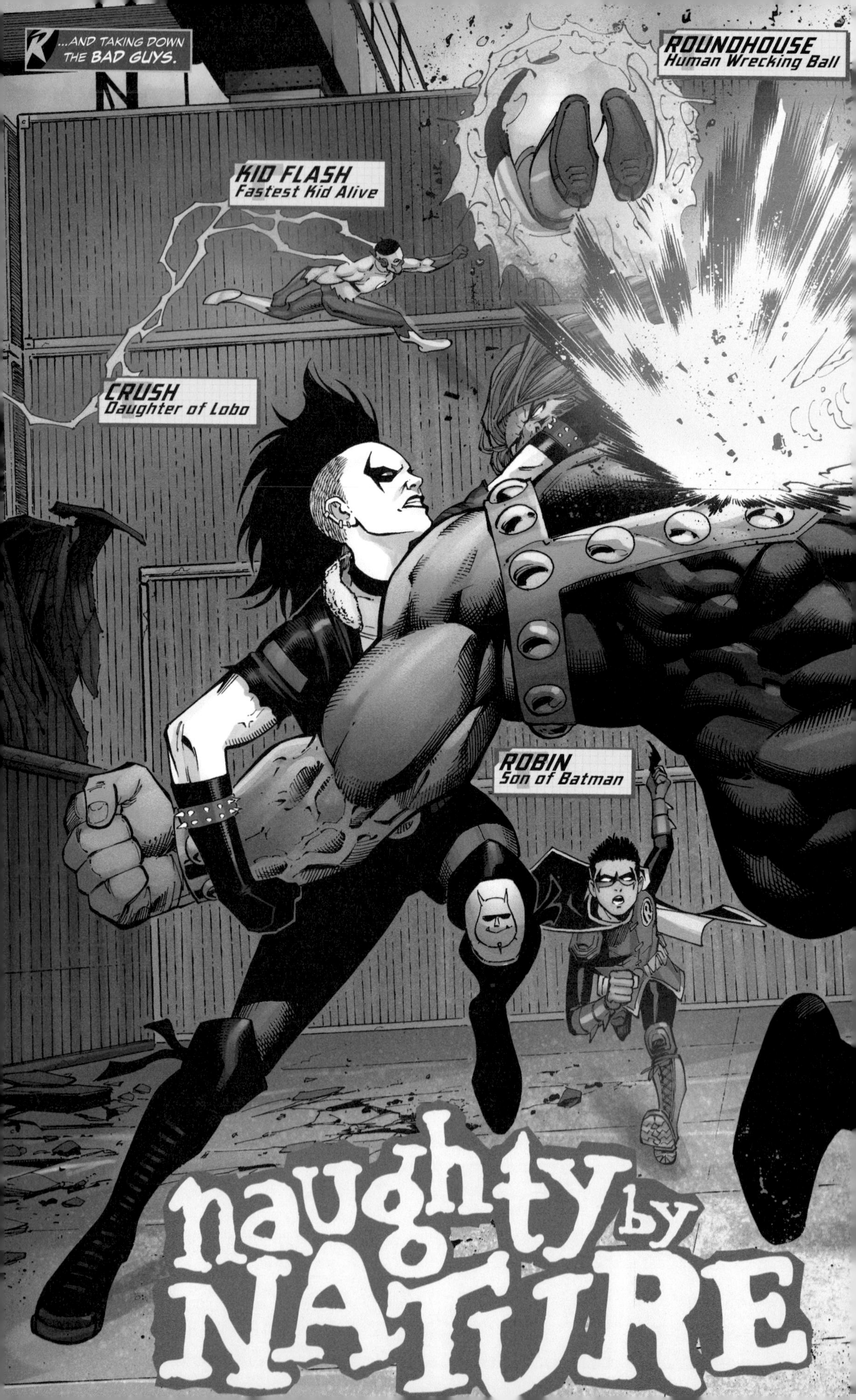
...AND TAKING DOWN THE BAD GUYS.
ROUNDHOUSE Human Wrecking Ball
KID FLASH Fastest Kid Alive
CRUSH Daughter of Lobo
ROBIN Son of Batman
naughty by NATURE

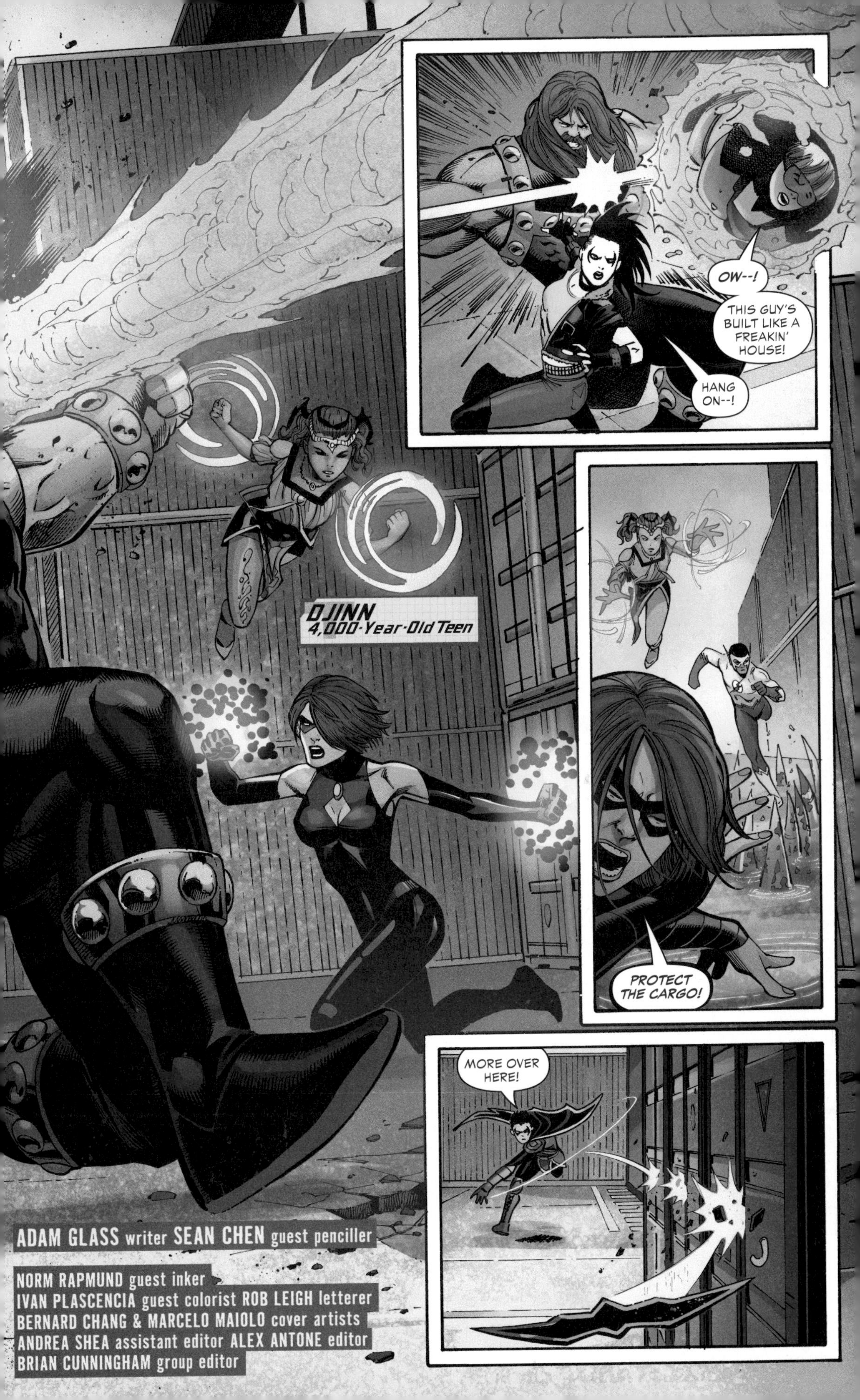
OW--!
THIS GUY'S BUILT LIKE A FREAKIN' HOUSE!
HANG ON--!
DJINN
4,000-Year-Old Teen
PROTECT THE CARGO!
MORE OVER HERE!
ADAM GLASS writer SEAN CHEN guest penciller
NORM RAPMUND guest inker
IVAN PLASCENCIA guest colorist ROB LEIGH letterer
BERNARD CHANG & MARCELO MAIOLO cover artists
ANDREA SHEA assistant editor ALEX ANTONE editor
BRIAN CUNNINGHAM group editor

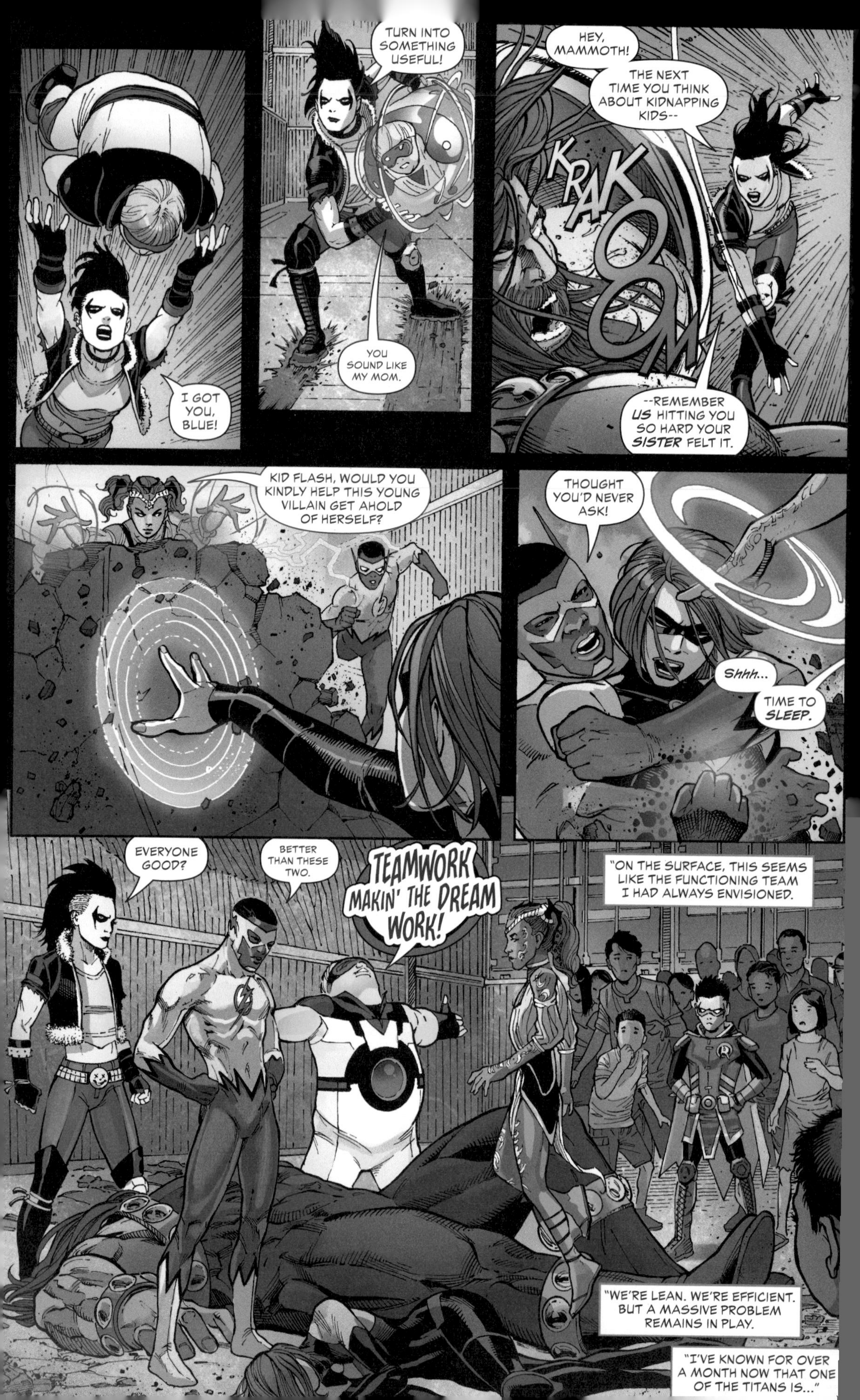

I GOT YOU, BLUE!
TURN INTO SOMETHING USEFUL!
YOU SOUND LIKE MY MOM.
HEY, MAMMOTH!
THE NEXT TIME YOU THINK ABOUT KIDNAPPING KIDS--
KRAKOOOM
--REMEMBER US HITTING YOU SO HARD YOUR SISTER FELT IT.
KID FLASH, WOULD YOU KINDLY HELP THIS YOUNG VILLAIN GET AHOLD OF HERSELF?
THOUGHT YOU'D NEVER ASK!
Shhh...
TIME TO SLEEP.
EVERYONE GOOD?
BETTER THAN THESE TWO.
TEAMWORK MAKIN' THE DREAM WORK!
"ON THE SURFACE, THIS SEEMS LIKE THE FUNCTIONING TEAM I HAD ALWAYS ENVISIONED.
"WE'RE LEAN. WE'RE EFFICIENT. BUT A MASSIVE PROBLEM REMAINS IN PLAY.
"I'VE KNOWN FOR OVER A MONTH NOW THAT ONE OF THE TITANS IS..."

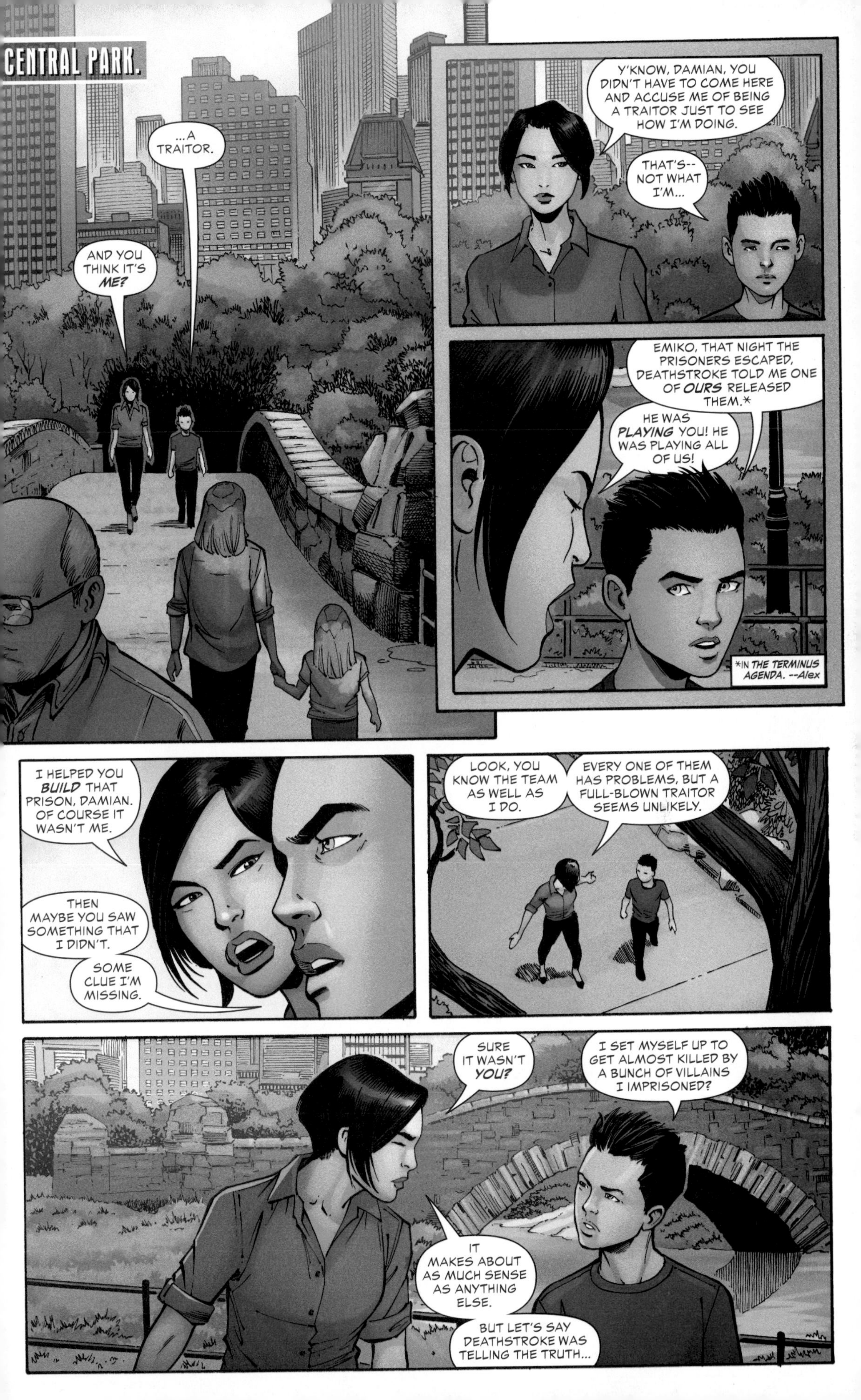
CENTRAL PARK.
AND YOU THINK IT'S *ME?*
...A TRAITOR.
Y'KNOW, DAMIAN, YOU DIDN'T HAVE TO COME HERE AND ACCUSE ME OF BEING A TRAITOR JUST TO SEE HOW I'M DOING.
THAT'S-- NOT WHAT I'M...
EMIKO, THAT NIGHT THE PRISONERS ESCAPED, DEATHSTROKE TOLD ME ONE OF *OURS* RELEASED THEM.*
HE WAS *PLAYING* YOU! HE WAS PLAYING ALL OF US!
*IN *THE TERMINUS AGENDA.* --*Alex*
I HELPED YOU *BUILD* THAT PRISON, DAMIAN. OF COURSE IT WASN'T ME.
THEN MAYBE YOU SAW SOMETHING THAT I DIDN'T.
SOME CLUE I'M MISSING.
LOOK, YOU KNOW THE TEAM AS WELL AS I DO.
EVERY ONE OF THEM HAS PROBLEMS, BUT A FULL-BLOWN TRAITOR SEEMS UNLIKELY.
SURE IT WASN'T *YOU?*
I SET MYSELF UP TO GET ALMOST KILLED BY A BUNCH OF VILLAINS I IMPRISONED?
IT MAKES ABOUT AS MUCH SENSE AS ANYTHING ELSE.
BUT LET'S SAY DEATHSTROKE WAS TELLING THE TRUTH...

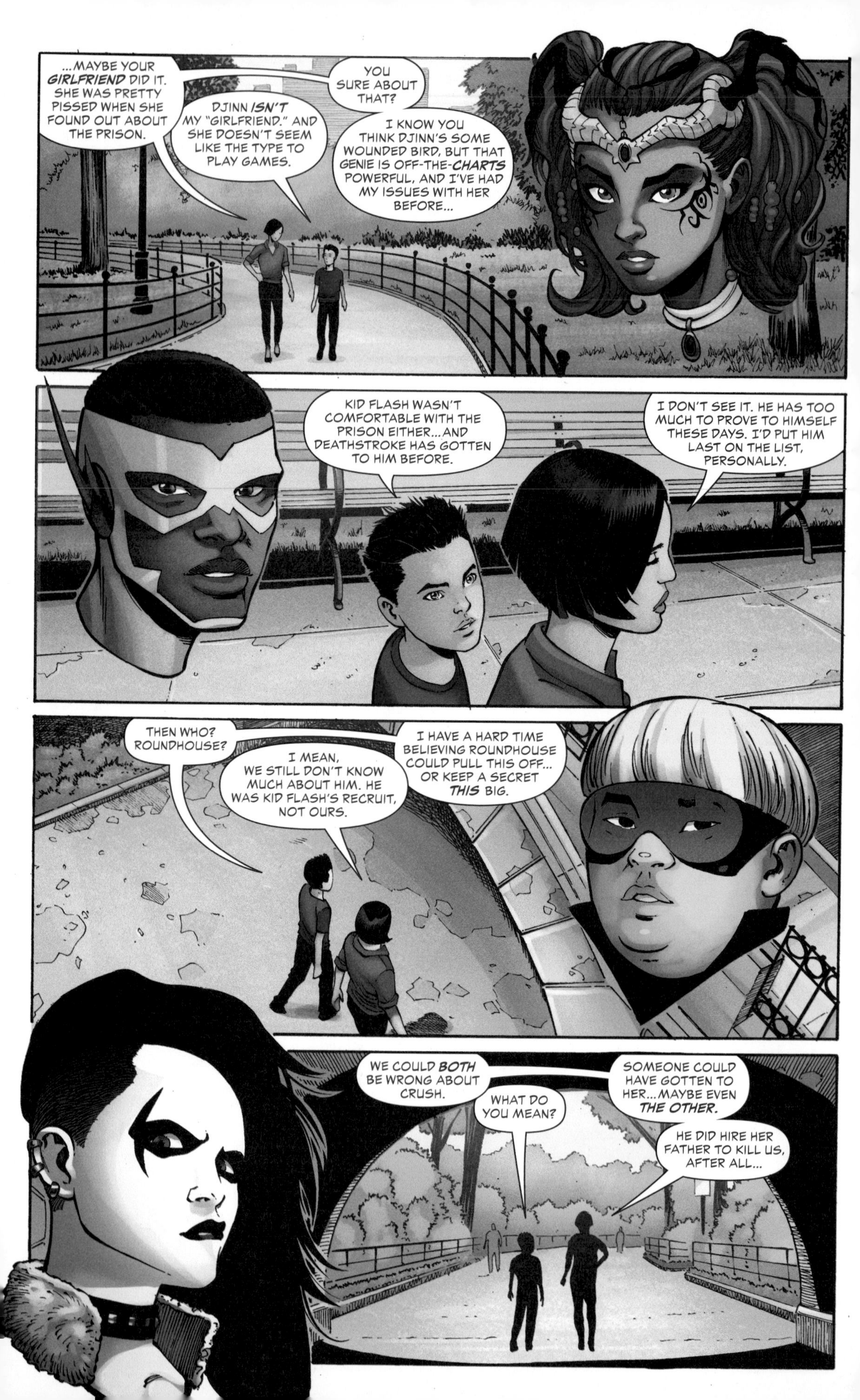
...MAYBE YOUR GIRLFRIEND DID IT. SHE WAS PRETTY PISSED WHEN SHE FOUND OUT ABOUT THE PRISON.
YOU SURE ABOUT THAT?
DJINN ISN'T MY "GIRLFRIEND." AND SHE DOESN'T SEEM LIKE THE TYPE TO PLAY GAMES.
I KNOW YOU THINK DJINN'S SOME WOUNDED BIRD, BUT THAT GENIE IS OFF-THE-CHARTS POWERFUL, AND I'VE HAD MY ISSUES WITH HER BEFORE...
KID FLASH WASN'T COMFORTABLE WITH THE PRISON EITHER...AND DEATHSTROKE HAS GOTTEN TO HIM BEFORE.
I DON'T SEE IT. HE HAS TOO MUCH TO PROVE TO HIMSELF THESE DAYS. I'D PUT HIM LAST ON THE LIST, PERSONALLY.
THEN WHO? ROUNDHOUSE?
I HAVE A HARD TIME BELIEVING ROUNDHOUSE COULD PULL THIS OFF... OR KEEP A SECRET THIS BIG.
I MEAN, WE STILL DON'T KNOW MUCH ABOUT HIM. HE WAS KID FLASH'S RECRUIT, NOT OURS.
WE COULD BOTH BE WRONG ABOUT CRUSH.
WHAT DO YOU MEAN?
SOMEONE COULD HAVE GOTTEN TO HER...MAYBE EVEN THE OTHER.
HE DID HIRE HER FATHER TO KILL US, AFTER ALL...

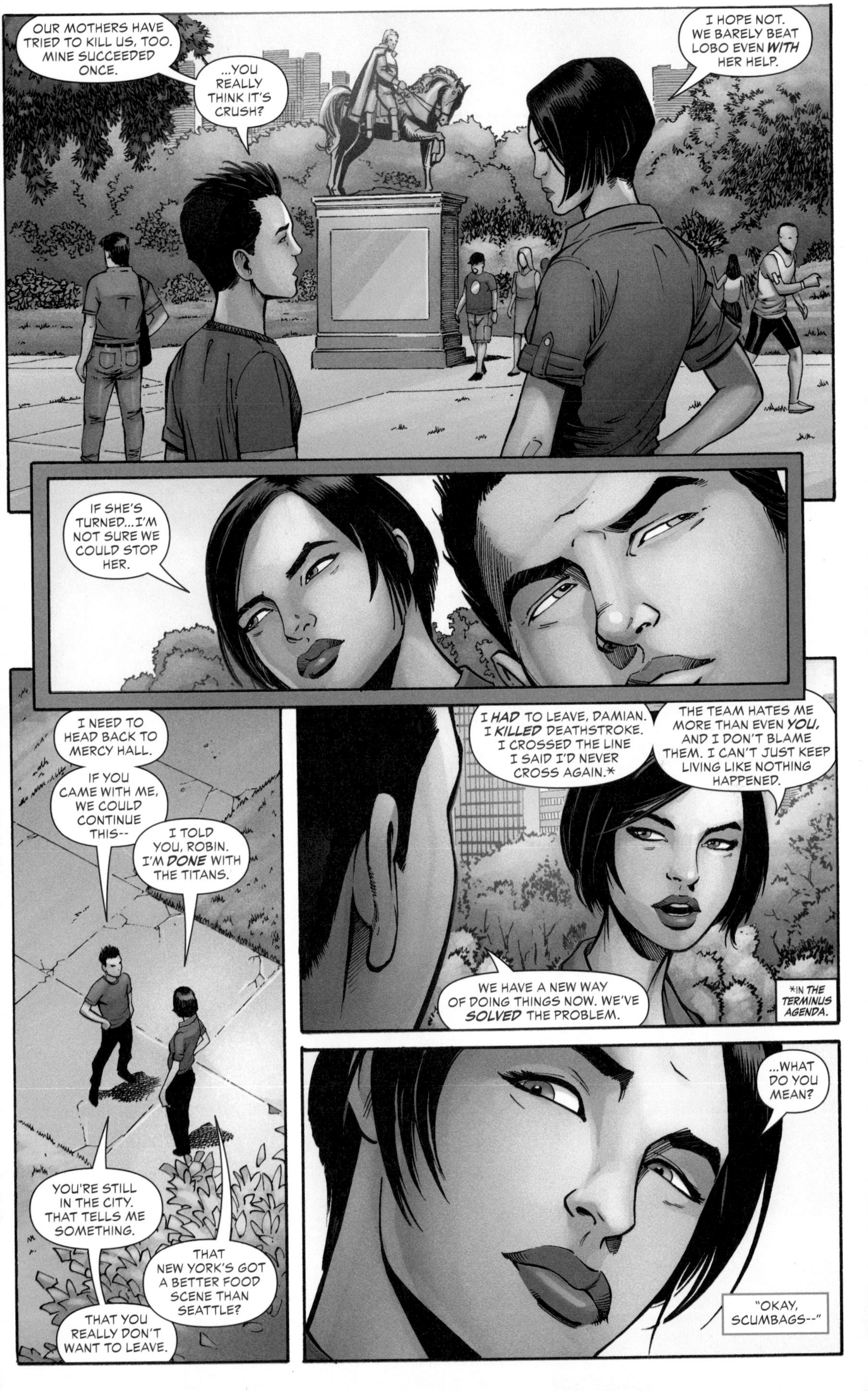
OUR MOTHERS HAVE TRIED TO KILL US, TOO. MINE SUCCEEDED ONCE.
...YOU REALLY THINK IT'S CRUSH?
I HOPE NOT. WE BARELY BEAT LOBO EVEN *WITH* HER HELP.
IF SHE'S TURNED...I'M NOT SURE WE COULD STOP HER.
I NEED TO HEAD BACK TO MERCY HALL.
IF YOU CAME WITH ME, WE COULD CONTINUE THIS--
I TOLD YOU, ROBIN. I'M *DONE* WITH THE TITANS.
YOU'RE STILL IN THE CITY. THAT TELLS ME SOMETHING.
THAT NEW YORK'S GOT A BETTER FOOD SCENE THAN SEATTLE?
THAT YOU REALLY DON'T WANT TO LEAVE.
I *HAD* TO LEAVE, DAMIAN. I *KILLED* DEATHSTROKE. I CROSSED THE LINE I SAID I'D NEVER CROSS AGAIN.*
THE TEAM HATES ME MORE THAN EVEN *YOU,* AND I DON'T BLAME THEM. I CAN'T JUST KEEP LIVING LIKE NOTHING HAPPENED.
WE HAVE A NEW WAY OF DOING THINGS NOW. WE'VE *SOLVED* THE PROBLEM.
*IN *THE TERMINUS AGENDA*.
...WHAT DO YOU MEAN?
"OKAY, SCUMBAGS--"

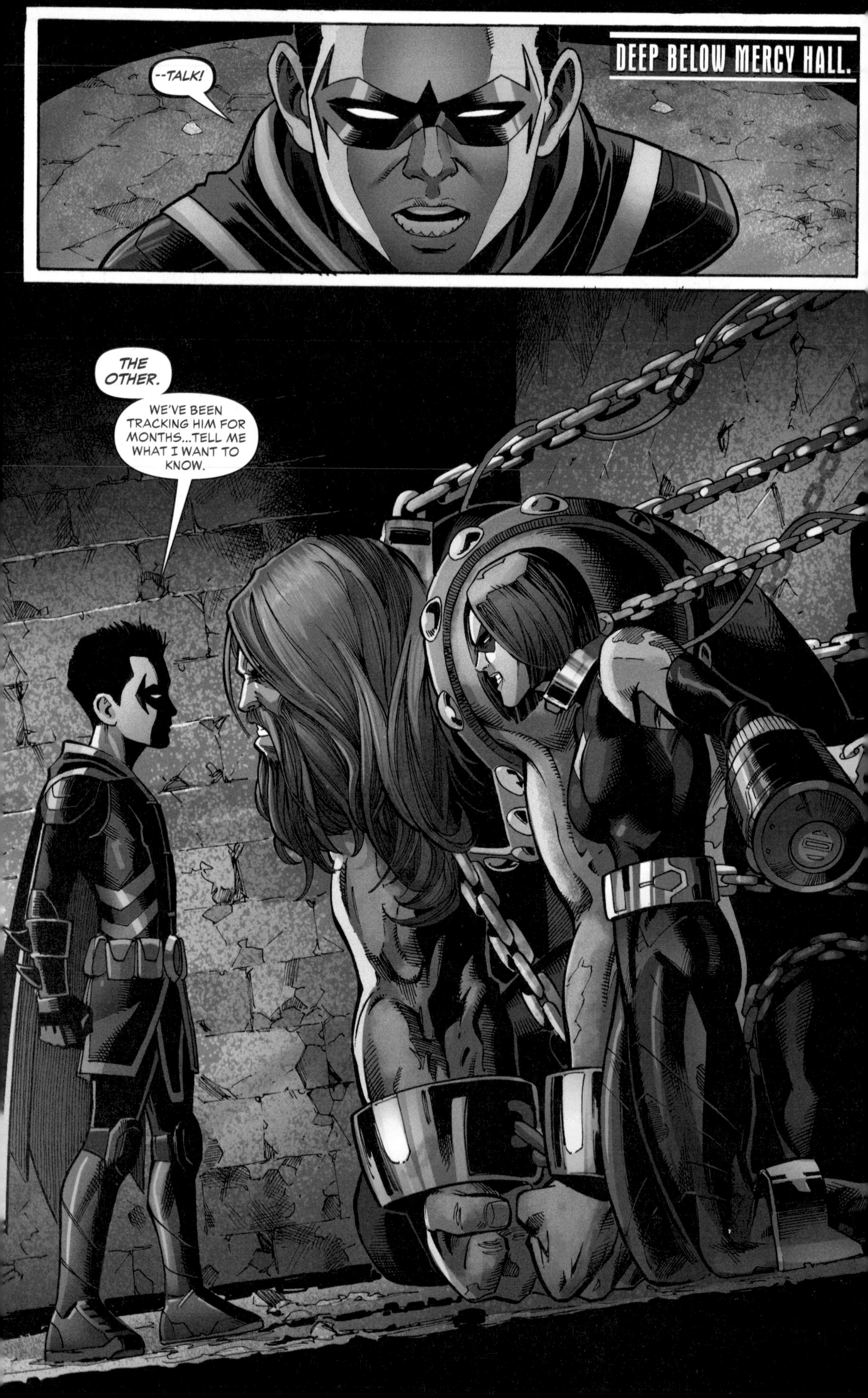
DEEP BELOW MERCY HALL.
--TALK!
THE OTHER.
WE'VE BEEN TRACKING HIM FOR MONTHS...TELL ME WHAT I WANT TO KNOW.

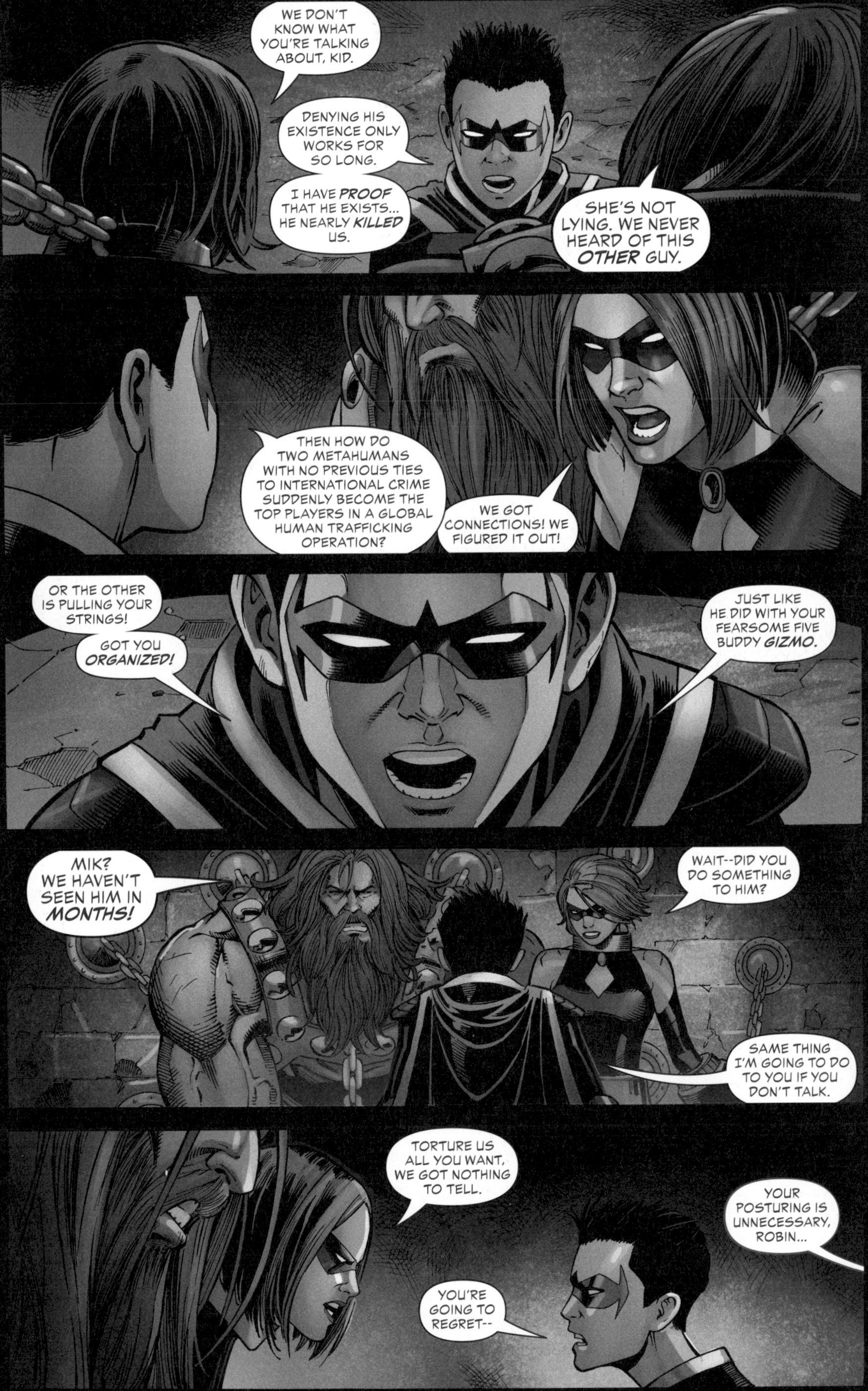
WE DON'T KNOW WHAT YOU'RE TALKING ABOUT, KID.
DENYING HIS EXISTENCE ONLY WORKS FOR SO LONG.
I HAVE PROOF THAT HE EXISTS... HE NEARLY KILLED US.
SHE'S NOT LYING. WE NEVER HEARD OF THIS OTHER GUY.
THEN HOW DO TWO METAHUMANS WITH NO PREVIOUS TIES TO INTERNATIONAL CRIME SUDDENLY BECOME THE TOP PLAYERS IN A GLOBAL HUMAN TRAFFICKING OPERATION?
WE GOT CONNECTIONS! WE FIGURED IT OUT!
OR THE OTHER IS PULLING YOUR STRINGS!
GOT YOU ORGANIZED!
JUST LIKE HE DID WITH YOUR FEARSOME FIVE BUDDY GIZMO.
MIK? WE HAVEN'T SEEN HIM IN MONTHS!
WAIT--DID YOU DO SOMETHING TO HIM?
SAME THING I'M GOING TO DO TO YOU IF YOU DON'T TALK.
TORTURE US ALL YOU WANT, WE GOT NOTHING TO TELL.
YOU'RE GOING TO REGRET--
YOUR POSTURING IS UNNECESSARY, ROBIN...

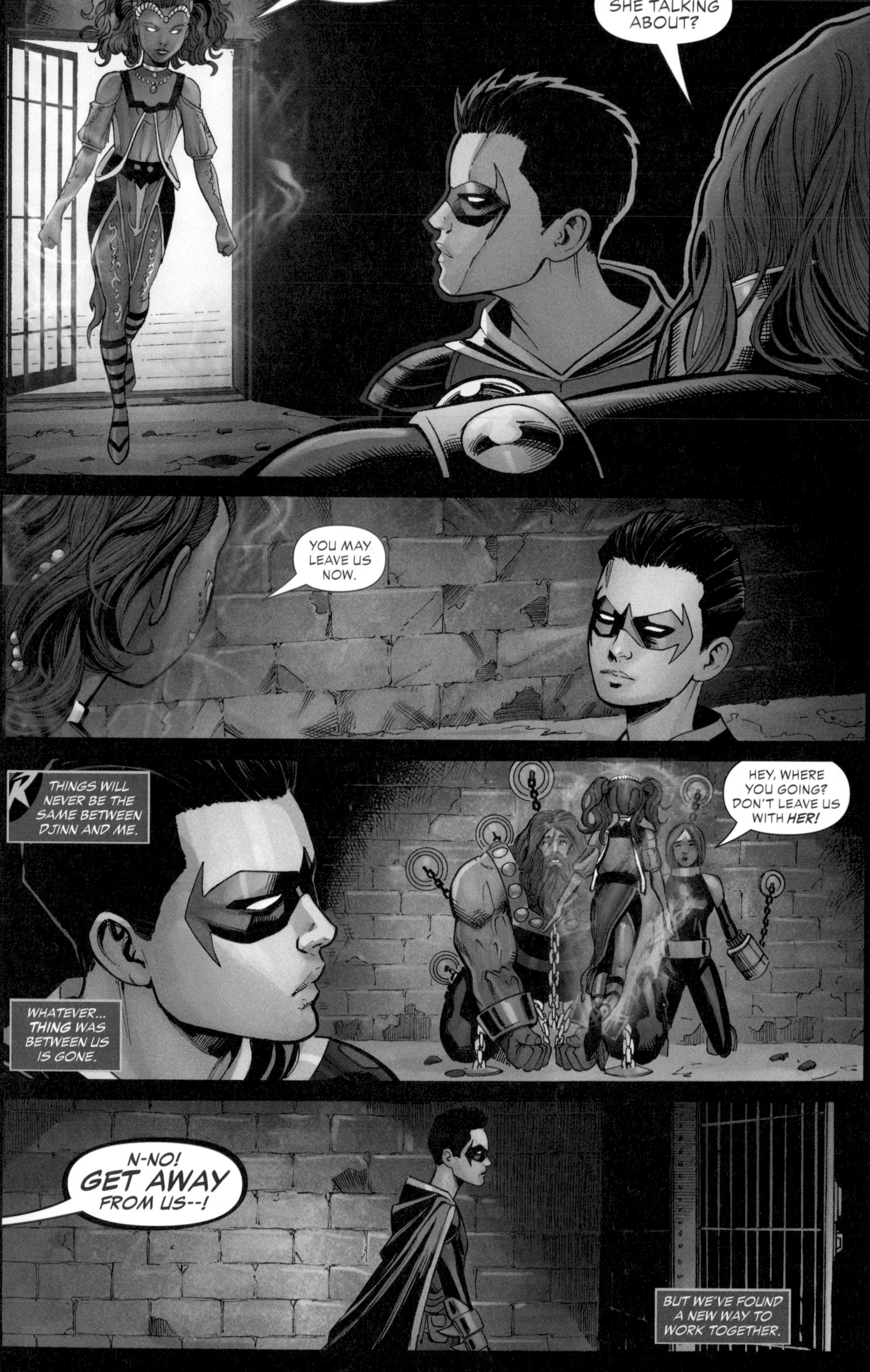

...I WILL KNOW ALL SOON ENOUGH.
THE HELL IS SHE TALKING ABOUT?
YOU MAY LEAVE US NOW.
THINGS WILL NEVER BE THE SAME BETWEEN DJINN AND ME.
HEY, WHERE YOU GOING? DON'T LEAVE US WITH HER!
WHATEVER... THING WAS BETWEEN US IS GONE.
N-NO! GET AWAY FROM US--!
BUT WE'VE FOUND A NEW WAY TO WORK TOGETHER.

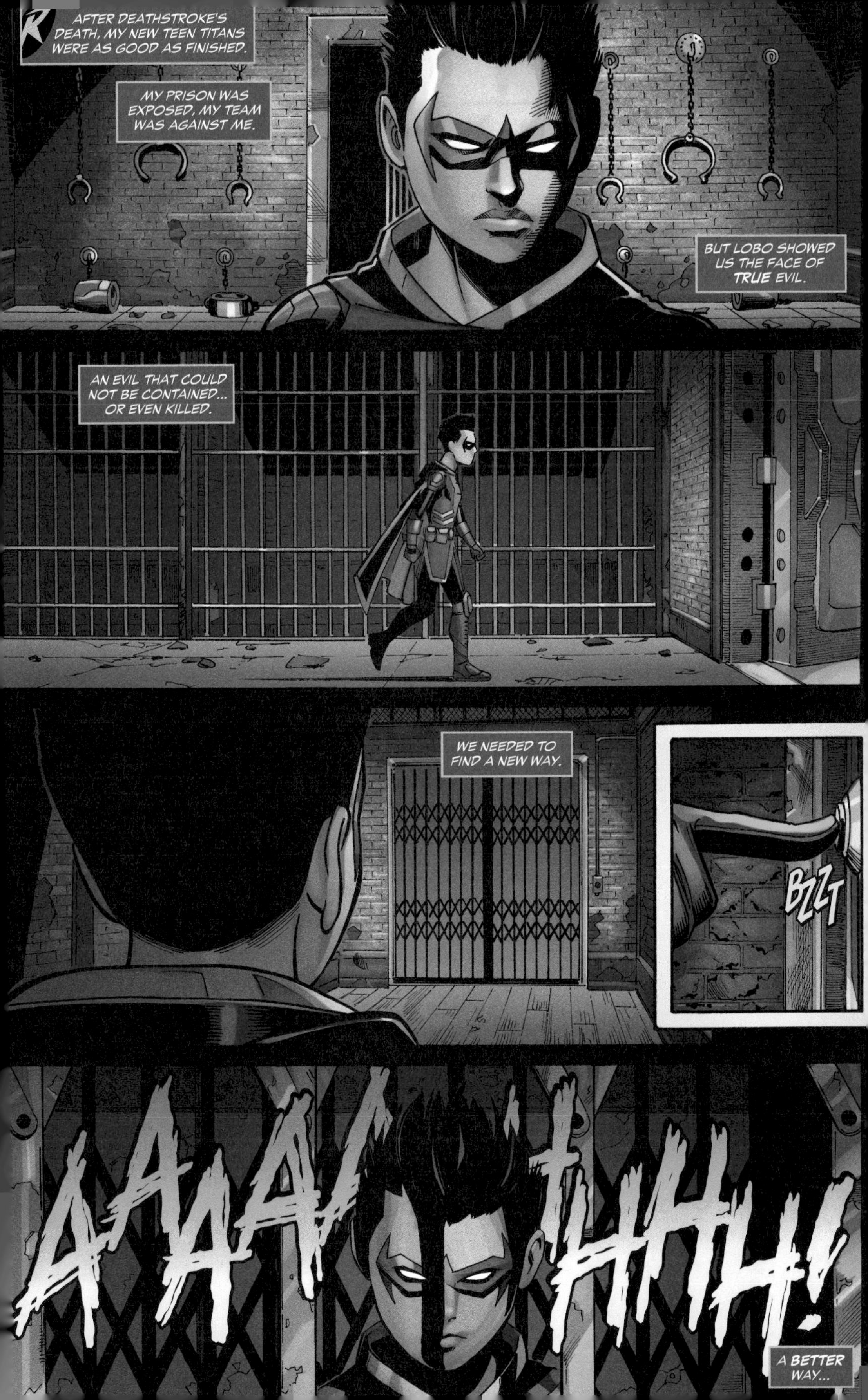
AFTER DEATHSTROKE'S DEATH, MY NEW TEEN TITANS WERE AS GOOD AS FINISHED.
MY PRISON WAS EXPOSED, MY TEAM WAS AGAINST ME.
BUT LOBO SHOWED US THE FACE OF TRUE EVIL.
AN EVIL THAT COULD NOT BE CONTAINED... OR EVEN KILLED.
WE NEEDED TO FIND A NEW WAY.
BZZT
AAAAHHH!
A BETTER WAY...

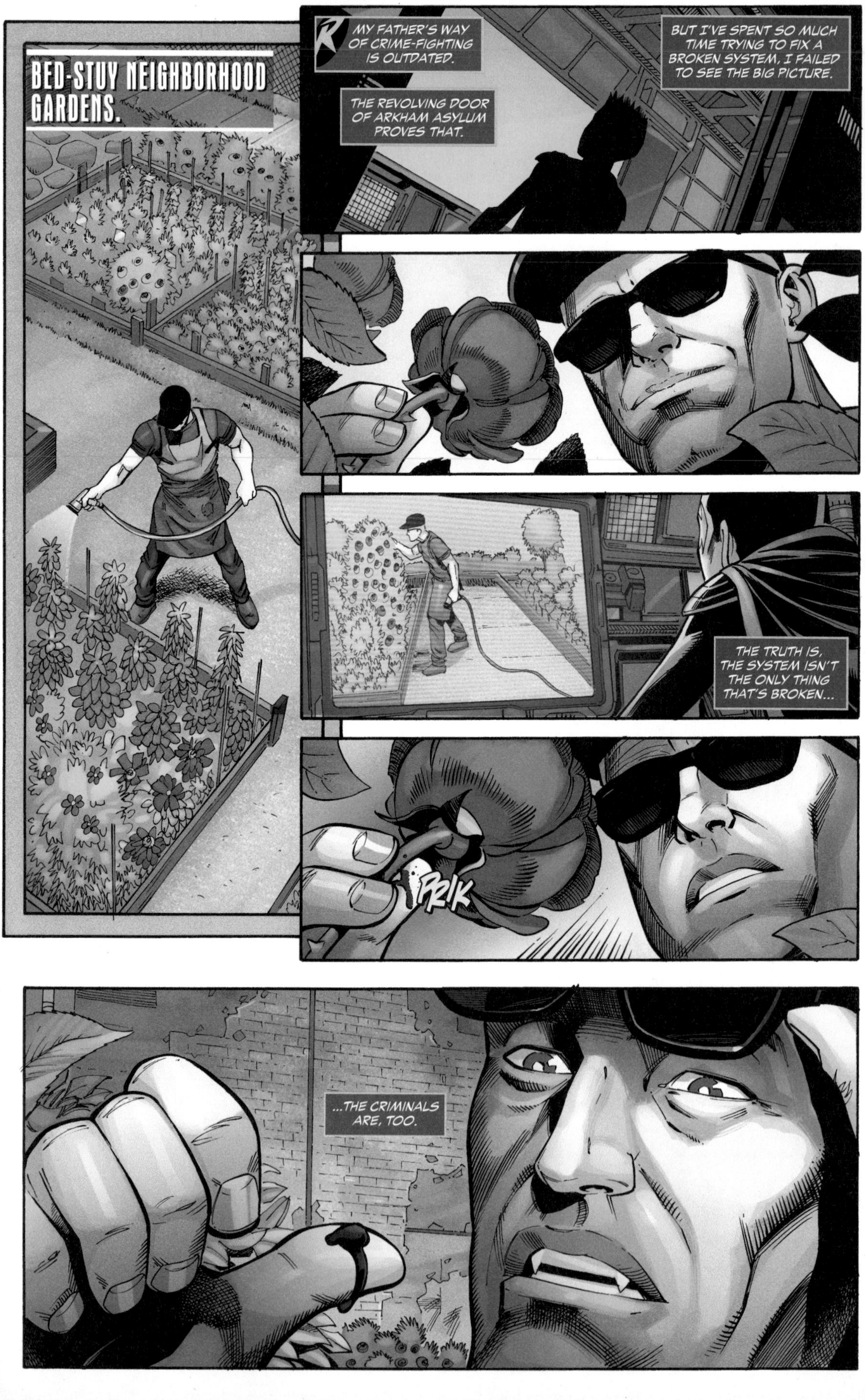
BED-STUY NEIGHBORHOOD GARDENS.
MY FATHER'S WAY OF CRIME-FIGHTING IS OUTDATED.
THE REVOLVING DOOR OF ARKHAM ASYLUM PROVES THAT.
BUT I'VE SPENT SO MUCH TIME TRYING TO FIX A BROKEN SYSTEM, I FAILED TO SEE THE BIG PICTURE.
THE TRUTH IS, THE SYSTEM ISN'T THE ONLY THING THAT'S BROKEN...
PRIK
...THE CRIMINALS ARE, TOO.

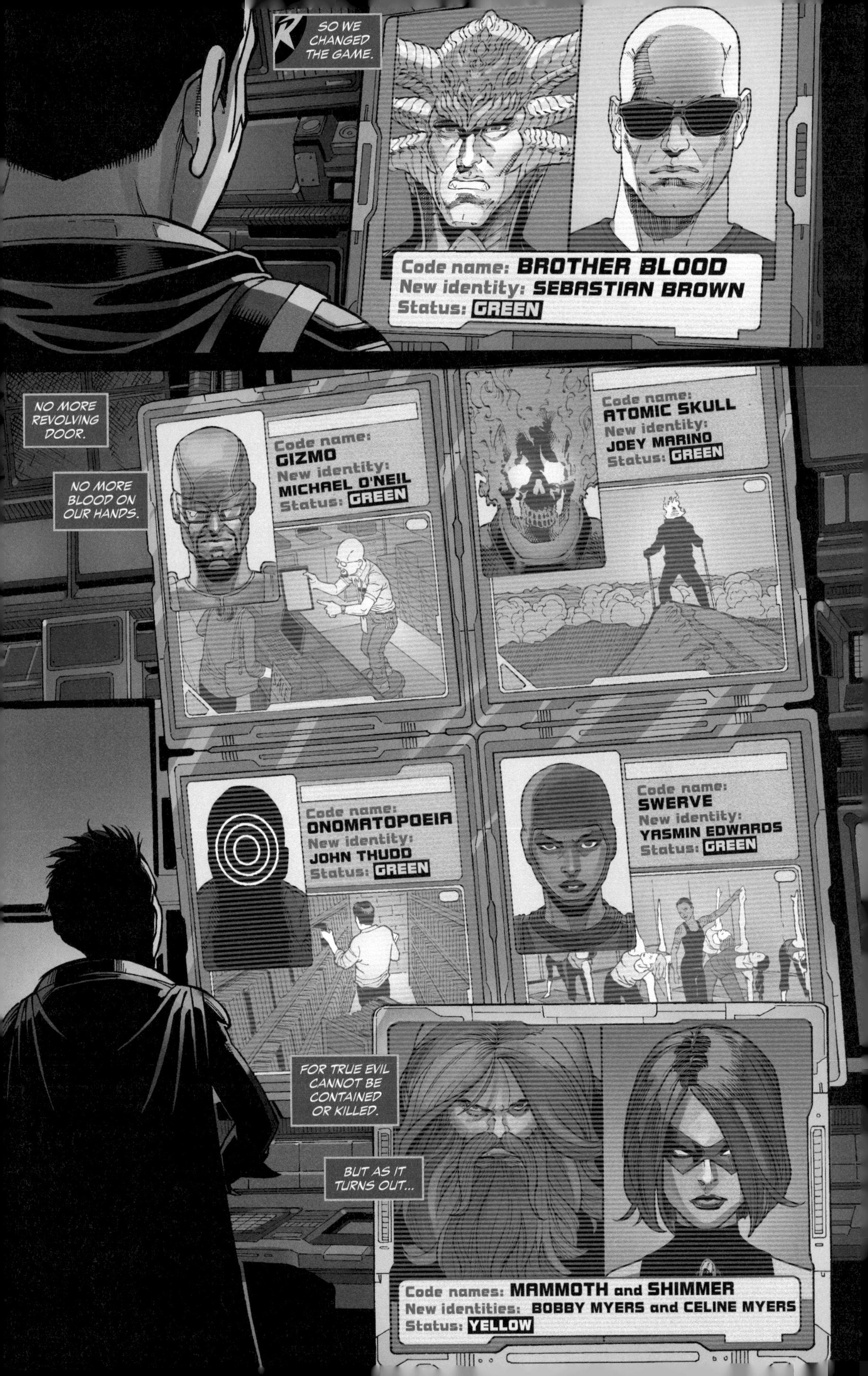
SO WE CHANGED THE GAME.
Code name: BROTHER BLOOD
New identity: SEBASTIAN BROWN
Status: GREEN
NO MORE REVOLVING DOOR.
NO MORE BLOOD ON OUR HANDS.
Code name: GIZMO
New identity: MICHAEL O'NEIL
Status: GREEN
Code name: ATOMIC SKULL
New identity: JOEY MARINO
Status: GREEN
Code name: ONOMATOPOEIA
New identity: JOHN THUDD
Status: GREEN
Code name: SWERVE
New identity: YASMIN EDWARDS
Status: GREEN
FOR TRUE EVIL CANNOT BE CONTAINED OR KILLED.
BUT AS IT TURNS OUT...
Code names: MAMMOTH and SHIMMER
New identities: BOBBY MYERS and CELINE MYERS
Status: YELLOW

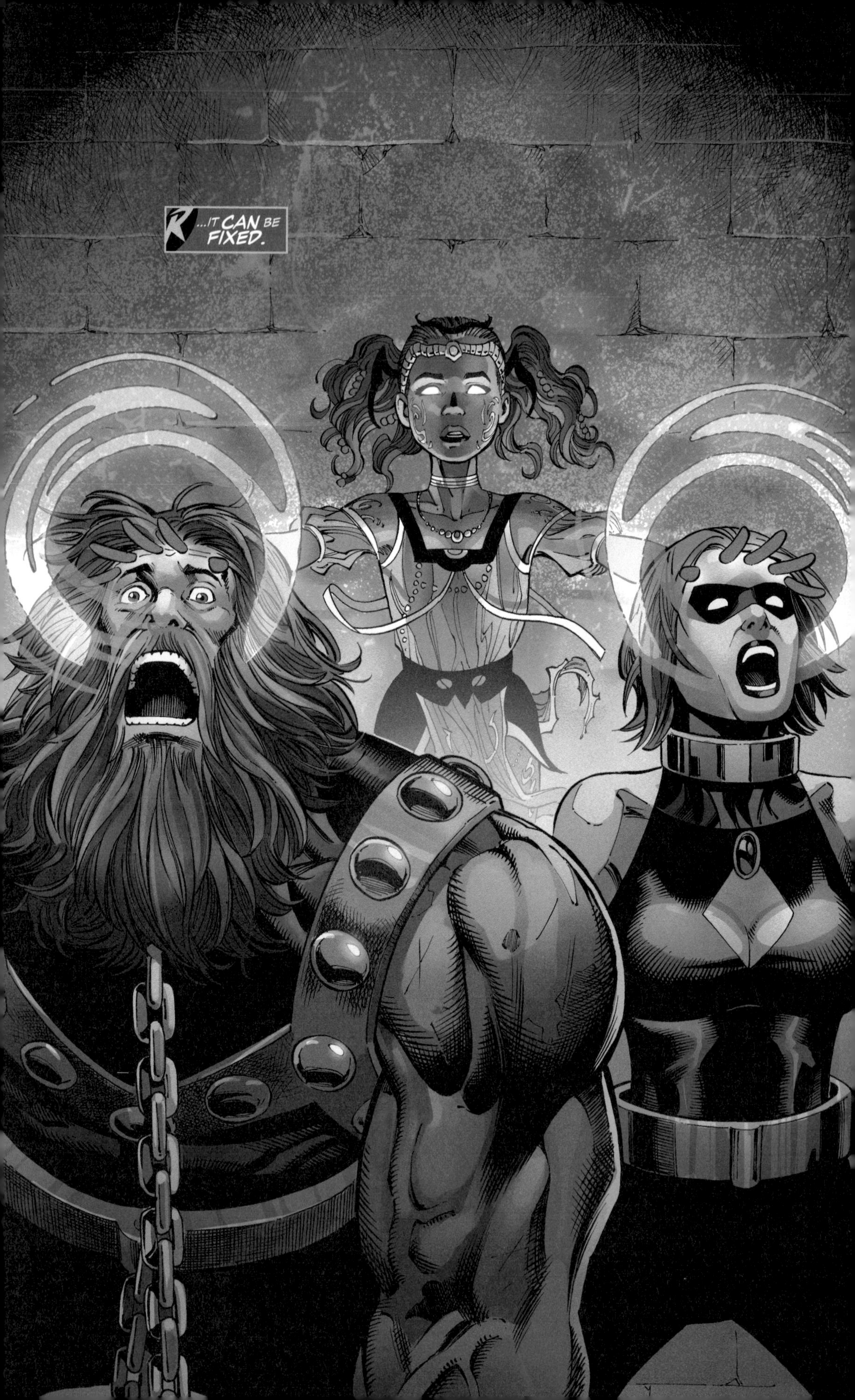
...IT CAN BE FIXED.

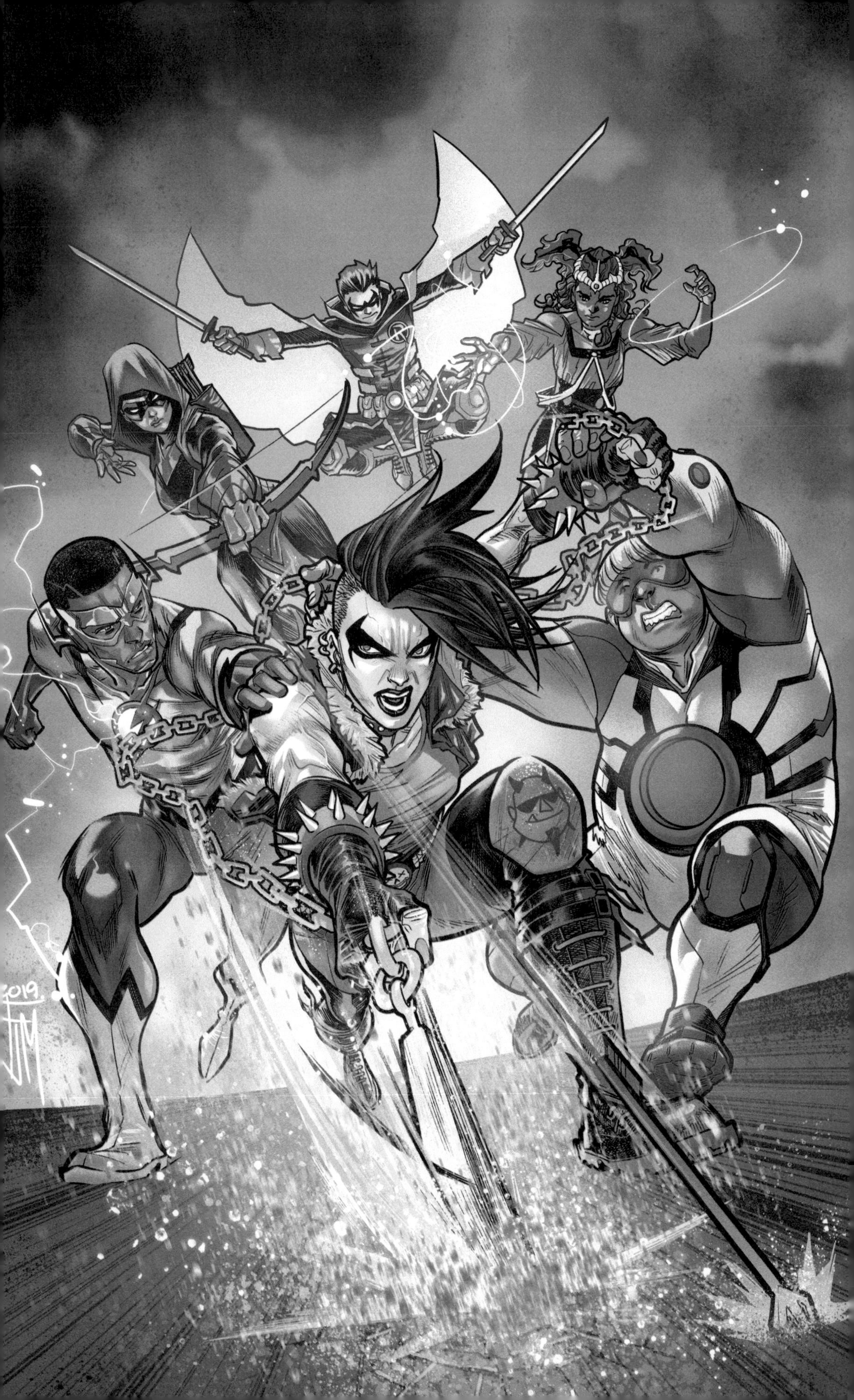

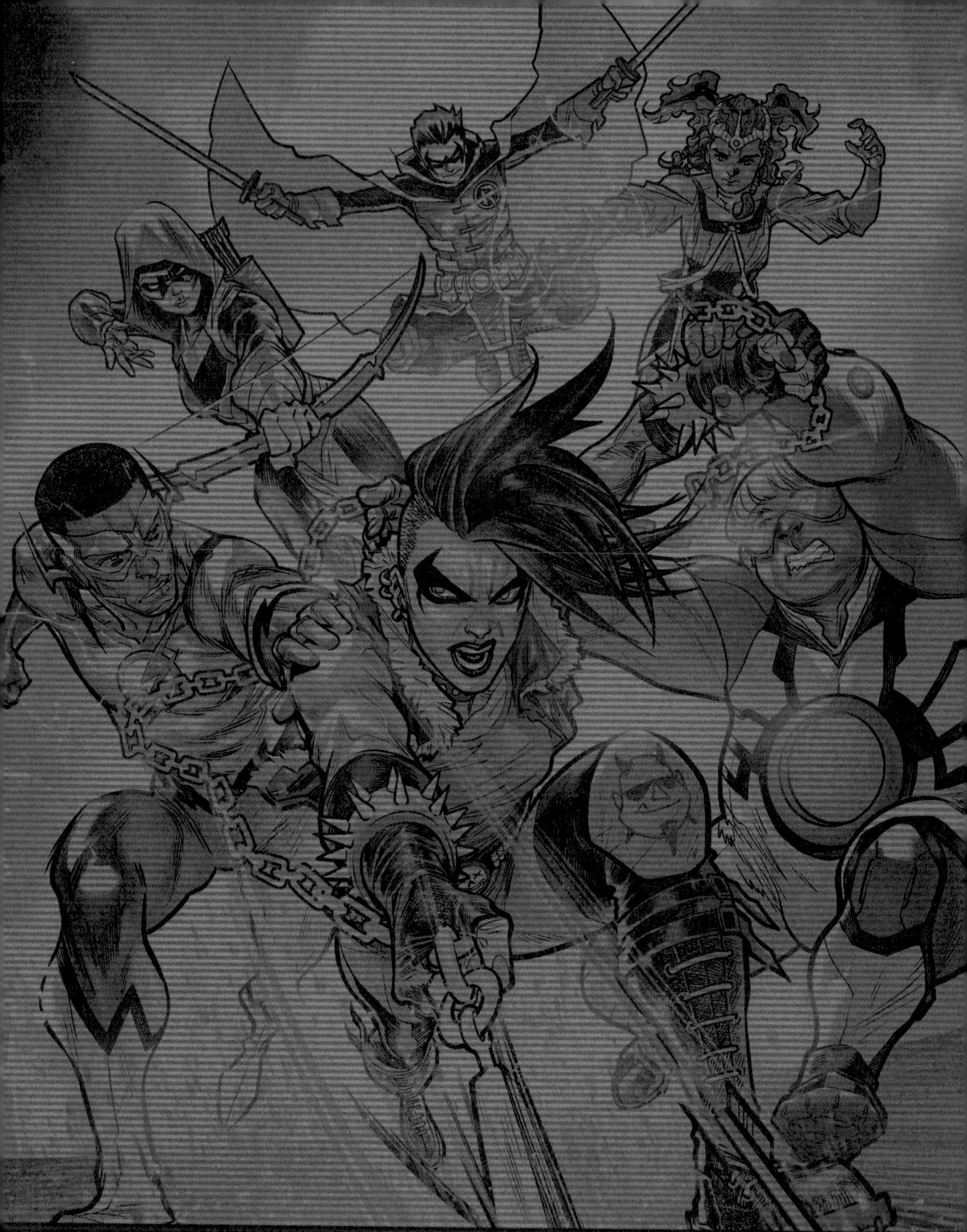

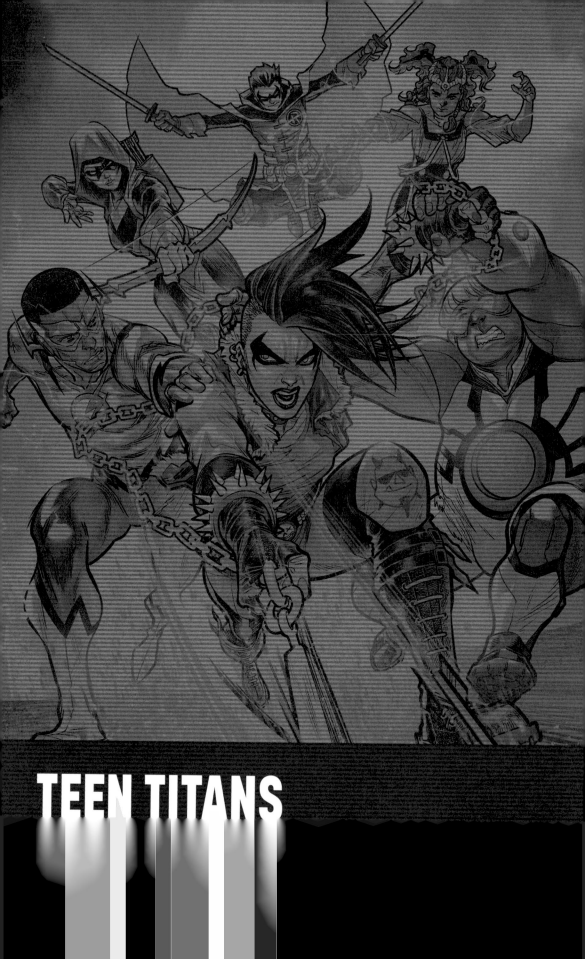

TEEN TITANS

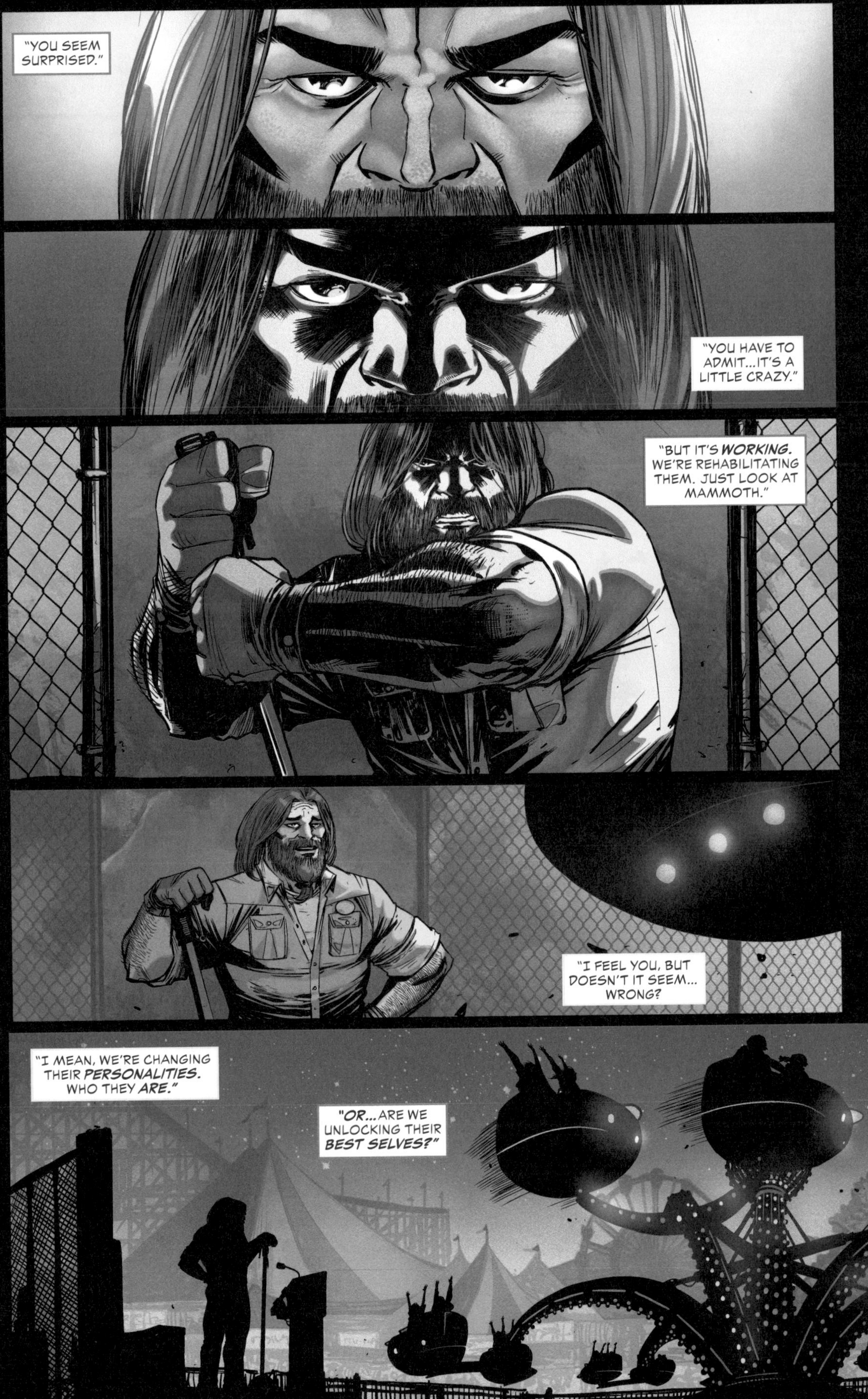
"YOU SEEM SURPRISED."
"YOU HAVE TO ADMIT...IT'S A LITTLE CRAZY."
"BUT IT'S *WORKING.* WE'RE REHABILITATING THEM. JUST LOOK AT MAMMOTH."
"I FEEL YOU, BUT DOESN'T IT SEEM... WRONG?
"I MEAN, WE'RE CHANGING THEIR *PERSONALITIES.* WHO THEY *ARE.*"
"*OR...* ARE WE UNLOCKING THEIR *BEST SELVES?*"

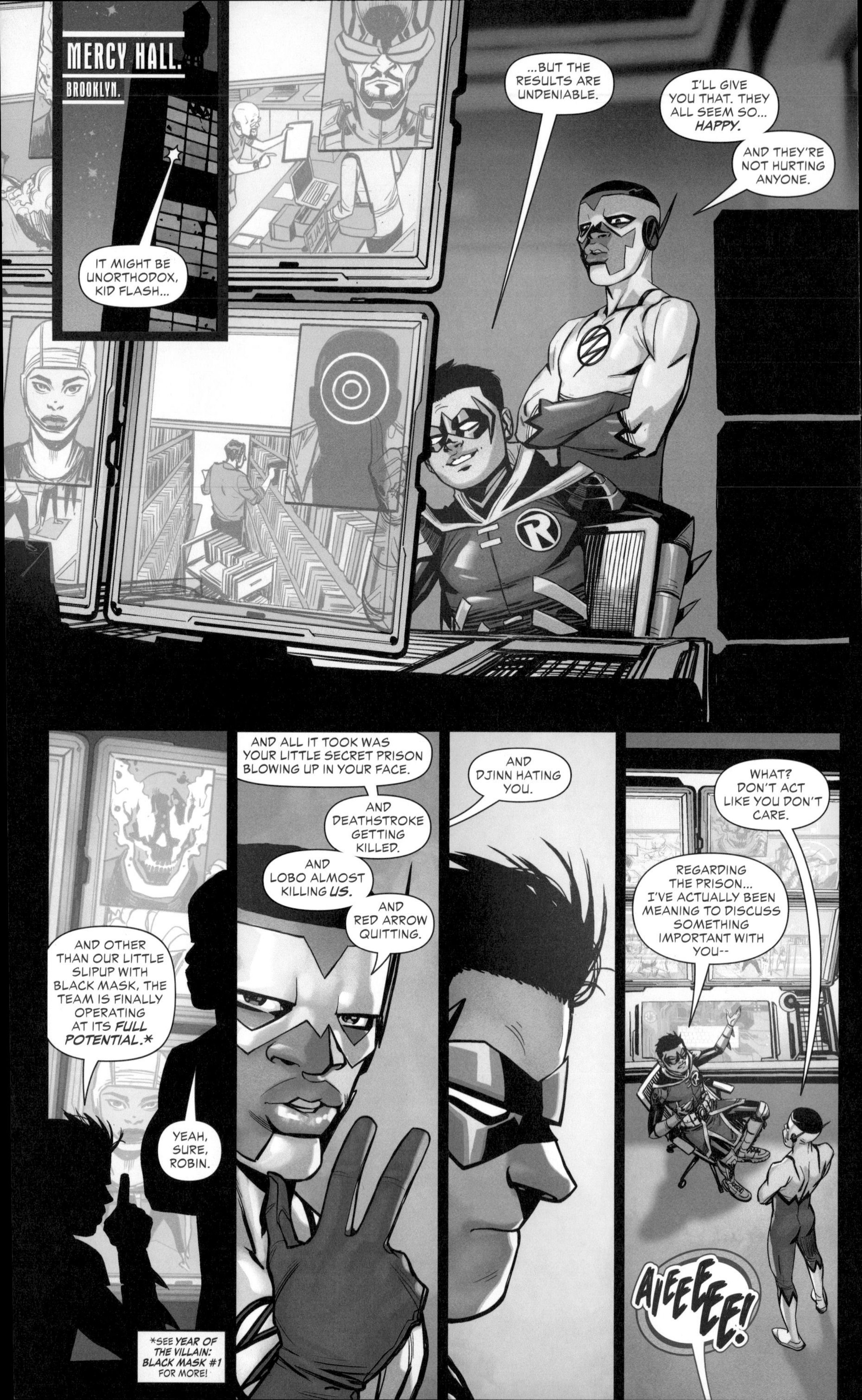
MERCY HALL.
BROOKLYN.
IT MIGHT BE UNORTHODOX, KID FLASH...
...BUT THE RESULTS ARE UNDENIABLE.
I'LL GIVE YOU THAT. THEY ALL SEEM SO... HAPPY.
AND THEY'RE NOT HURTING ANYONE.
AND OTHER THAN OUR LITTLE SLIPUP WITH BLACK MASK, THE TEAM IS FINALLY OPERATING AT ITS FULL POTENTIAL.*
YEAH, SURE, ROBIN.
*SEE YEAR OF THE VILLAIN: BLACK MASK #1 FOR MORE!
AND ALL IT TOOK WAS YOUR LITTLE SECRET PRISON BLOWING UP IN YOUR FACE.
AND DEATHSTROKE GETTING KILLED.
AND LOBO ALMOST KILLING US.
AND RED ARROW QUITTING.
AND DJINN HATING YOU.
WHAT? DON'T ACT LIKE YOU DON'T CARE.
REGARDING THE PRISON... I'VE ACTUALLY BEEN MEANING TO DISCUSS SOMETHING IMPORTANT WITH YOU--
AIEEEEEE!

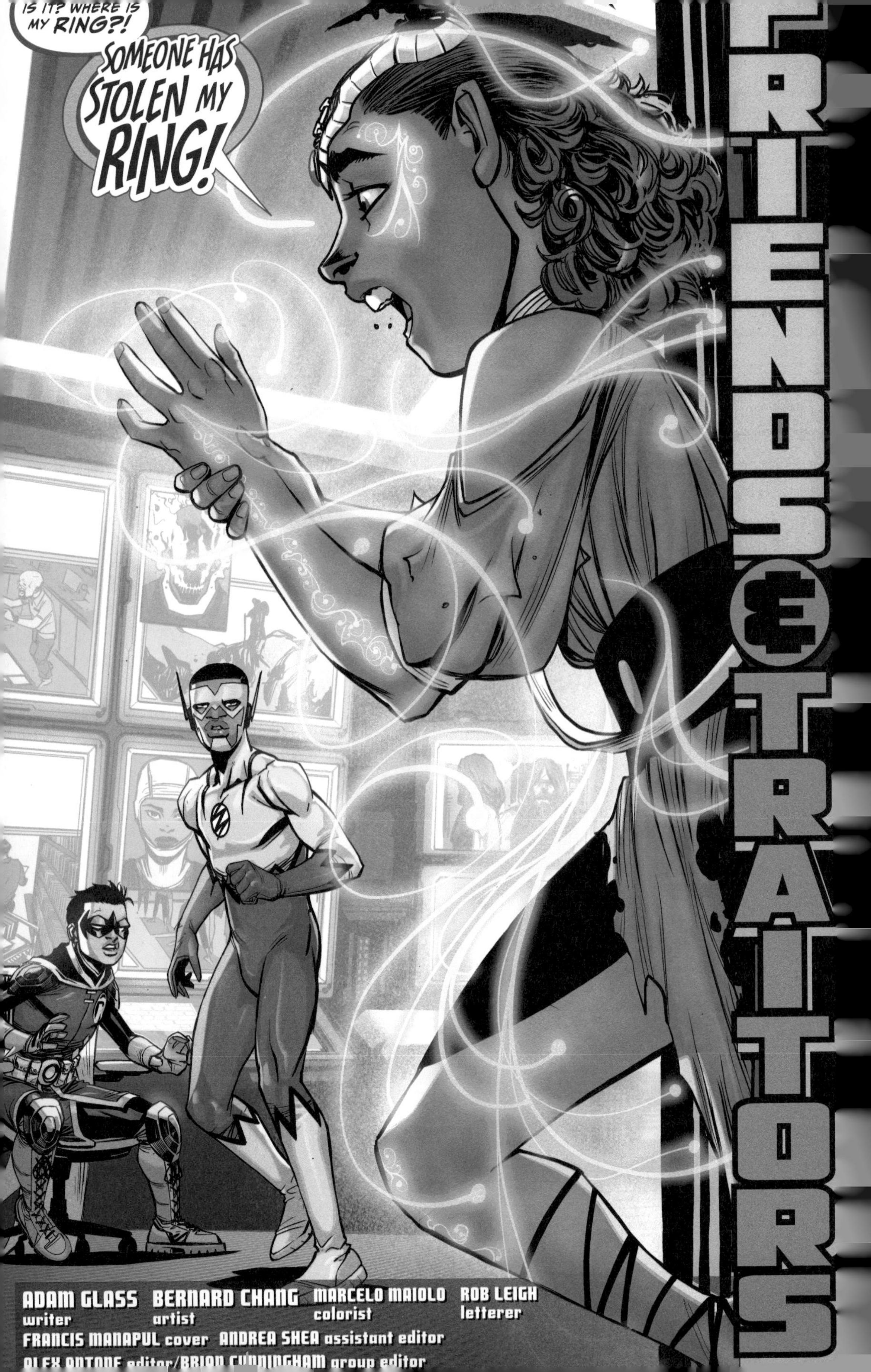
IS IT? WHERE IS MY RING?!
SOMEONE HAS STOLEN MY RING!
FRIENDS & TRAITORS
ADAM GLASS writer
BERNARD CHANG artist
MARCELO MAIOLO colorist
ROB LEIGH letterer
FRANCIS MANAPUL cover
ANDREA SHEA assistant editor
ALEX ANTONE editor/BRIAN CUNNINGHAM group editor

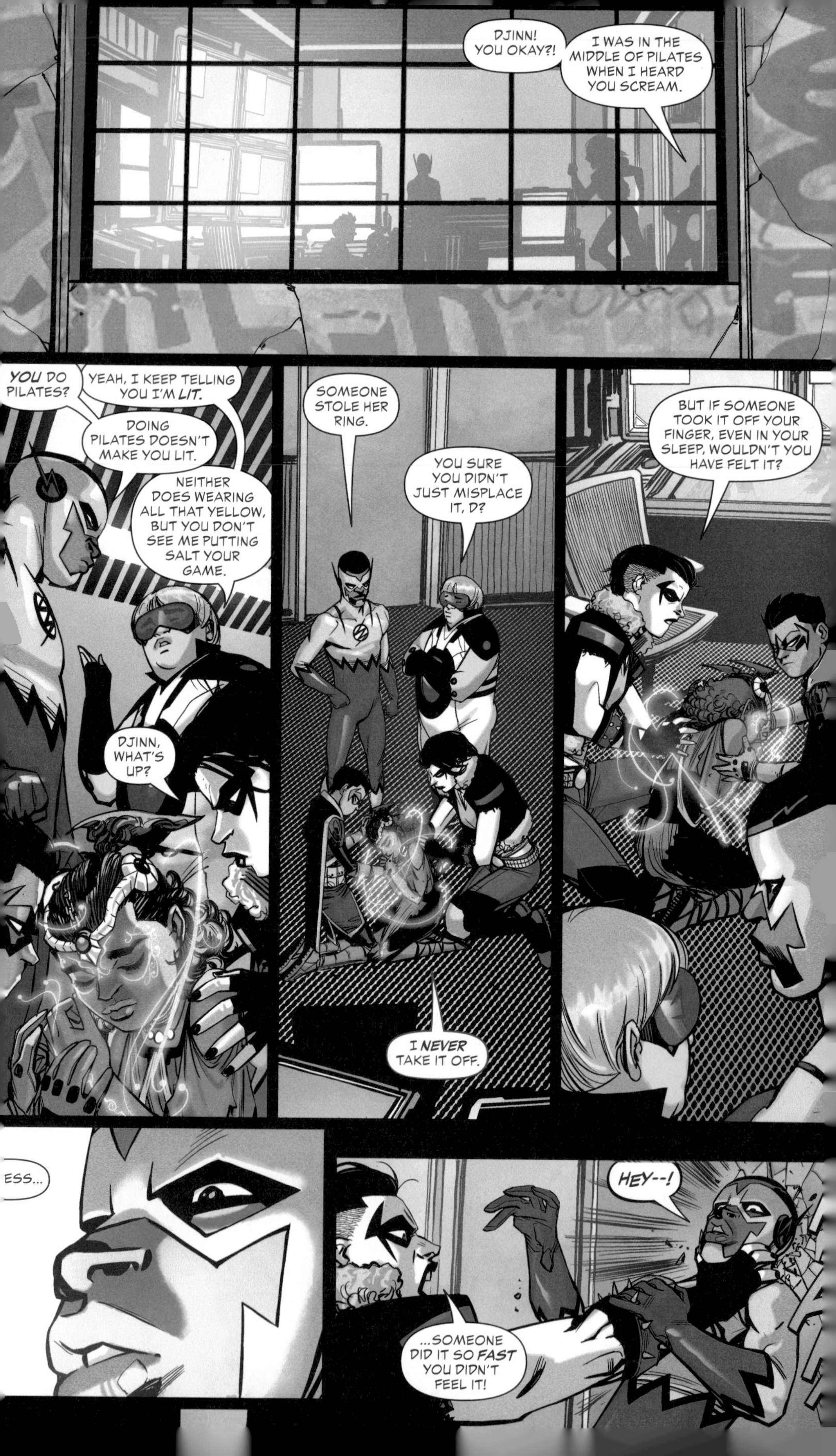
DJINN! YOU OKAY?!
I WAS IN THE MIDDLE OF PILATES WHEN I HEARD YOU SCREAM.
YOU DO PILATES?
YEAH, I KEEP TELLING YOU I'M LIT.
DOING PILATES DOESN'T MAKE YOU LIT.
NEITHER DOES WEARING ALL THAT YELLOW, BUT YOU DON'T SEE ME PUTTING SALT YOUR GAME.
DJINN, WHAT'S UP?
SOMEONE STOLE HER RING.
YOU SURE YOU DIDN'T JUST MISPLACE IT, D?
I NEVER TAKE IT OFF.
BUT IF SOMEONE TOOK IT OFF YOUR FINGER, EVEN IN YOUR SLEEP, WOULDN'T YOU HAVE FELT IT?
ESS...
HEY--!
...SOMEONE DID IT SO FAST YOU DIDN'T FEEL IT!

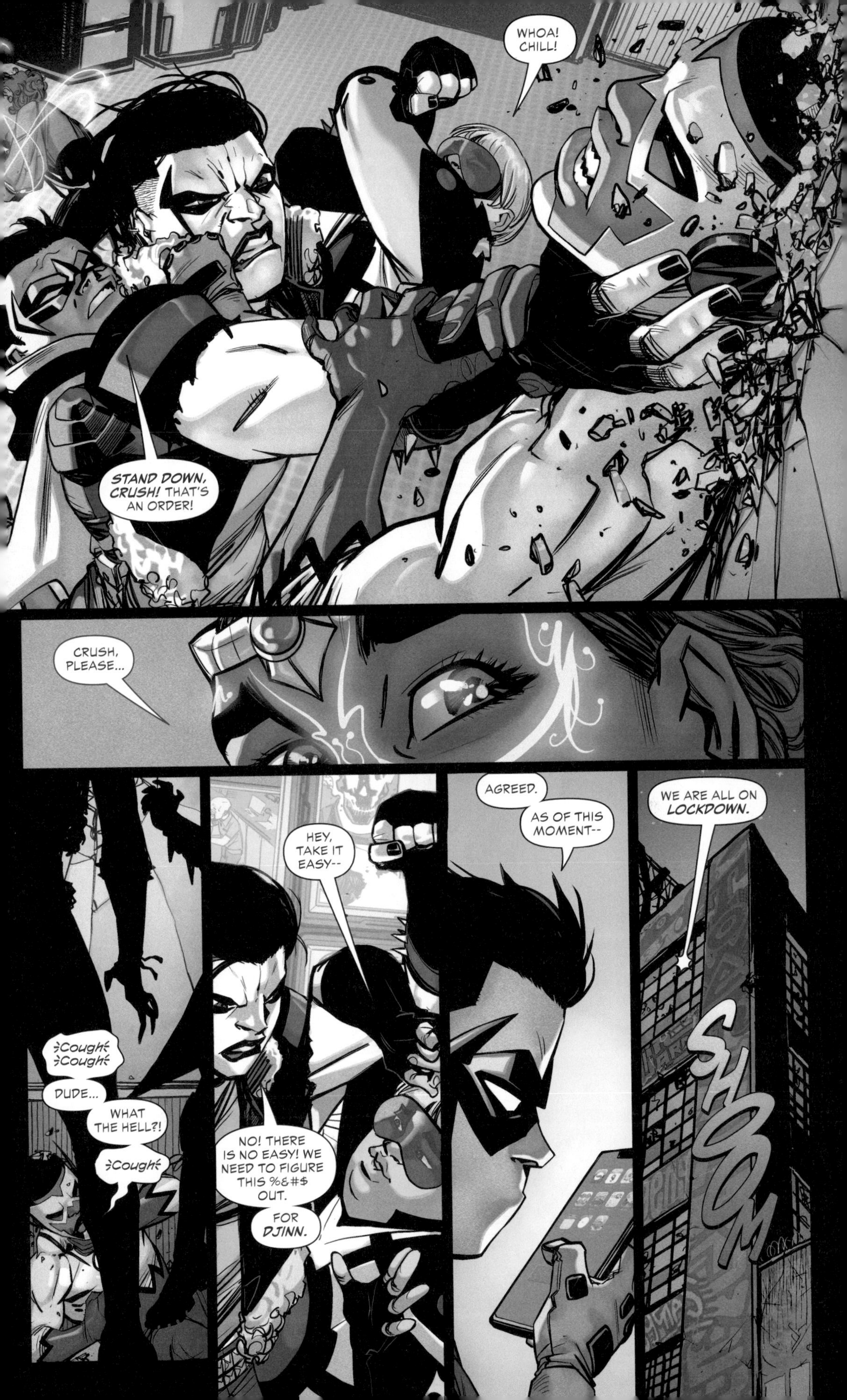
WHOA! CHILL!
STAND DOWN, CRUSH! THAT'S AN ORDER!
CRUSH, PLEASE...
¦Cough¦ ¦Cough¦
DUDE...
WHAT THE HELL?!
¦Cough¦
HEY, TAKE IT EASY--
NO! THERE IS NO EASY! WE NEED TO FIGURE THIS %&#$ OUT.
FOR DJINN.
AGREED.
AS OF THIS MOMENT--
WE ARE ALL ON LOCKDOWN.
SHOOM

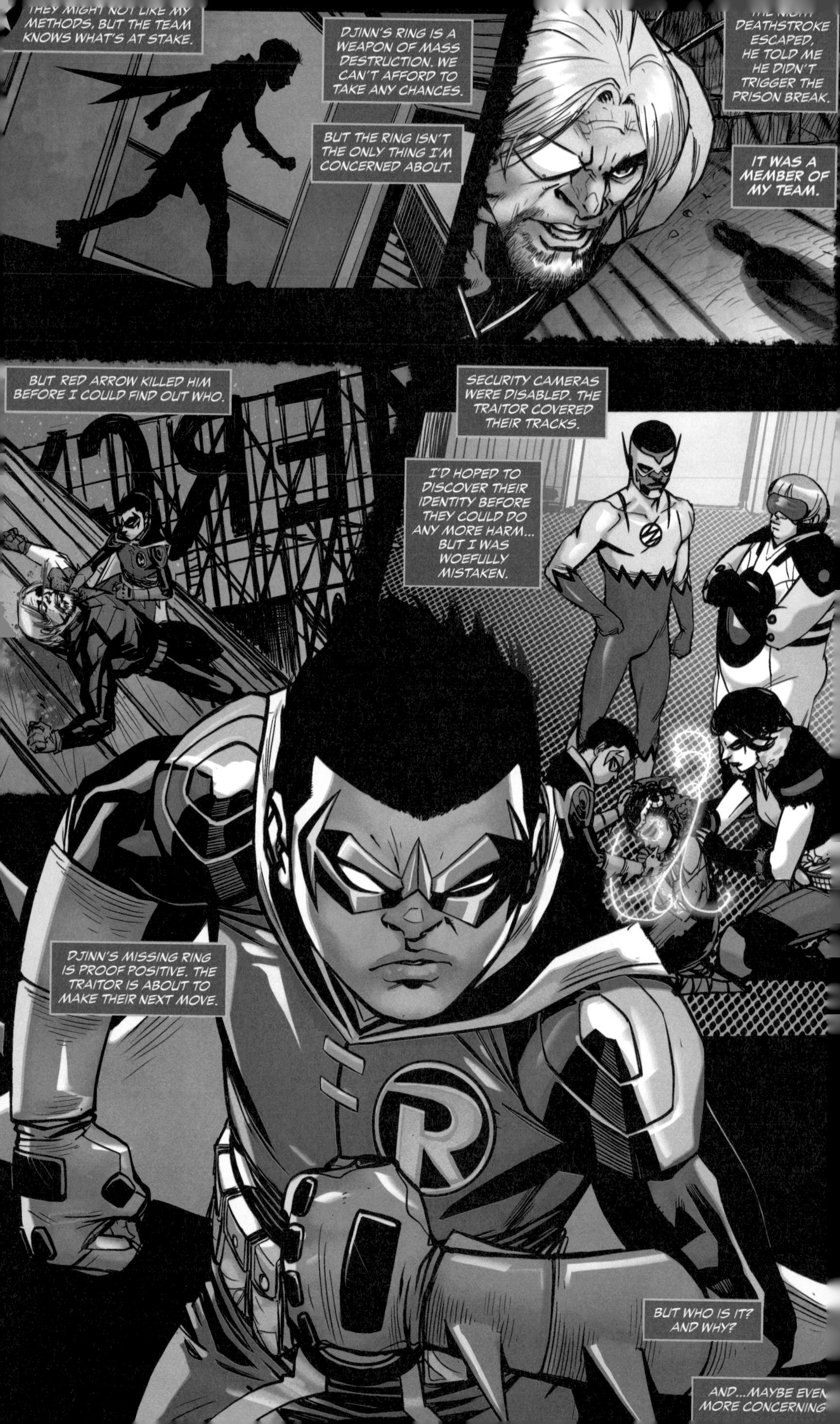
THEY MIGHT NOT LIKE MY METHODS, BUT THE TEAM KNOWS WHAT'S AT STAKE.
DJINN'S RING IS A WEAPON OF MASS DESTRUCTION. WE CAN'T AFFORD TO TAKE ANY CHANCES.
BUT THE RING ISN'T THE ONLY THING I'M CONCERNED ABOUT.
DEATHSTROKE ESCAPED, HE TOLD ME HE DIDN'T TRIGGER THE PRISON BREAK.
IT WAS A MEMBER OF MY TEAM.
BUT RED ARROW KILLED HIM BEFORE I COULD FIND OUT WHO.
SECURITY CAMERAS WERE DISABLED. THE TRAITOR COVERED THEIR TRACKS.
I'D HOPED TO DISCOVER THEIR IDENTITY BEFORE THEY COULD DO ANY MORE HARM... BUT I WAS WOEFULLY MISTAKEN.
DJINN'S MISSING RING IS PROOF POSITIVE. THE TRAITOR IS ABOUT TO MAKE THEIR NEXT MOVE.
BUT WHO IS IT? AND WHY?
AND...MAYBE EVEN MORE CONCERNING

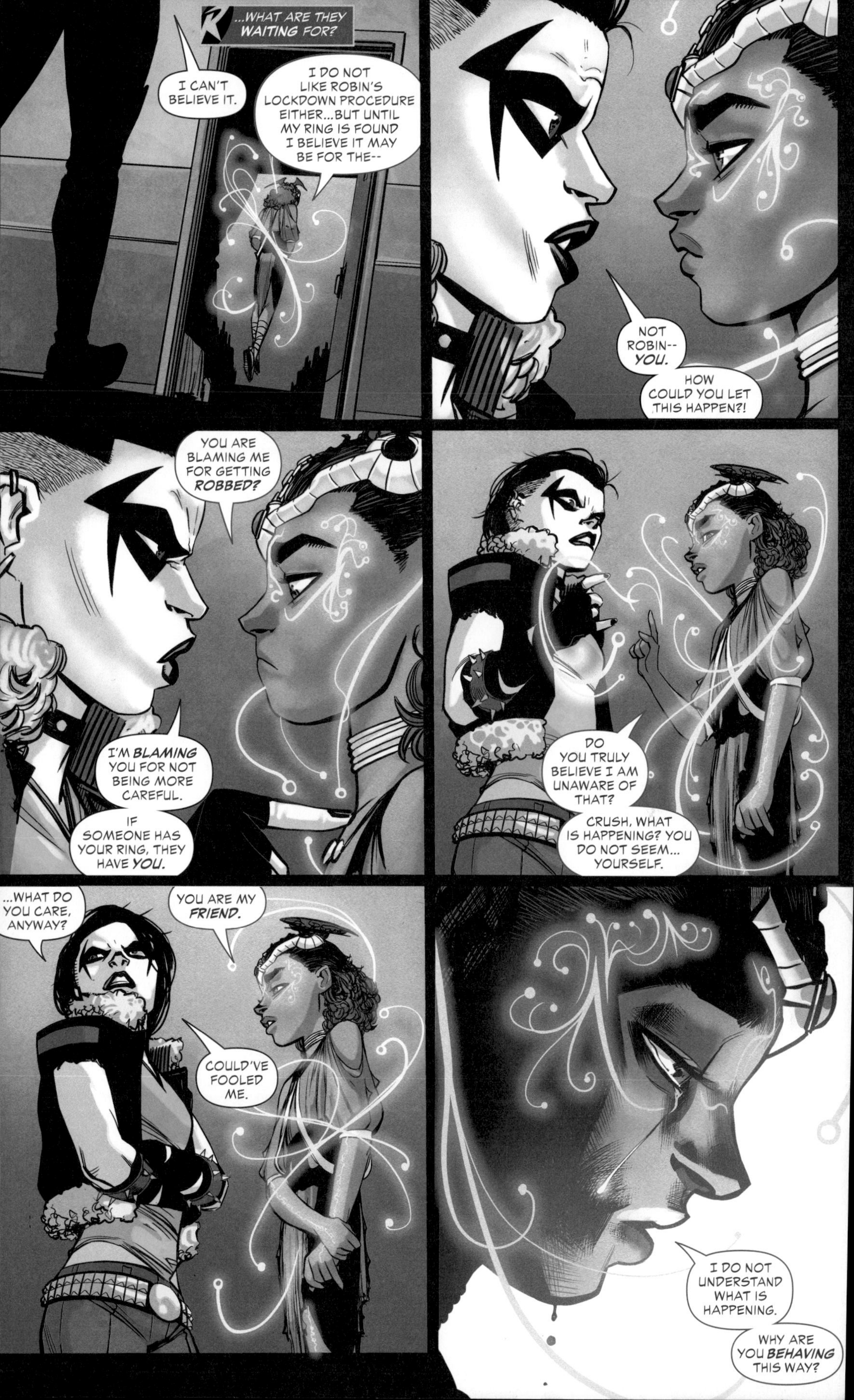
...WHAT ARE THEY WAITING FOR?
I CAN'T BELIEVE IT.
I DO NOT LIKE ROBIN'S LOCKDOWN PROCEDURE EITHER...BUT UNTIL MY RING IS FOUND I BELIEVE IT MAY BE FOR THE--
NOT ROBIN-- YOU.
HOW COULD YOU LET THIS HAPPEN?!
YOU ARE BLAMING ME FOR GETTING ROBBED?
I'M BLAMING YOU FOR NOT BEING MORE CAREFUL.
IF SOMEONE HAS YOUR RING, THEY HAVE YOU.
DO YOU TRULY BELIEVE I AM UNAWARE OF THAT?
CRUSH, WHAT IS HAPPENING? YOU DO NOT SEEM... YOURSELF.
...WHAT DO YOU CARE, ANYWAY?
YOU ARE MY FRIEND.
COULD'VE FOOLED ME.
I DO NOT UNDERSTAND WHAT IS HAPPENING.
WHY ARE YOU BEHAVING THIS WAY?

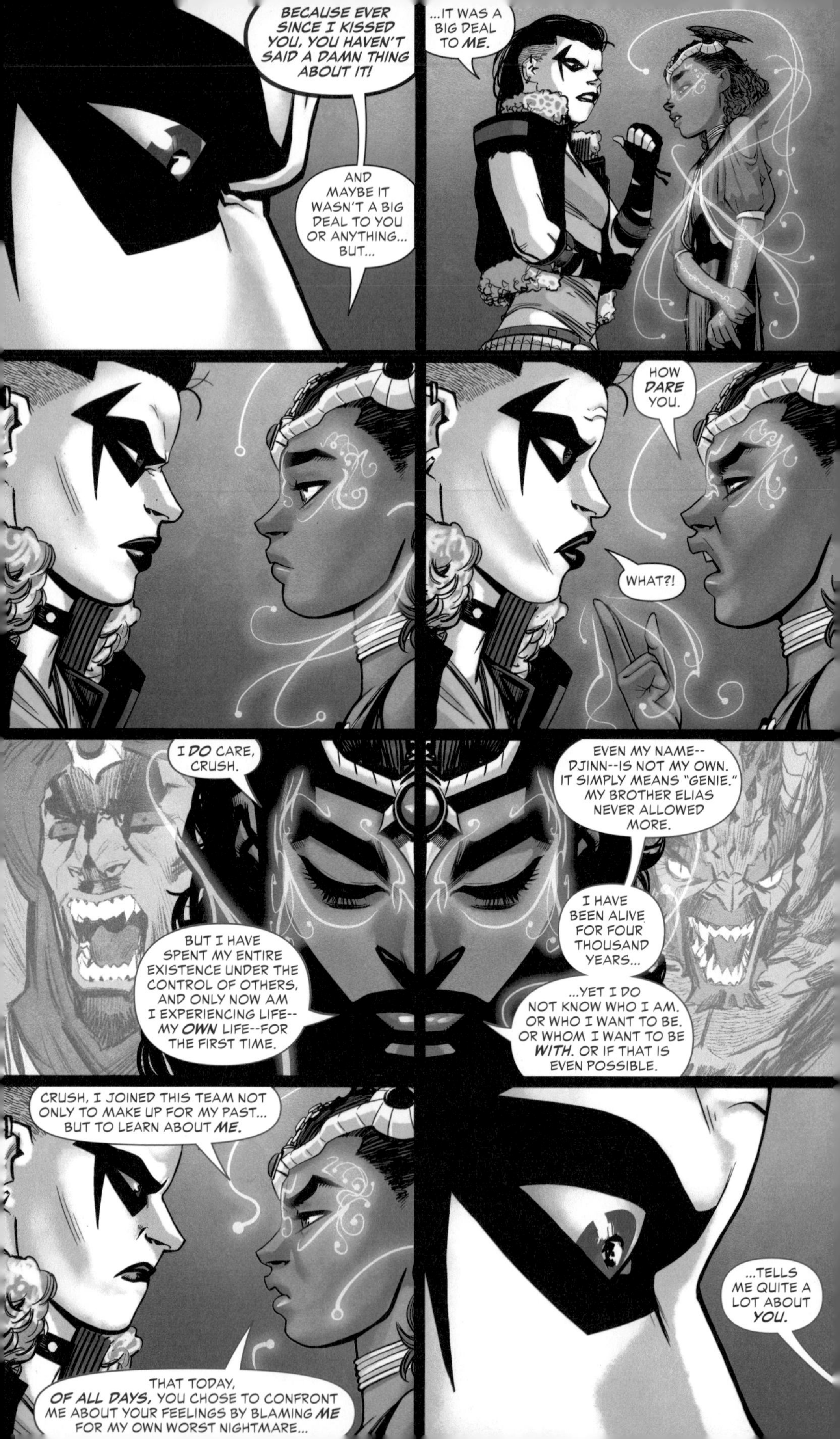
BECAUSE EVER SINCE I KISSED YOU, YOU HAVEN'T SAID A DAMN THING ABOUT IT!
AND MAYBE IT WASN'T A BIG DEAL TO YOU OR ANYTHING... BUT...
...IT WAS A BIG DEAL TO ME.
HOW DARE YOU.
WHAT?!
I DO CARE, CRUSH.
BUT I HAVE SPENT MY ENTIRE EXISTENCE UNDER THE CONTROL OF OTHERS, AND ONLY NOW AM I EXPERIENCING LIFE--MY OWN LIFE--FOR THE FIRST TIME.
EVEN MY NAME--DJINN--IS NOT MY OWN. IT SIMPLY MEANS "GENIE." MY BROTHER ELIAS NEVER ALLOWED MORE.
I HAVE BEEN ALIVE FOR FOUR THOUSAND YEARS...
...YET I DO NOT KNOW WHO I AM. OR WHO I WANT TO BE. OR WHOM I WANT TO BE WITH. OR IF THAT IS EVEN POSSIBLE.
CRUSH, I JOINED THIS TEAM NOT ONLY TO MAKE UP FOR MY PAST... BUT TO LEARN ABOUT ME.
THAT TODAY, OF ALL DAYS, YOU CHOSE TO CONFRONT ME ABOUT YOUR FEELINGS BY BLAMING ME FOR MY OWN WORST NIGHTMARE...
...TELLS ME QUITE A LOT ABOUT YOU.

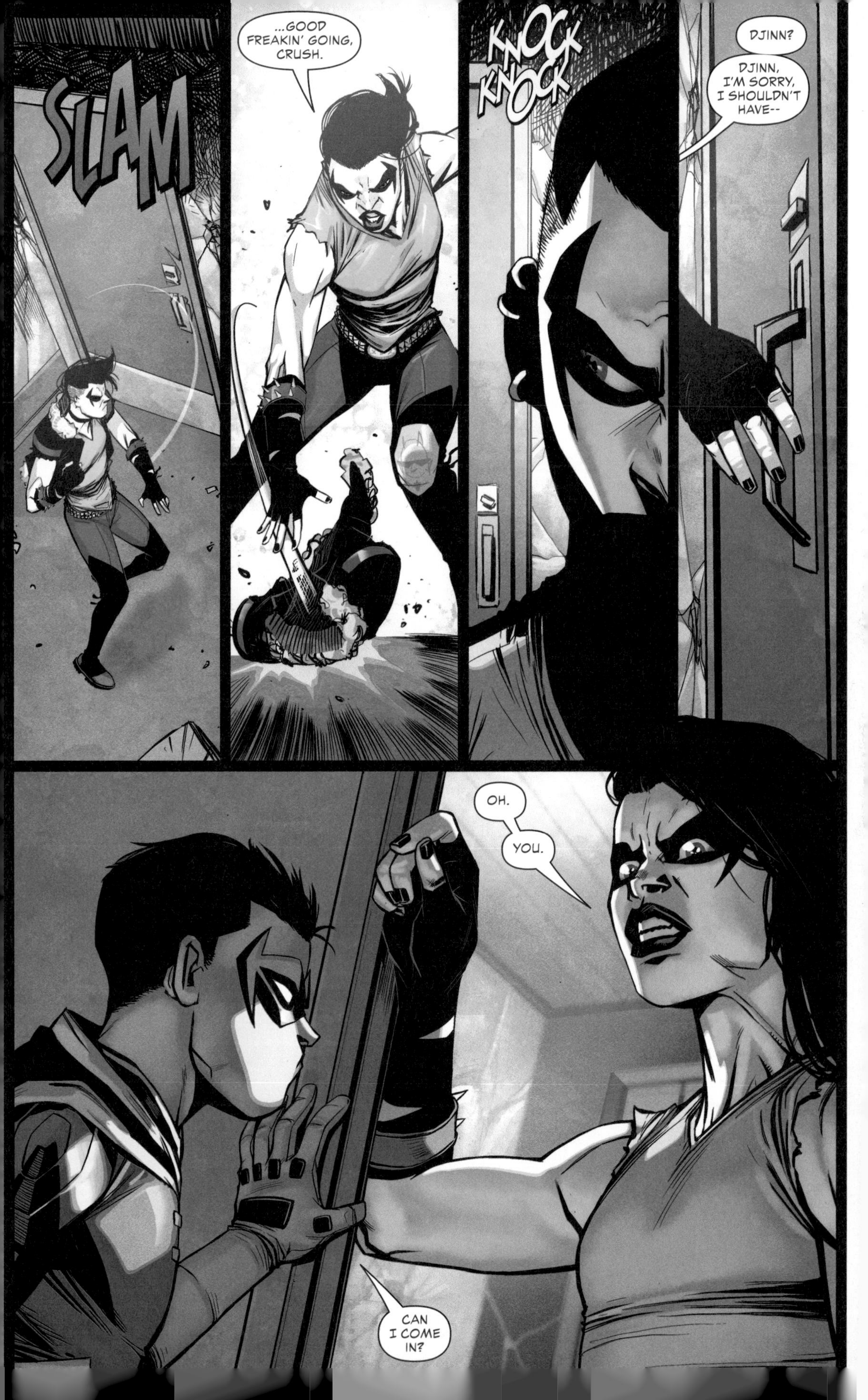
SLAM
...GOOD FREAKIN' GOING, CRUSH.
KNOCK KNOCK
DJINN?
DJINN, I'M SORRY, I SHOULDN'T HAVE--
OH.
YOU.
CAN I COME IN?

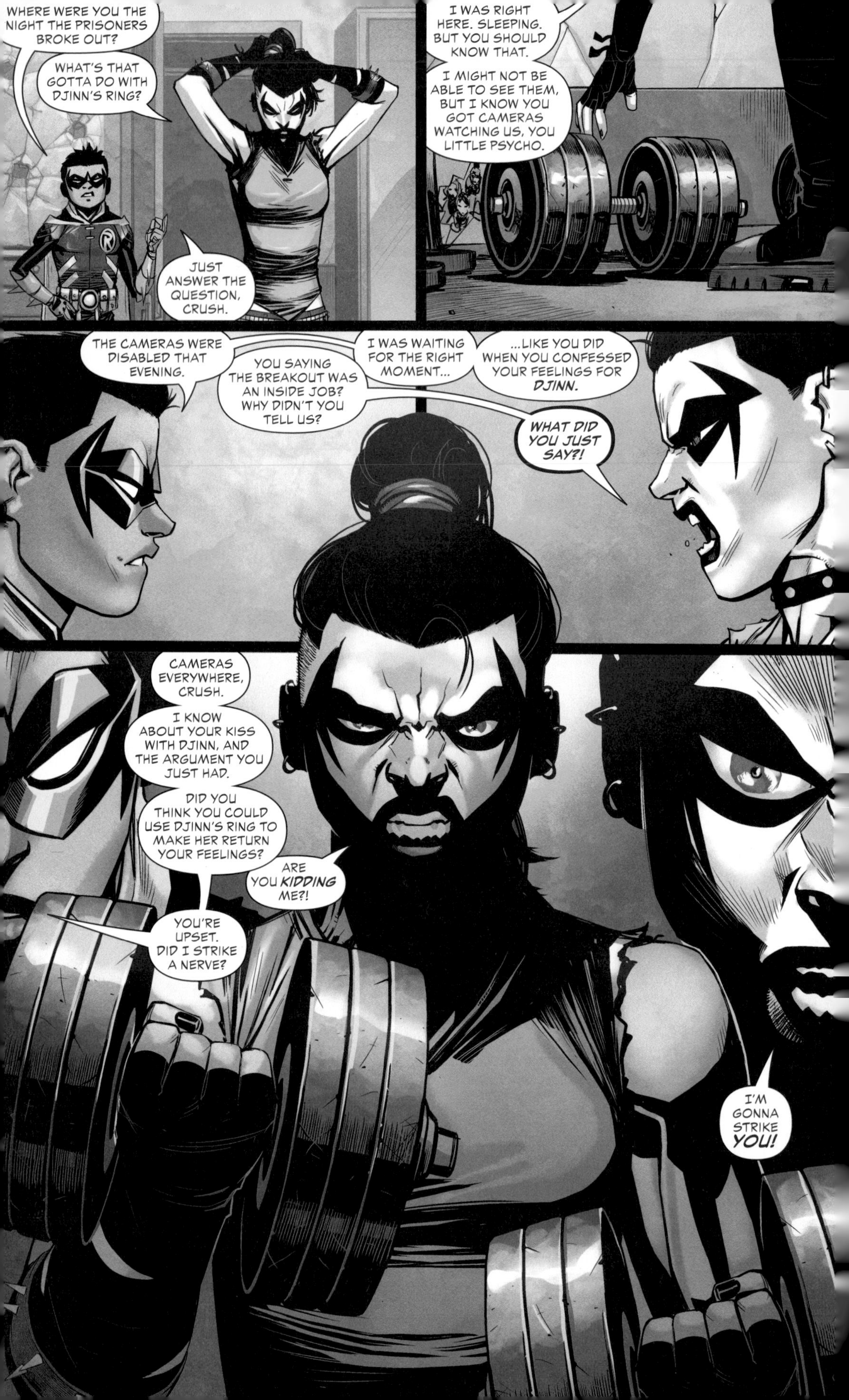
WHERE WERE YOU THE NIGHT THE PRISONERS BROKE OUT?
WHAT'S THAT GOTTA DO WITH DJINN'S RING?
JUST ANSWER THE QUESTION, CRUSH.
I WAS RIGHT HERE. SLEEPING. BUT YOU SHOULD KNOW THAT.
I MIGHT NOT BE ABLE TO SEE THEM, BUT I KNOW YOU GOT CAMERAS WATCHING US, YOU LITTLE PSYCHO.
THE CAMERAS WERE DISABLED THAT EVENING.
YOU SAYING THE BREAKOUT WAS AN INSIDE JOB? WHY DIDN'T YOU TELL US?
I WAS WAITING FOR THE RIGHT MOMENT...
...LIKE YOU DID WHEN YOU CONFESSED YOUR FEELINGS FOR DJINN.
WHAT DID YOU JUST SAY?!
CAMERAS EVERYWHERE, CRUSH.
I KNOW ABOUT YOUR KISS WITH DJINN, AND THE ARGUMENT YOU JUST HAD.
DID YOU THINK YOU COULD USE DJINN'S RING TO MAKE HER RETURN YOUR FEELINGS?
ARE YOU KIDDING ME?!
YOU'RE UPSET. DID I STRIKE A NERVE?
I'M GONNA STRIKE YOU!

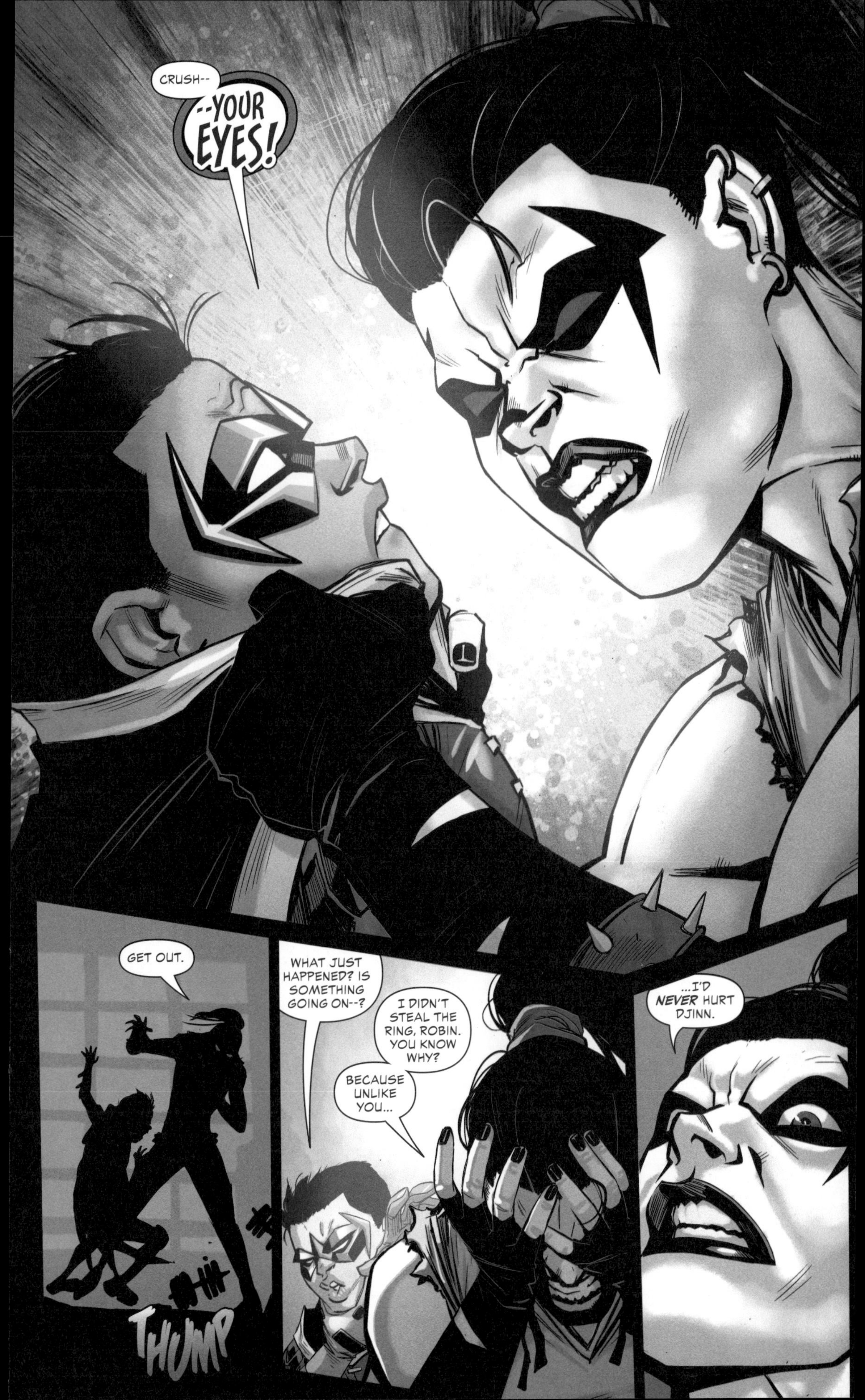
CRUSH--
--YOUR EYES!
GET OUT.
THUMP
WHAT JUST HAPPENED? IS SOMETHING GOING ON--?
I DIDN'T STEAL THE RING, ROBIN. YOU KNOW WHY?
BECAUSE UNLIKE YOU...
...I'D NEVER HURT DJINN.

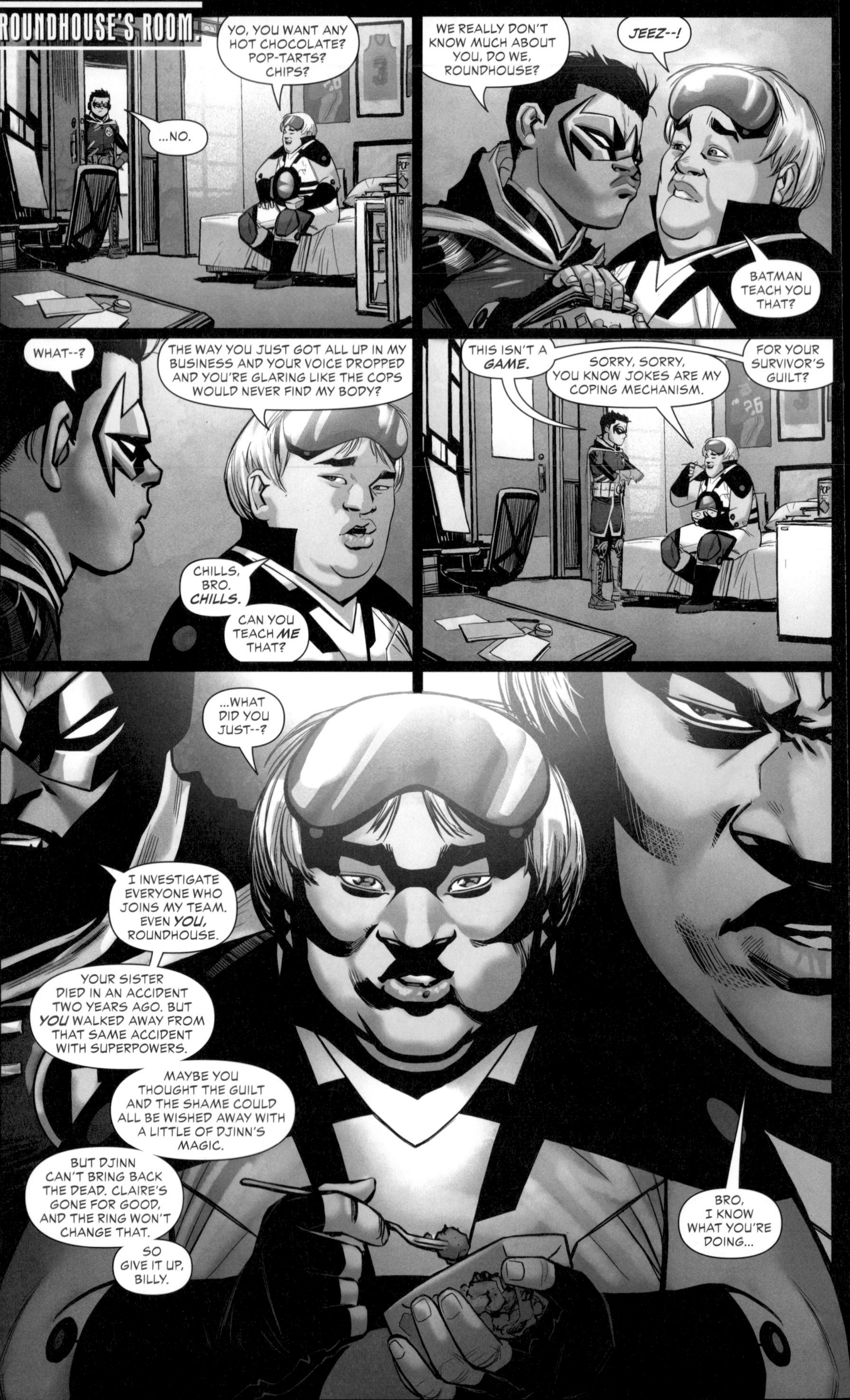

ROUNDHOUSE'S ROOM.
YO, YOU WANT ANY HOT CHOCOLATE? POP-TARTS? CHIPS?
...NO.
WE REALLY DON'T KNOW MUCH ABOUT YOU, DO WE, ROUNDHOUSE?
JEEZ--!
BATMAN TEACH YOU THAT?
WHAT--?
THE WAY YOU JUST GOT ALL UP IN MY BUSINESS AND YOUR VOICE DROPPED AND YOU'RE GLARING LIKE THE COPS WOULD NEVER FIND MY BODY?
CHILLS, BRO. CHILLS.
CAN YOU TEACH ME THAT?
FOR YOUR SURVIVOR'S GUILT?
SORRY, SORRY, YOU KNOW JOKES ARE MY COPING MECHANISM.
THIS ISN'T A GAME.
...WHAT DID YOU JUST--?
I INVESTIGATE EVERYONE WHO JOINS MY TEAM. EVEN YOU, ROUNDHOUSE.
YOUR SISTER DIED IN AN ACCIDENT TWO YEARS AGO. BUT YOU WALKED AWAY FROM THAT SAME ACCIDENT WITH SUPERPOWERS.
MAYBE YOU THOUGHT THE GUILT AND THE SHAME COULD ALL BE WISHED AWAY WITH A LITTLE OF DJINN'S MAGIC.
BUT DJINN CAN'T BRING BACK THE DEAD. CLAIRE'S GONE FOR GOOD, AND THE RING WON'T CHANGE THAT.
SO GIVE IT UP, BILLY.
BRO, I KNOW WHAT YOU'RE DOING...

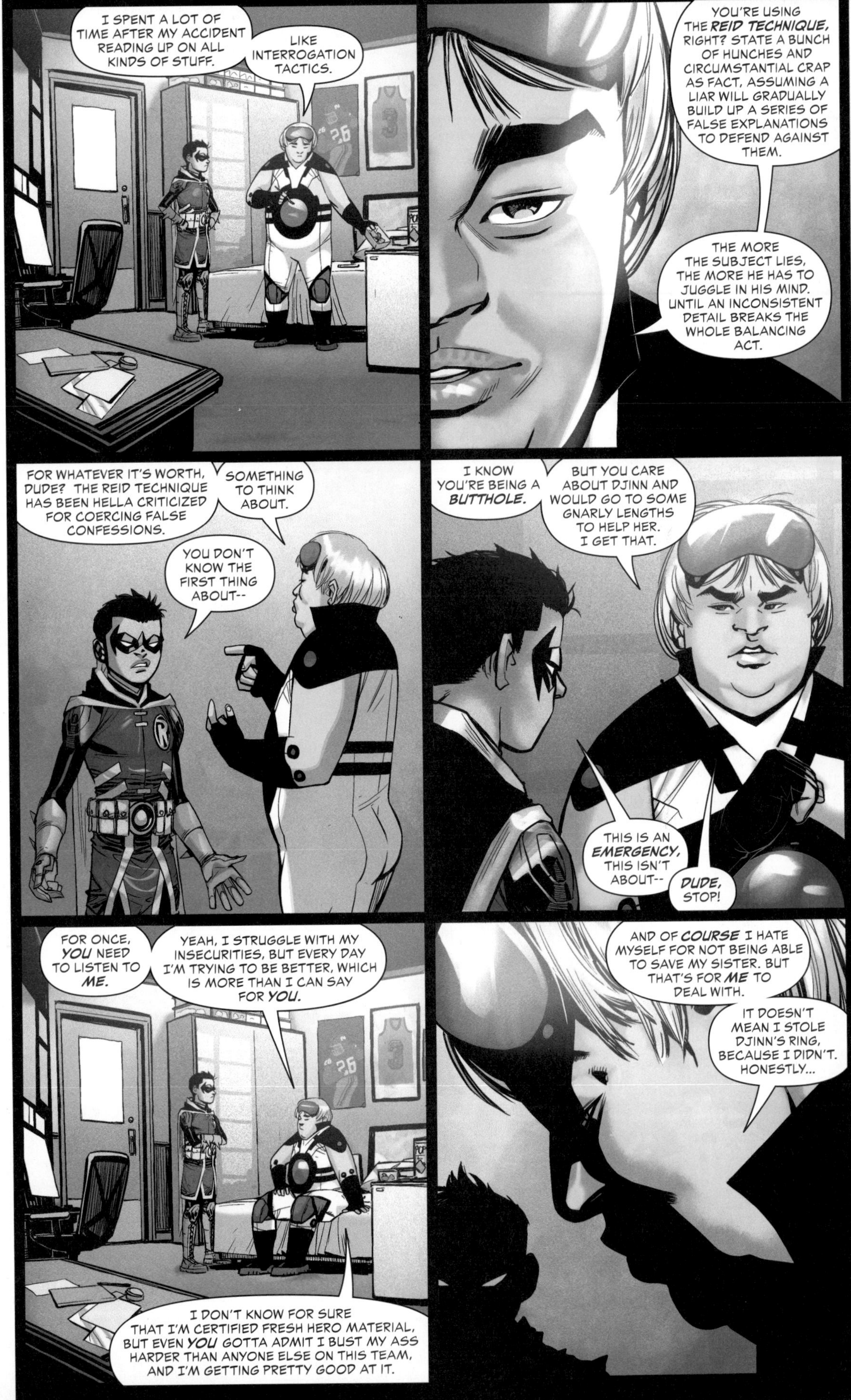
I SPENT A LOT OF TIME AFTER MY ACCIDENT READING UP ON ALL KINDS OF STUFF.
LIKE INTERROGATION TACTICS.
YOU'RE USING THE *REID TECHNIQUE,* RIGHT? STATE A BUNCH OF HUNCHES AND CIRCUMSTANTIAL CRAP AS FACT, ASSUMING A LIAR WILL GRADUALLY BUILD UP A SERIES OF FALSE EXPLANATIONS TO DEFEND AGAINST THEM.
THE MORE THE SUBJECT LIES, THE MORE HE HAS TO JUGGLE IN HIS MIND. UNTIL AN INCONSISTENT DETAIL BREAKS THE WHOLE BALANCING ACT.
FOR WHATEVER IT'S WORTH, DUDE? THE REID TECHNIQUE HAS BEEN HELLA CRITICIZED FOR COERCING FALSE CONFESSIONS.
SOMETHING TO THINK ABOUT.
YOU DON'T KNOW THE FIRST THING ABOUT--
I KNOW YOU'RE BEING A *BUTTHOLE.*
BUT YOU CARE ABOUT DJINN AND WOULD GO TO SOME GNARLY LENGTHS TO HELP HER. I GET THAT.
THIS IS AN *EMERGENCY,* THIS ISN'T ABOUT--
DUDE, STOP!
FOR ONCE, *YOU* NEED TO LISTEN TO *ME.*
YEAH, I STRUGGLE WITH MY INSECURITIES, BUT EVERY DAY I'M TRYING TO BE BETTER, WHICH IS MORE THAN I CAN SAY FOR *YOU.*
I DON'T KNOW FOR SURE THAT I'M CERTIFIED FRESH HERO MATERIAL, BUT EVEN *YOU* GOTTA ADMIT I BUST MY ASS HARDER THAN ANYONE ELSE ON THIS TEAM, AND I'M GETTING PRETTY GOOD AT IT.
AND OF *COURSE* I HATE MYSELF FOR NOT BEING ABLE TO SAVE MY SISTER. BUT THAT'S FOR *ME* TO DEAL WITH.
IT DOESN'T MEAN I STOLE DJINN'S RING, BECAUSE I DIDN'T. HONESTLY...

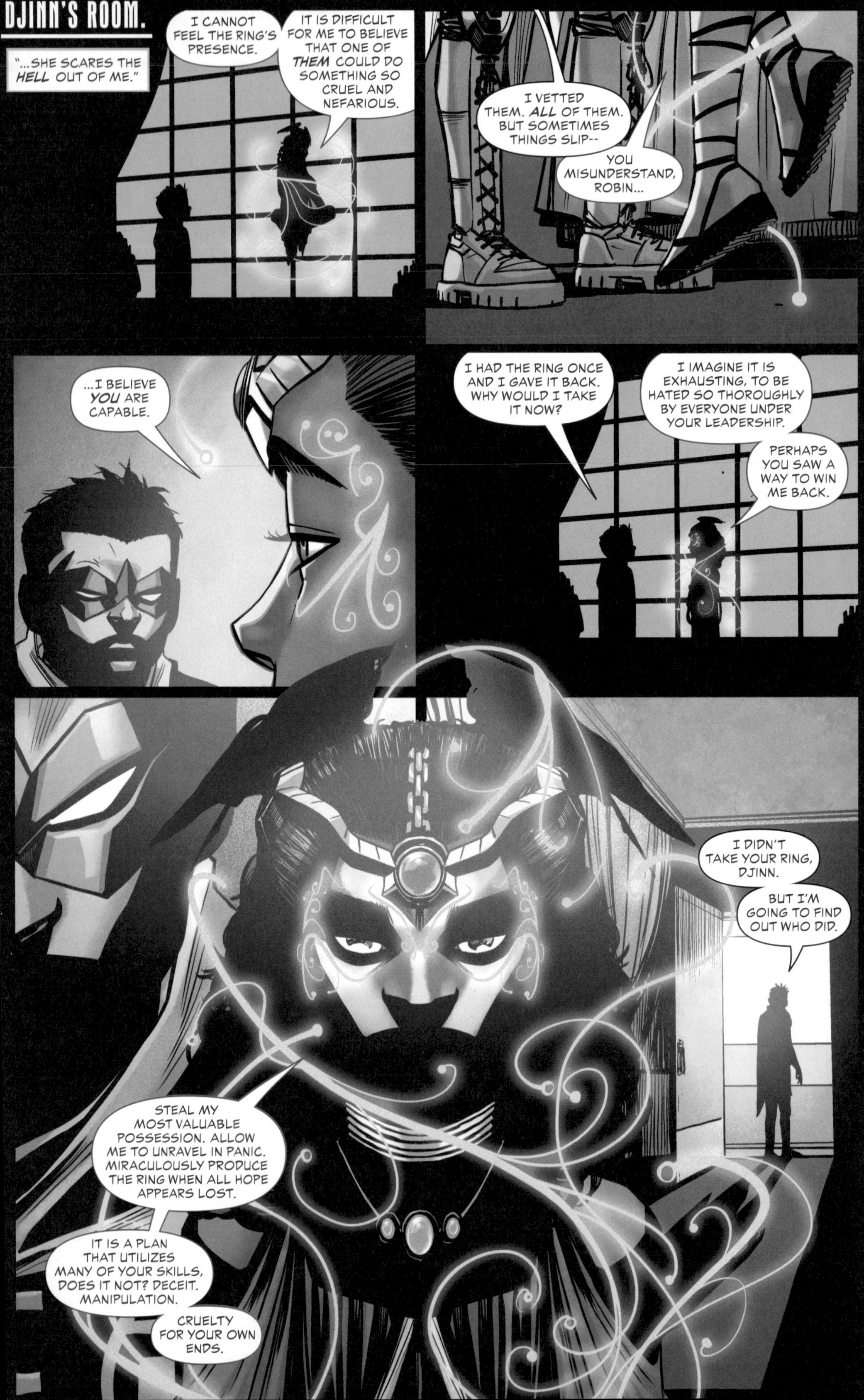
DJINN'S ROOM.
"...SHE SCARES THE *HELL* OUT OF ME."
I CANNOT FEEL THE RING'S PRESENCE.
IT IS DIFFICULT FOR ME TO BELIEVE THAT ONE OF *THEM* COULD DO SOMETHING SO CRUEL AND NEFARIOUS.
I VETTED THEM. *ALL* OF THEM. BUT SOMETIMES THINGS SLIP--
YOU MISUNDERSTAND, ROBIN...
...I BELIEVE *YOU* ARE CAPABLE.
I HAD THE RING ONCE AND I GAVE IT BACK. WHY WOULD I TAKE IT NOW?
I IMAGINE IT IS EXHAUSTING, TO BE HATED SO THOROUGHLY BY EVERYONE UNDER YOUR LEADERSHIP.
PERHAPS YOU SAW A WAY TO WIN ME BACK.
STEAL MY MOST VALUABLE POSSESSION. ALLOW ME TO UNRAVEL IN PANIC. MIRACULOUSLY PRODUCE THE RING WHEN ALL HOPE APPEARS LOST.
IT IS A PLAN THAT UTILIZES MANY OF YOUR SKILLS, DOES IT NOT? DECEIT. MANIPULATION.
CRUELTY FOR YOUR OWN ENDS.
I DIDN'T TAKE YOUR RING, DJINN.
BUT I'M GOING TO FIND OUT WHO DID.

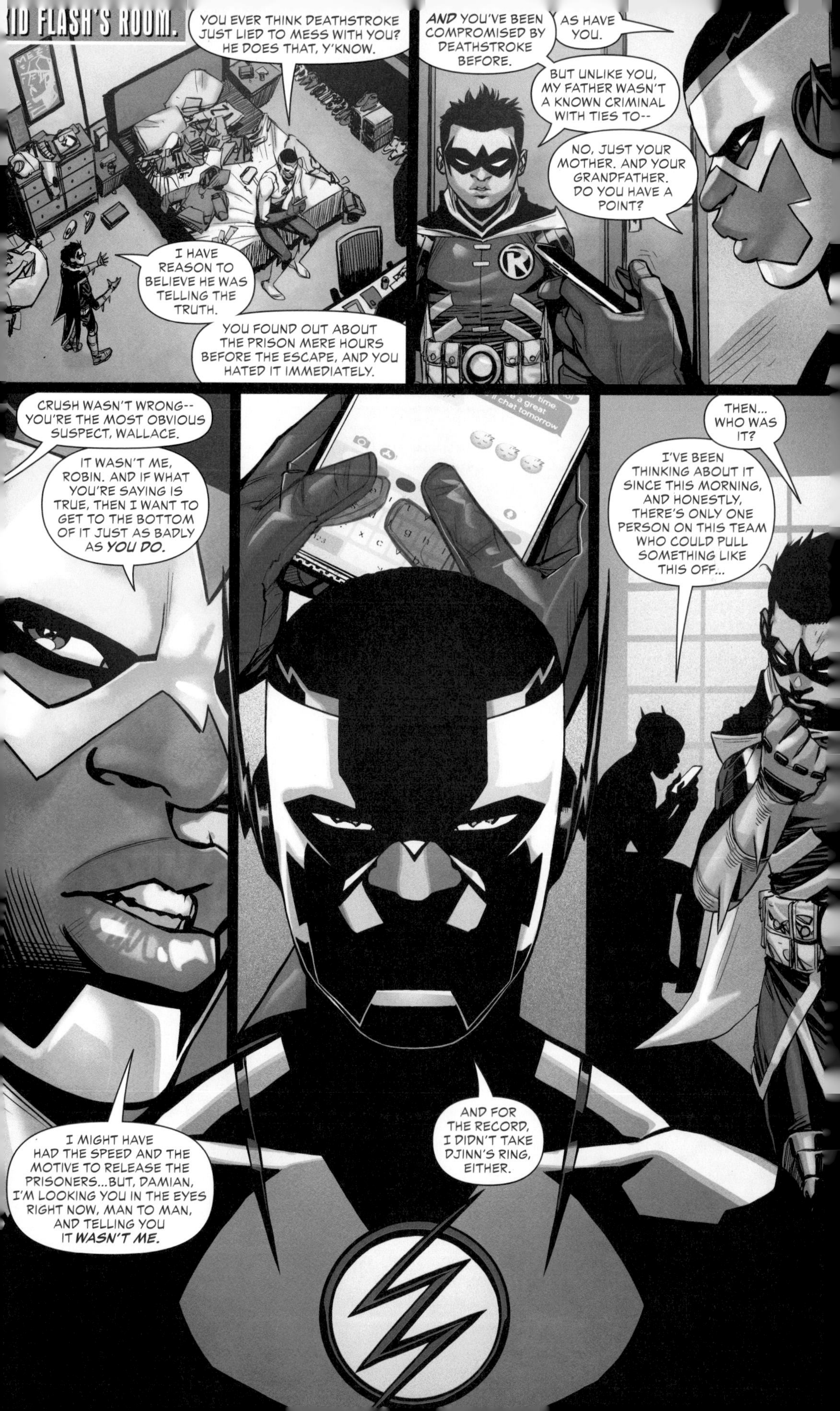
ID FLASH'S ROOM.
YOU EVER THINK DEATHSTROKE JUST LIED TO MESS WITH YOU? HE DOES THAT, Y'KNOW.
I HAVE REASON TO BELIEVE HE WAS TELLING THE TRUTH.
YOU FOUND OUT ABOUT THE PRISON MERE HOURS BEFORE THE ESCAPE, AND YOU HATED IT IMMEDIATELY.
AND YOU'VE BEEN COMPROMISED BY DEATHSTROKE BEFORE.
AS HAVE YOU.
BUT UNLIKE YOU, MY FATHER WASN'T A KNOWN CRIMINAL WITH TIES TO--
NO, JUST YOUR MOTHER. AND YOUR GRANDFATHER. DO YOU HAVE A POINT?
CRUSH WASN'T WRONG-- YOU'RE THE MOST OBVIOUS SUSPECT, WALLACE.
IT WASN'T ME, ROBIN. AND IF WHAT YOU'RE SAYING IS TRUE, THEN I WANT TO GET TO THE BOTTOM OF IT JUST AS BADLY AS ***YOU DO.***
I MIGHT HAVE HAD THE SPEED AND THE MOTIVE TO RELEASE THE PRISONERS...BUT, DAMIAN, I'M LOOKING YOU IN THE EYES RIGHT NOW, MAN TO MAN, AND TELLING YOU IT ***WASN'T ME.***
AND FOR THE RECORD, I DIDN'T TAKE DJINN'S RING, EITHER.
THEN... WHO WAS IT?
I'VE BEEN THINKING ABOUT IT SINCE THIS MORNING, AND HONESTLY, THERE'S ONLY ONE PERSON ON THIS TEAM WHO COULD PULL SOMETHING LIKE THIS OFF...

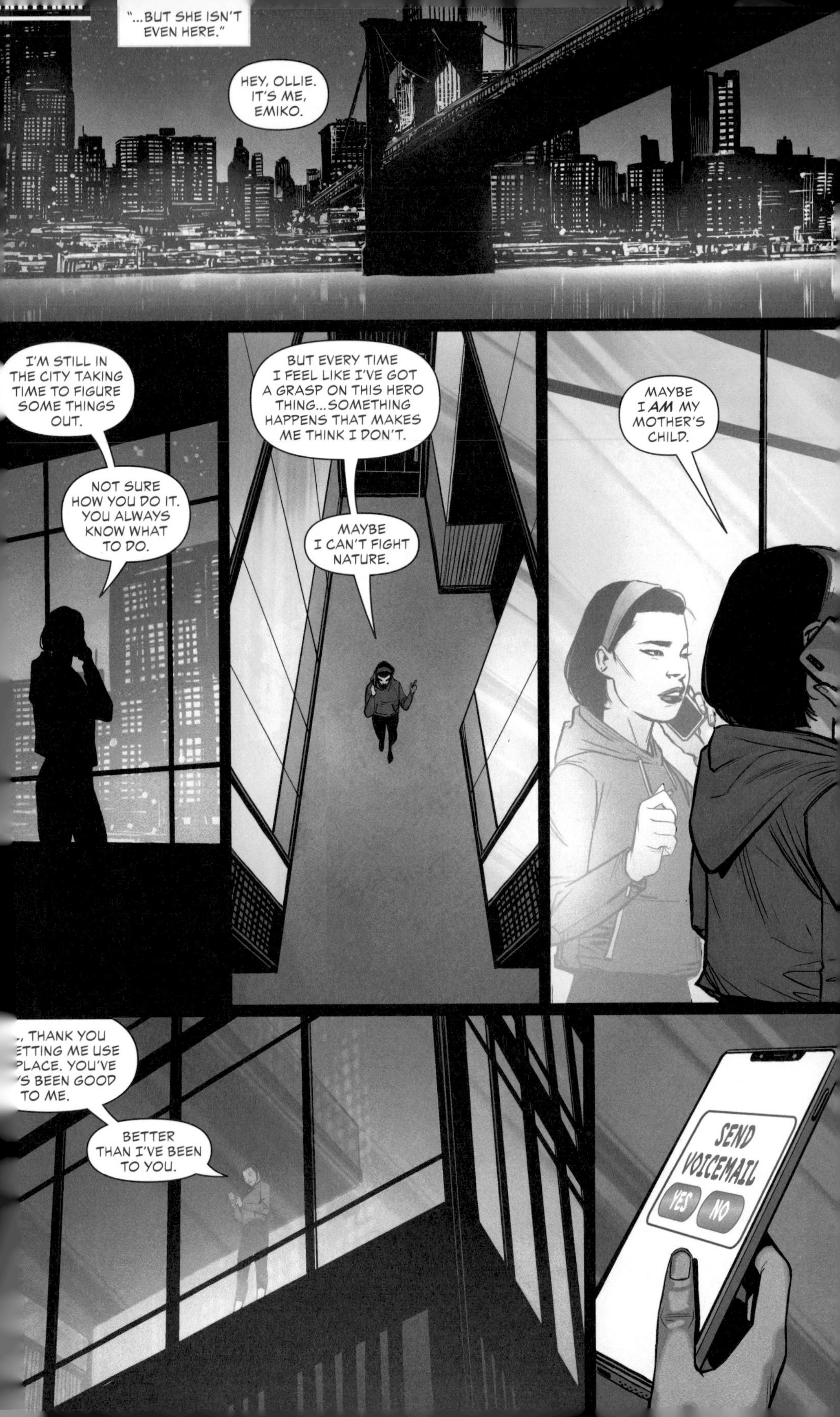

"...BUT SHE ISN'T EVEN HERE."
HEY, OLLIE. IT'S ME, EMIKO.
I'M STILL IN THE CITY TAKING TIME TO FIGURE SOME THINGS OUT.
NOT SURE HOW YOU DO IT. YOU ALWAYS KNOW WHAT TO DO.
BUT EVERY TIME I FEEL LIKE I'VE GOT A GRASP ON THIS HERO THING...SOMETHING HAPPENS THAT MAKES ME THINK I DON'T.
MAYBE I CAN'T FIGHT NATURE.
MAYBE I AM MY MOTHER'S CHILD.
THANK YOU ETTING ME USE PLACE. YOU'VE 'S BEEN GOOD TO ME.
BETTER THAN I'VE BEEN TO YOU.
SEND VOICEMAIL
YES
NO

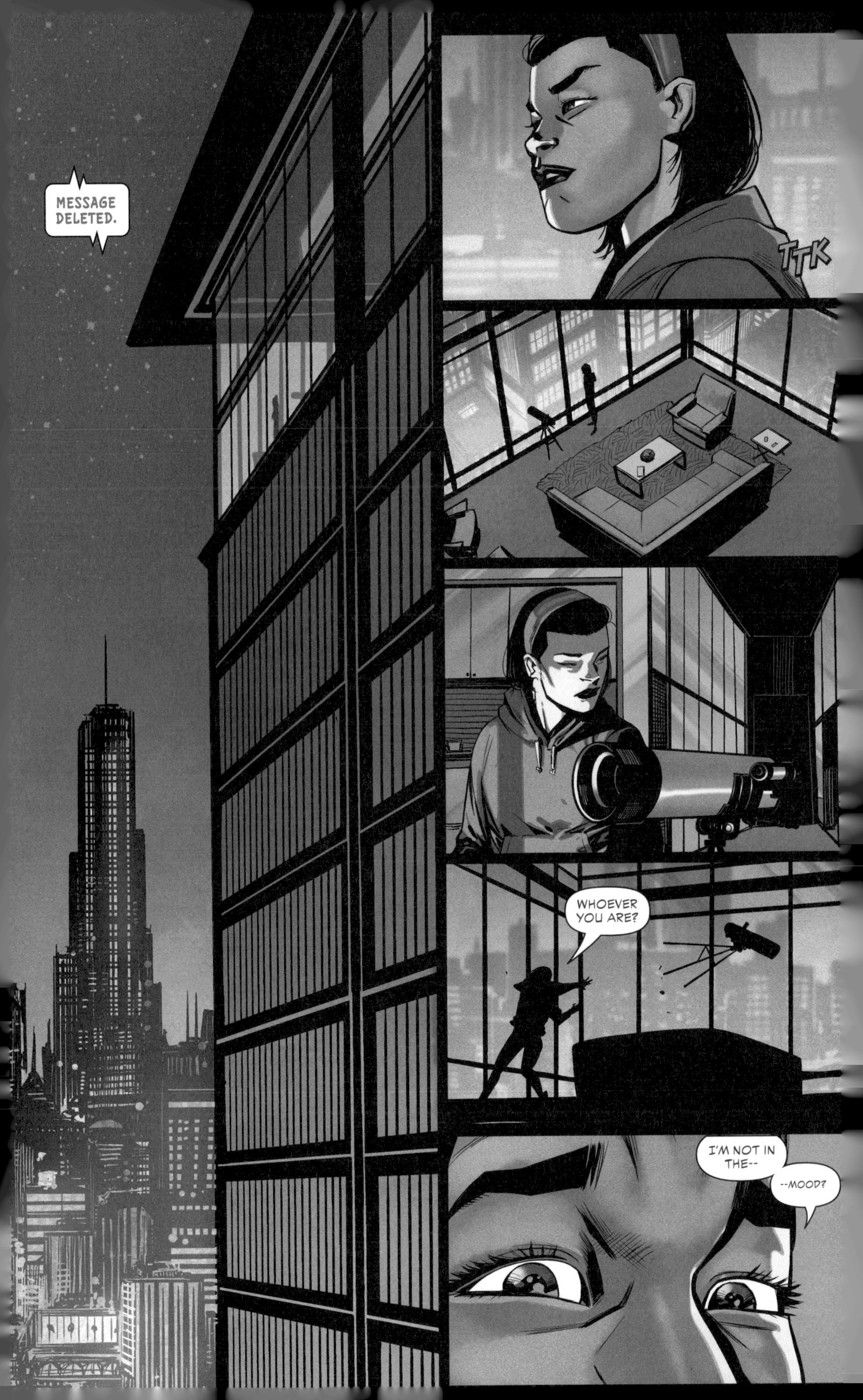
MESSAGE DELETED.
TTK
WHOEVER YOU ARE?
I'M NOT IN THE--
--MOOD?

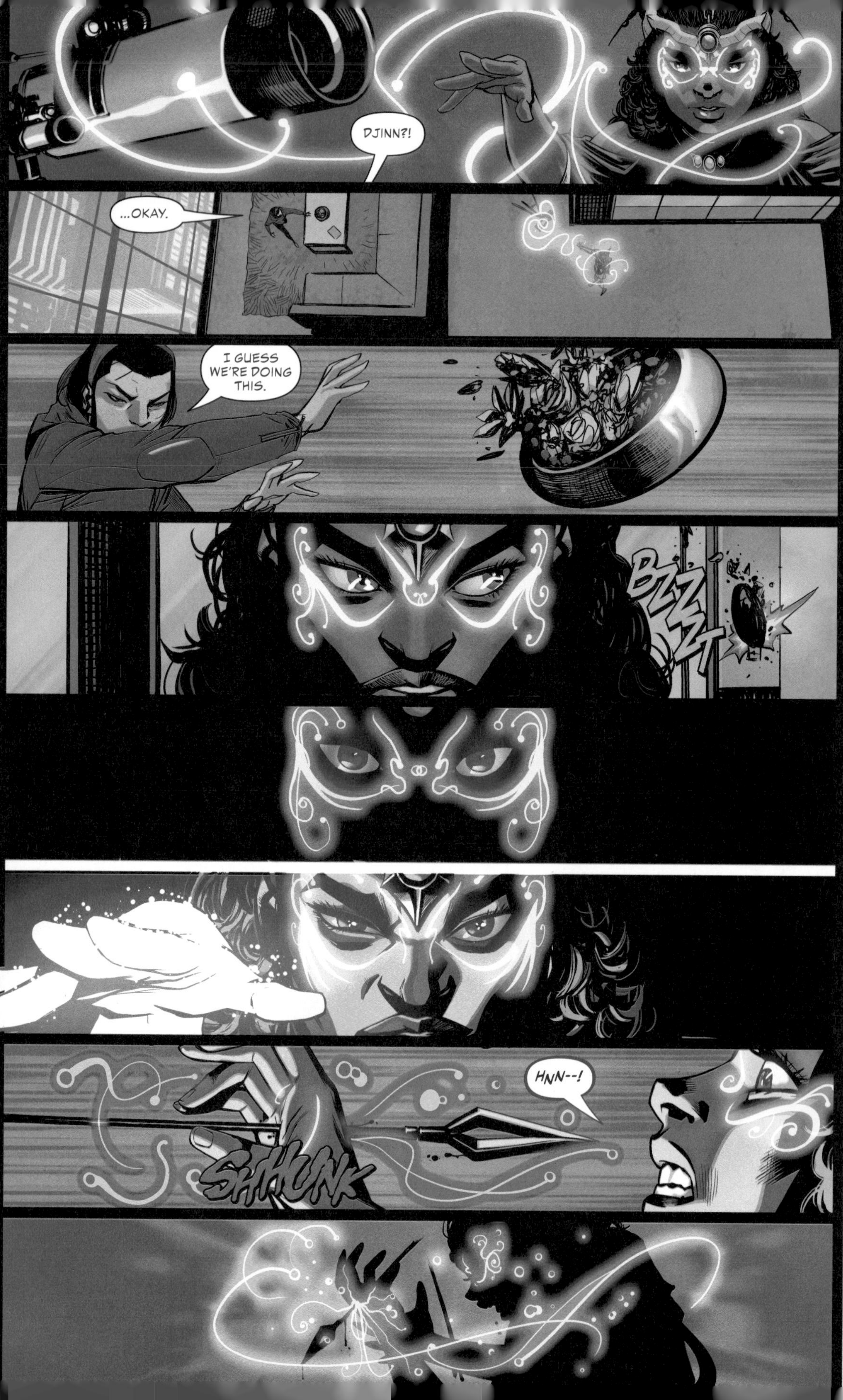
DJINN?!
...OKAY.
I GUESS WE'RE DOING THIS.
BZZZT
HNN--!
SHHUNK

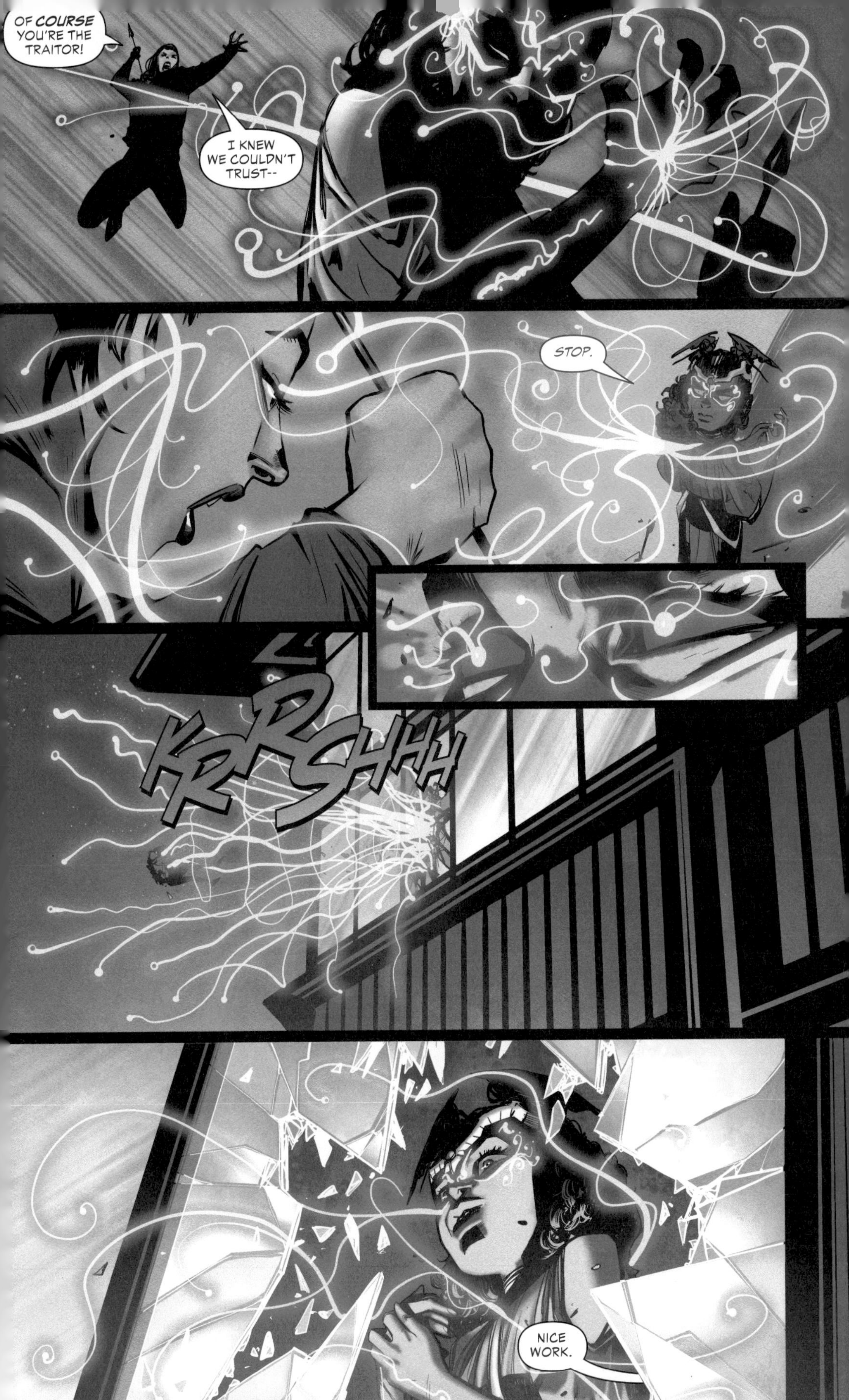
OF COURSE YOU'RE THE TRAITOR!
I KNEW WE COULDN'T TRUST--
STOP.
KRRSHHH
NICE WORK.

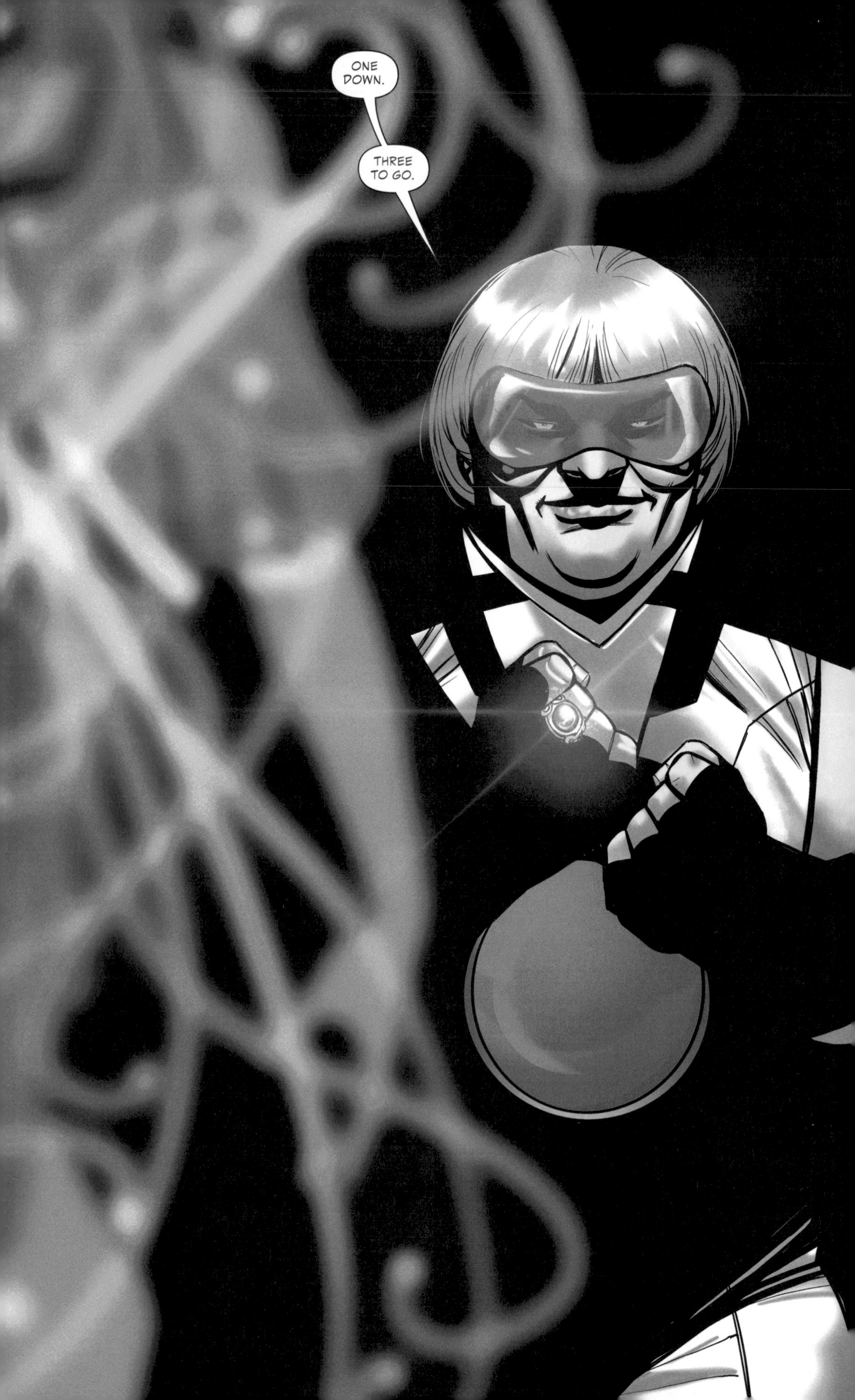
ONE DOWN.
THREE TO GO.

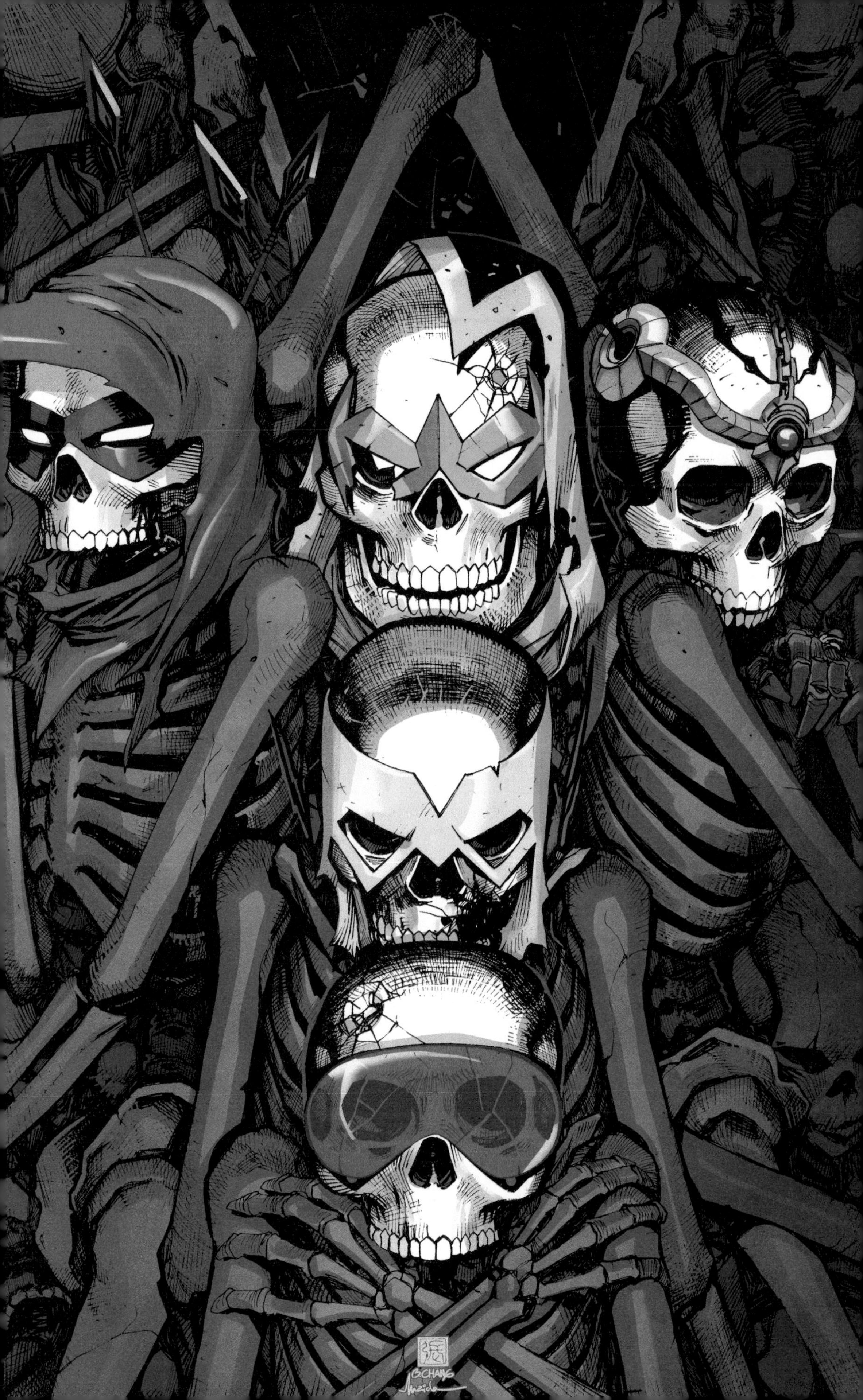
B.CHANG

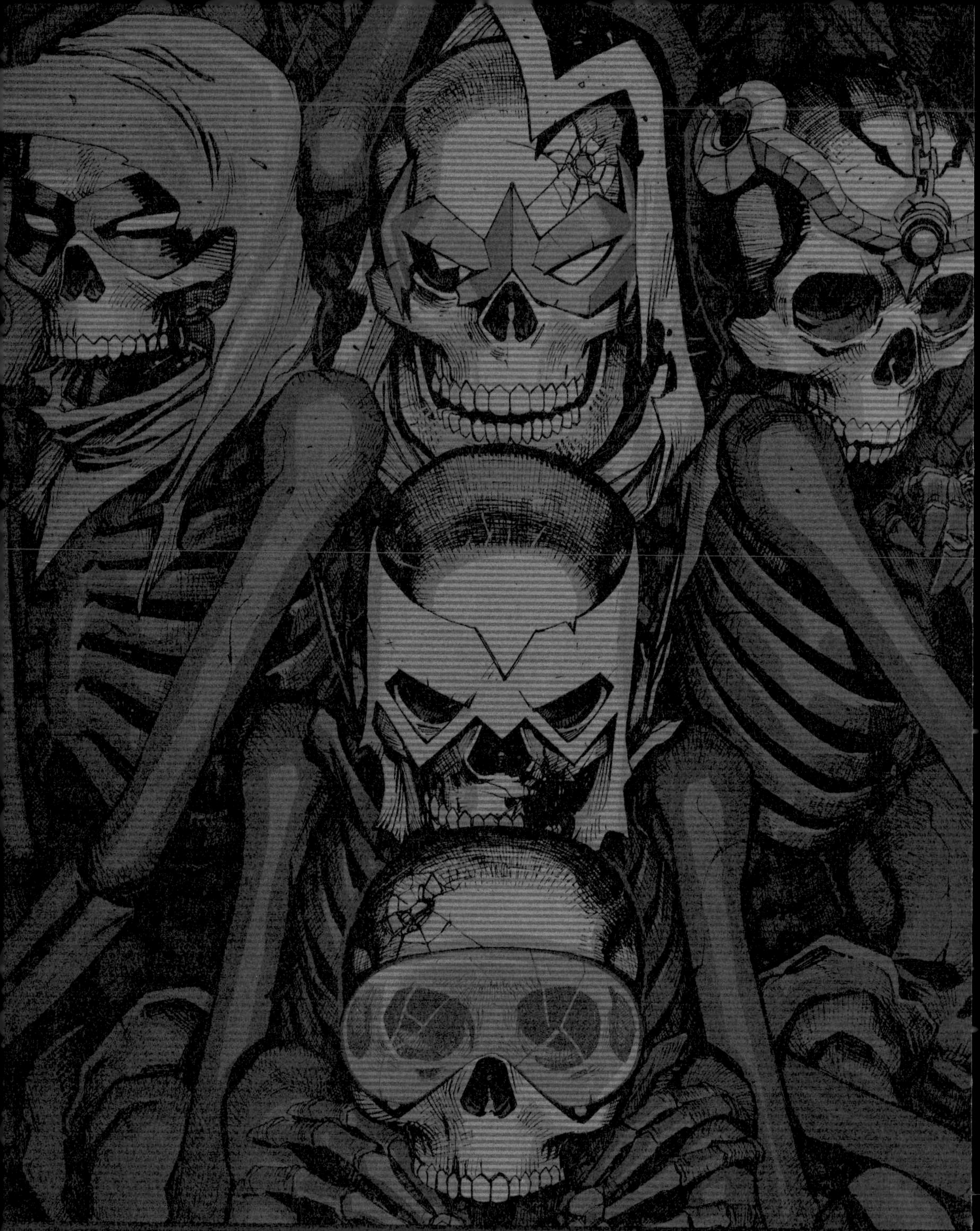

TEEN TITANS
#35

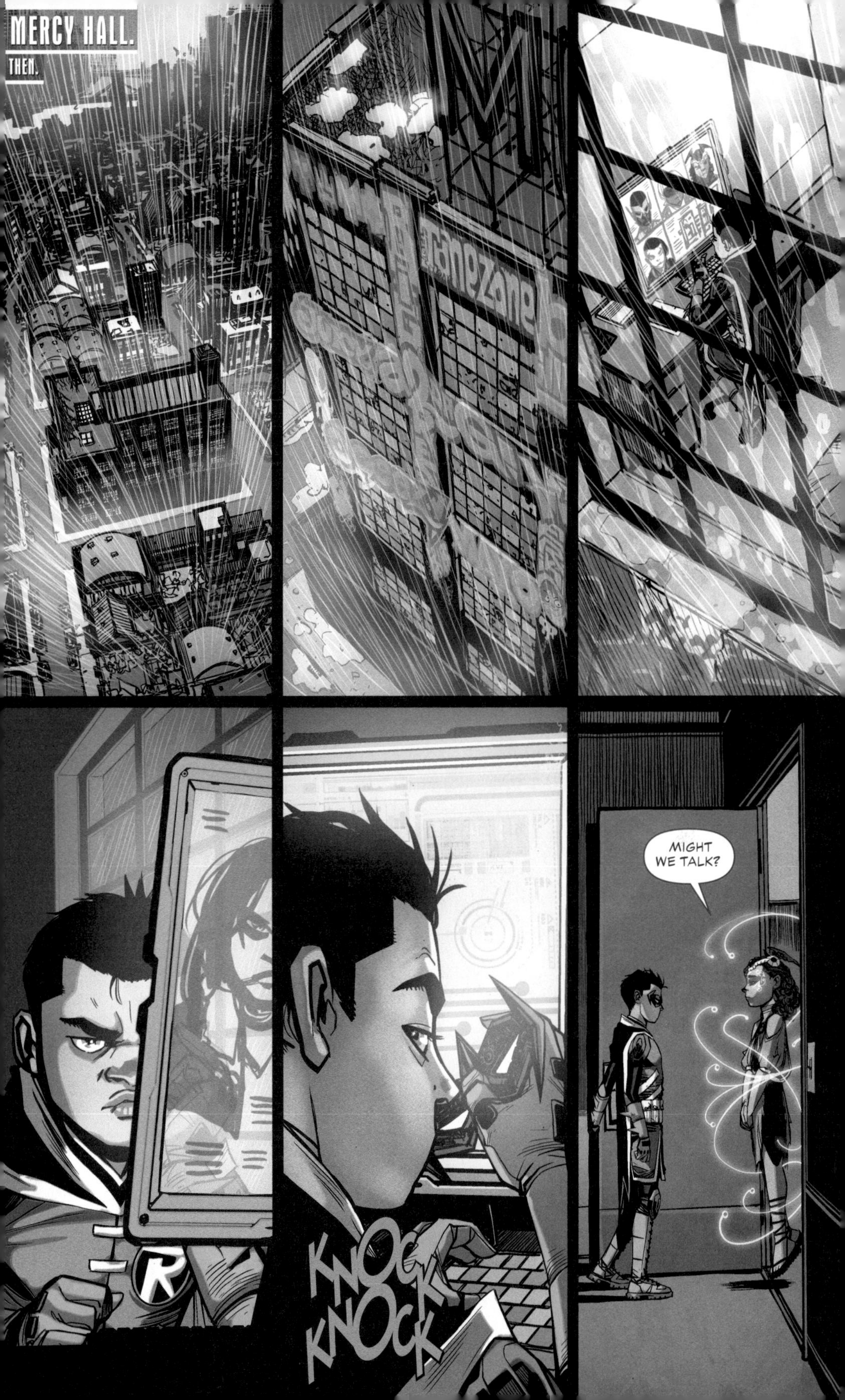
MERCY HALL.
THEN.
MIGHT WE TALK?
KNOCK KNOCK

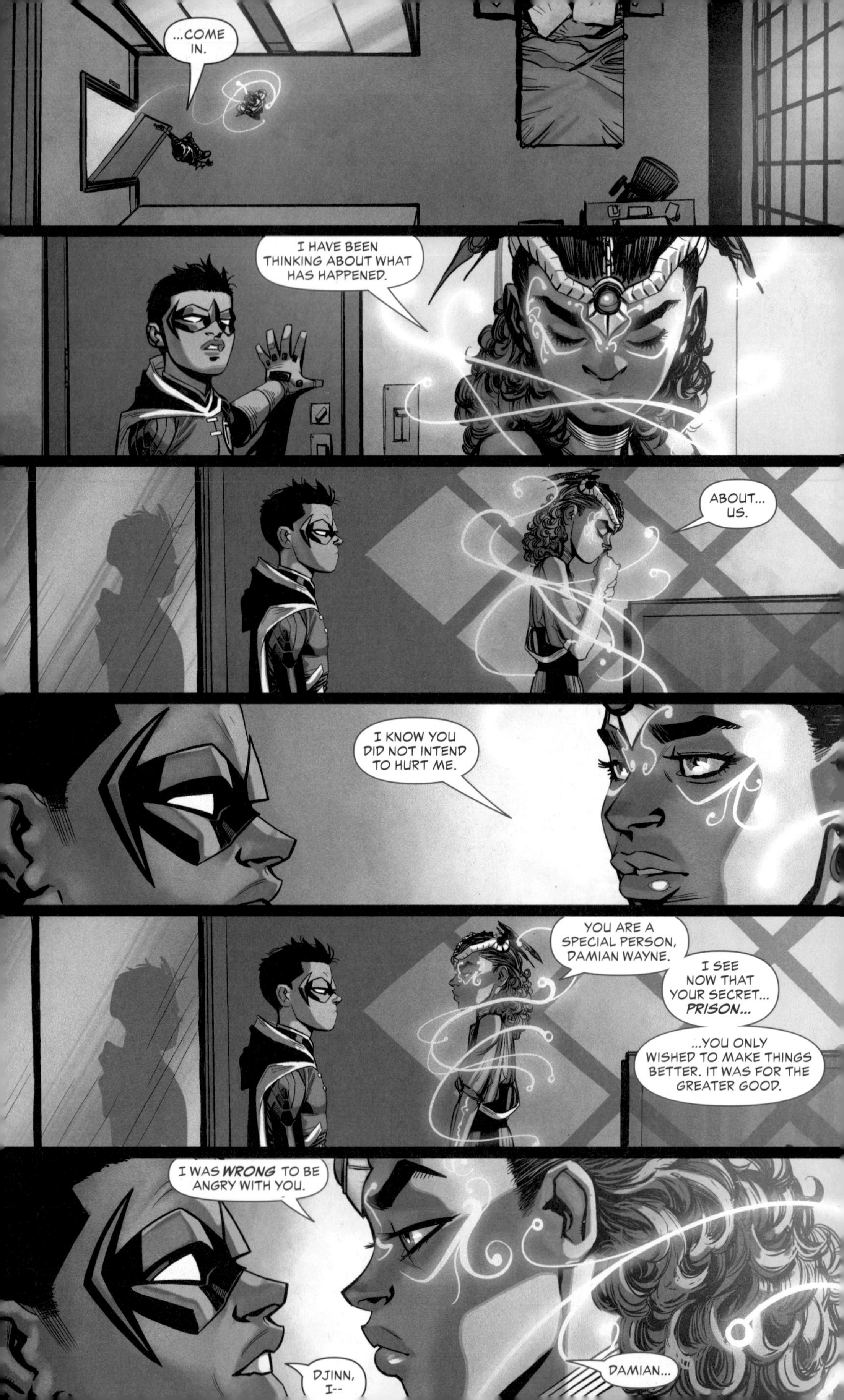
...COME IN.
I HAVE BEEN THINKING ABOUT WHAT HAS HAPPENED.
ABOUT... US.
I KNOW YOU DID NOT INTEND TO HURT ME.
YOU ARE A SPECIAL PERSON, DAMIAN WAYNE.
I SEE NOW THAT YOUR SECRET... PRISON...
...YOU ONLY WISHED TO MAKE THINGS BETTER. IT WAS FOR THE GREATER GOOD.
I WAS WRONG TO BE ANGRY WITH YOU.
DJINN, I--
DAMIAN...

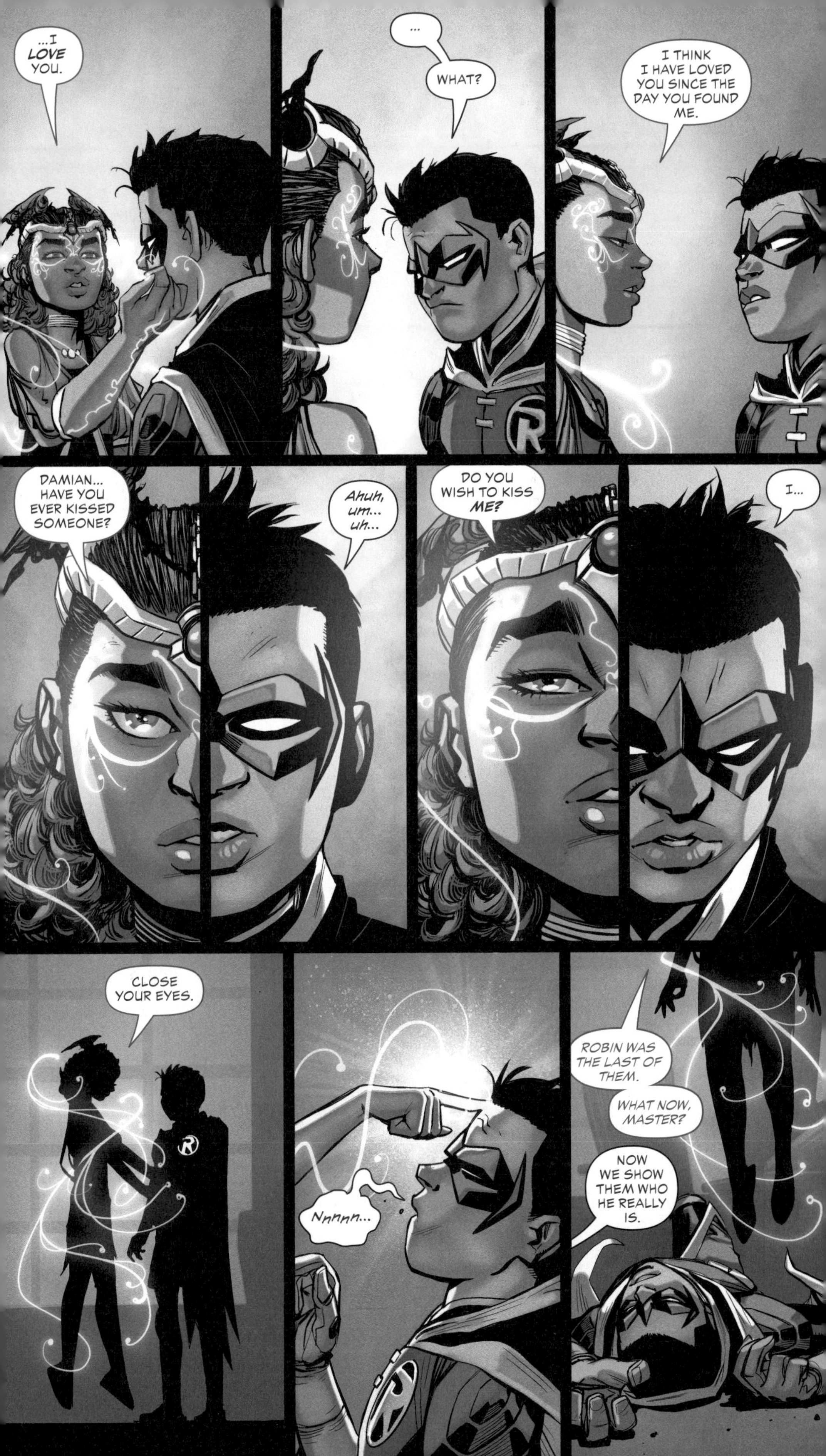
...I LOVE YOU.
...
WHAT?
I THINK I HAVE LOVED YOU SINCE THE DAY YOU FOUND ME.
DAMIAN... HAVE YOU EVER KISSED SOMEONE?
Ahuh, um... uh...
DO YOU WISH TO KISS ME?
I...
CLOSE YOUR EYES.
Nnnnn...
ROBIN WAS THE LAST OF THEM.
WHAT NOW, MASTER?
NOW WE SHOW THEM WHO HE REALLY IS.

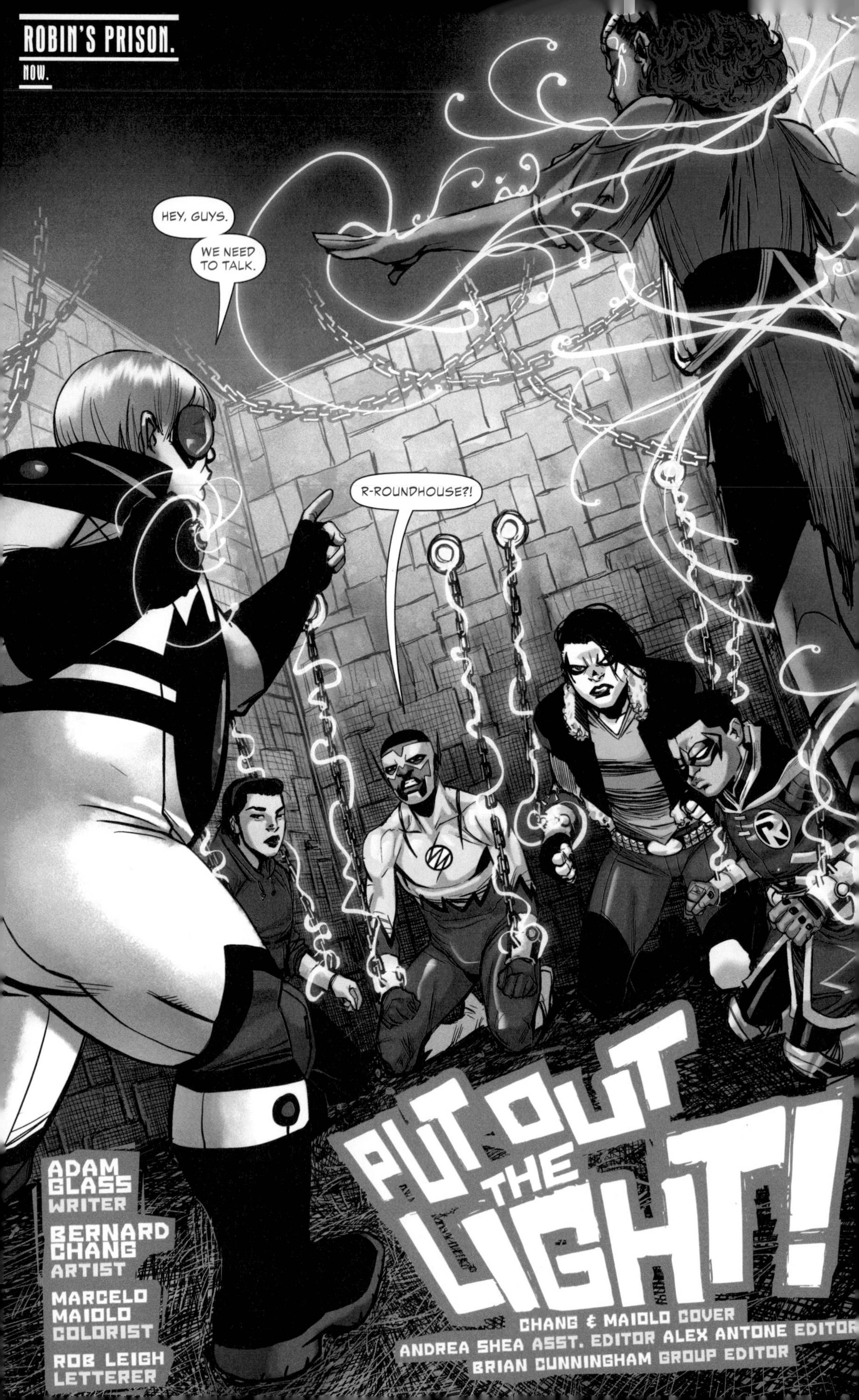
ROBIN'S PRISON.
NOW.
HEY, GUYS.
WE NEED TO TALK.
R-ROUNDHOUSE?!
PUT OUT THE LIGHT!
ADAM GLASS WRITER
BERNARD CHANG ARTIST
MARCELO MAIOLO COLORIST
ROB LEIGH LETTERER
CHANG & MAIOLO COVER
ANDREA SHEA ASST. EDITOR ALEX ANTONE EDITOR
BRIAN CUNNINGHAM GROUP EDITOR

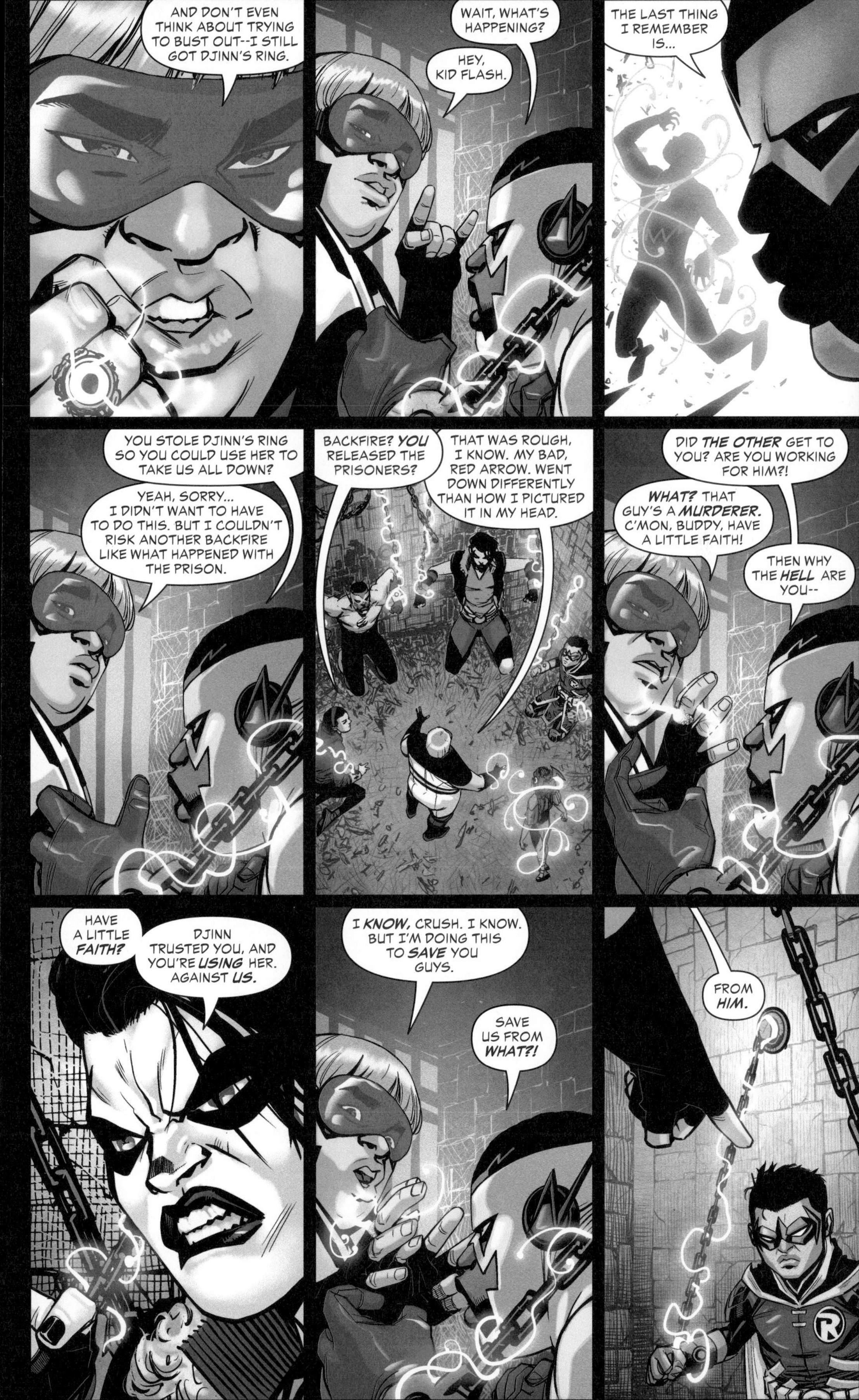
AND DON'T EVEN THINK ABOUT TRYING TO BUST OUT--I STILL GOT DJINN'S RING.
WAIT, WHAT'S HAPPENING?
HEY, KID FLASH.
THE LAST THING I REMEMBER IS...
YOU STOLE DJINN'S RING SO YOU COULD USE HER TO TAKE US ALL DOWN?
YEAH, SORRY... I DIDN'T WANT TO HAVE TO DO THIS. BUT I COULDN'T RISK ANOTHER BACKFIRE LIKE WHAT HAPPENED WITH THE PRISON.
BACKFIRE? *YOU* RELEASED THE PRISONERS?
THAT WAS ROUGH, I KNOW. MY BAD, RED ARROW. WENT DOWN DIFFERENTLY THAN HOW I PICTURED IT IN MY HEAD.
DID *THE OTHER* GET TO YOU? ARE YOU WORKING FOR HIM?!
WHAT? THAT GUY'S A *MURDERER.* C'MON, BUDDY, HAVE A LITTLE FAITH!
THEN WHY THE *HELL* ARE YOU--
HAVE A LITTLE *FAITH?*
DJINN TRUSTED YOU, AND YOU'RE *USING* HER. AGAINST *US.*
I *KNOW,* CRUSH. I KNOW. BUT I'M DOING THIS TO *SAVE* YOU GUYS.
SAVE US FROM *WHAT?!*
FROM *HIM.*

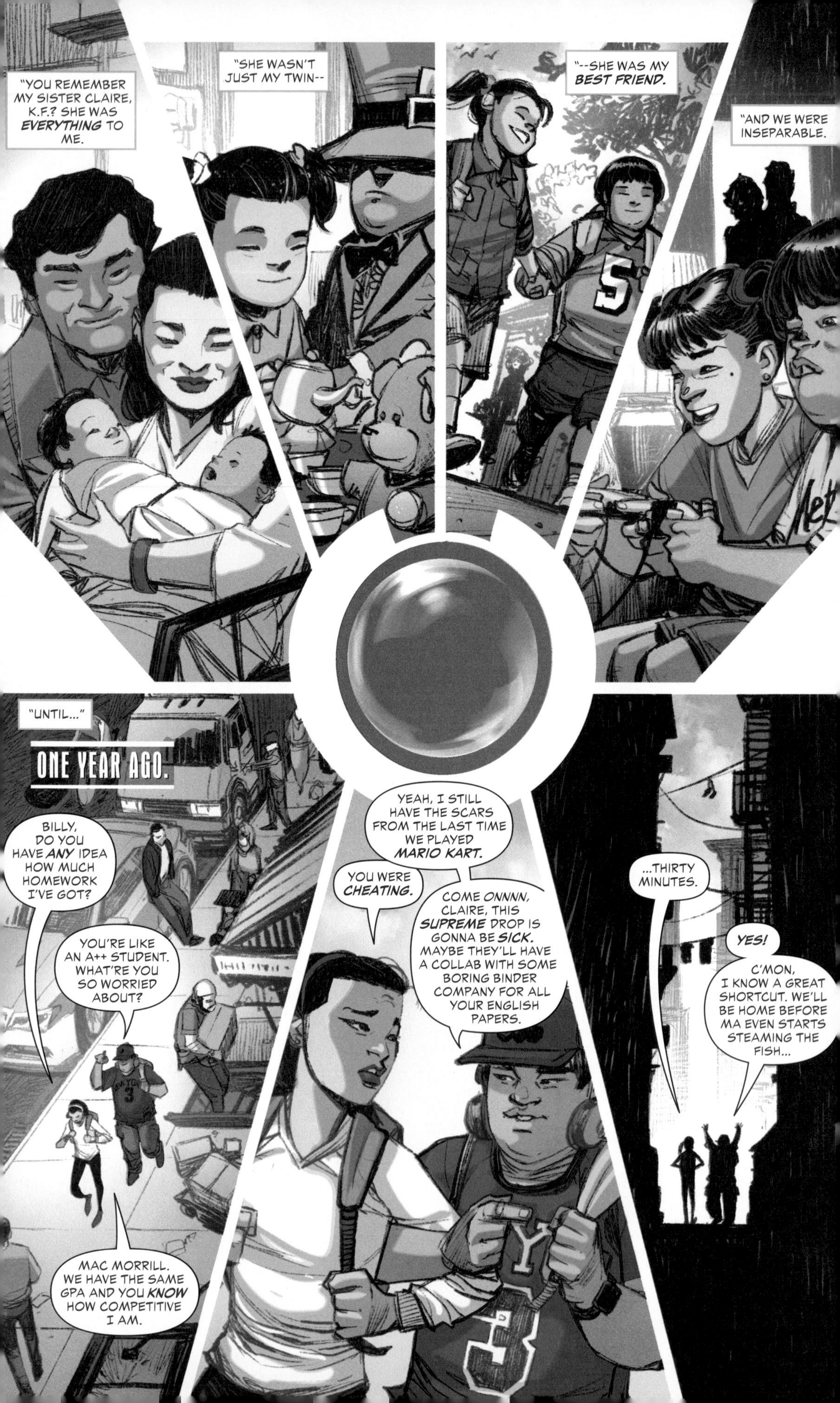
"YOU REMEMBER MY SISTER CLAIRE, K.F.? SHE WAS *EVERYTHING* TO ME.
"SHE WASN'T JUST MY TWIN--
"--SHE WAS MY *BEST FRIEND.*
"AND WE WERE INSEPARABLE.
"UNTIL..."
ONE YEAR AGO.
BILLY, DO YOU HAVE *ANY* IDEA HOW MUCH HOMEWORK I'VE GOT?
YOU'RE LIKE AN A++ STUDENT. WHAT'RE YOU SO WORRIED ABOUT?
MAC MORRILL. WE HAVE THE SAME GPA AND YOU *KNOW* HOW COMPETITIVE I AM.
YEAH, I STILL HAVE THE SCARS FROM THE LAST TIME WE PLAYED *MARIO KART.*
YOU WERE *CHEATING.*
COME *ONNNN*, CLAIRE, THIS *SUPREME* DROP IS GONNA BE *SICK.* MAYBE THEY'LL HAVE A COLLAB WITH SOME BORING BINDER COMPANY FOR ALL YOUR ENGLISH PAPERS.
...THIRTY MINUTES.
YES!
C'MON, I KNOW A GREAT SHORTCUT. WE'LL BE HOME BEFORE MA EVEN STARTS STEAMING THE FISH...

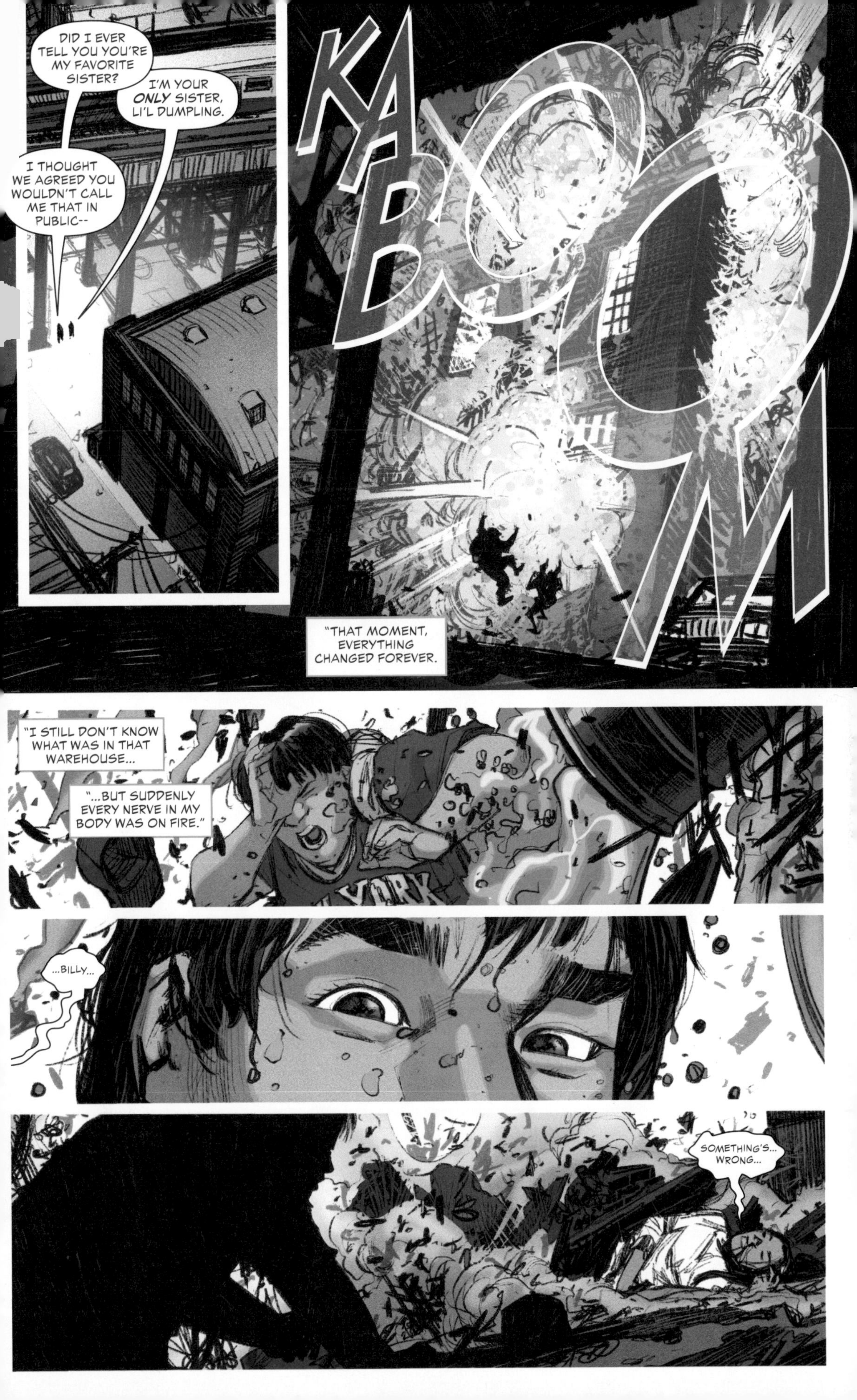
DID I EVER TELL YOU YOU'RE MY FAVORITE SISTER?
I'M YOUR ONLY SISTER, LI'L DUMPLING.
I THOUGHT WE AGREED YOU WOULDN'T CALL ME THAT IN PUBLIC--
KABOOM
"THAT MOMENT, EVERYTHING CHANGED FOREVER.
"I STILL DON'T KNOW WHAT WAS IN THAT WAREHOUSE...
"...BUT SUDDENLY EVERY NERVE IN MY BODY WAS ON FIRE."
...BILLY...
SOMETHING'S... WRONG...

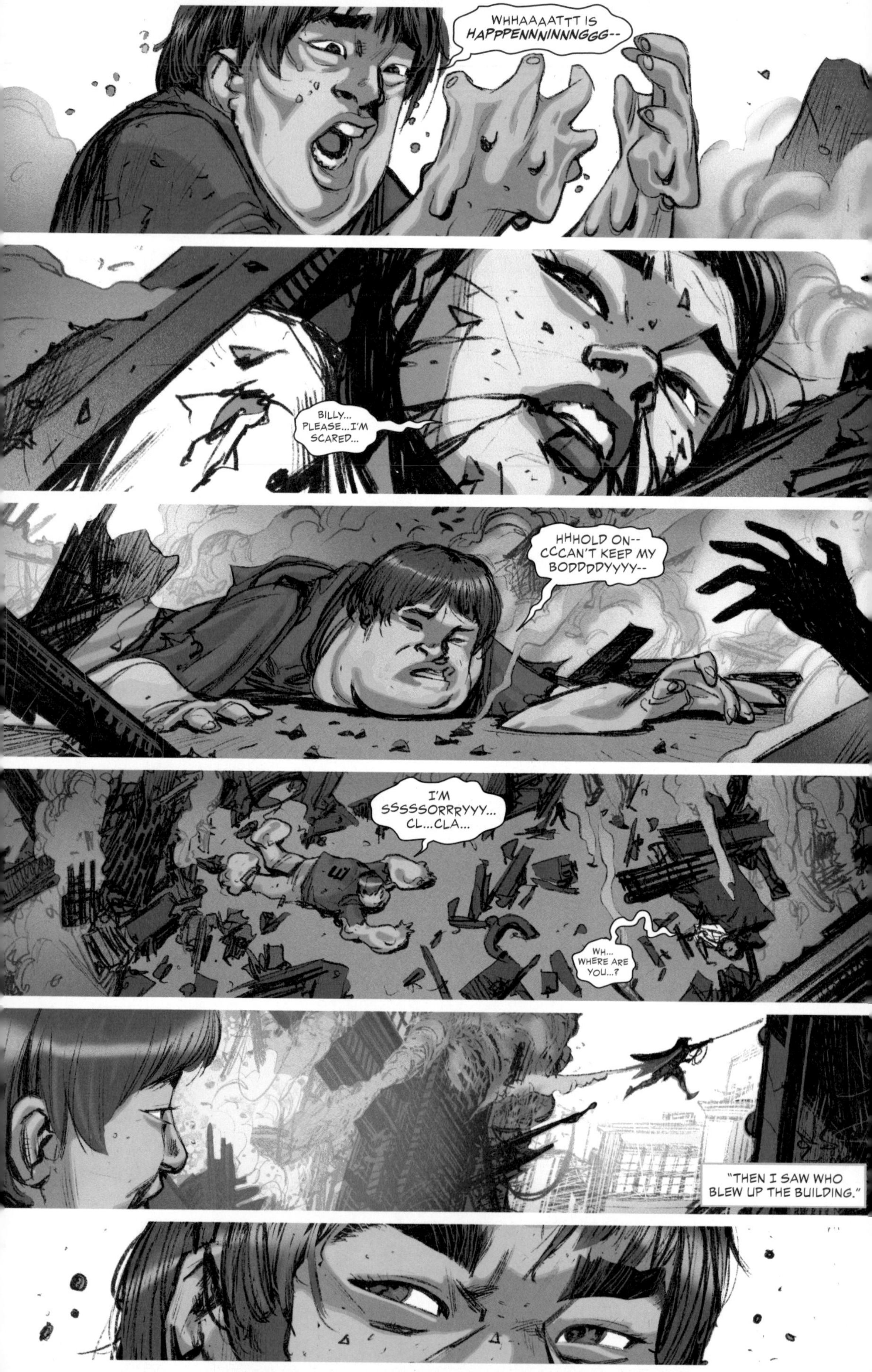
WHHAAAATTT IS HAPPPENNNINNNGGG--
BILLY... PLEASE...I'M SCARED...
HHHOLD ON-- CCCAN'T KEEP MY BODDDDYYYY--
I'M SSSSSORRRYYY... CL...CLA...
WH... WHERE ARE YOU...?
"THEN I SAW WHO BLEW UP THE BUILDING."

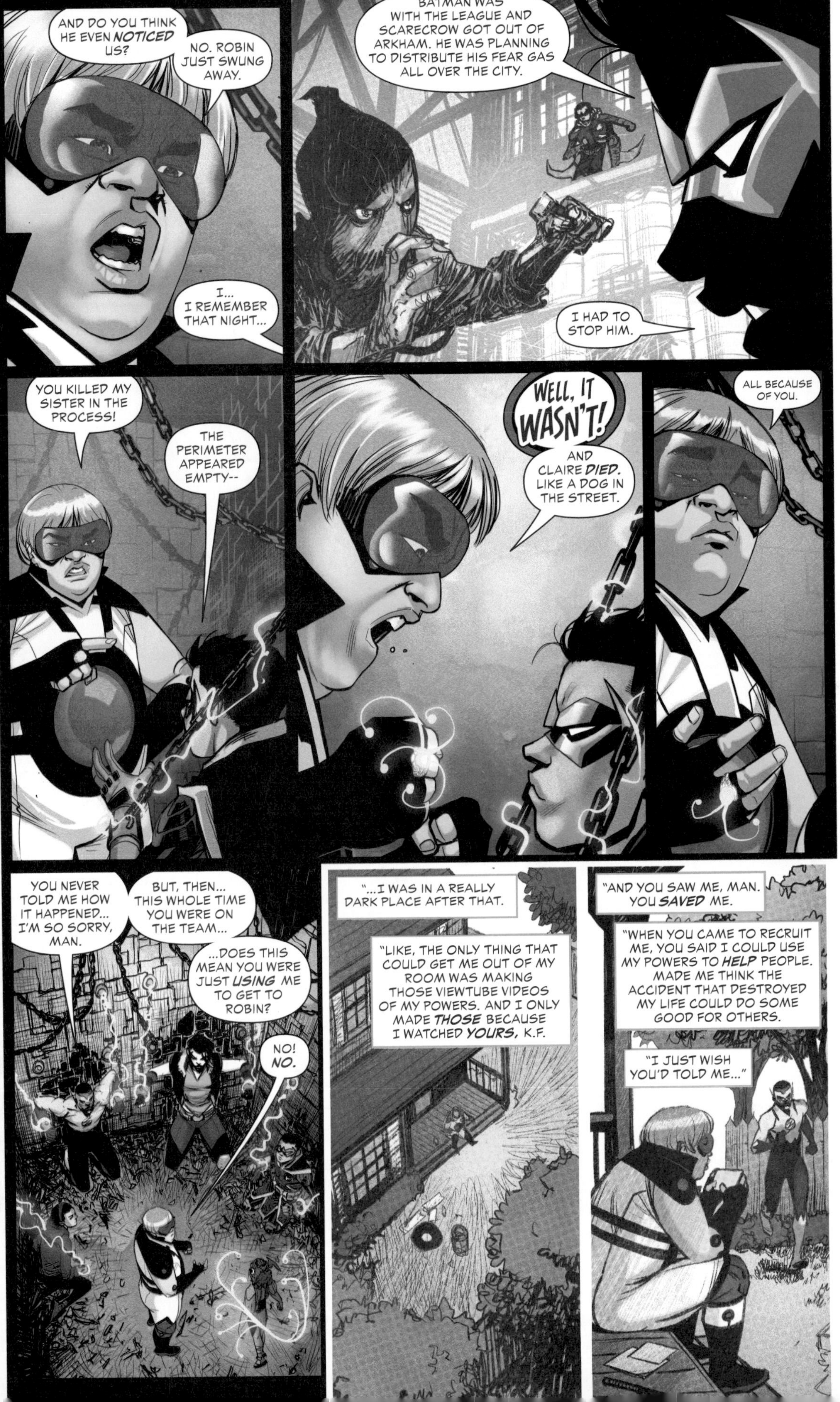
AND DO YOU THINK HE EVEN *NOTICED* US?
NO. ROBIN JUST SWUNG AWAY.
I... I REMEMBER THAT NIGHT...
BATMAN WAS WITH THE LEAGUE AND SCARECROW GOT OUT OF ARKHAM. HE WAS PLANNING TO DISTRIBUTE HIS FEAR GAS ALL OVER THE CITY.
I HAD TO STOP HIM.
YOU KILLED MY SISTER IN THE PROCESS!
THE PERIMETER APPEARED EMPTY--
WELL, IT WASN'T!
AND CLAIRE *DIED.* LIKE A DOG IN THE STREET.
ALL BECAUSE OF YOU.
YOU NEVER TOLD ME HOW IT HAPPENED... I'M SO SORRY, MAN.
BUT, THEN... THIS WHOLE TIME YOU WERE ON THE TEAM...
...DOES THIS MEAN YOU WERE JUST *USING* ME TO GET TO ROBIN?
NO! *NO.*
"...I WAS IN A REALLY DARK PLACE AFTER THAT.
"LIKE, THE ONLY THING THAT COULD GET ME OUT OF MY ROOM WAS MAKING THOSE VIEWTUBE VIDEOS OF MY POWERS. AND I ONLY MADE *THOSE* BECAUSE I WATCHED *YOURS,* K.F.
"AND YOU SAW ME, MAN. YOU *SAVED* ME.
"WHEN YOU CAME TO RECRUIT ME, YOU SAID I COULD USE MY POWERS TO *HELP* PEOPLE. MADE ME THINK THE ACCIDENT THAT DESTROYED MY LIFE COULD DO SOME GOOD FOR OTHERS.
"I JUST WISH YOU'D TOLD ME..."

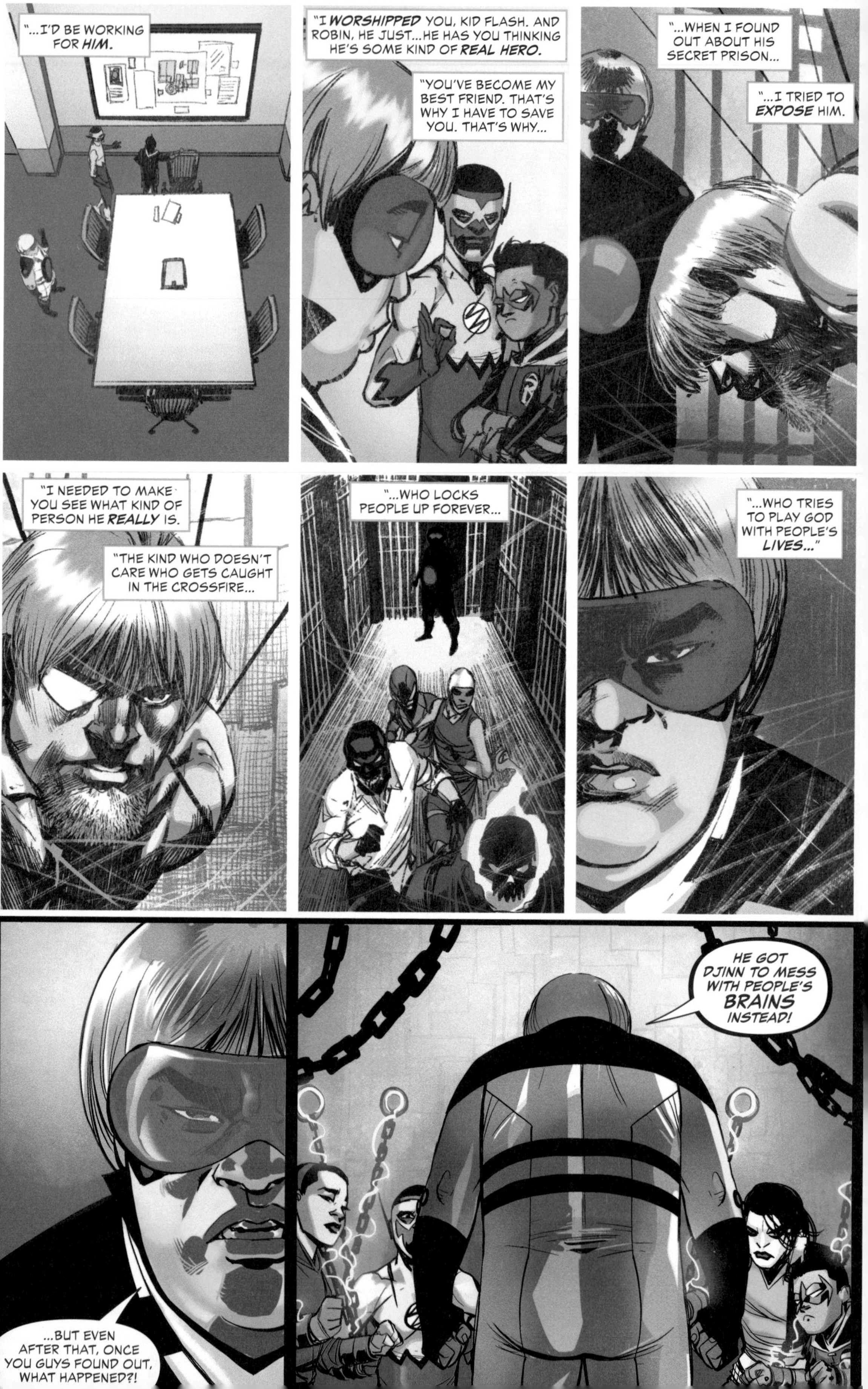
"...I'D BE WORKING FOR HIM.
"I WORSHIPPED YOU, KID FLASH. AND ROBIN, HE JUST...HE HAS YOU THINKING HE'S SOME KIND OF REAL HERO.
"YOU'VE BECOME MY BEST FRIEND. THAT'S WHY I HAVE TO SAVE YOU. THAT'S WHY...
"...WHEN I FOUND OUT ABOUT HIS SECRET PRISON...
"...I TRIED TO EXPOSE HIM.
"I NEEDED TO MAKE YOU SEE WHAT KIND OF PERSON HE REALLY IS.
"THE KIND WHO DOESN'T CARE WHO GETS CAUGHT IN THE CROSSFIRE...
"...WHO LOCKS PEOPLE UP FOREVER...
"...WHO TRIES TO PLAY GOD WITH PEOPLE'S LIVES..."
...BUT EVEN AFTER THAT, ONCE YOU GUYS FOUND OUT, WHAT HAPPENED?!
HE GOT DJINN TO MESS WITH PEOPLE'S BRAINS INSTEAD!

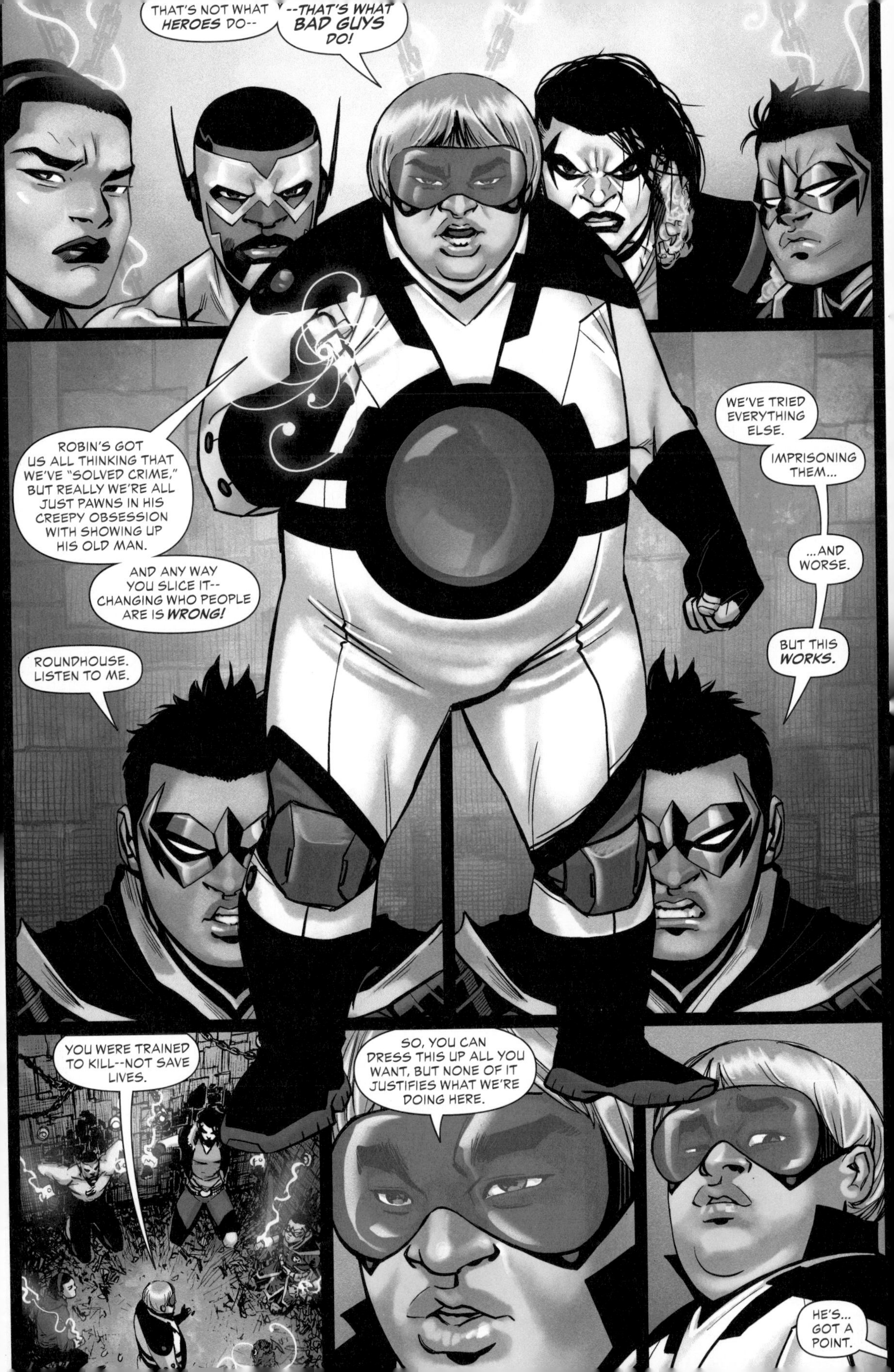

THAT'S NOT WHAT HEROES DO--
--THAT'S WHAT BAD GUYS DO!
ROBIN'S GOT US ALL THINKING THAT WE'VE "SOLVED CRIME," BUT REALLY WE'RE ALL JUST PAWNS IN HIS CREEPY OBSESSION WITH SHOWING UP HIS OLD MAN.
AND ANY WAY YOU SLICE IT--CHANGING WHO PEOPLE ARE IS WRONG!
WE'VE TRIED EVERYTHING ELSE.
IMPRISONING THEM...
...AND WORSE.
BUT THIS WORKS.
ROUNDHOUSE. LISTEN TO ME.
YOU WERE TRAINED TO KILL--NOT SAVE LIVES.
SO, YOU CAN DRESS THIS UP ALL YOU WANT, BUT NONE OF IT JUSTIFIES WHAT WE'RE DOING HERE.
HE'S... GOT A POINT.

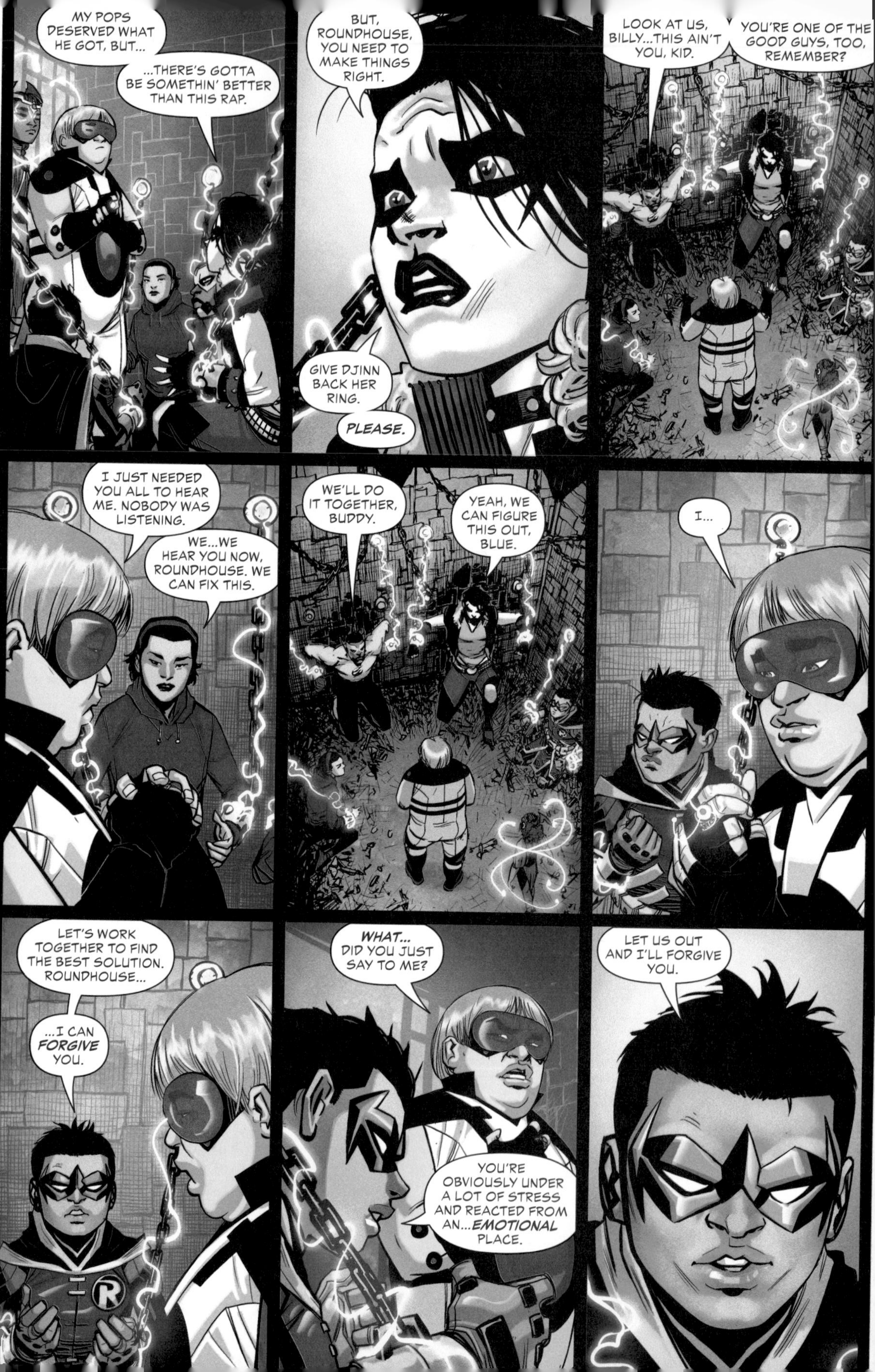
MY POPS DESERVED WHAT HE GOT, BUT...
...THERE'S GOTTA BE SOMETHIN' BETTER THAN THIS RAP.
BUT, ROUNDHOUSE, YOU NEED TO MAKE THINGS RIGHT.
GIVE DJINN BACK HER RING.
PLEASE.
LOOK AT US, BILLY...THIS AIN'T YOU, KID.
YOU'RE ONE OF THE GOOD GUYS, TOO, REMEMBER?
I JUST NEEDED YOU ALL TO HEAR ME. NOBODY WAS LISTENING.
WE...WE HEAR YOU NOW, ROUNDHOUSE. WE CAN FIX THIS.
WE'LL DO IT TOGETHER, BUDDY.
YEAH, WE CAN FIGURE THIS OUT, BLUE.
I...
LET'S WORK TOGETHER TO FIND THE BEST SOLUTION. ROUNDHOUSE...
...I CAN FORGIVE YOU.
WHAT... DID YOU JUST SAY TO ME?
YOU'RE OBVIOUSLY UNDER A LOT OF STRESS AND REACTED FROM AN...EMOTIONAL PLACE.
LET US OUT AND I'LL FORGIVE YOU.

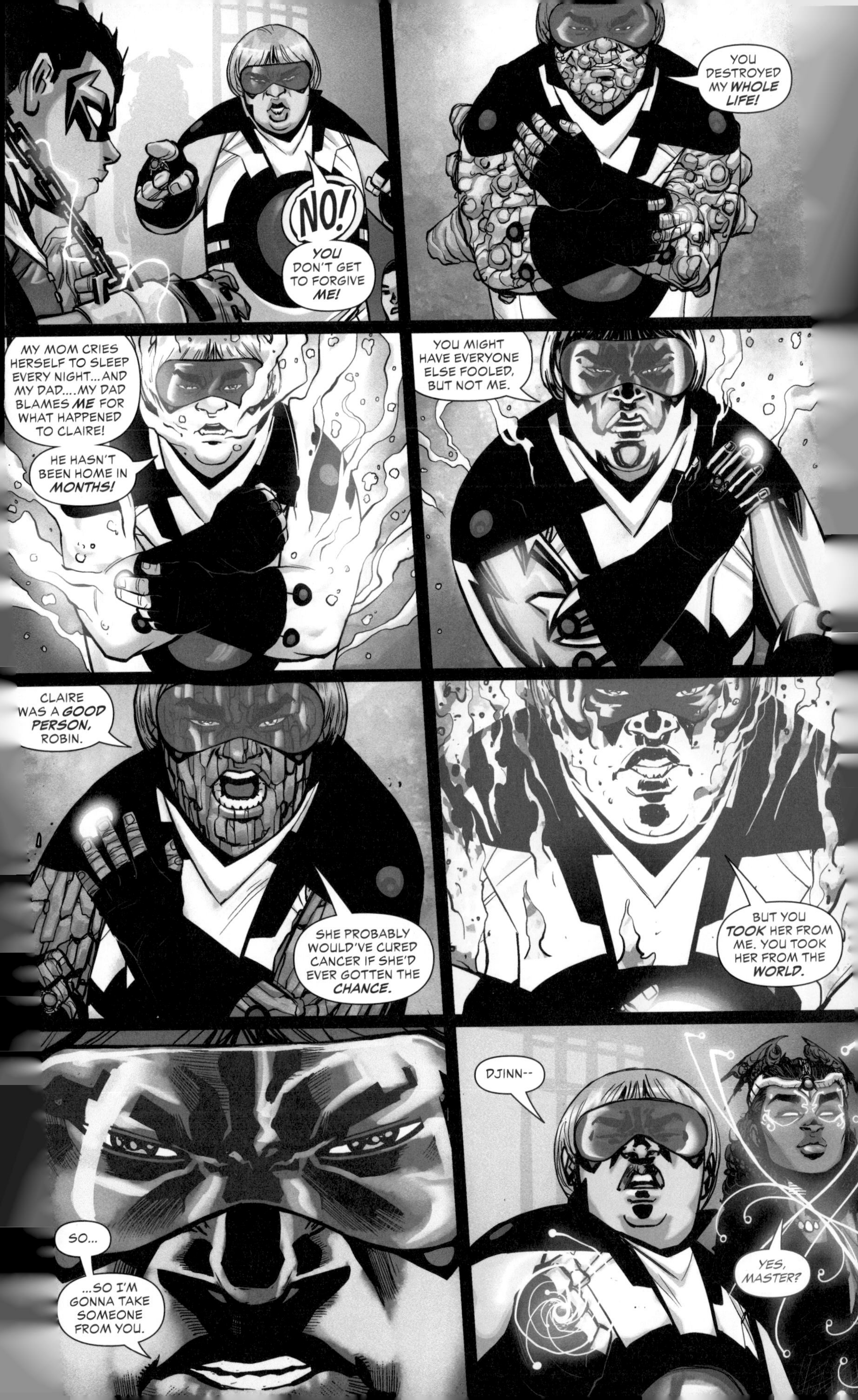
NO!
YOU DON'T GET TO FORGIVE ME!
YOU DESTROYED MY WHOLE LIFE!
MY MOM CRIES HERSELF TO SLEEP EVERY NIGHT...AND MY DAD....MY DAD BLAMES ME FOR WHAT HAPPENED TO CLAIRE!
HE HASN'T BEEN HOME IN MONTHS!
YOU MIGHT HAVE EVERYONE ELSE FOOLED, BUT NOT ME.
CLAIRE WAS A GOOD PERSON, ROBIN.
SHE PROBABLY WOULD'VE CURED CANCER IF SHE'D EVER GOTTEN THE CHANCE.
BUT YOU TOOK HER FROM ME. YOU TOOK HER FROM THE WORLD.
SO...
...SO I'M GONNA TAKE SOMEONE FROM YOU.
DJINN--
YES, MASTER?

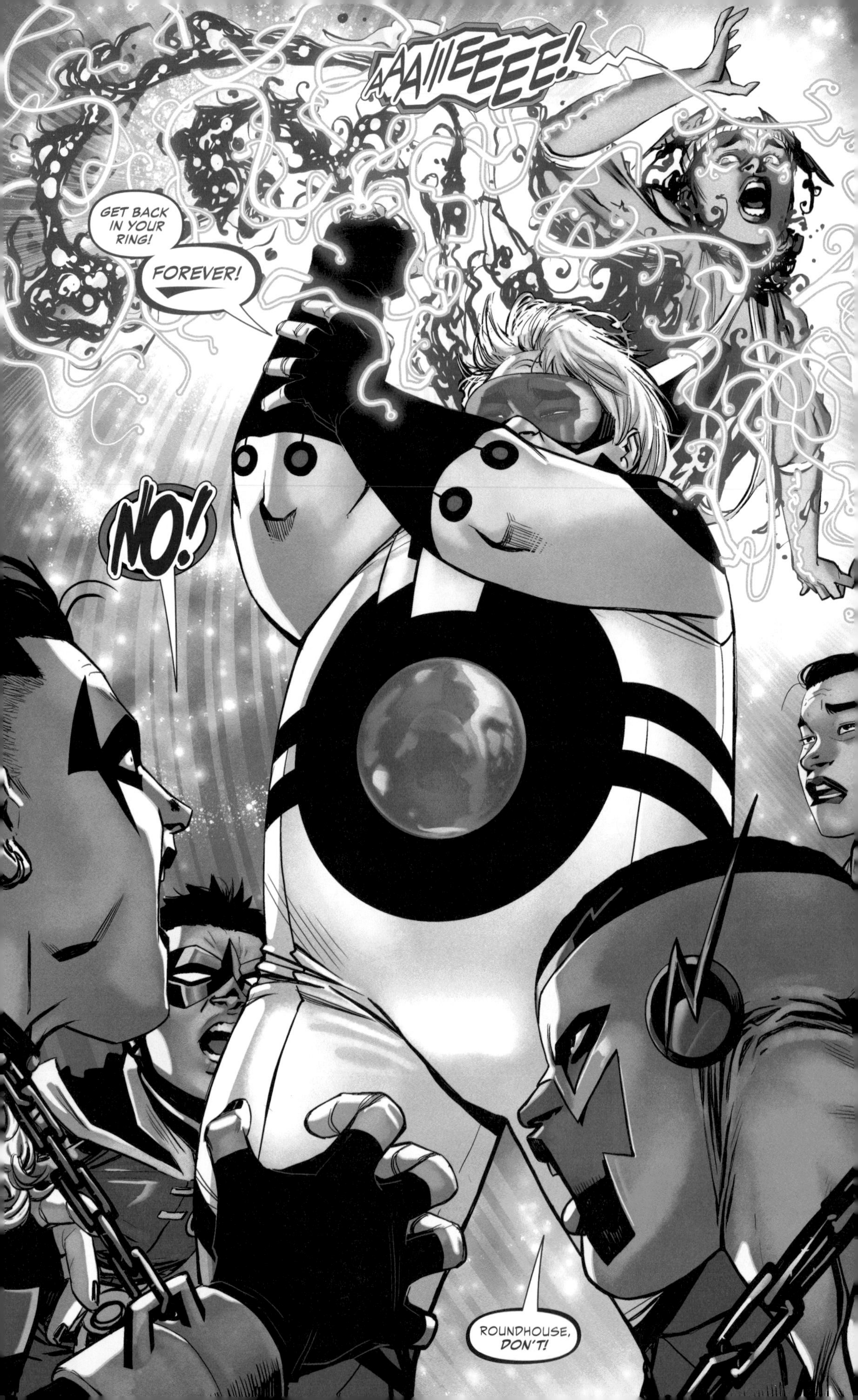
AAAIIIEEEEE!
GET BACK IN YOUR RING!
FOREVER!
NO!
ROUNDHOUSE, DON'T!

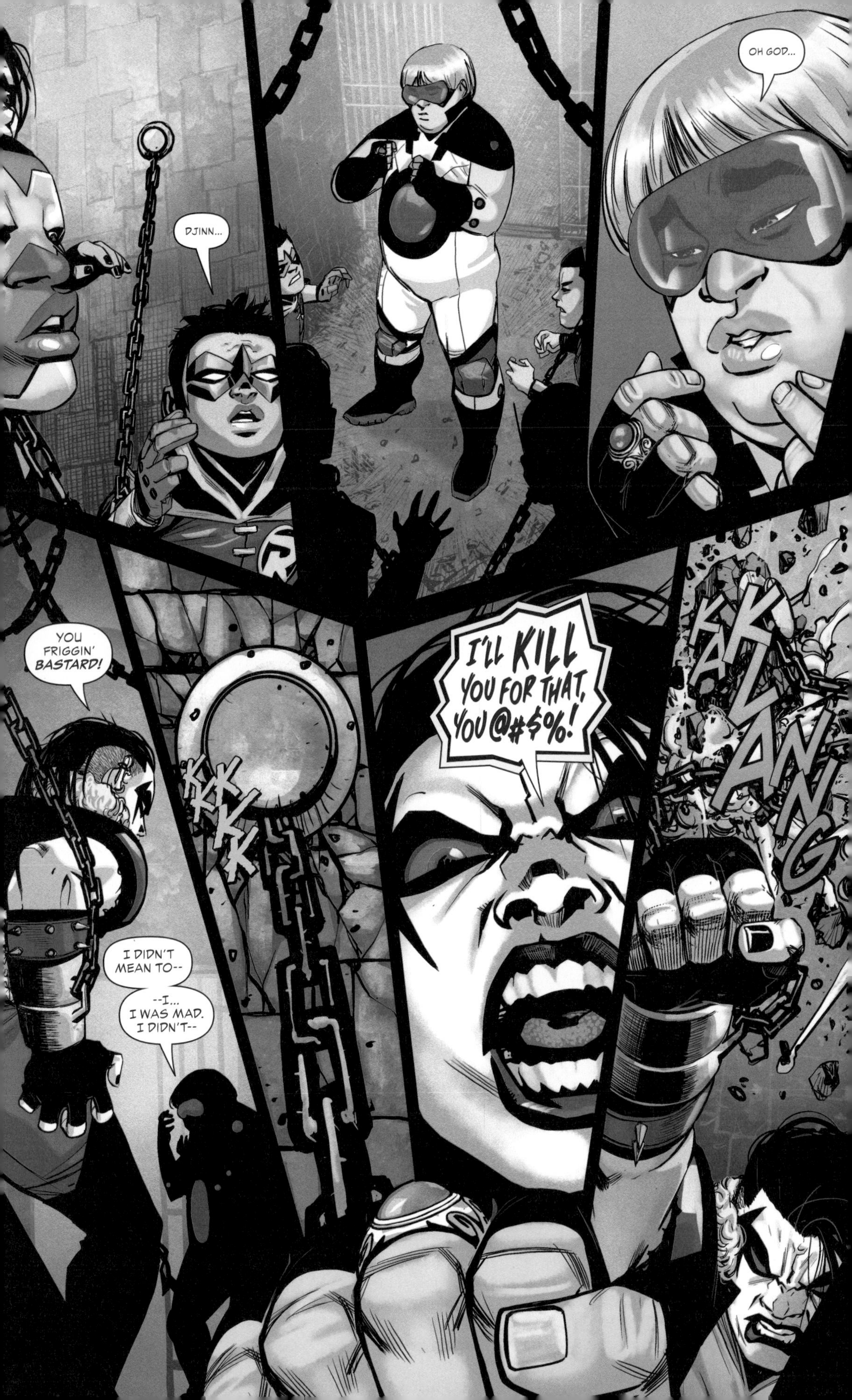
DJINN...
OH GOD...
YOU FRIGGIN' BASTARD!
I DIDN'T MEAN TO--
--I... I WAS MAD. I DIDN'T--
KKKKK
I'LL KILL YOU FOR THAT, YOU @#$%!
KAKLANG

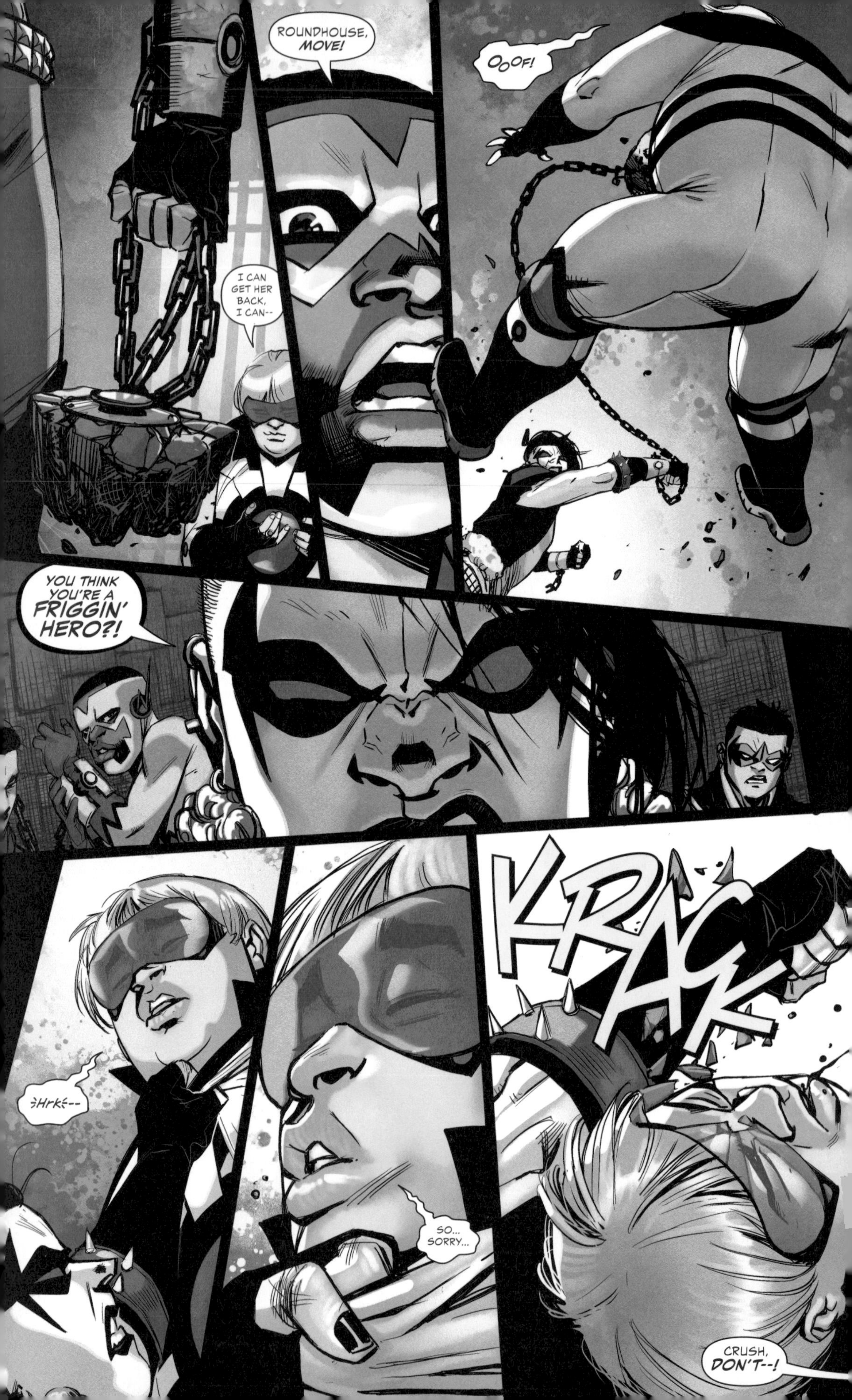
ROUNDHOUSE, MOVE!
I CAN GET HER BACK, I CAN--
OOOF!
YOU THINK YOU'RE A FRIGGIN' HERO?!
HRK--
SO... SORRY...
KRAK
CRUSH, DON'T--!

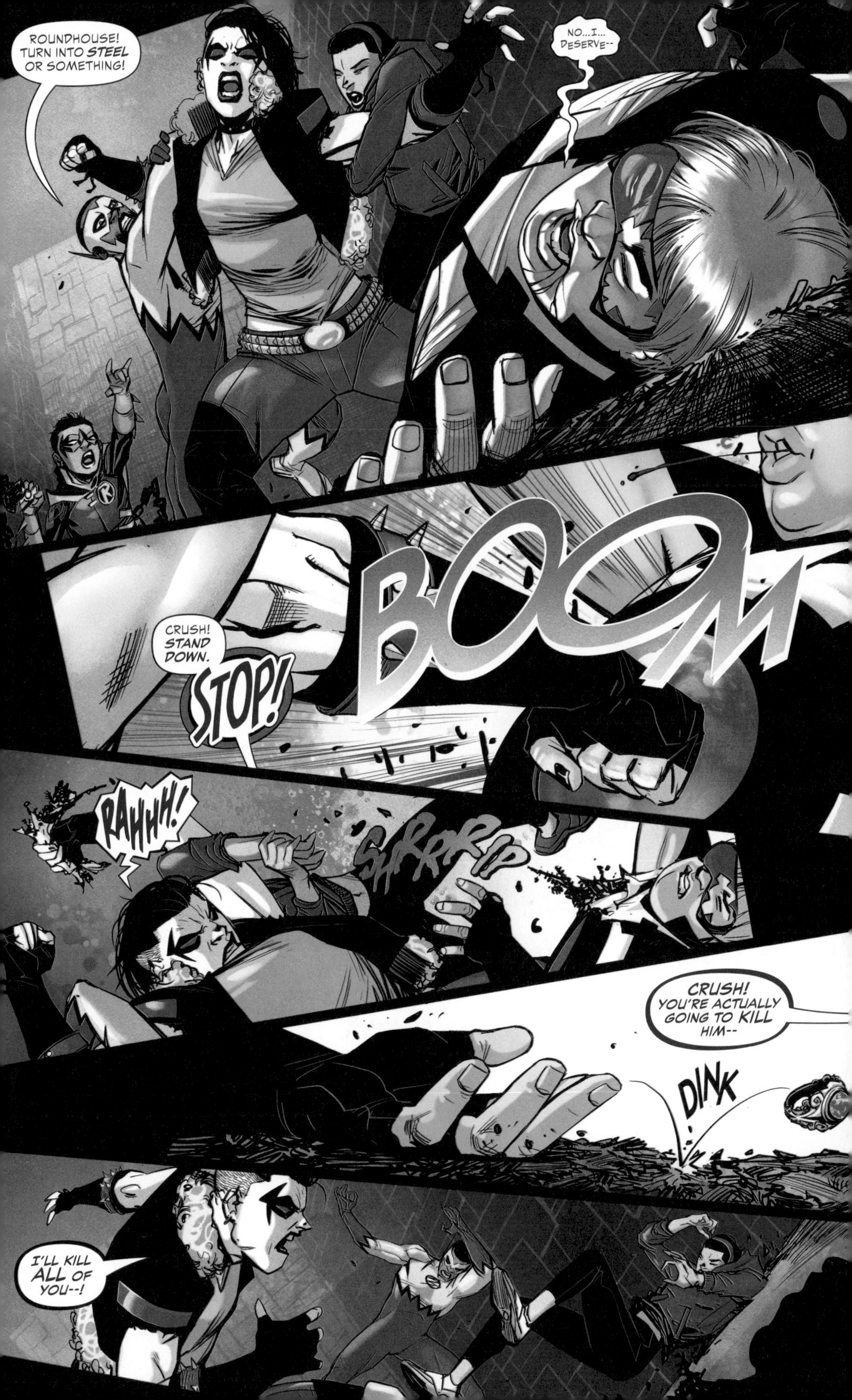
ROUNDHOUSE! TURN INTO STEEL OR SOMETHING!
NO...I... DESERVE--
BOOM
CRUSH! STAND DOWN.
STOP!
RAHHH!
SHRRRIP
CRUSH! YOU'RE ACTUALLY GOING TO KILL HIM--
DINK
I'LL KILL ALL OF YOU--!

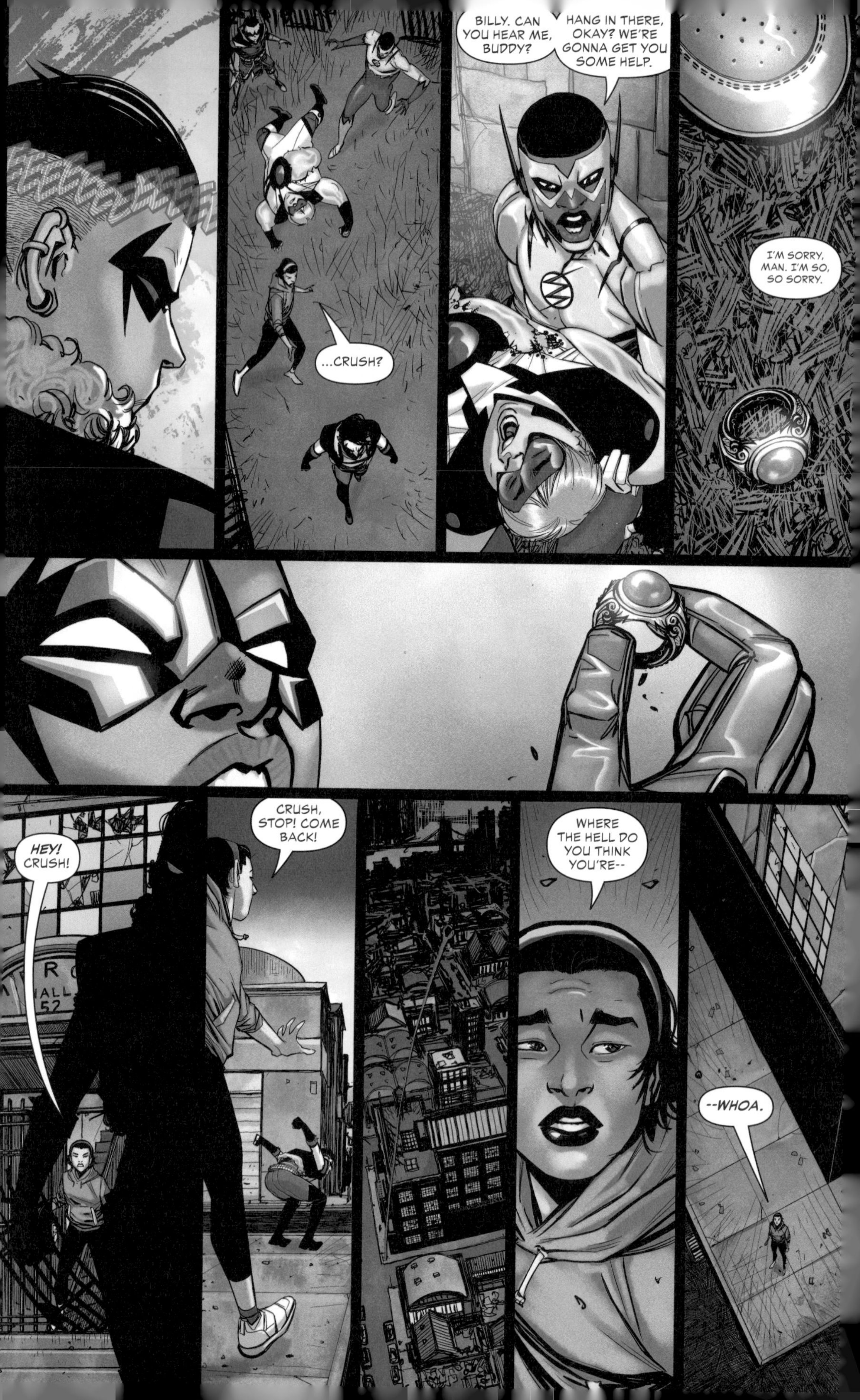
...CRUSH?
BILLY. CAN YOU HEAR ME, BUDDY?
HANG IN THERE, OKAY? WE'RE GONNA GET YOU SOME HELP.
I'M SORRY, MAN. I'M SO, SO SORRY.
HEY! CRUSH!
CRUSH, STOP! COME BACK!
WHERE THE HELL DO YOU THINK YOU'RE--
--WHOA.

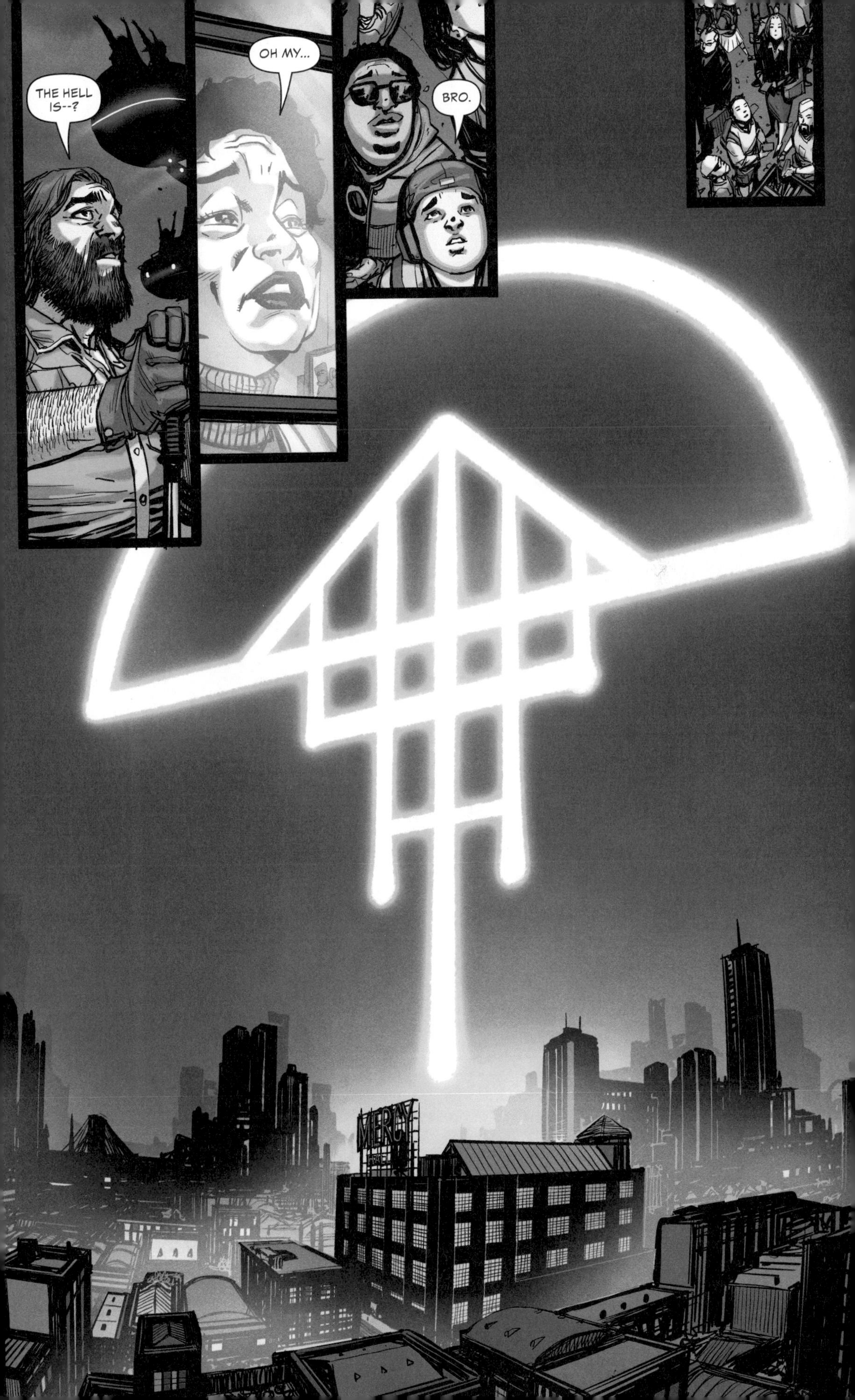
THE HELL IS--?
OH MY...
BRO.

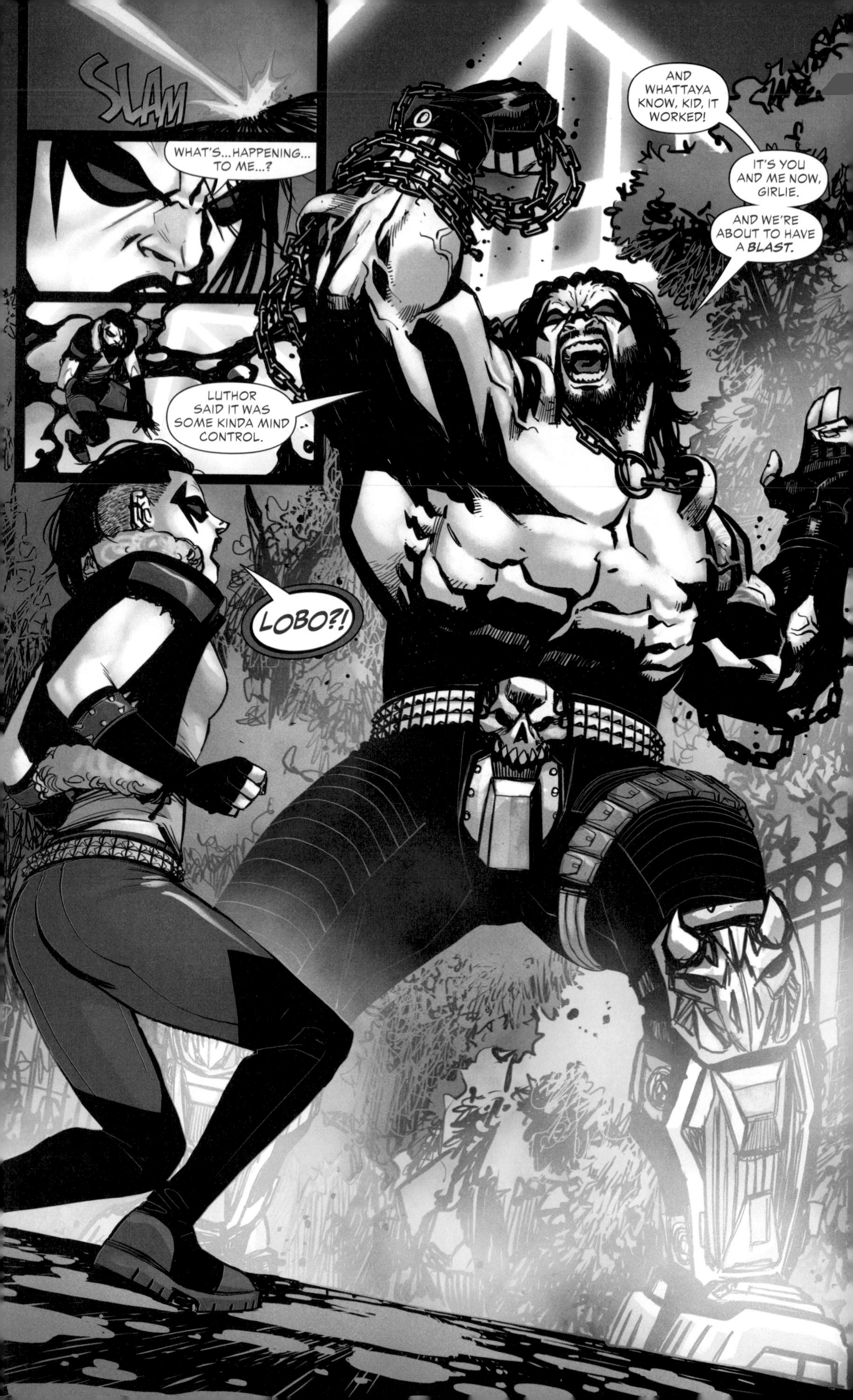
SLAM
WHAT'S...HAPPENING... TO ME...?
LUTHOR SAID IT WAS SOME KINDA MIND CONTROL.
AND WHATTAYA KNOW, KID, IT WORKED!
IT'S YOU AND ME NOW, GIRLIE.
AND WE'RE ABOUT TO HAVE A BLAST.
LOBO?!

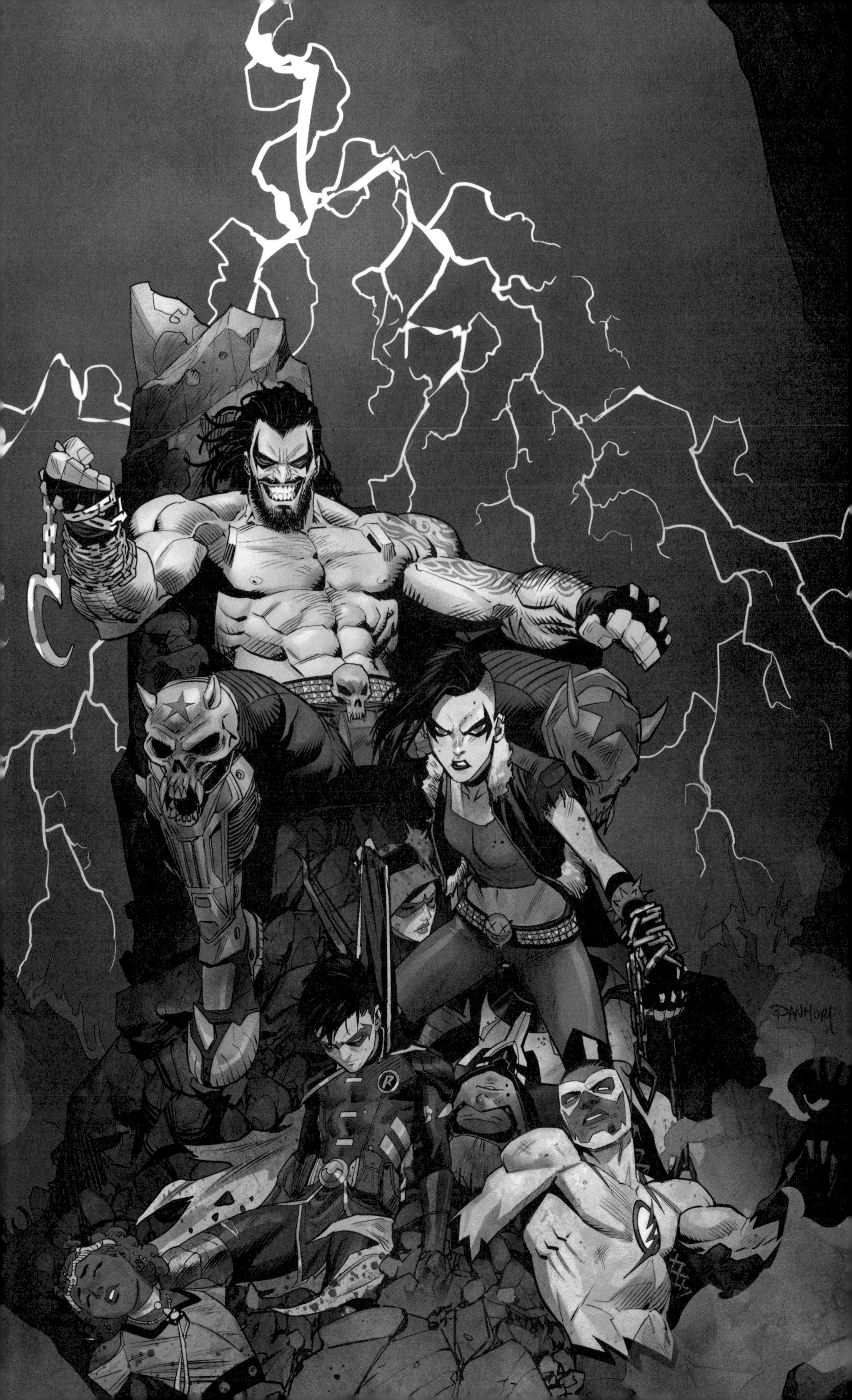

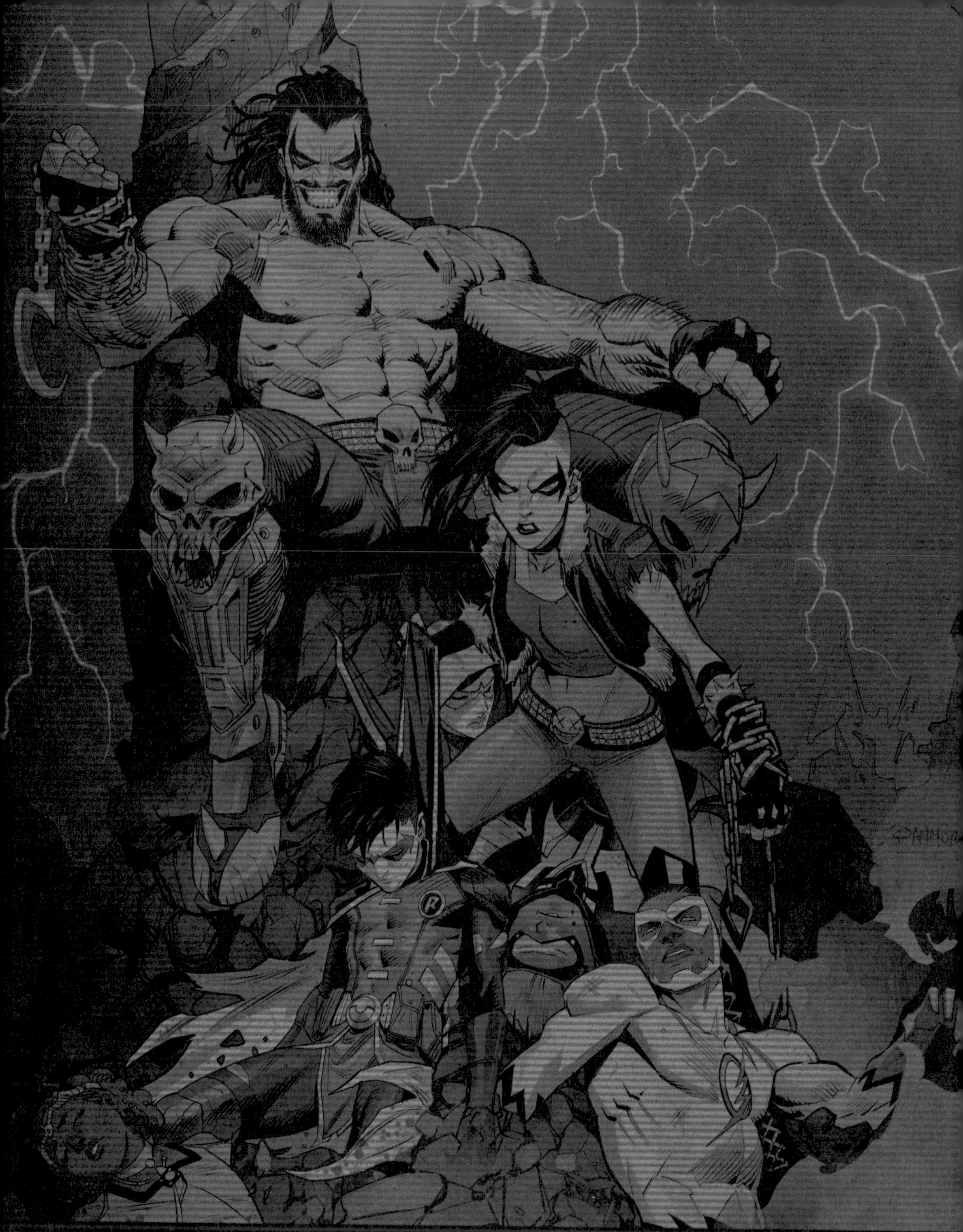

TEEN TITANS
#36

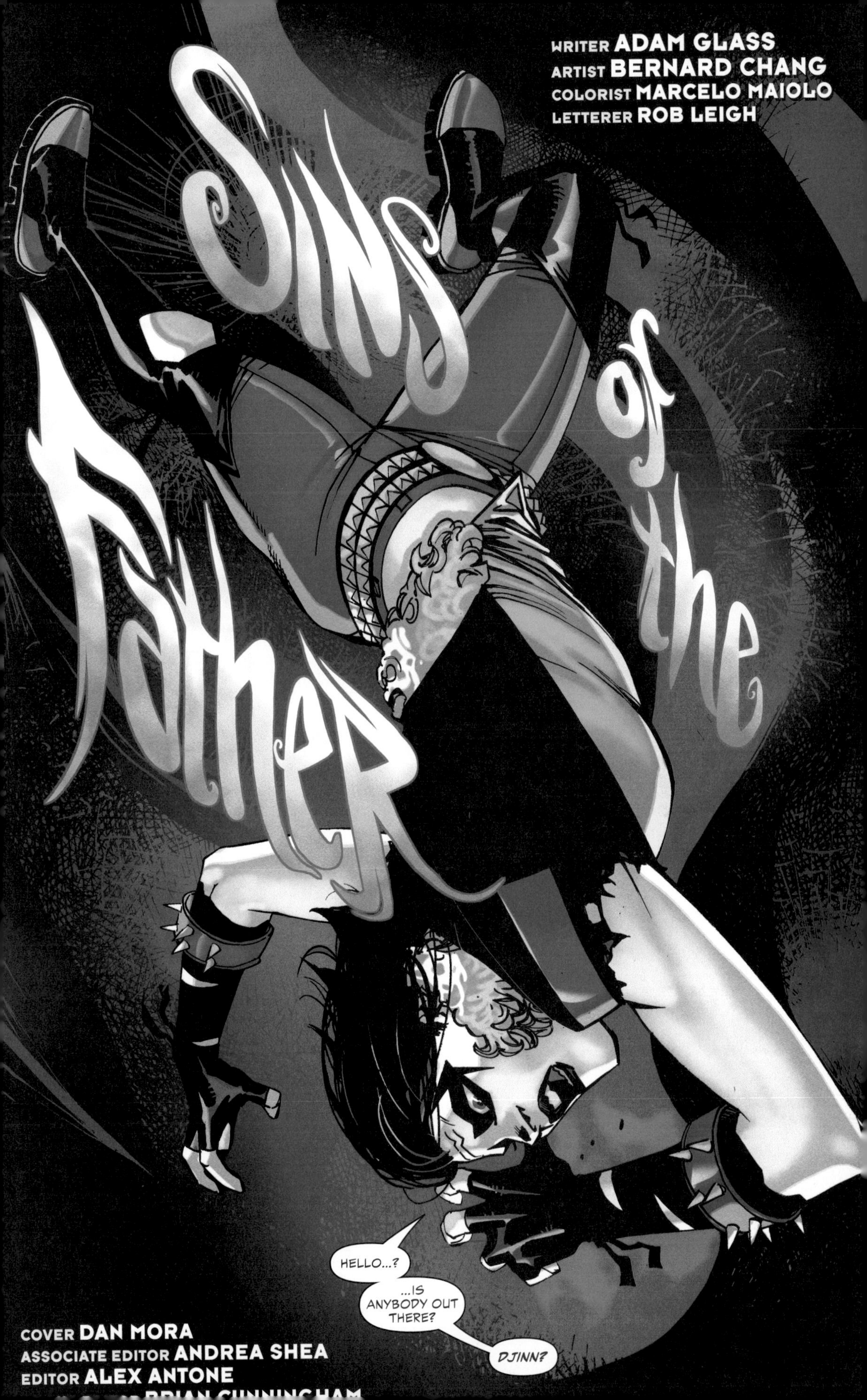
Sins of the Father
WRITER ADAM GLASS
ARTIST BERNARD CHANG
COLORIST MARCELO MAIOLO
LETTERER ROB LEIGH
HELLO...?
...IS ANYBODY OUT THERE?
DJINN?
COVER DAN MORA
ASSOCIATE EDITOR ANDREA SHEA
EDITOR ALEX ANTONE

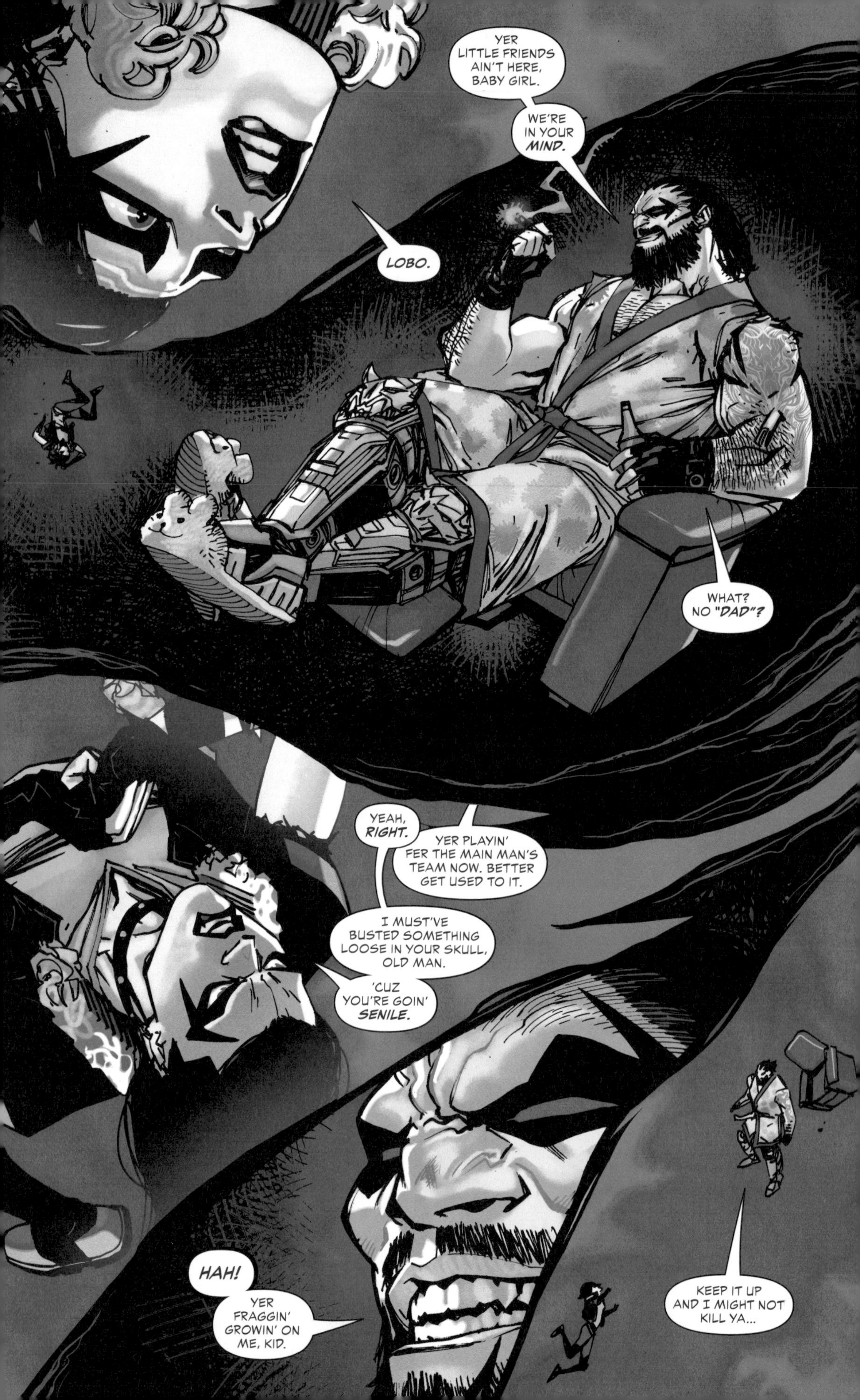
YER LITTLE FRIENDS AIN'T HERE, BABY GIRL.
WE'RE IN YOUR *MIND.*
LOBO.
WHAT? NO *"DAD"*?
YEAH, *RIGHT.*
YER PLAYIN' FER THE MAIN MAN'S TEAM NOW. BETTER GET USED TO IT.
I MUST'VE BUSTED SOMETHING LOOSE IN YOUR SKULL, OLD MAN.
'CUZ YOU'RE GOIN' *SENILE.*
KEEP IT UP AND I MIGHT NOT KILL YA...
HAH!
YER FRAGGIN' GROWIN' ON ME, KID.

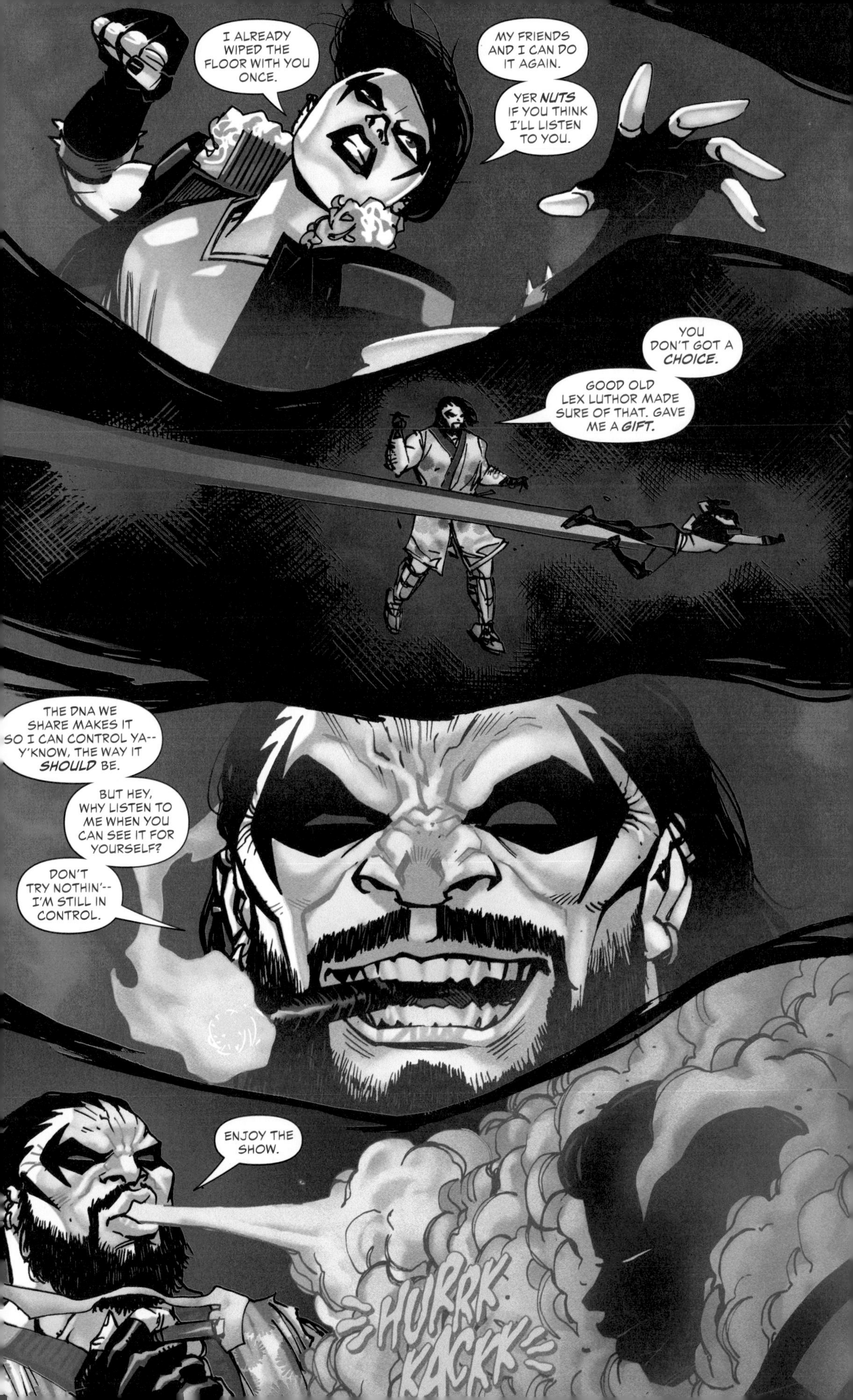

I ALREADY WIPED THE FLOOR WITH YOU ONCE.
MY FRIENDS AND I CAN DO IT AGAIN.
YER NUTS IF YOU THINK I'LL LISTEN TO YOU.
YOU DON'T GOT A CHOICE.
GOOD OLD LEX LUTHOR MADE SURE OF THAT. GAVE ME A GIFT.
THE DNA WE SHARE MAKES IT SO I CAN CONTROL YA-- Y'KNOW, THE WAY IT SHOULD BE.
BUT HEY, WHY LISTEN TO ME WHEN YOU CAN SEE IT FOR YOURSELF?
DON'T TRY NOTHIN'-- I'M STILL IN CONTROL.
ENJOY THE SHOW.
HURRK
KACKK

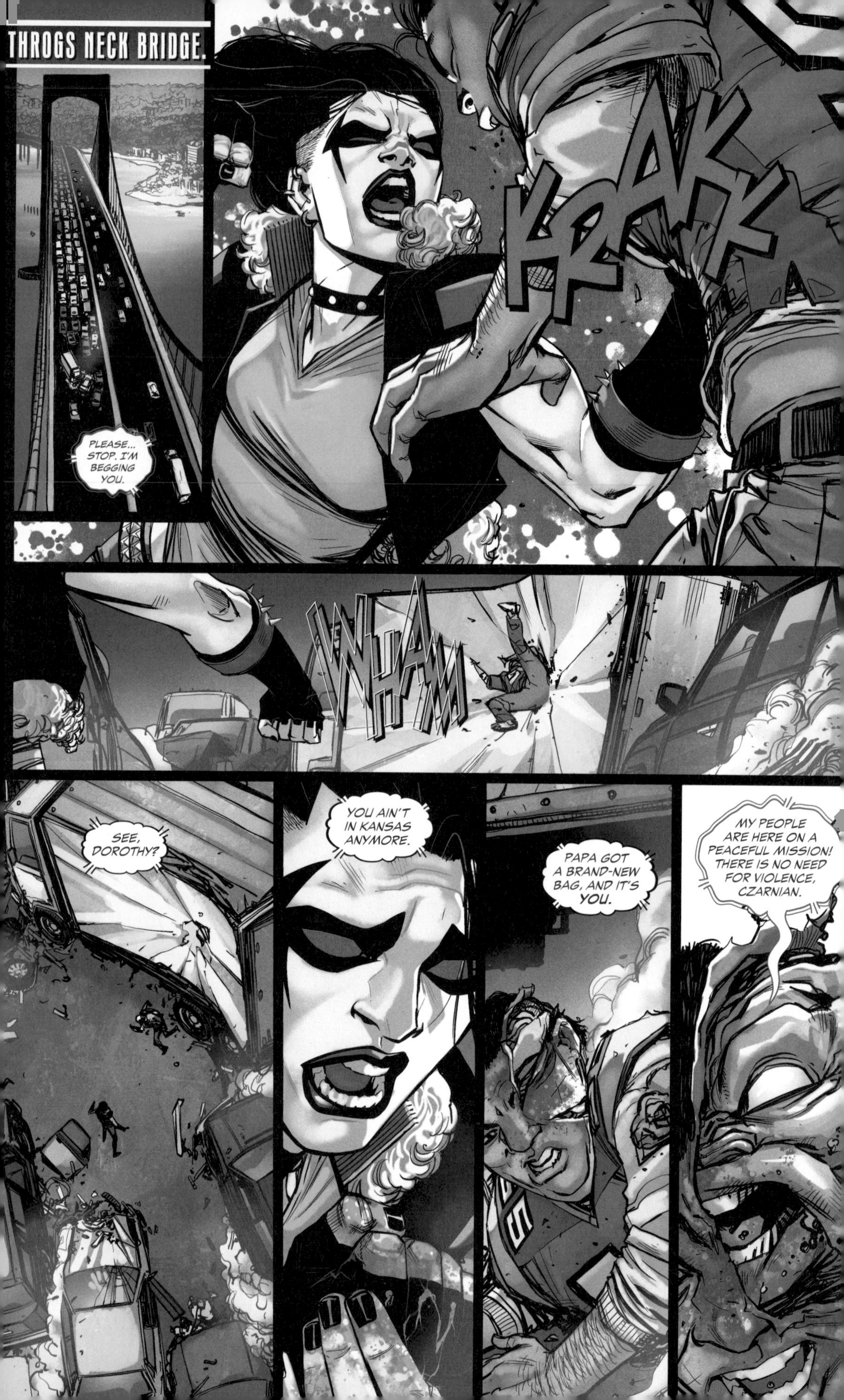
THROGS NECK BRIDGE.
PLEASE... STOP. I'M BEGGING YOU.
KRAKK
WHAM
SEE, DOROTHY?
YOU AIN'T IN KANSAS ANYMORE.
PAPA GOT A BRAND-NEW BAG, AND IT'S YOU.
MY PEOPLE ARE HERE ON A PEACEFUL MISSION! THERE IS NO NEED FOR VIOLENCE, CZARNIAN.

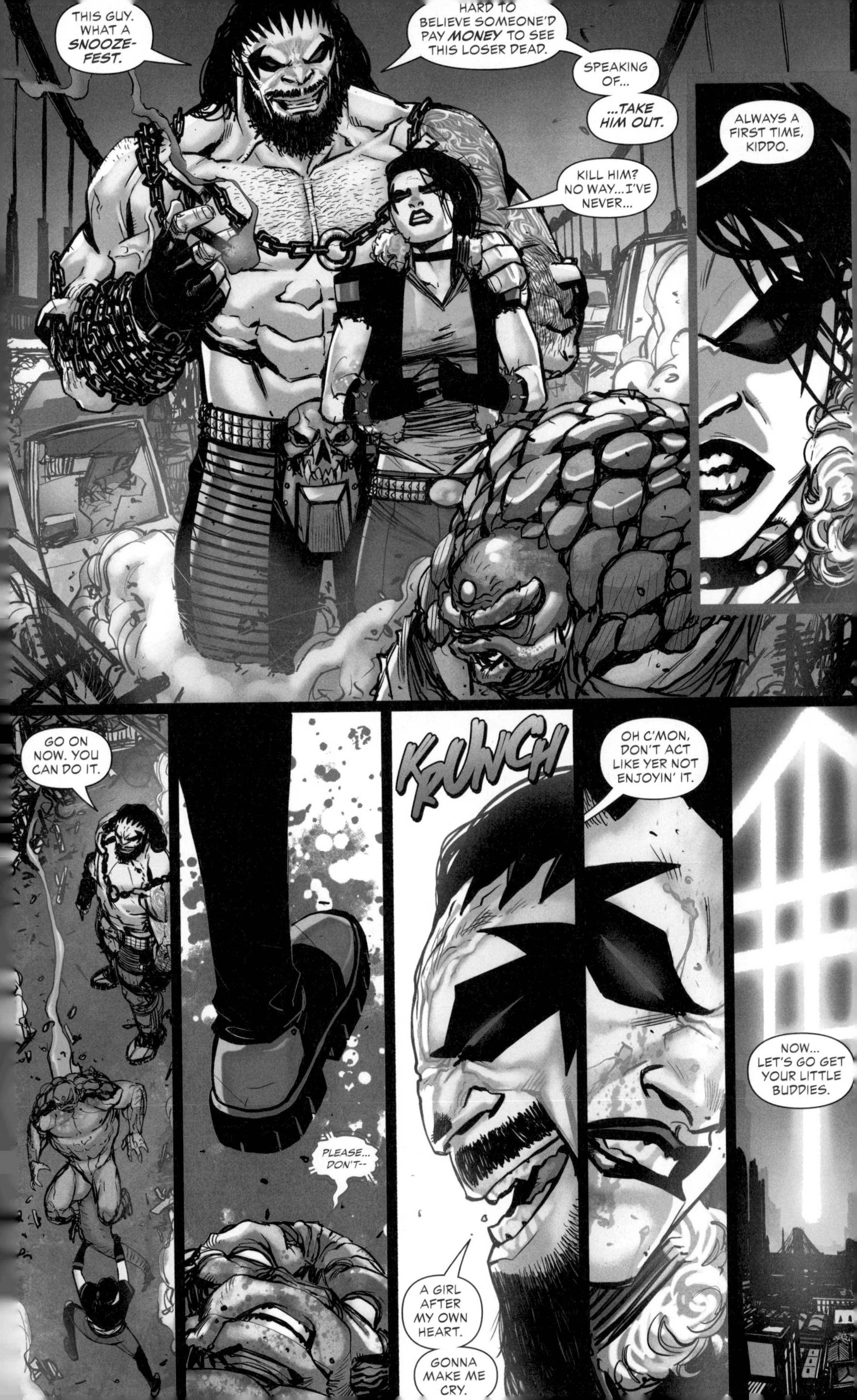
THIS GUY. WHAT A SNOOZE-FEST.
HARD TO BELIEVE SOMEONE'D PAY MONEY TO SEE THIS LOSER DEAD.
SPEAKING OF...
...TAKE HIM OUT.
KILL HIM? NO WAY...I'VE NEVER...
ALWAYS A FIRST TIME, KIDDO.
GO ON NOW. YOU CAN DO IT.
PLEASE... DON'T--
KRUNCH
OH C'MON, DON'T ACT LIKE YER NOT ENJOYIN' IT.
A GIRL AFTER MY OWN HEART.
GONNA MAKE ME CRY.
NOW... LET'S GO GET YOUR LITTLE BUDDIES.

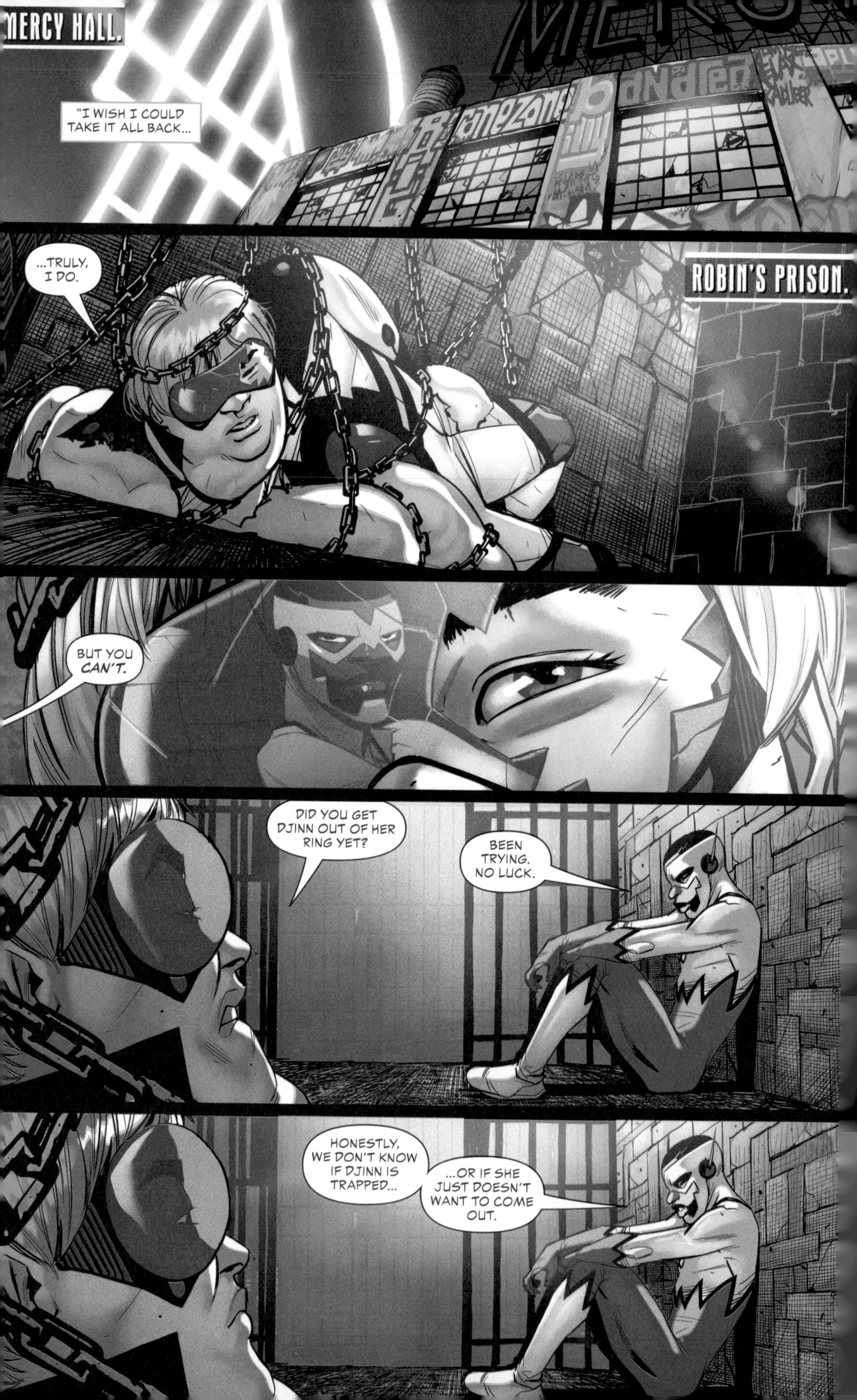
MERCY HALL.
"I WISH I COULD TAKE IT ALL BACK...
...TRULY, I DO.
ROBIN'S PRISON.
BUT YOU *CAN'T.*
DID YOU GET DJINN OUT OF HER RING YET?
BEEN TRYING. NO LUCK.
HONESTLY, WE DON'T KNOW IF DJINN IS TRAPPED...
...OR IF SHE JUST DOESN'T WANT TO COME OUT.

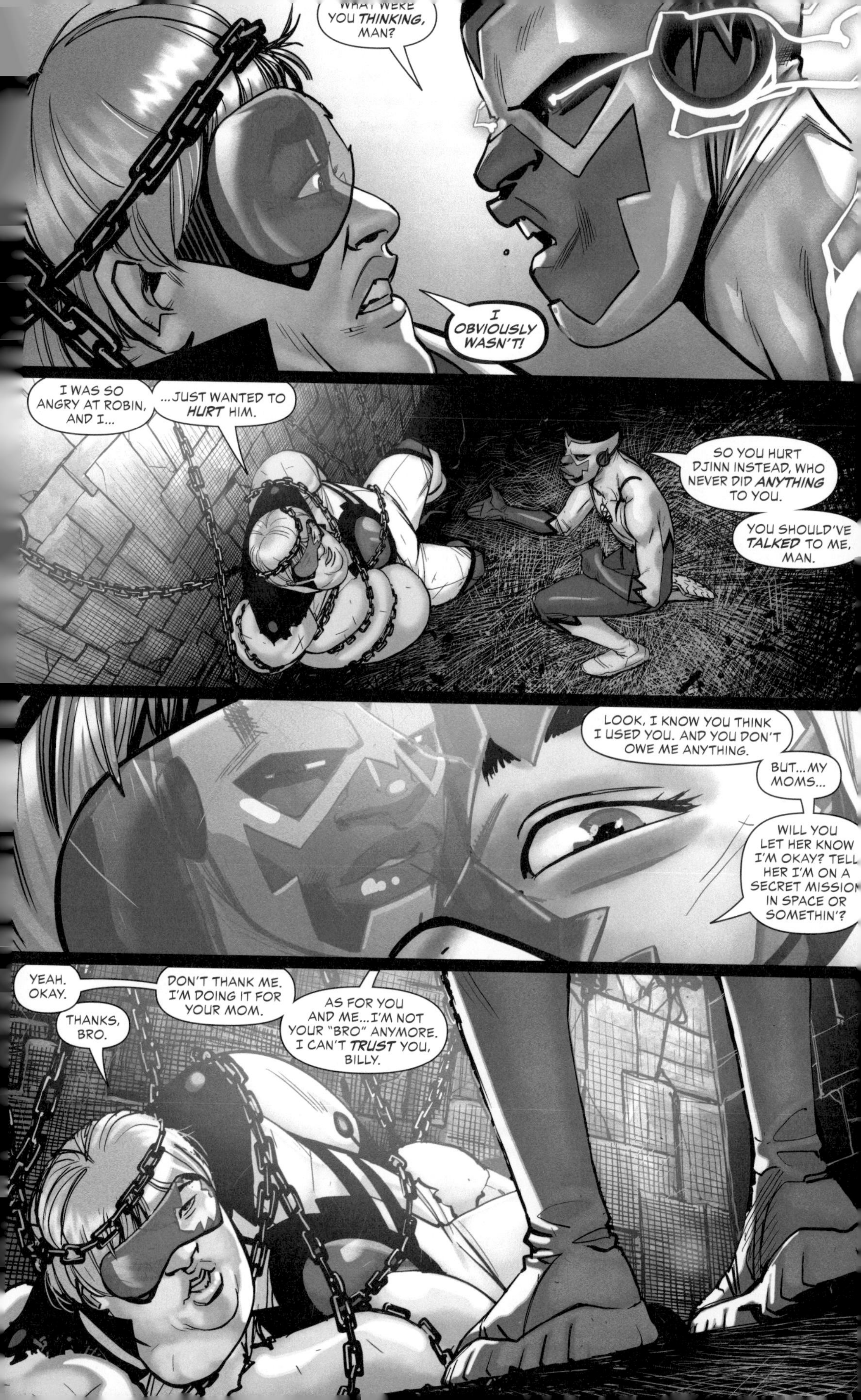
WHAT WERE YOU THINKING, MAN?
I OBVIOUSLY WASN'T!
I WAS SO ANGRY AT ROBIN, AND I...
...JUST WANTED TO HURT HIM.
SO YOU HURT DJINN INSTEAD, WHO NEVER DID ANYTHING TO YOU.
YOU SHOULD'VE TALKED TO ME, MAN.
LOOK, I KNOW YOU THINK I USED YOU. AND YOU DON'T OWE ME ANYTHING.
BUT...MY MOMS...
WILL YOU LET HER KNOW I'M OKAY? TELL HER I'M ON A SECRET MISSION IN SPACE OR SOMETHIN'?
YEAH. OKAY.
THANKS, BRO.
DON'T THANK ME. I'M DOING IT FOR YOUR MOM.
AS FOR YOU AND ME...I'M NOT YOUR "BRO" ANYMORE. I CAN'T TRUST YOU, BILLY.

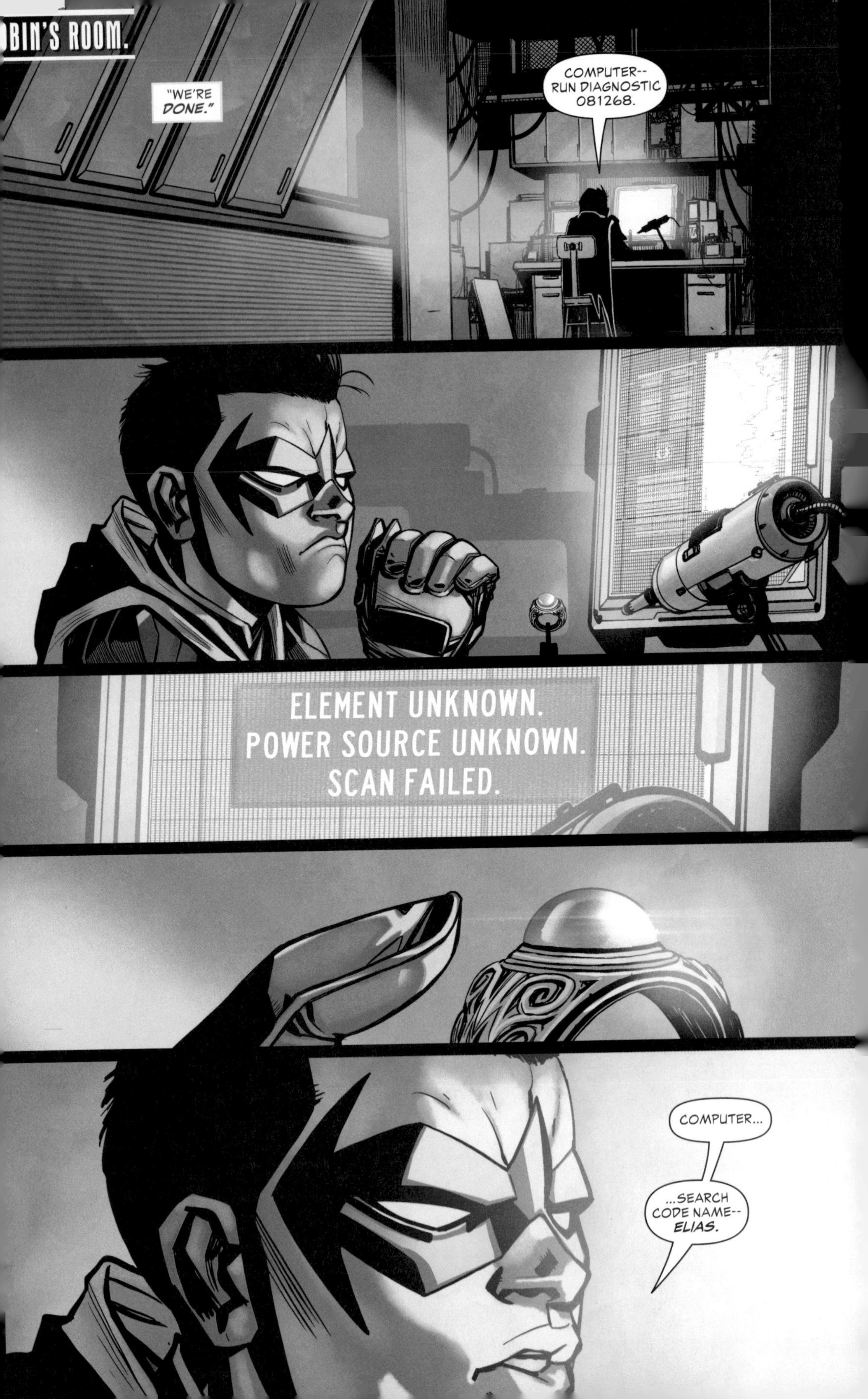
BIN'S ROOM.
"WE'RE DONE."
COMPUTER-- RUN DIAGNOSTIC 081268.
ELEMENT UNKNOWN.
POWER SOURCE UNKNOWN.
SCAN FAILED.
COMPUTER...
...SEARCH CODE NAME-- ELIAS.

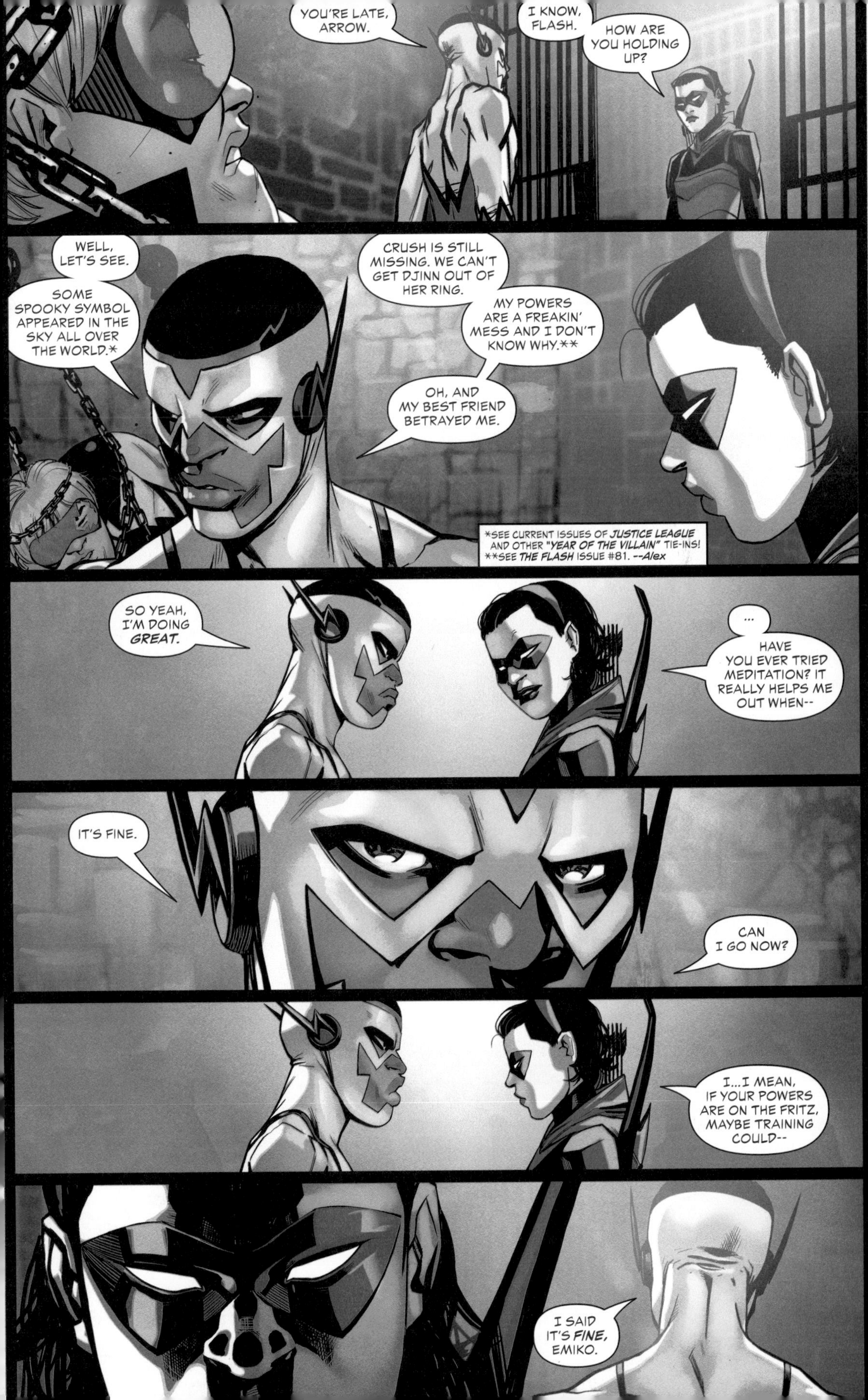
YOU'RE LATE, ARROW.
I KNOW, FLASH.
HOW ARE YOU HOLDING UP?
WELL, LET'S SEE.
SOME SPOOKY SYMBOL APPEARED IN THE SKY ALL OVER THE WORLD.*
CRUSH IS STILL MISSING. WE CAN'T GET DJINN OUT OF HER RING.
MY POWERS ARE A FREAKIN' MESS AND I DON'T KNOW WHY.**
OH, AND MY BEST FRIEND BETRAYED ME.
*SEE CURRENT ISSUES OF JUSTICE LEAGUE AND OTHER "YEAR OF THE VILLAIN" TIE-INS!
**SEE THE FLASH ISSUE #81. --Alex
SO YEAH, I'M DOING GREAT.
...
HAVE YOU EVER TRIED MEDITATION? IT REALLY HELPS ME OUT WHEN--
IT'S FINE.
CAN I GO NOW?
I...I MEAN, IF YOUR POWERS ARE ON THE FRITZ, MAYBE TRAINING COULD--
I SAID IT'S FINE, EMIKO.

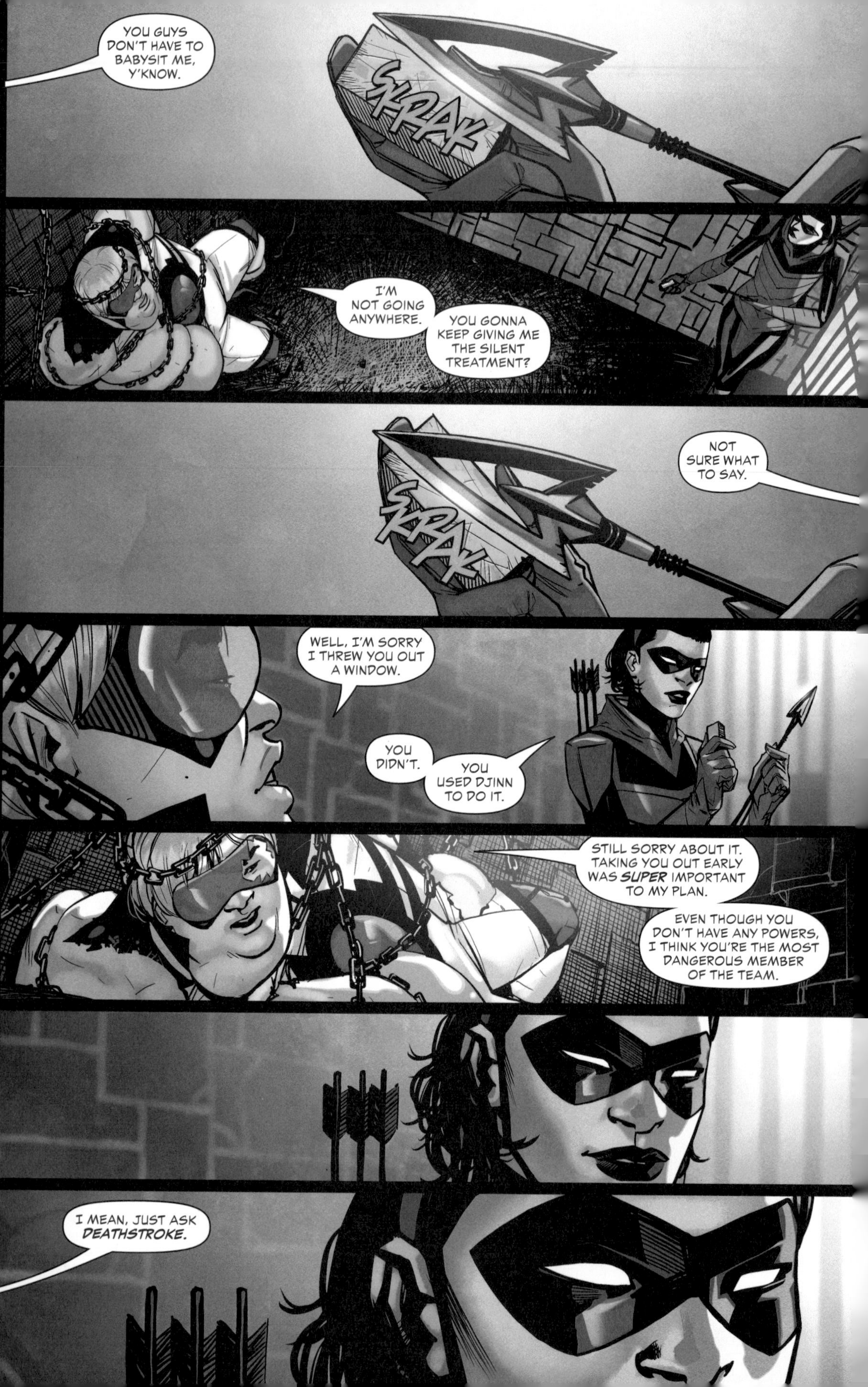
YOU GUYS DON'T HAVE TO BABYSIT ME, Y'KNOW.
SKRAK
I'M NOT GOING ANYWHERE.
YOU GONNA KEEP GIVING ME THE SILENT TREATMENT?
NOT SURE WHAT TO SAY.
SKRAK
WELL, I'M SORRY I THREW YOU OUT A WINDOW.
YOU DIDN'T.
YOU USED DJINN TO DO IT.
STILL SORRY ABOUT IT. TAKING YOU OUT EARLY WAS SUPER IMPORTANT TO MY PLAN.
EVEN THOUGH YOU DON'T HAVE ANY POWERS, I THINK YOU'RE THE MOST DANGEROUS MEMBER OF THE TEAM.
I MEAN, JUST ASK DEATHSTROKE.

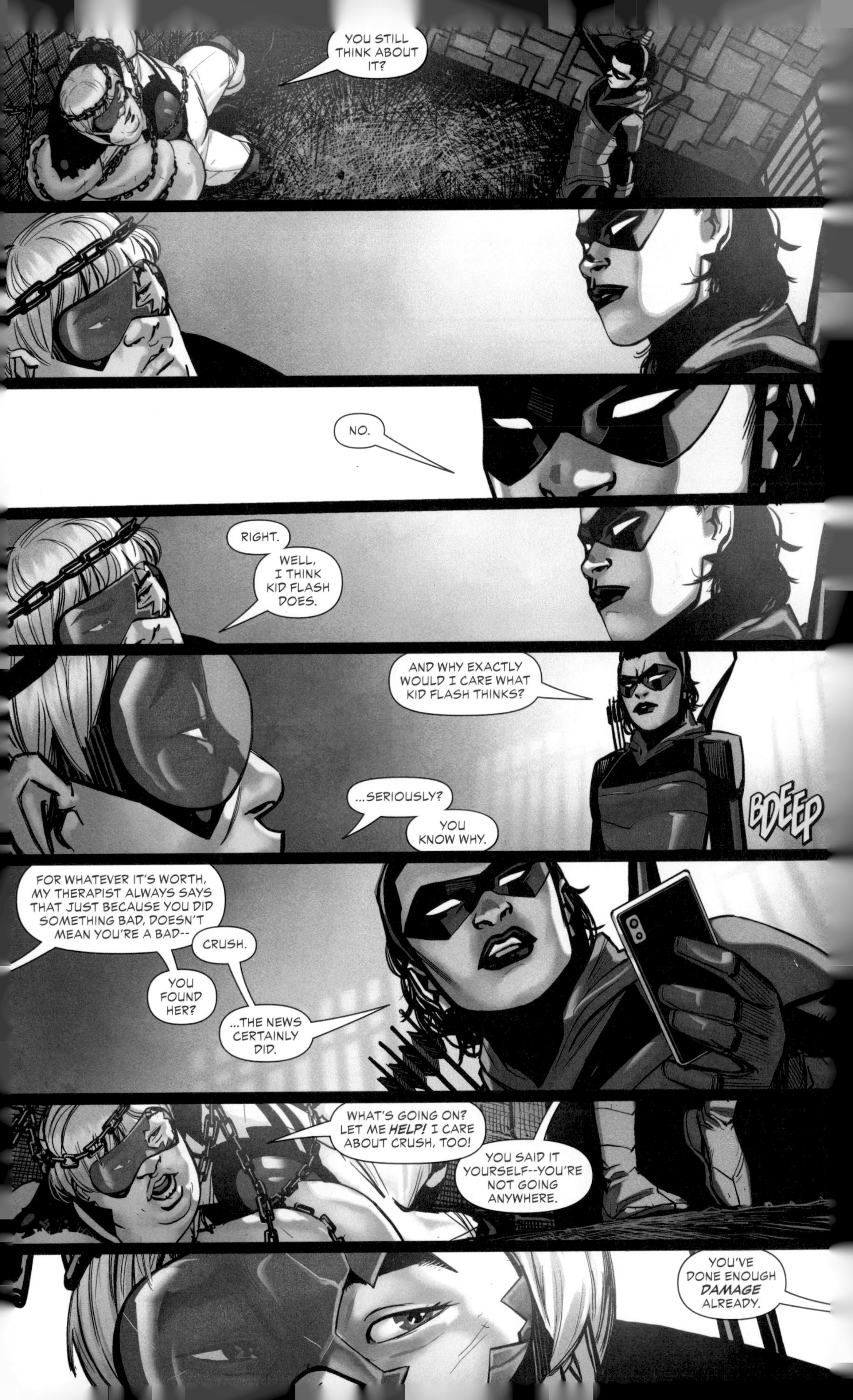

YOU STILL THINK ABOUT IT?
NO.
RIGHT.
WELL, I THINK KID FLASH DOES.
AND WHY EXACTLY WOULD I CARE WHAT KID FLASH THINKS?
...SERIOUSLY?
YOU KNOW WHY.
BDEEP
FOR WHATEVER IT'S WORTH, MY THERAPIST ALWAYS SAYS THAT JUST BECAUSE YOU DID SOMETHING BAD, DOESN'T MEAN YOU'RE A BAD--
CRUSH.
YOU FOUND HER?
...THE NEWS CERTAINLY DID.
WHAT'S GOING ON? LET ME HELP! I CARE ABOUT CRUSH, TOO!
YOU SAID IT YOURSELF--YOU'RE NOT GOING ANYWHERE.
YOU'VE DONE ENOUGH DAMAGE ALREADY.

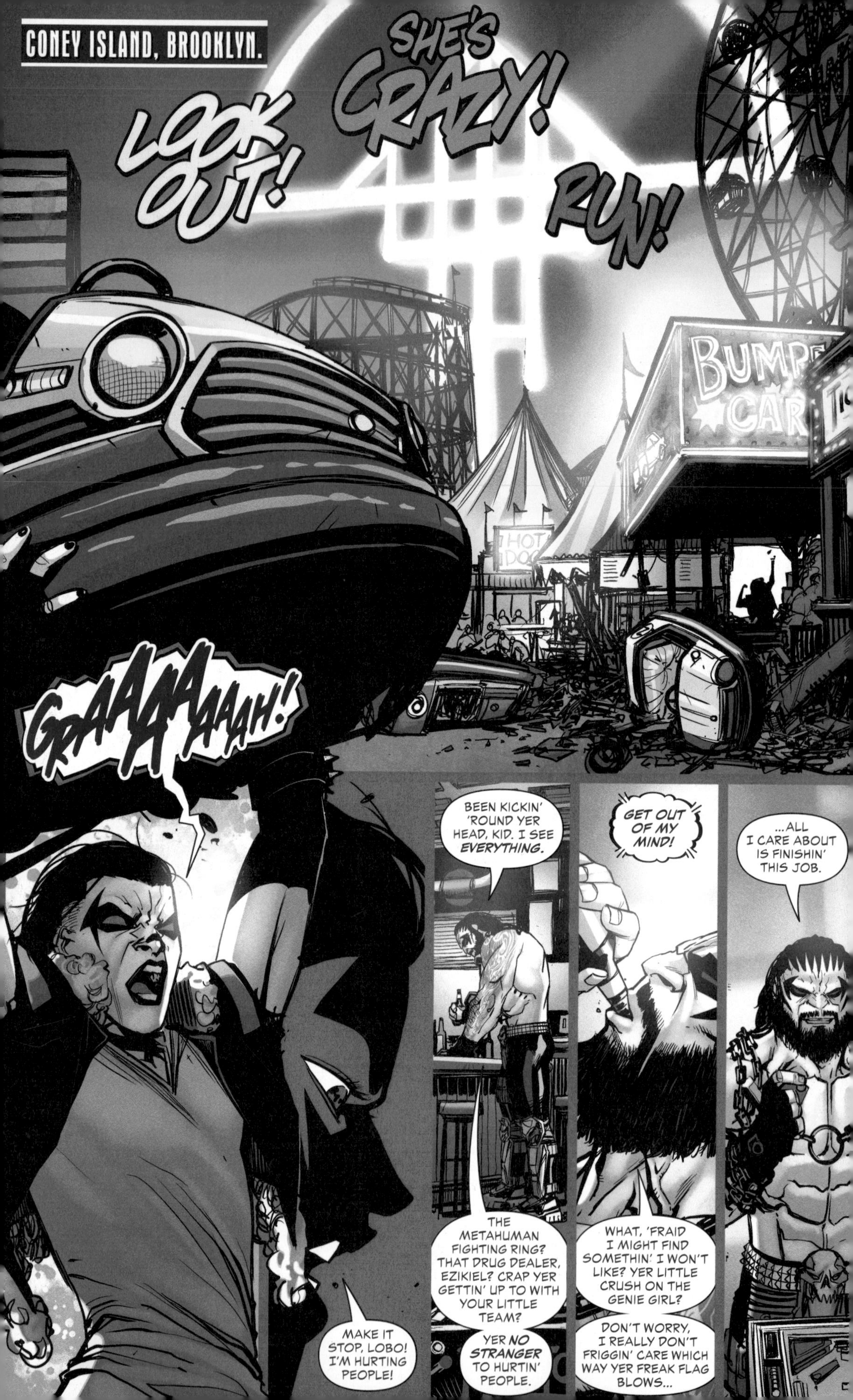

CONEY ISLAND, BROOKLYN.
LOOK OUT!
SHE'S CRAZY!
RUN!
BUMPER CARS
HOT DOG
GRAAAAAAAAH!
MAKE IT STOP, LOBO! I'M HURTING PEOPLE!
BEEN KICKIN' 'ROUND YER HEAD, KID. I SEE EVERYTHING.
THE METAHUMAN FIGHTING RING? THAT DRUG DEALER, EZIKIEL? CRAP YER GETTIN' UP TO WITH YOUR LITTLE TEAM?
YER NO STRANGER TO HURTIN' PEOPLE.
GET OUT OF MY MIND!
WHAT, 'FRAID I MIGHT FIND SOMETHIN' I WON'T LIKE? YER LITTLE CRUSH ON THE GENIE GIRL?
DON'T WORRY, I REALLY DON'T FRIGGIN' CARE WHICH WAY YER FREAK FLAG BLOWS...
...ALL I CARE ABOUT IS FINISHIN' THIS JOB.

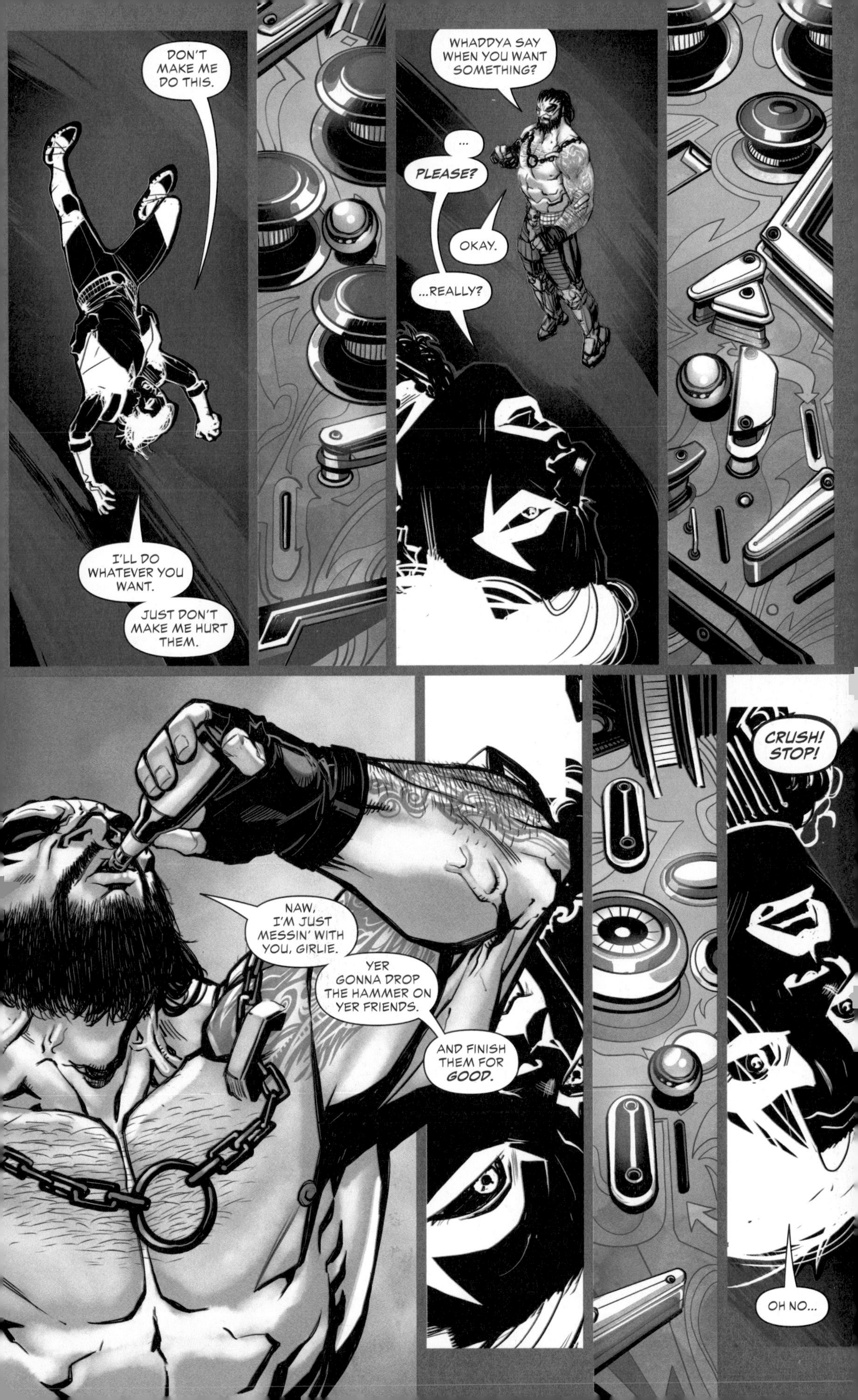
DON'T MAKE ME DO THIS.
I'LL DO WHATEVER YOU WANT.
JUST DON'T MAKE ME HURT THEM.
WHADDYA SAY WHEN YOU WANT SOMETHING?
...
PLEASE?
OKAY.
...REALLY?
NAW, I'M JUST MESSIN' WITH YOU, GIRLIE.
YER GONNA DROP THE HAMMER ON YER FRIENDS.
AND FINISH THEM FOR GOOD.
CRUSH! STOP!
OH NO...

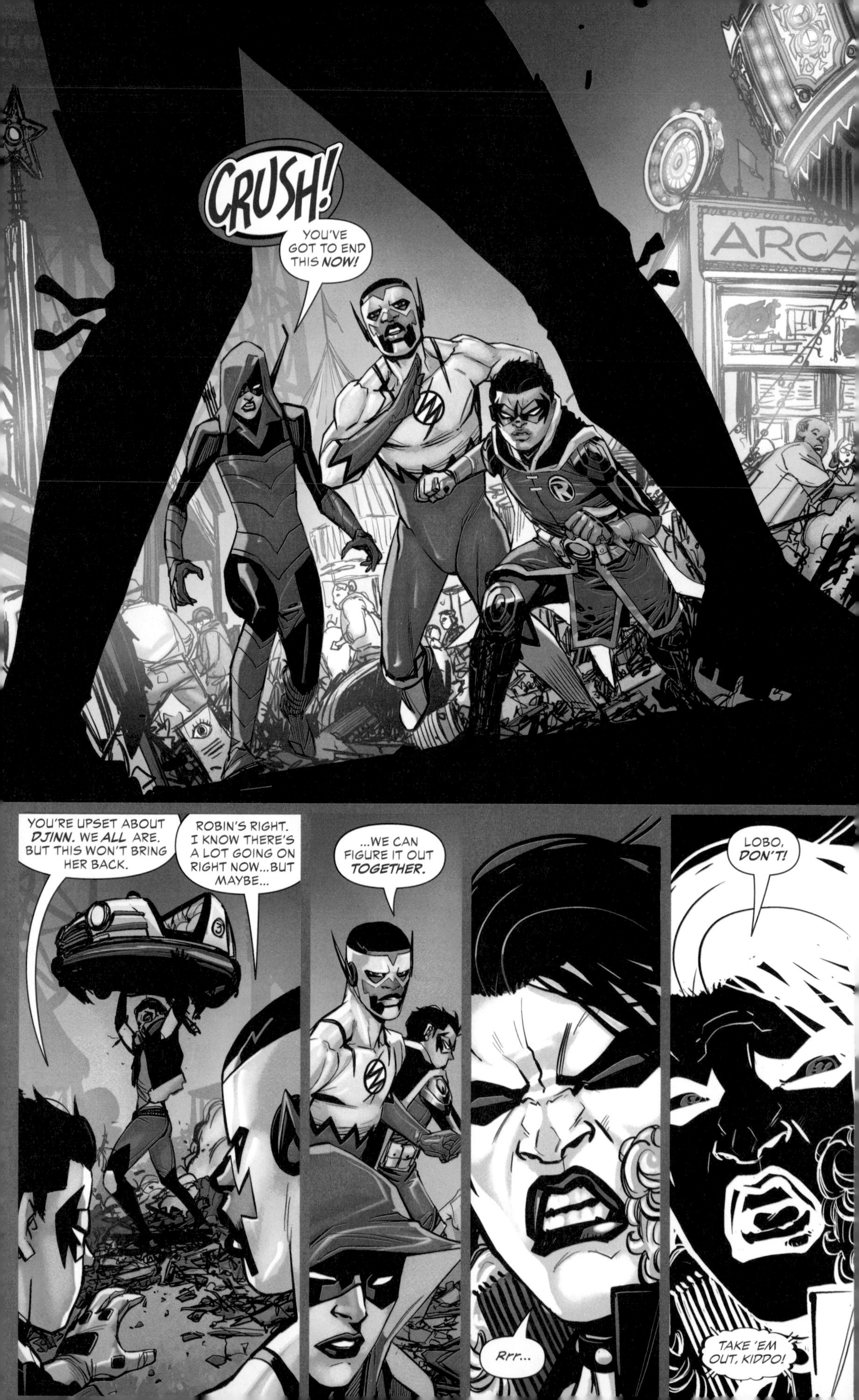
CRUSH!
YOU'VE GOT TO END THIS NOW!
YOU'RE UPSET ABOUT DJINN. WE ALL ARE. BUT THIS WON'T BRING HER BACK.
ROBIN'S RIGHT. I KNOW THERE'S A LOT GOING ON RIGHT NOW...BUT MAYBE...
...WE CAN FIGURE IT OUT TOGETHER.
Rrr...
LOBO, DON'T!
TAKE 'EM OUT, KIDDO!

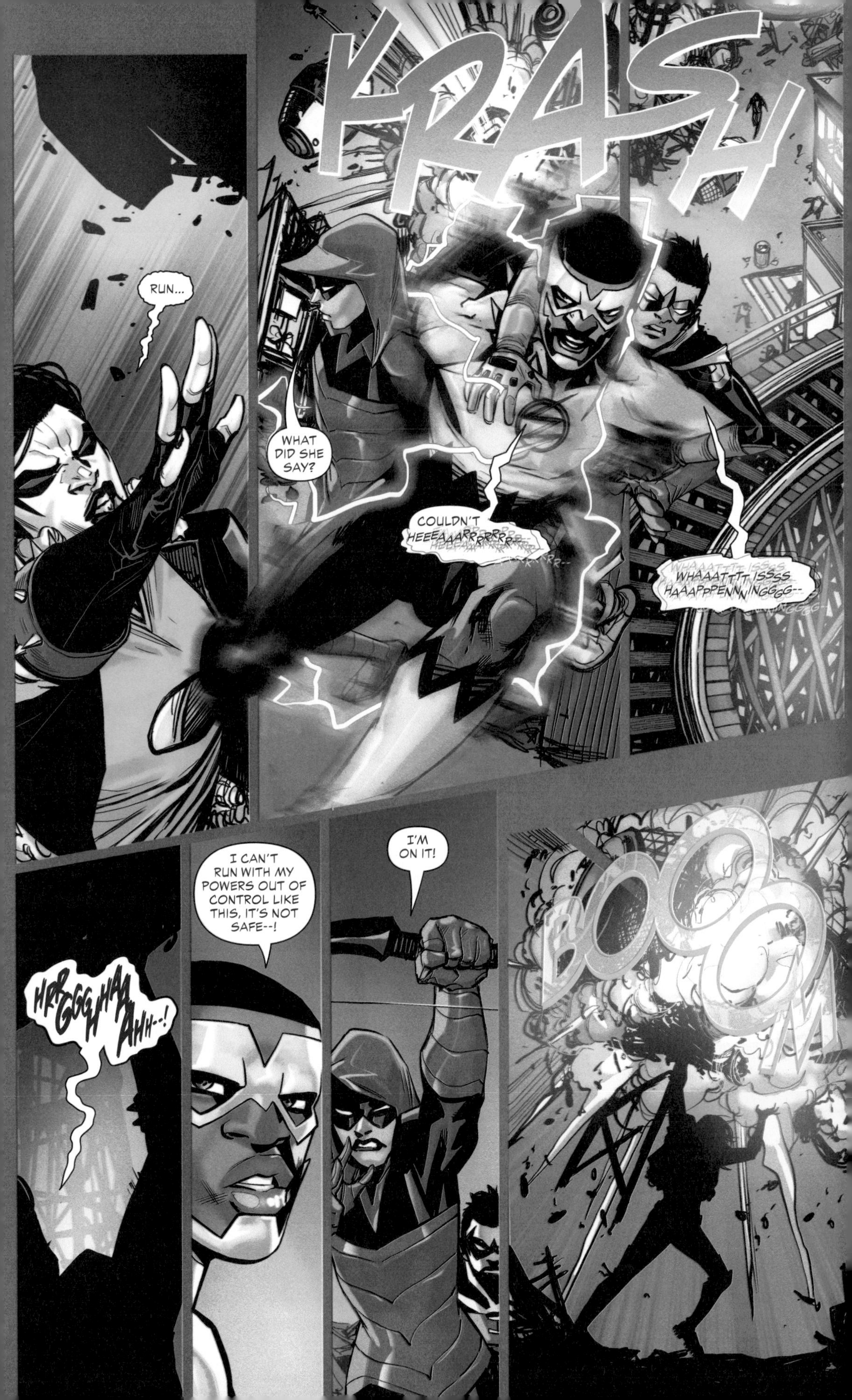
KRASH
RUN...
WHAT DID SHE SAY?
COULDN'T HEEEAAARRRRRR--
WHAAATTTT ISSSS HAAAPPPENNNINGGGG--
HRRGGGHHAAAHH--!
I CAN'T RUN WITH MY POWERS OUT OF CONTROL LIKE THIS, IT'S NOT SAFE--!
I'M ON IT!
BOOOOM

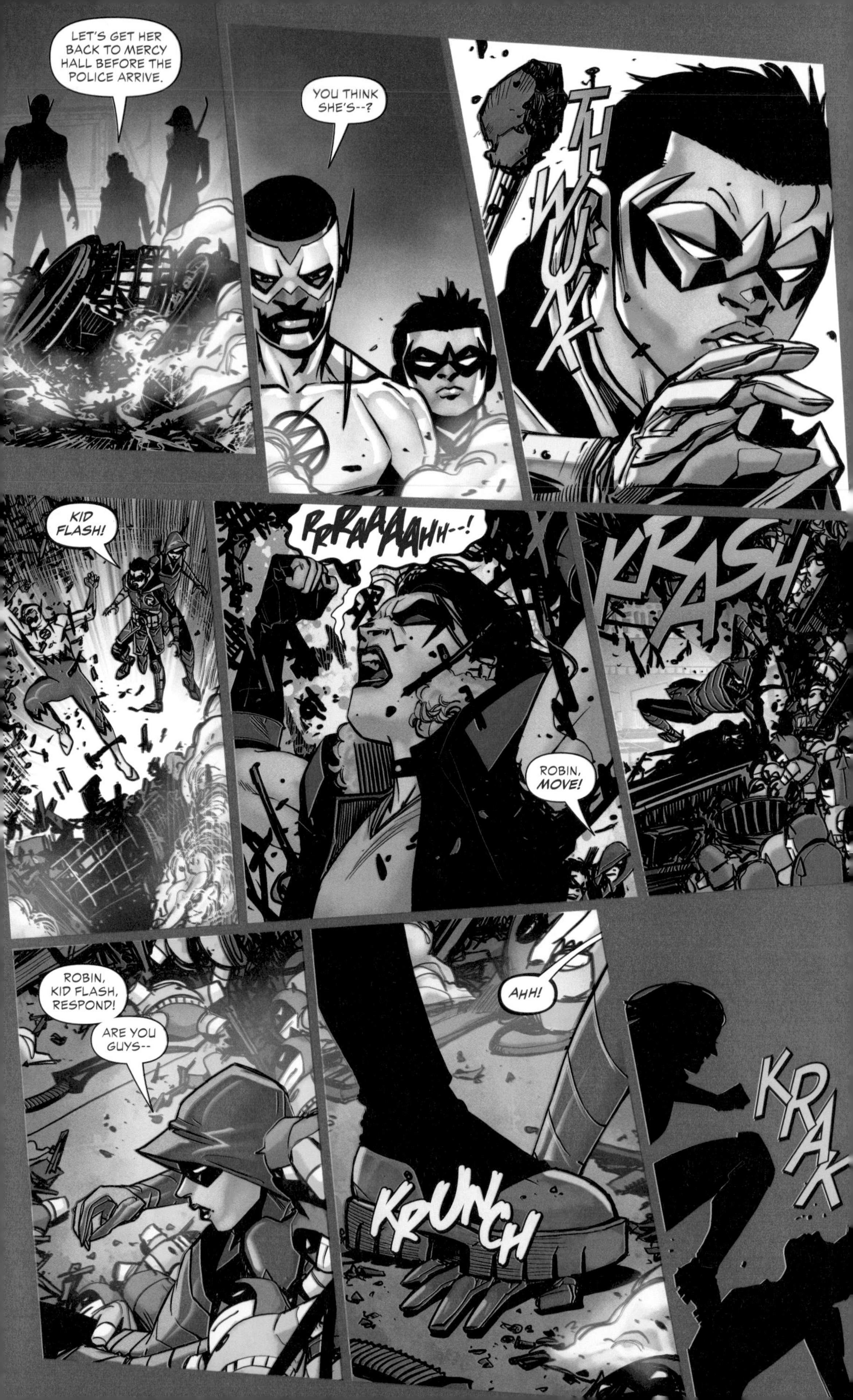
LET'S GET HER BACK TO MERCY HALL BEFORE THE POLICE ARRIVE.
YOU THINK SHE'S--?
THWUNK
KID FLASH!
RRRAAAAAHH--!
ROBIN, MOVE!
KRASH
ROBIN, KID FLASH, RESPOND!
ARE YOU GUYS--
AHH!
KRUNCH
KRAK

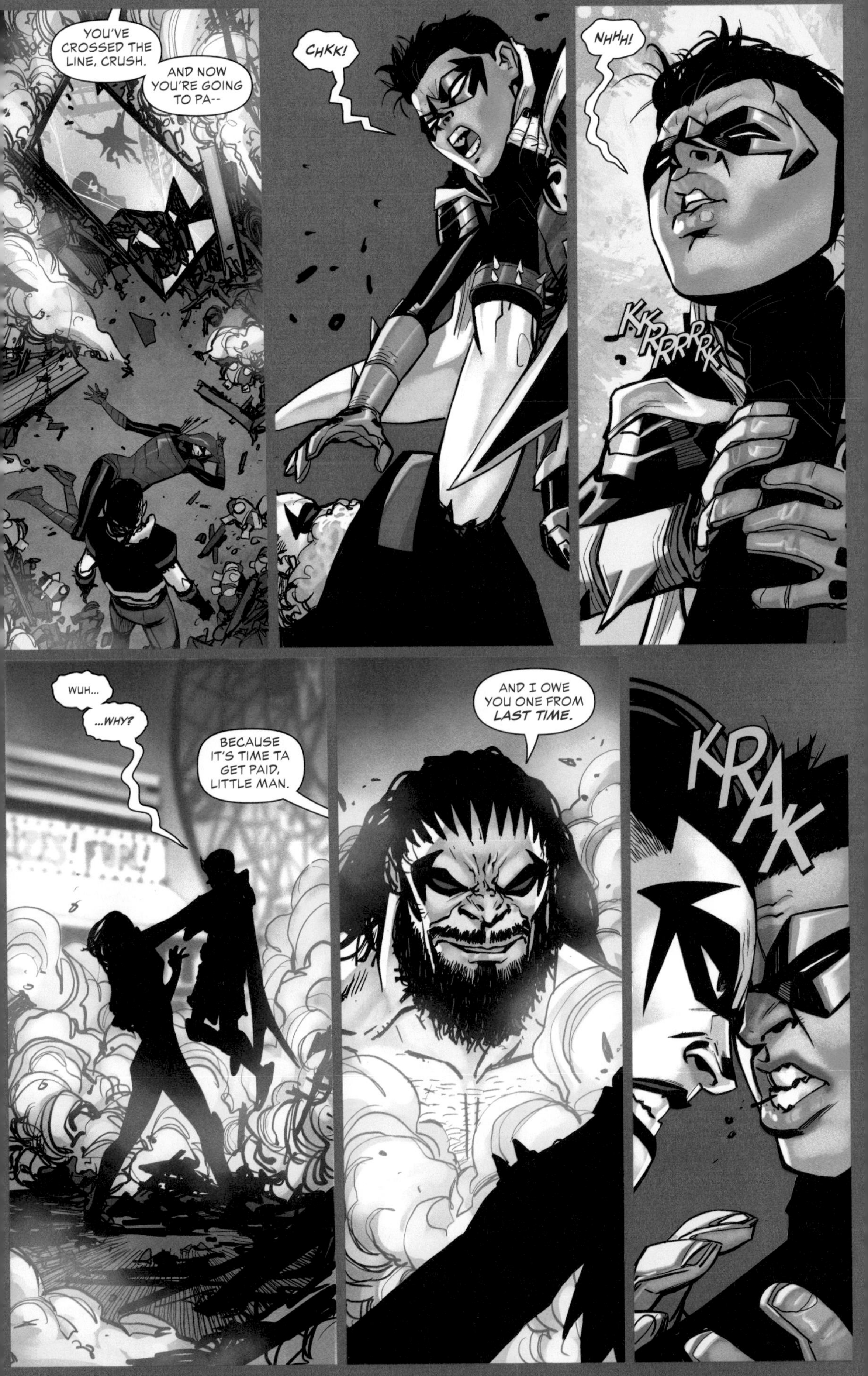

YOU'VE CROSSED THE LINE, CRUSH.
AND NOW YOU'RE GOING TO PA--
CHKK!
NHHH!
KKRRRRRK
WUH...
...WHY?
BECAUSE IT'S TIME TA GET PAID, LITTLE MAN.
AND I OWE YOU ONE FROM LAST TIME.
KRAK

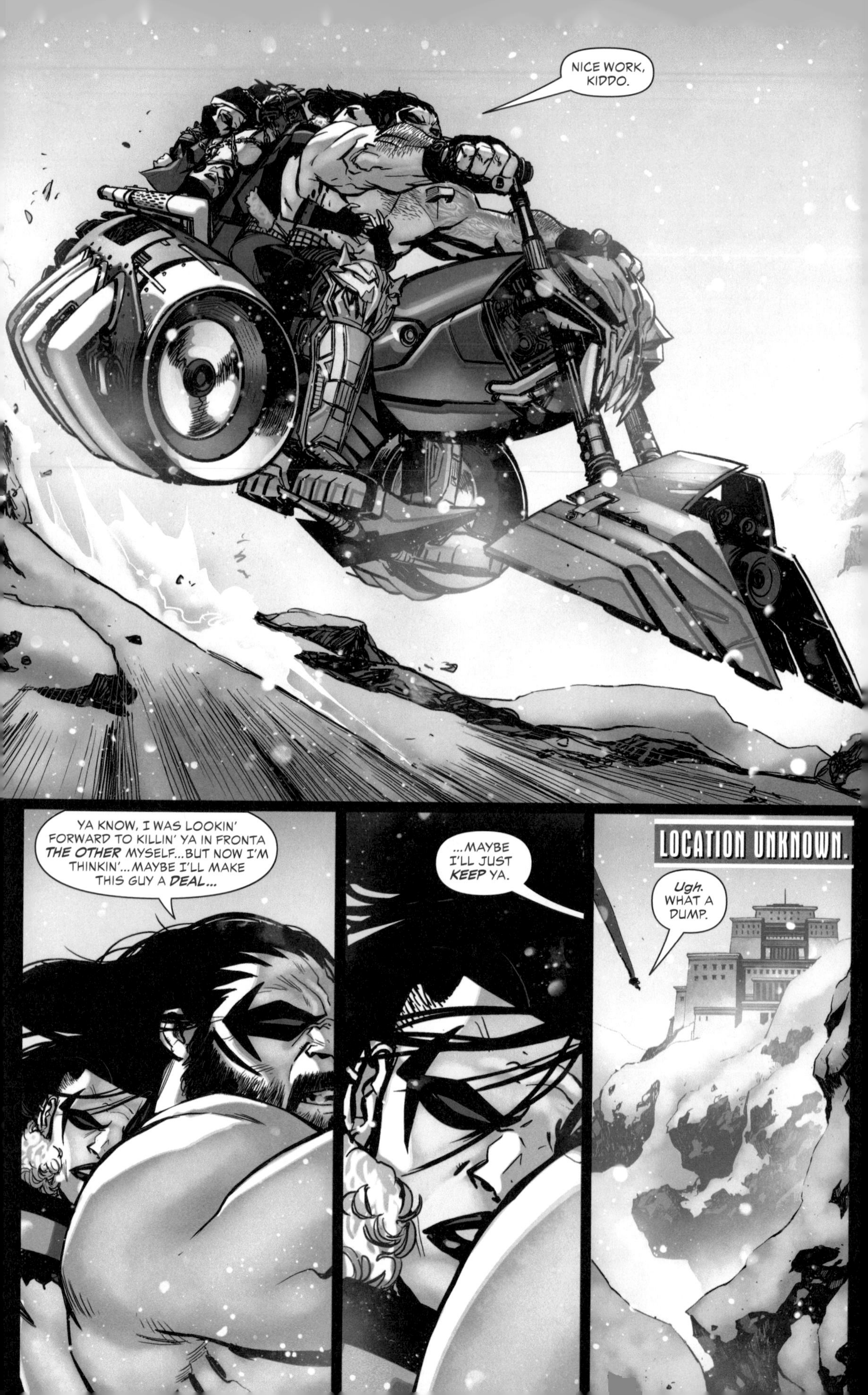
NICE WORK, KIDDO.
YA KNOW, I WAS LOOKIN' FORWARD TO KILLIN' YA IN FRONTA *THE OTHER* MYSELF...BUT NOW I'M THINKIN'...MAYBE I'LL MAKE THIS GUY A *DEAL*...
...MAYBE I'LL JUST *KEEP* YA.
LOCATION UNKNOWN.
Ugh. WHAT A DUMP.

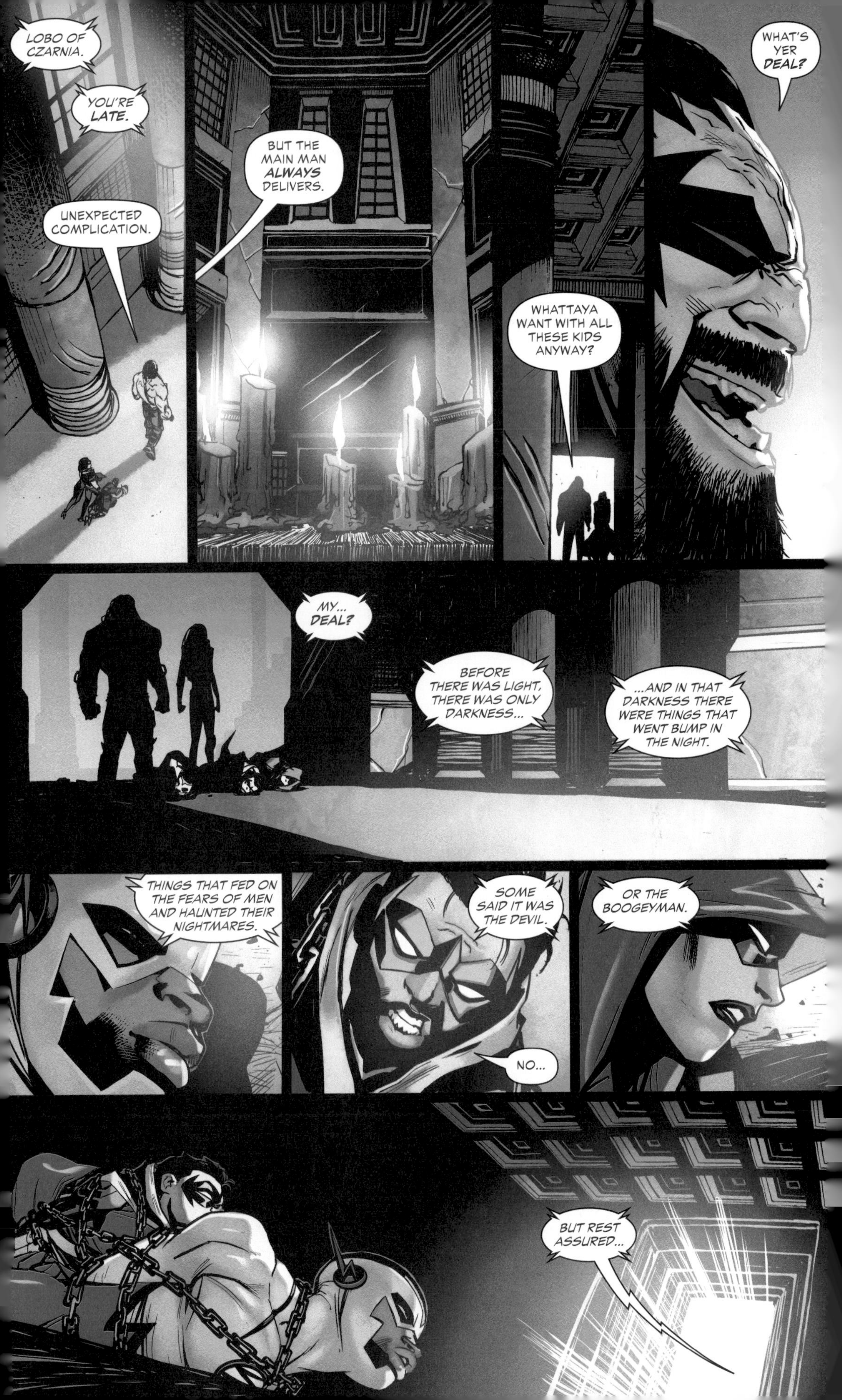

LOBO OF CZARNIA.
YOU'RE LATE.
UNEXPECTED COMPLICATION.
BUT THE MAIN MAN ALWAYS DELIVERS.
WHAT'S YER DEAL?
WHATTAYA WANT WITH ALL THESE KIDS ANYWAY?
MY... DEAL?
BEFORE THERE WAS LIGHT, THERE WAS ONLY DARKNESS...
...AND IN THAT DARKNESS THERE WERE THINGS THAT WENT BUMP IN THE NIGHT.
THINGS THAT FED ON THE FEARS OF MEN AND HAUNTED THEIR NIGHTMARES.
SOME SAID IT WAS THE DEVIL.
NO...
OR THE BOOGEYMAN.
BUT REST ASSURED...

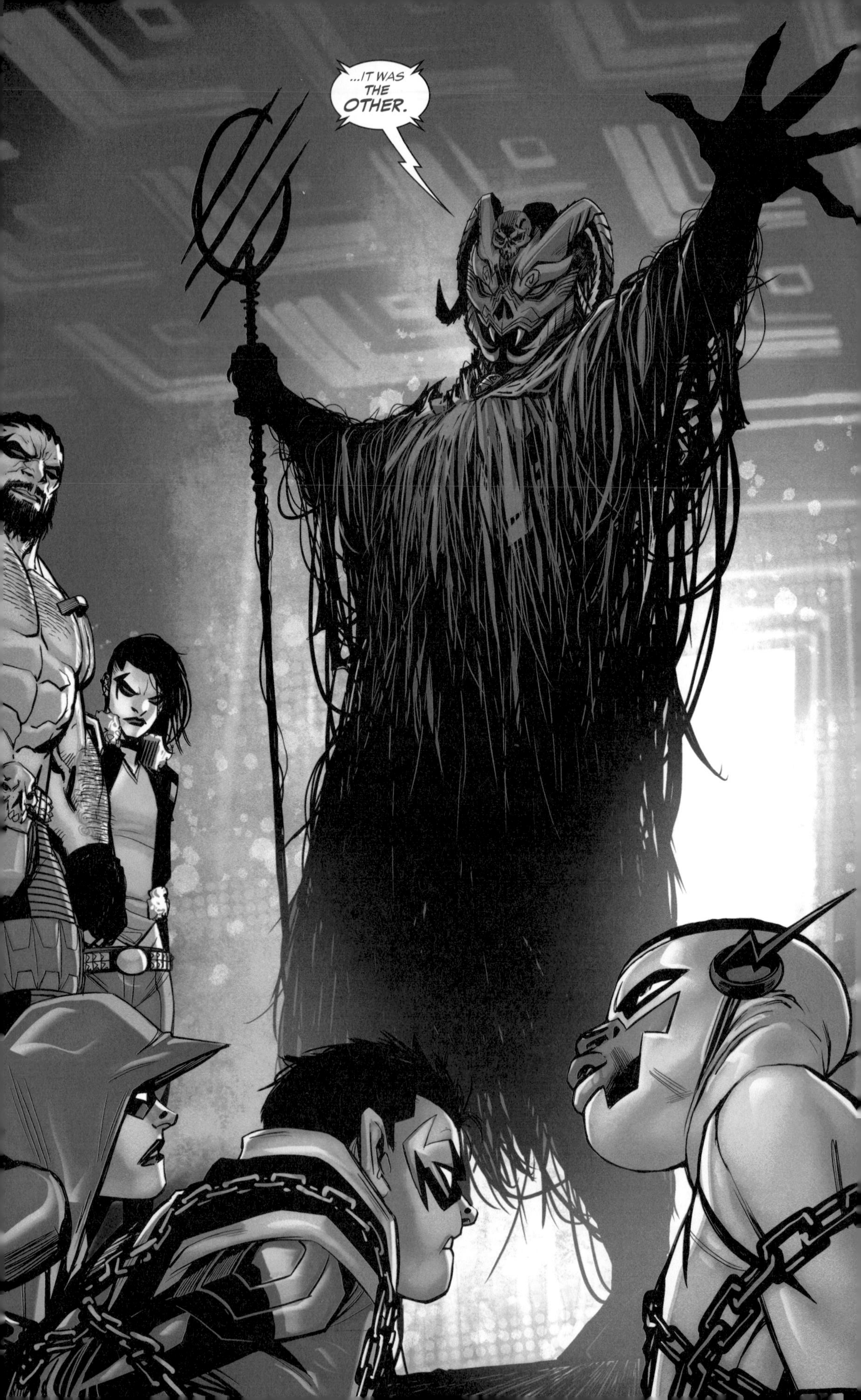
...IT WAS THE OTHER.

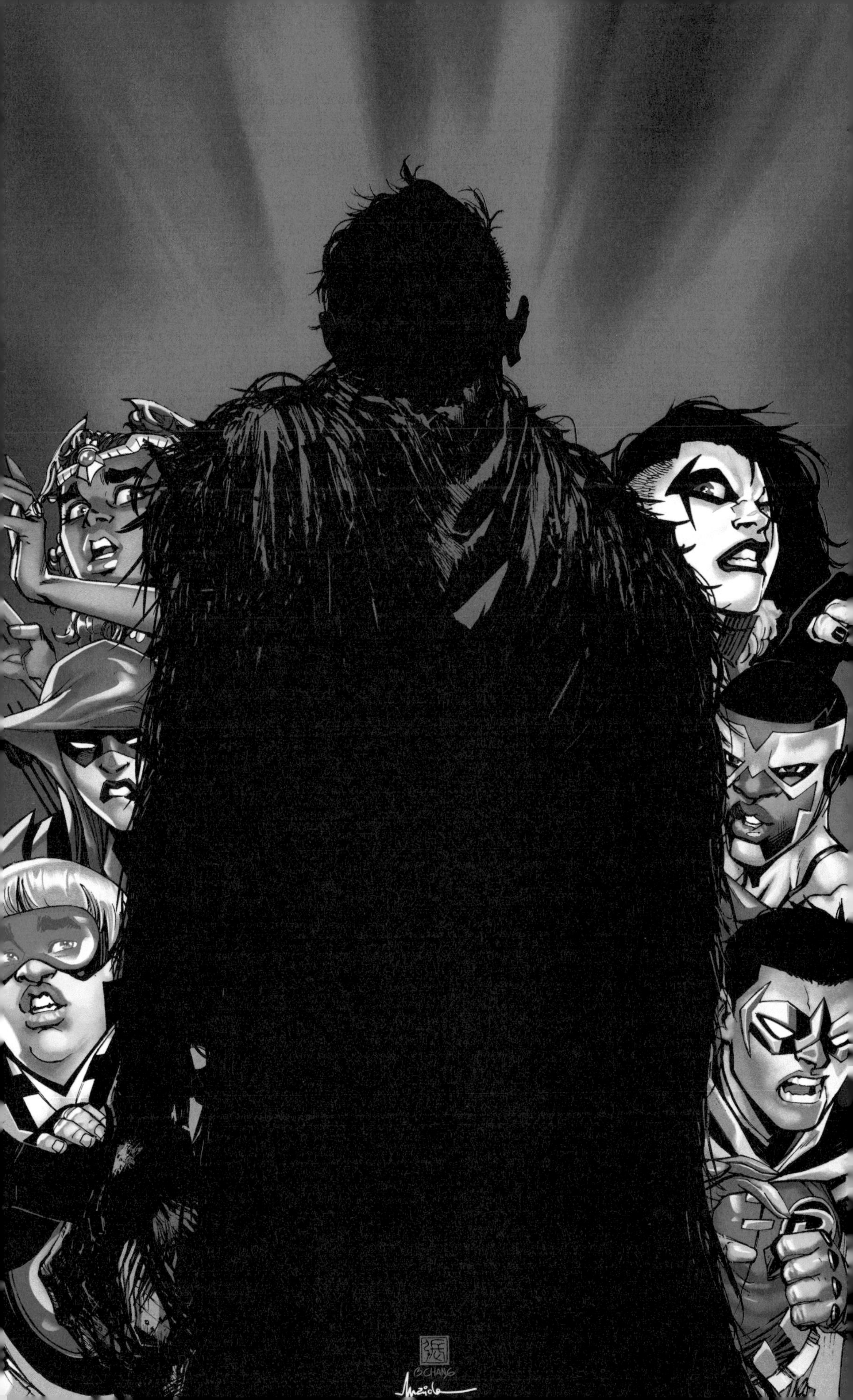
B.CHANG

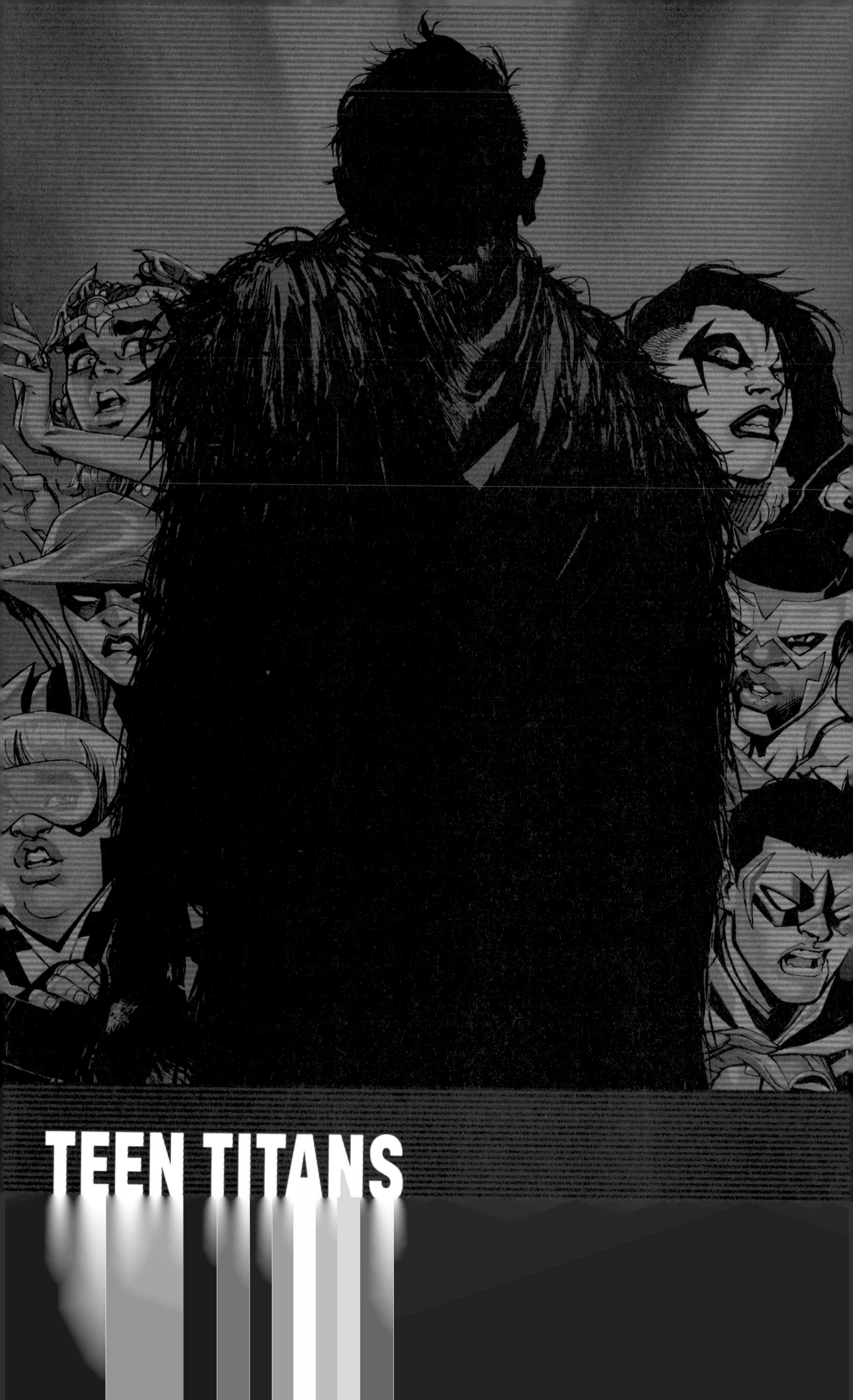
TEEN TITANS

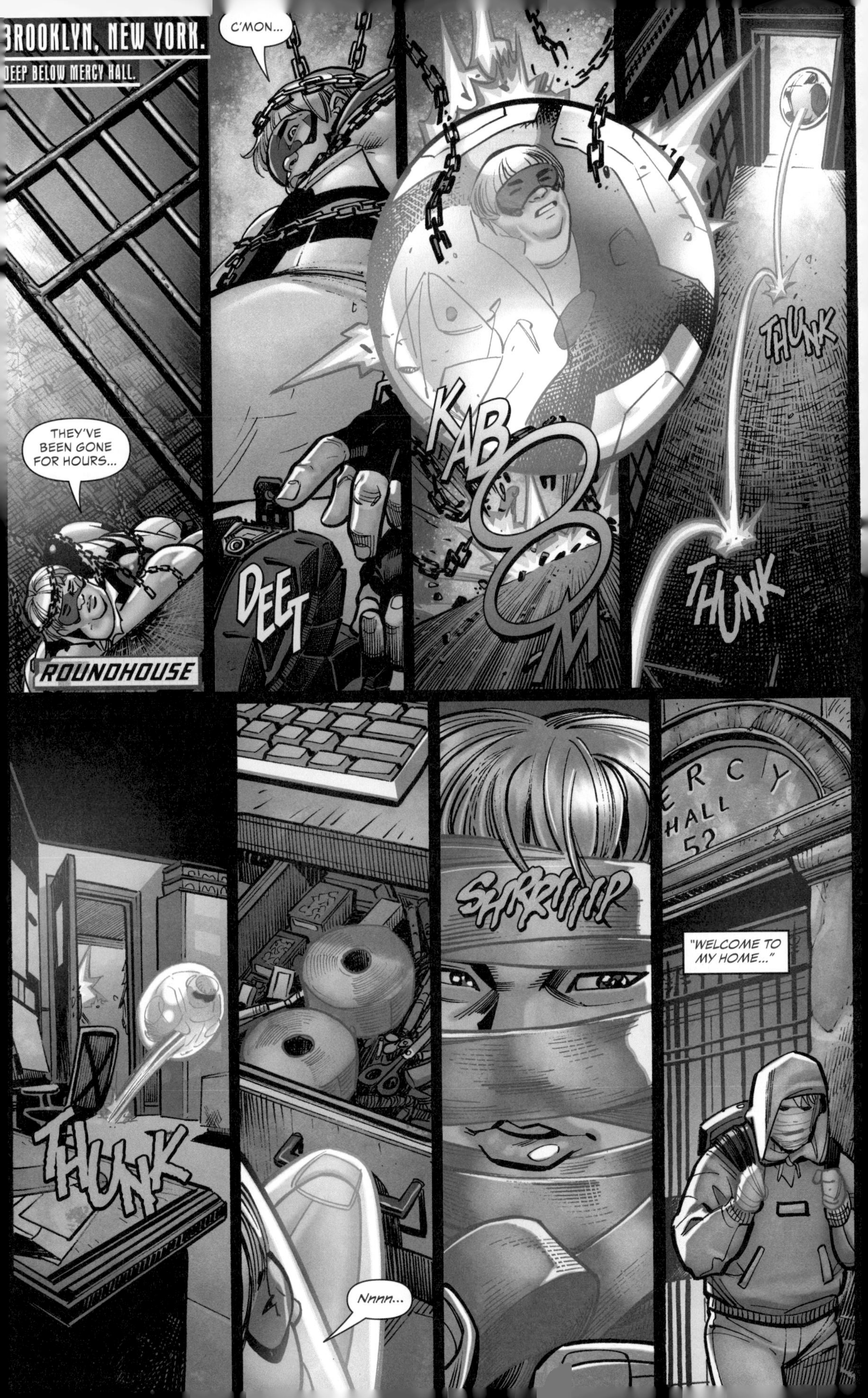
BROOKLYN, NEW YORK.
DEEP BELOW MERCY HALL.
THEY'VE BEEN GONE FOR HOURS...
ROUNDHOUSE
C'MON...
DEET
KABOOM
THUNK
THUNK
THUNK
SHRRIIIIP
Nnnn...
ERCY HALL 52
"WELCOME TO MY HOME..."

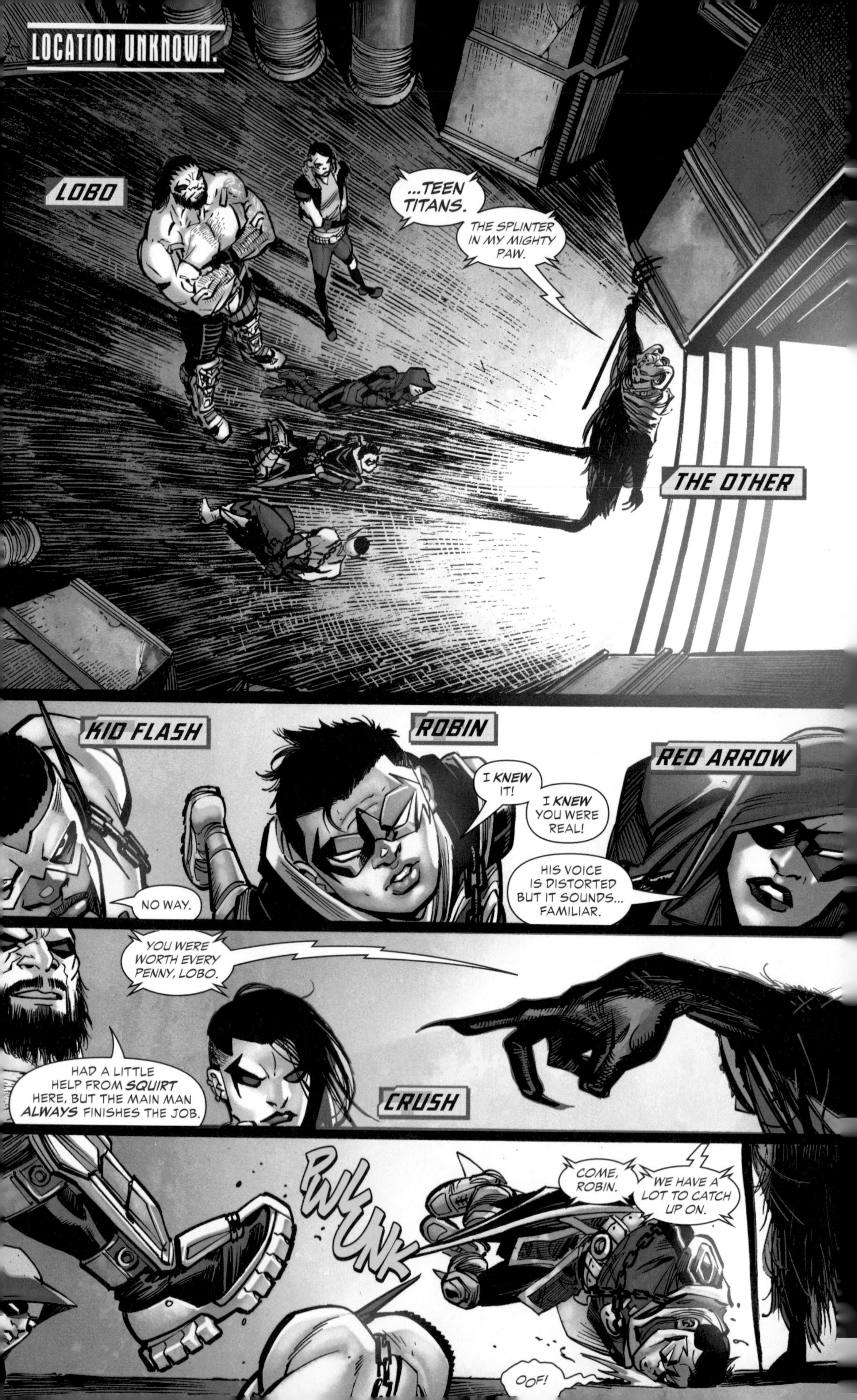
LOCATION UNKNOWN.
LOBO
...TEEN TITANS.
THE SPLINTER IN MY MIGHTY PAW.
THE OTHER
KID FLASH
ROBIN
RED ARROW
I KNEW IT!
I KNEW YOU WERE REAL!
NO WAY.
HIS VOICE IS DISTORTED BUT IT SOUNDS... FAMILIAR.
YOU WERE WORTH EVERY PENNY, LOBO.
HAD A LITTLE HELP FROM SQUIRT HERE, BUT THE MAIN MAN ALWAYS FINISHES THE JOB.
CRUSH
PWUNK
COME, ROBIN.
WE HAVE A LOT TO CATCH UP ON.
OOF!

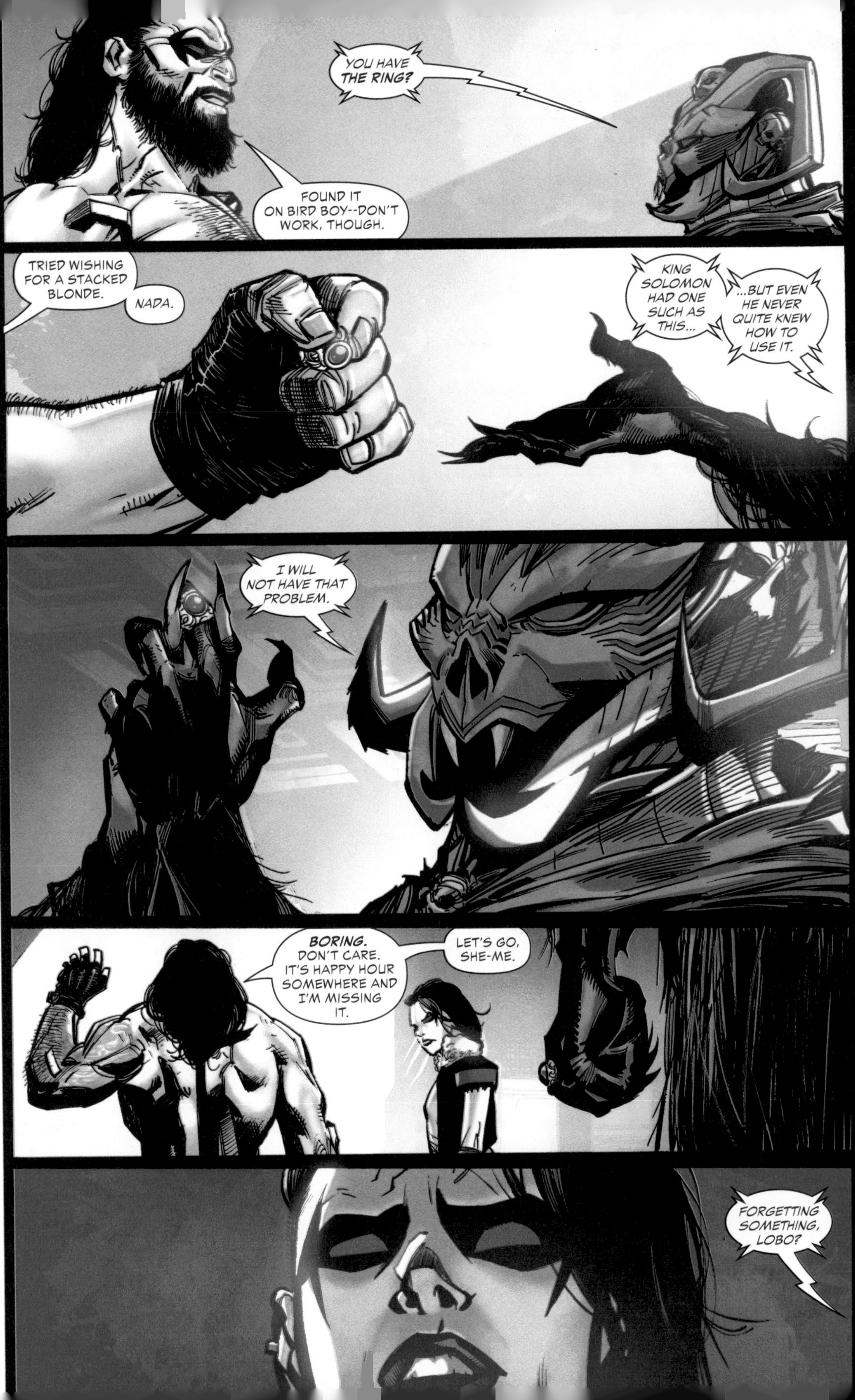
YOU HAVE THE RING?
FOUND IT ON BIRD BOY--DON'T WORK, THOUGH.
TRIED WISHING FOR A STACKED BLONDE.
NADA.
KING SOLOMON HAD ONE SUCH AS THIS...
...BUT EVEN HE NEVER QUITE KNEW HOW TO USE IT.
I WILL NOT HAVE THAT PROBLEM.
BORING. DON'T CARE. IT'S HAPPY HOUR SOMEWHERE AND I'M MISSING IT.
LET'S GO, SHE-ME.
FORGETTING SOMETHING, LOBO?

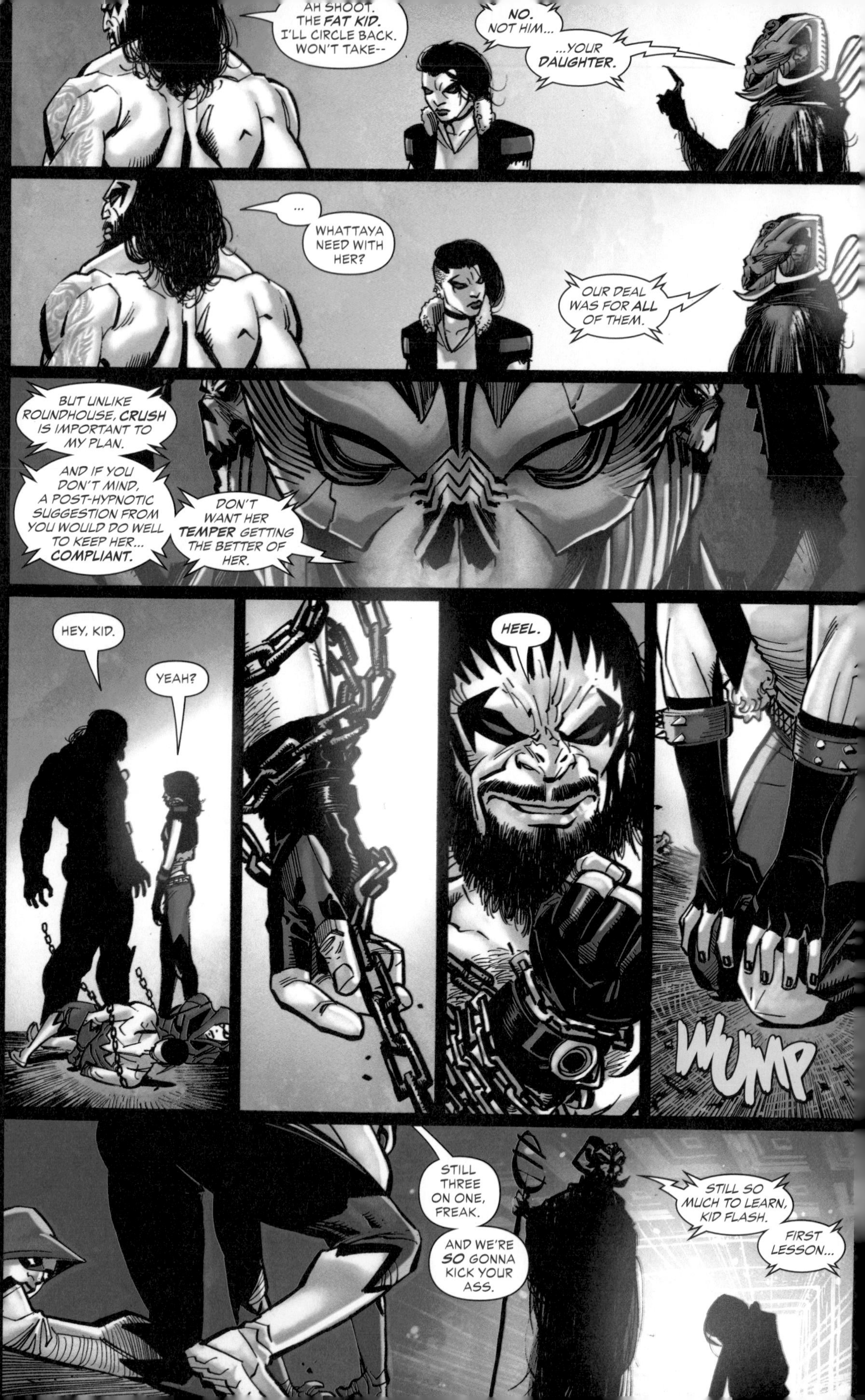
AH SHOOT. THE FAT KID. I'LL CIRCLE BACK. WON'T TAKE--
NO. NOT HIM...
...YOUR DAUGHTER.
...
WHATTAYA NEED WITH HER?
OUR DEAL WAS FOR ALL OF THEM.
BUT UNLIKE ROUNDHOUSE, CRUSH IS IMPORTANT TO MY PLAN.
AND IF YOU DON'T MIND, A POST-HYPNOTIC SUGGESTION FROM YOU WOULD DO WELL TO KEEP HER... COMPLIANT.
DON'T WANT HER TEMPER GETTING THE BETTER OF HER.
HEY, KID.
YEAH?
HEEL.
WUMP
STILL THREE ON ONE, FREAK.
AND WE'RE SO GONNA KICK YOUR ASS.
STILL SO MUCH TO LEARN, KID FLASH.
FIRST LESSON...

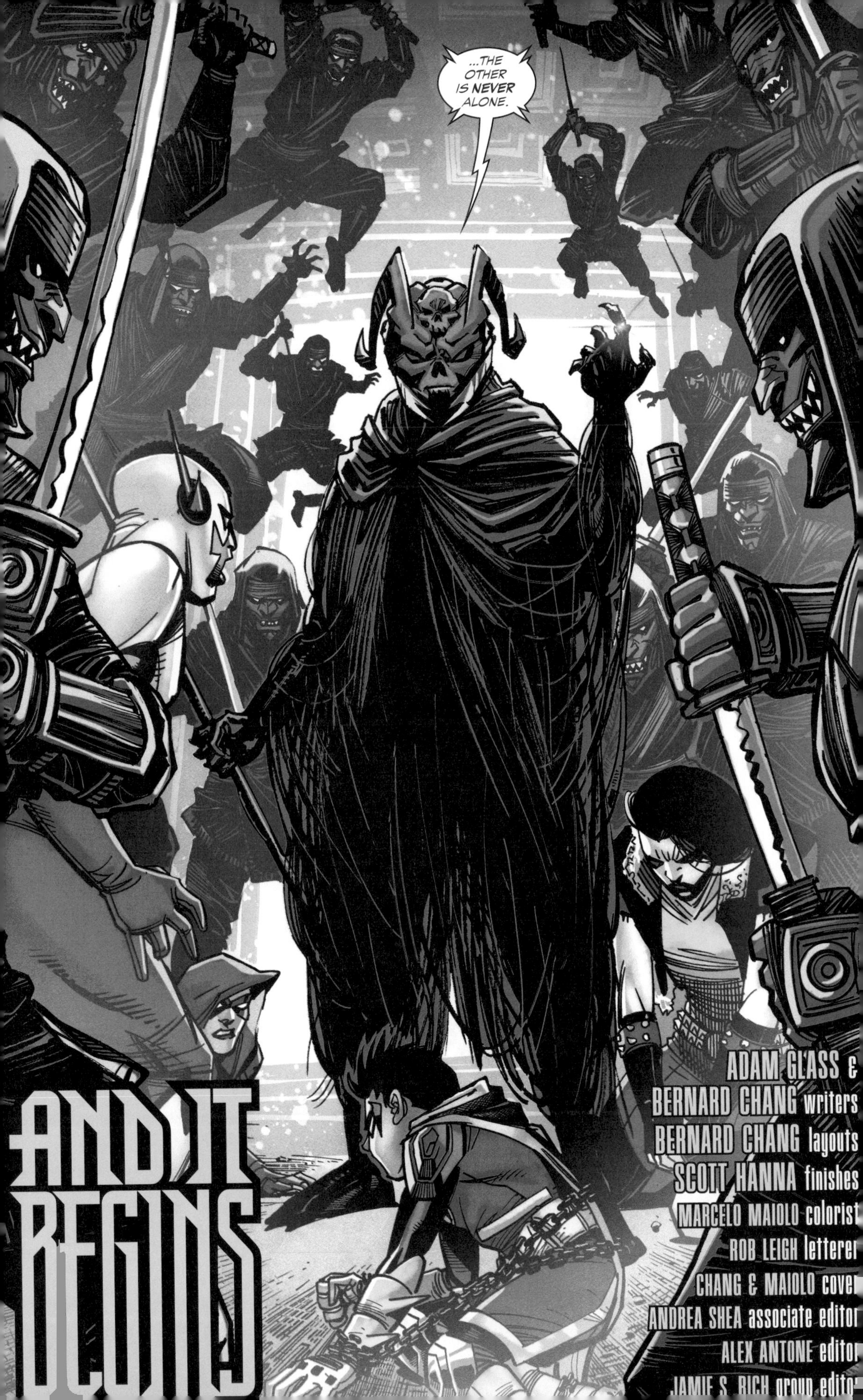
...THE OTHER IS NEVER ALONE.
AND IT BEGINS
ADAM GLASS &
BERNARD CHANG writers
BERNARD CHANG layouts
SCOTT HANNA finishes
MARCELO MAIOLO colorist
ROB LEIGH letterer
CHANG & MAIOLO cover
ANDREA SHEA associate editor
ALEX ANTONE editor

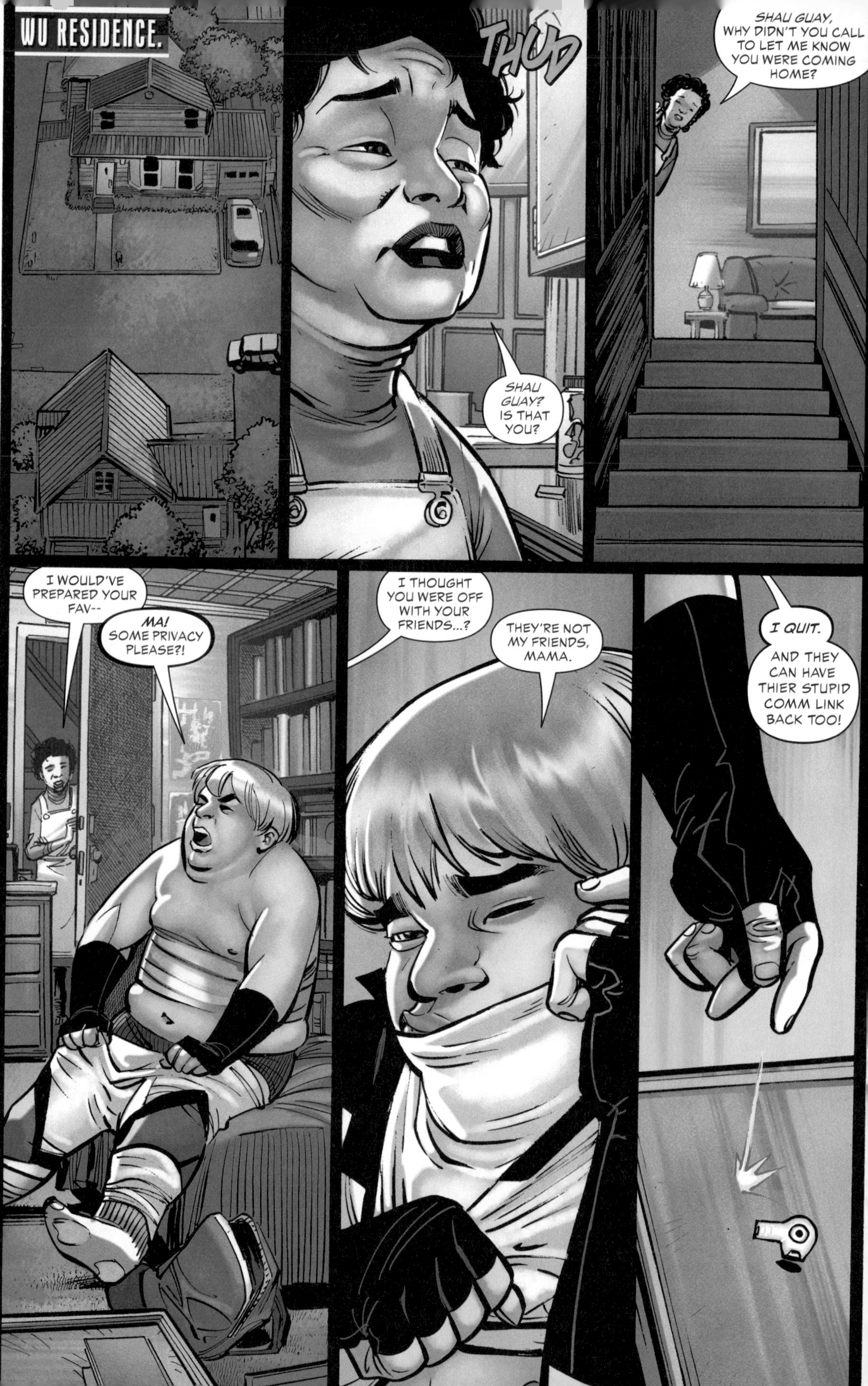
WU RESIDENCE.
THUD
SHAU GUAY? IS THAT YOU?
SHAU GUAY, WHY DIDN'T YOU CALL TO LET ME KNOW YOU WERE COMING HOME?
I WOULD'VE PREPARED YOUR FAV--
MA! SOME PRIVACY PLEASE?!
I THOUGHT YOU WERE OFF WITH YOUR FRIENDS...?
THEY'RE NOT MY FRIENDS, MAMA.
I QUIT.
AND THEY CAN HAVE THIER STUPID COMM LINK BACK TOO!

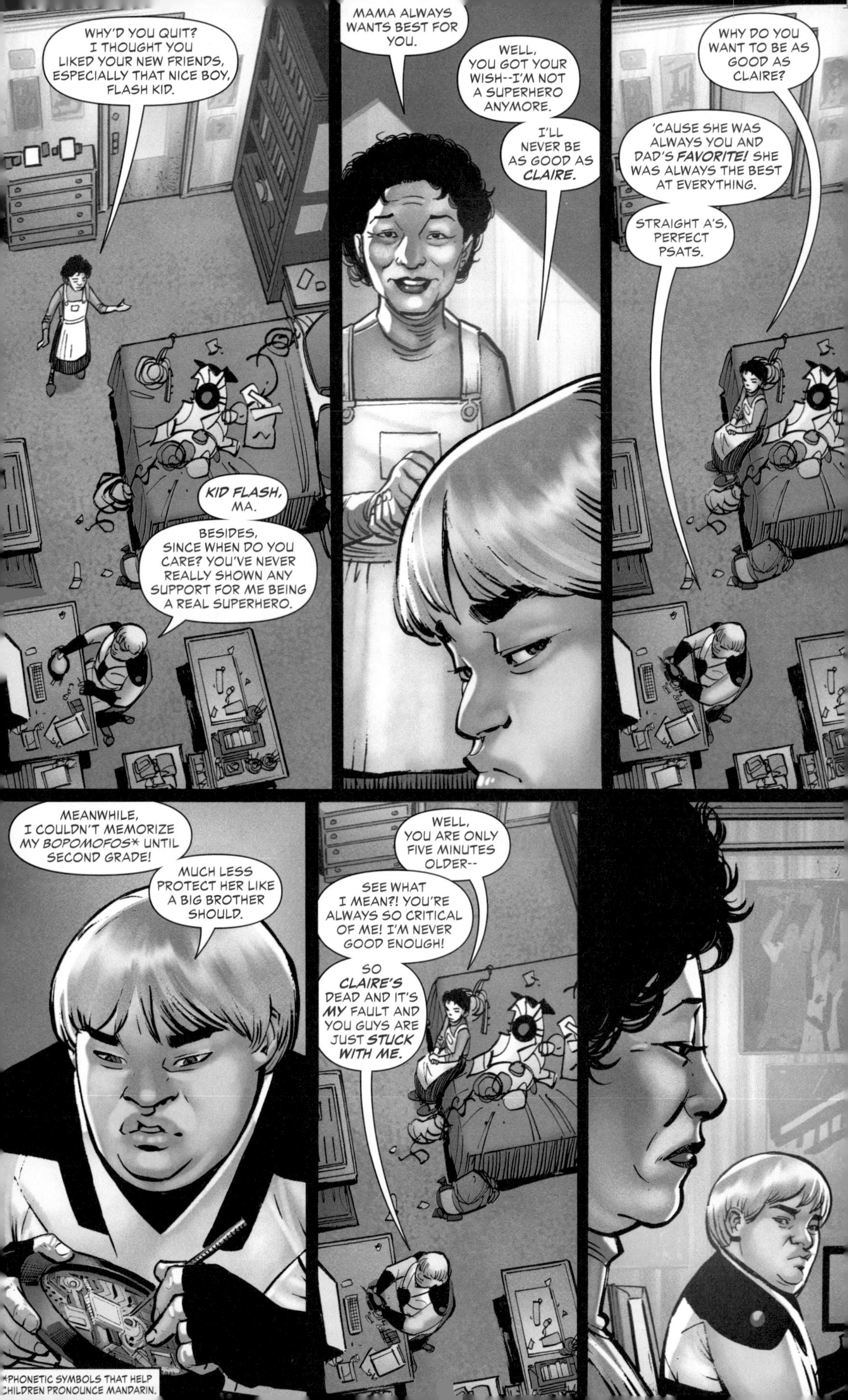
WHY'D YOU QUIT? I THOUGHT YOU LIKED YOUR NEW FRIENDS, ESPECIALLY THAT NICE BOY, FLASH KID.
KID FLASH, MA.
BESIDES, SINCE WHEN DO YOU CARE? YOU'VE NEVER REALLY SHOWN ANY SUPPORT FOR ME BEING A REAL SUPERHERO.
MAMA ALWAYS WANTS BEST FOR YOU.
WELL, YOU GOT YOUR WISH--I'M NOT A SUPERHERO ANYMORE.
I'LL NEVER BE AS GOOD AS CLAIRE.
WHY DO YOU WANT TO BE AS GOOD AS CLAIRE?
'CAUSE SHE WAS ALWAYS YOU AND DAD'S FAVORITE! SHE WAS ALWAYS THE BEST AT EVERYTHING.
STRAIGHT A'S, PERFECT PSATS.
MEANWHILE, I COULDN'T MEMORIZE MY BOPOMOFOS* UNTIL SECOND GRADE!
MUCH LESS PROTECT HER LIKE A BIG BROTHER SHOULD.
*PHONETIC SYMBOLS THAT HELP CHILDREN PRONOUNCE MANDARIN.
WELL, YOU ARE ONLY FIVE MINUTES OLDER--
SEE WHAT I MEAN?! YOU'RE ALWAYS SO CRITICAL OF ME! I'M NEVER GOOD ENOUGH!
SO CLAIRE'S DEAD AND IT'S MY FAULT AND YOU GUYS ARE JUST STUCK WITH ME.

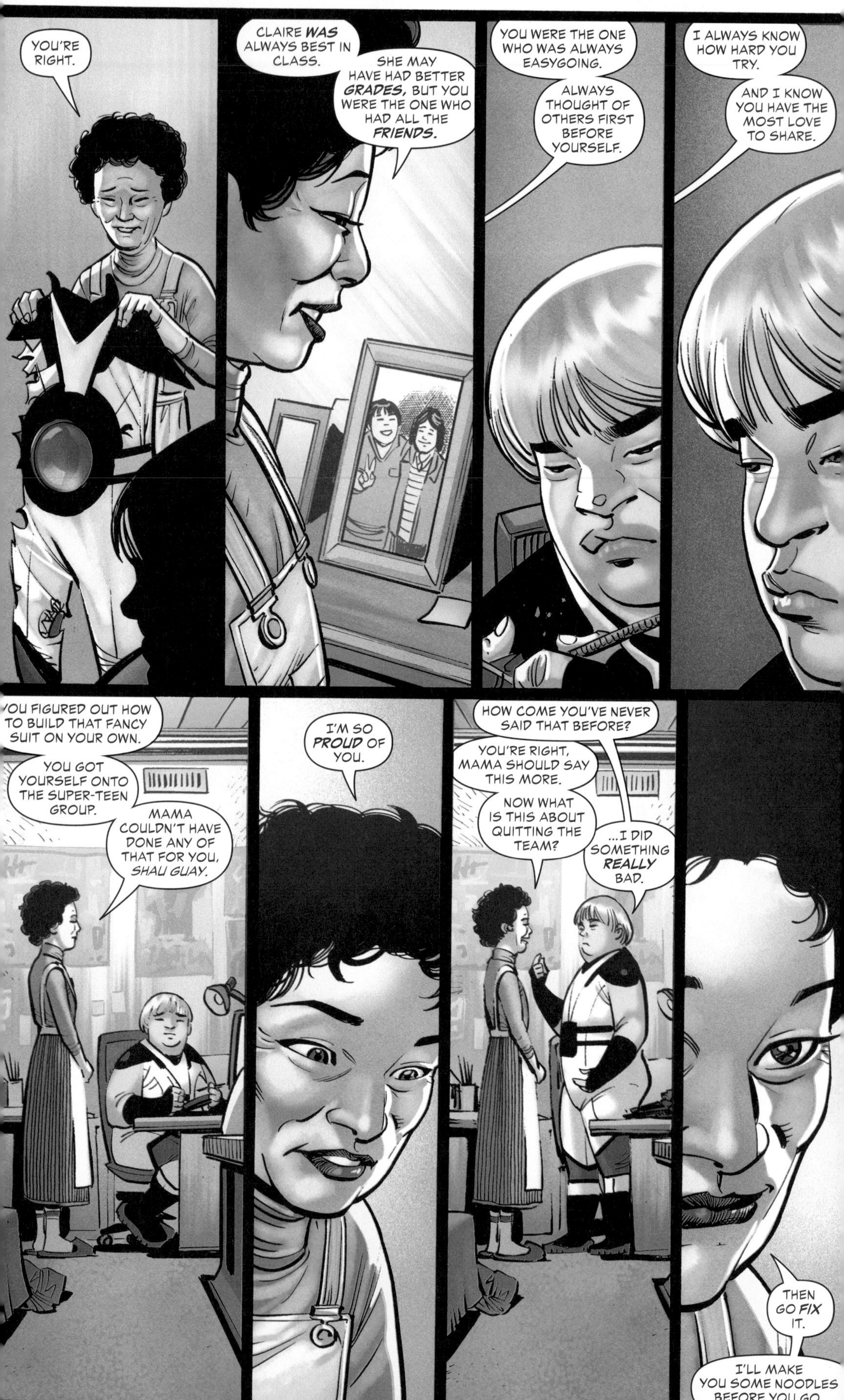
YOU'RE RIGHT.
CLAIRE WAS ALWAYS BEST IN CLASS.
SHE MAY HAVE HAD BETTER GRADES, BUT YOU WERE THE ONE WHO HAD ALL THE FRIENDS.
YOU WERE THE ONE WHO WAS ALWAYS EASYGOING.
ALWAYS THOUGHT OF OTHERS FIRST BEFORE YOURSELF.
I ALWAYS KNOW HOW HARD YOU TRY.
AND I KNOW YOU HAVE THE MOST LOVE TO SHARE.
YOU FIGURED OUT HOW TO BUILD THAT FANCY SUIT ON YOUR OWN.
YOU GOT YOURSELF ONTO THE SUPER-TEEN GROUP.
MAMA COULDN'T HAVE DONE ANY OF THAT FOR YOU, SHAU GUAY.
I'M SO PROUD OF YOU.
HOW COME YOU'VE NEVER SAID THAT BEFORE?
YOU'RE RIGHT, MAMA SHOULD SAY THIS MORE.
NOW WHAT IS THIS ABOUT QUITTING THE TEAM?
...I DID SOMETHING REALLY BAD.
THEN GO FIX IT.
I'LL MAKE YOU SOME NOODLES BEFORE YOU GO.

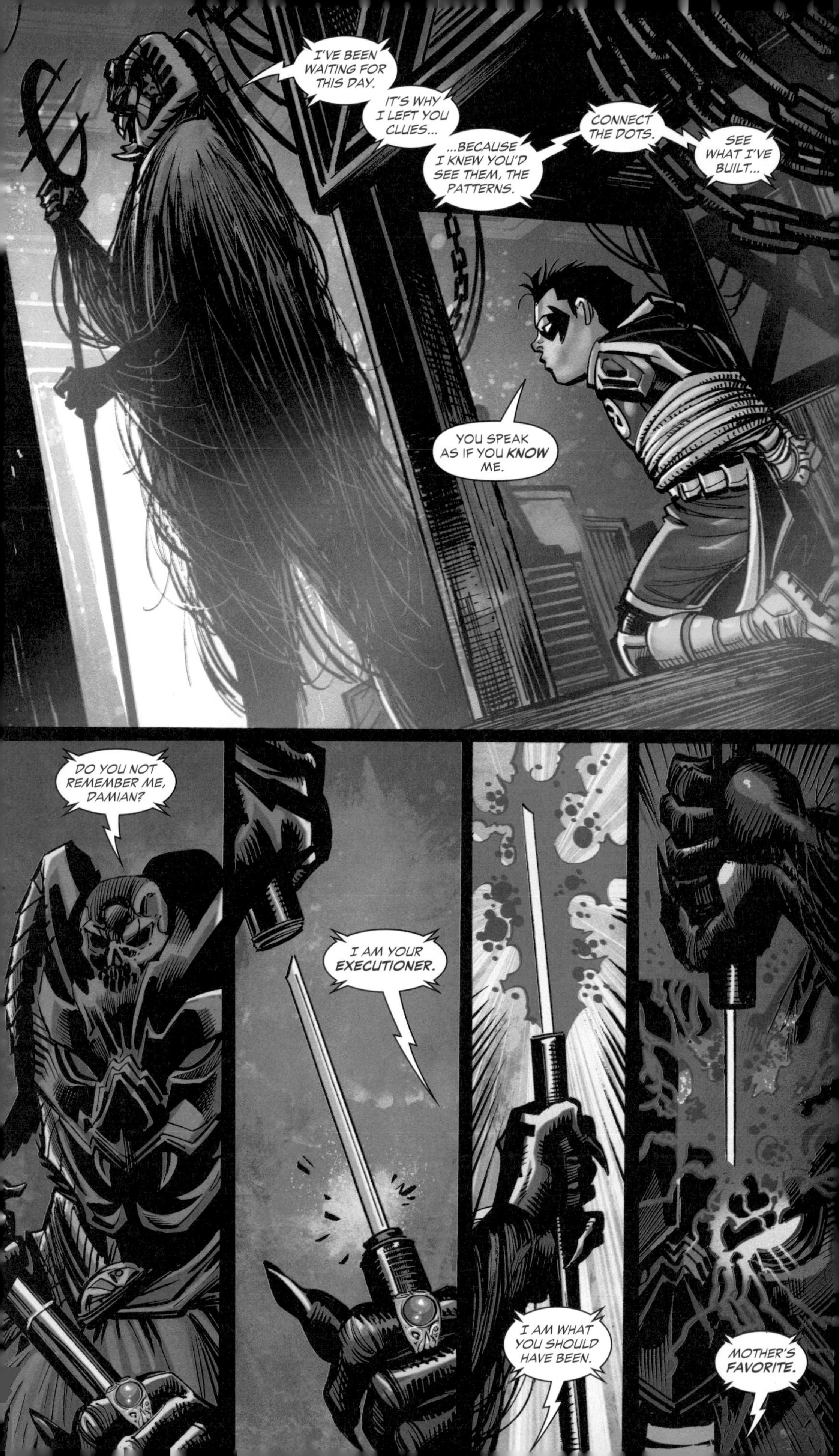
I'VE BEEN WAITING FOR THIS DAY.
IT'S WHY I LEFT YOU CLUES...
...BECAUSE I KNEW YOU'D SEE THEM, THE PATTERNS.
CONNECT THE DOTS.
SEE WHAT I'VE BUILT...
YOU SPEAK AS IF YOU **KNOW** ME.
DO YOU NOT REMEMBER ME, DAMIAN?
I AM YOUR **EXECUTIONER.**
I AM WHAT YOU SHOULD HAVE BEEN.
MOTHER'S **FAVORITE.**

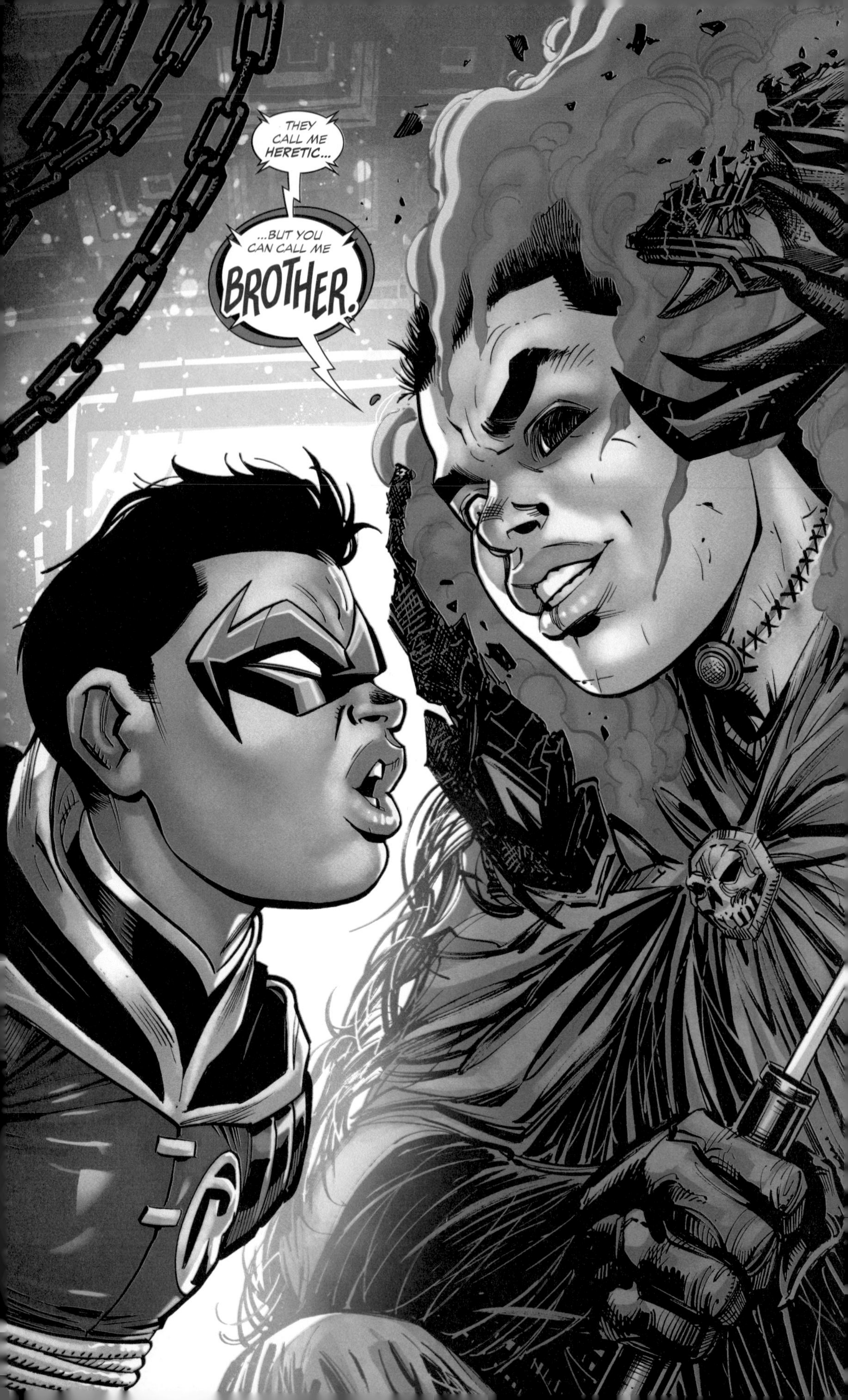
THEY CALL ME HERETIC...
...BUT YOU CAN CALL ME BROTHER.

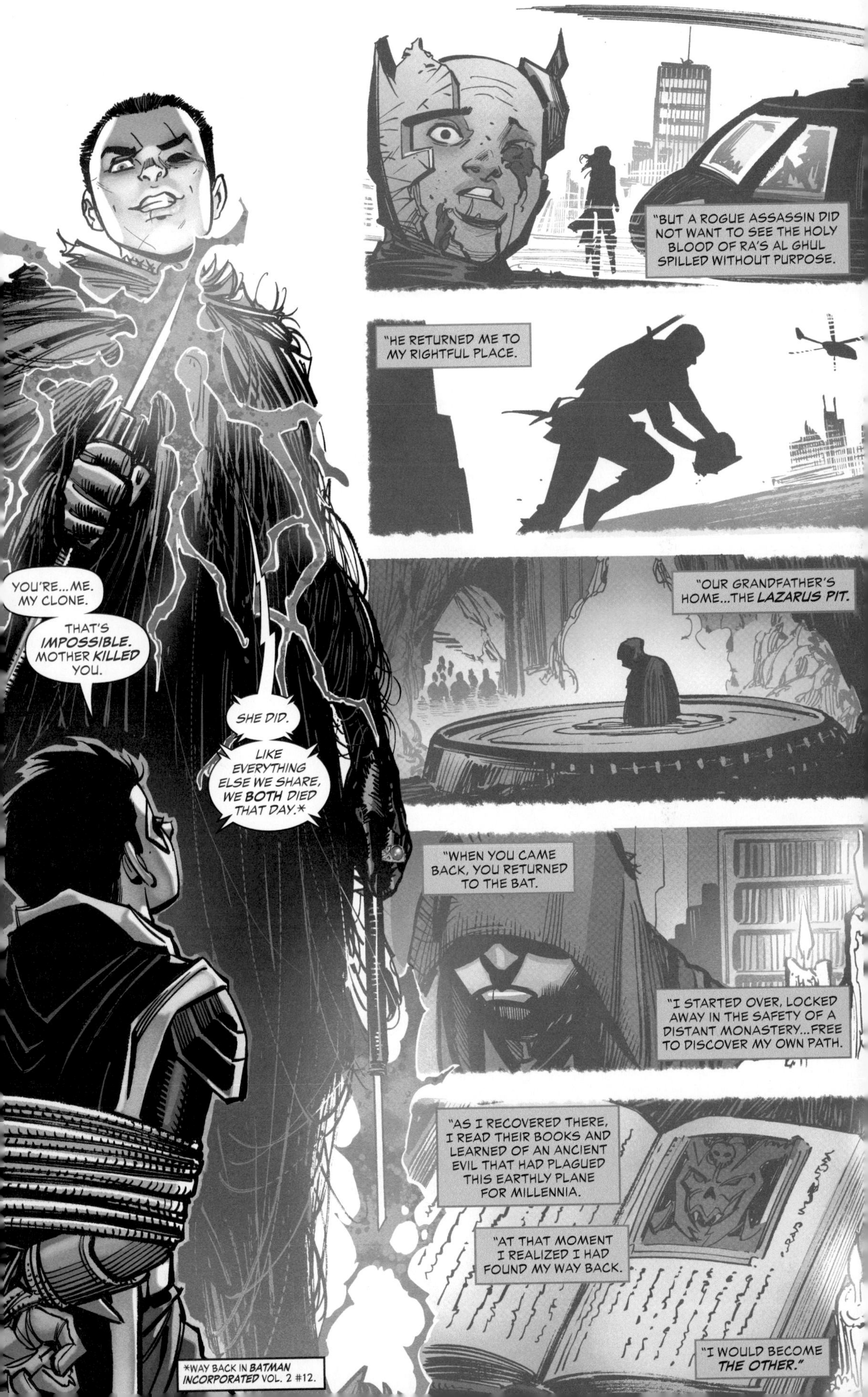

"BUT A ROGUE ASSASSIN DID NOT WANT TO SEE THE HOLY BLOOD OF RA'S AL GHUL SPILLED WITHOUT PURPOSE.
"HE RETURNED ME TO MY RIGHTFUL PLACE.
"OUR GRANDFATHER'S HOME...THE LAZARUS PIT.
"WHEN YOU CAME BACK, YOU RETURNED TO THE BAT.
"I STARTED OVER, LOCKED AWAY IN THE SAFETY OF A DISTANT MONASTERY...FREE TO DISCOVER MY OWN PATH.
"AS I RECOVERED THERE, I READ THEIR BOOKS AND LEARNED OF AN ANCIENT EVIL THAT HAD PLAGUED THIS EARTHLY PLANE FOR MILLENNIA.
"AT THAT MOMENT I REALIZED I HAD FOUND MY WAY BACK.
"I WOULD BECOME THE OTHER."
YOU'RE...ME. MY CLONE.
THAT'S IMPOSSIBLE. MOTHER KILLED YOU.
SHE DID.
LIKE EVERYTHING ELSE WE SHARE, WE BOTH DIED THAT DAY.*
*WAY BACK IN BATMAN INCORPORATED VOL. 2 #12.

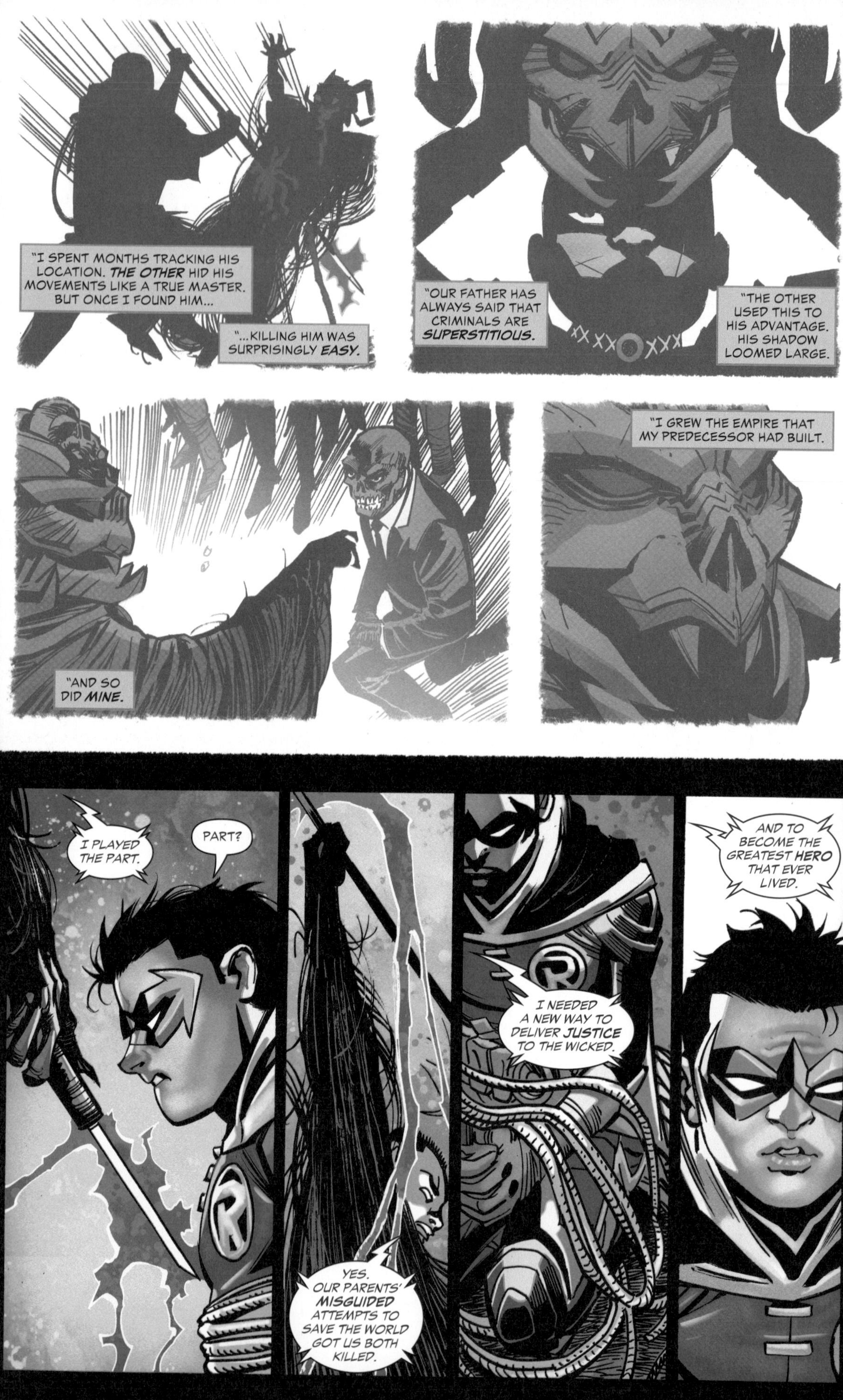

"I SPENT MONTHS TRACKING HIS LOCATION. THE OTHER HID HIS MOVEMENTS LIKE A TRUE MASTER. BUT ONCE I FOUND HIM...
"...KILLING HIM WAS SURPRISINGLY EASY.
"OUR FATHER HAS ALWAYS SAID THAT CRIMINALS ARE SUPERSTITIOUS.
"THE OTHER USED THIS TO HIS ADVANTAGE. HIS SHADOW LOOMED LARGE.
"AND SO DID MINE.
"I GREW THE EMPIRE THAT MY PREDECESSOR HAD BUILT.
I PLAYED THE PART.
PART?
YES. OUR PARENTS' MISGUIDED ATTEMPTS TO SAVE THE WORLD GOT US BOTH KILLED.
I NEEDED A NEW WAY TO DELIVER JUSTICE TO THE WICKED.
AND TO BECOME THE GREATEST HERO THAT EVER LIVED.

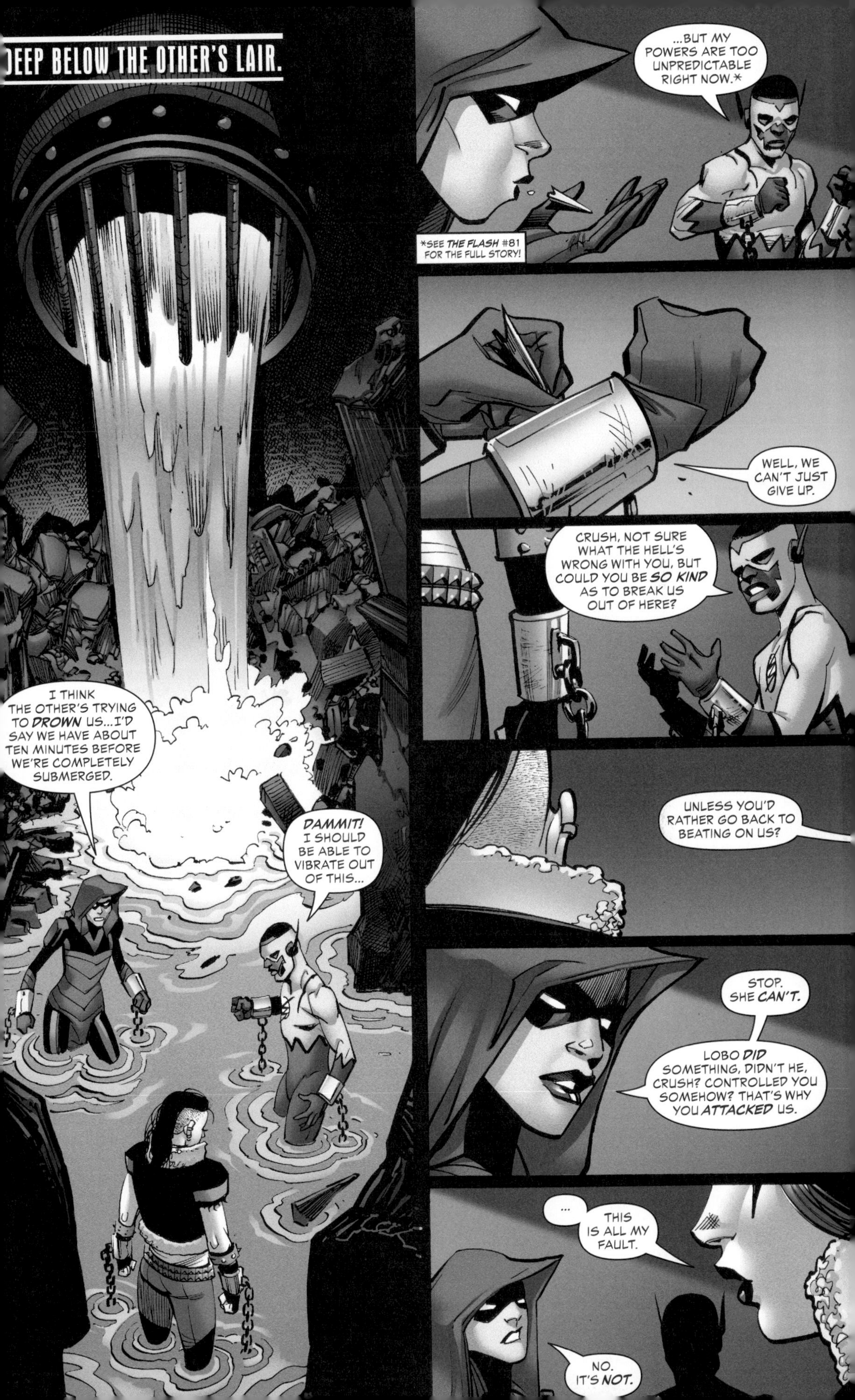

DEEP BELOW THE OTHER'S LAIR.
I THINK THE OTHER'S TRYING TO DROWN US...I'D SAY WE HAVE ABOUT TEN MINUTES BEFORE WE'RE COMPLETELY SUBMERGED.
DAMMIT! I SHOULD BE ABLE TO VIBRATE OUT OF THIS...
...BUT MY POWERS ARE TOO UNPREDICTABLE RIGHT NOW.*
*SEE THE FLASH #81 FOR THE FULL STORY!
WELL, WE CAN'T JUST GIVE UP.
CRUSH, NOT SURE WHAT THE HELL'S WRONG WITH YOU, BUT COULD YOU BE SO KIND AS TO BREAK US OUT OF HERE?
UNLESS YOU'D RATHER GO BACK TO BEATING ON US?
STOP. SHE CAN'T.
LOBO DID SOMETHING, DIDN'T HE, CRUSH? CONTROLLED YOU SOMEHOW? THAT'S WHY YOU ATTACKED US.
...
THIS IS ALL MY FAULT.
NO. IT'S NOT.

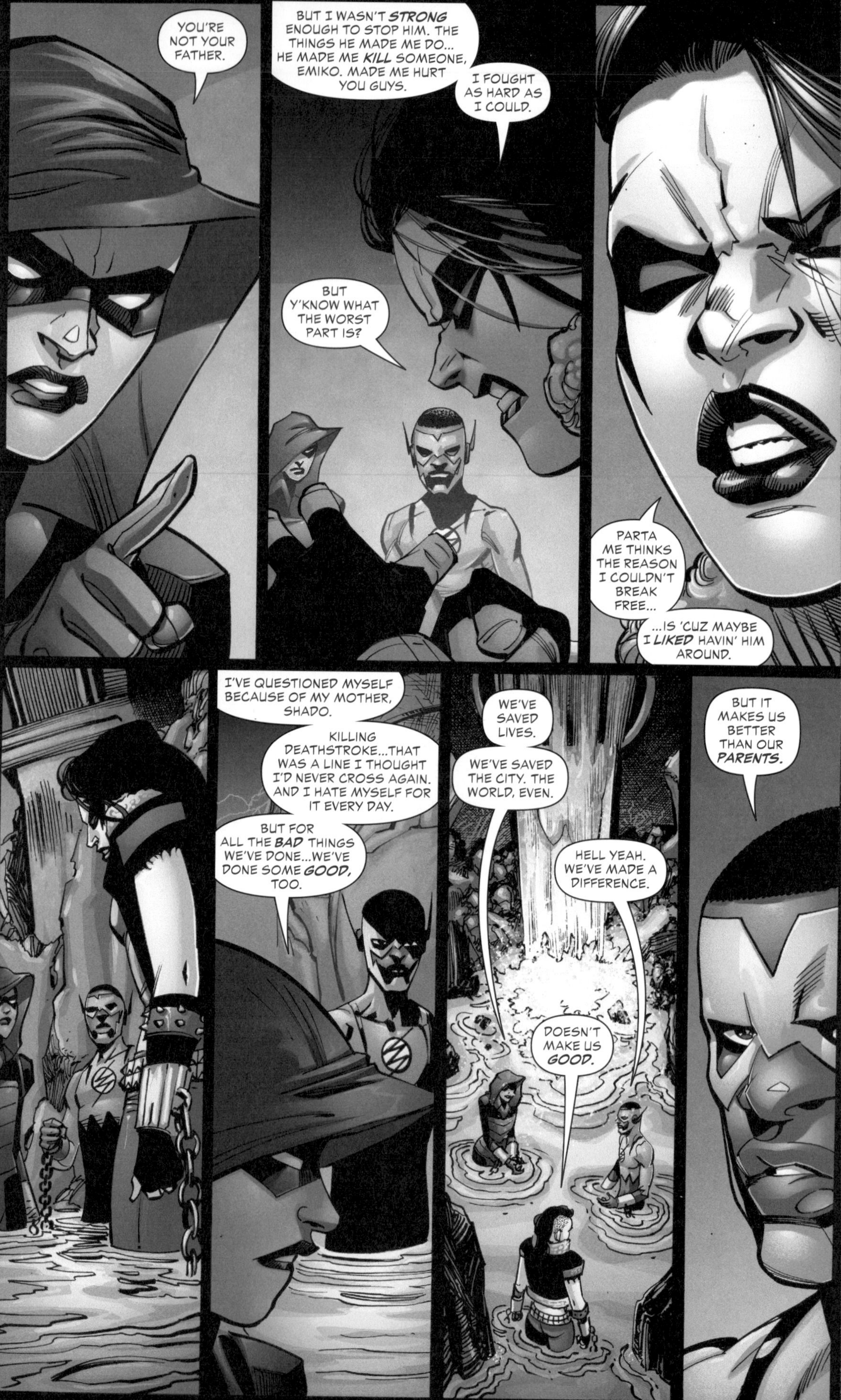
YOU'RE NOT YOUR FATHER.
BUT I WASN'T STRONG ENOUGH TO STOP HIM. THE THINGS HE MADE ME DO... HE MADE ME KILL SOMEONE, EMIKO. MADE ME HURT YOU GUYS.
I FOUGHT AS HARD AS I COULD.
BUT Y'KNOW WHAT THE WORST PART IS?
PARTA ME THINKS THE REASON I COULDN'T BREAK FREE...
...IS 'CUZ MAYBE I LIKED HAVIN' HIM AROUND.
I'VE QUESTIONED MYSELF BECAUSE OF MY MOTHER, SHADO.
KILLING DEATHSTROKE...THAT WAS A LINE I THOUGHT I'D NEVER CROSS AGAIN. AND I HATE MYSELF FOR IT EVERY DAY.
BUT FOR ALL THE BAD THINGS WE'VE DONE...WE'VE DONE SOME GOOD, TOO.
WE'VE SAVED LIVES.
WE'VE SAVED THE CITY. THE WORLD, EVEN.
HELL YEAH. WE'VE MADE A DIFFERENCE.
DOESN'T MAKE US GOOD.
BUT IT MAKES US BETTER THAN OUR PARENTS.

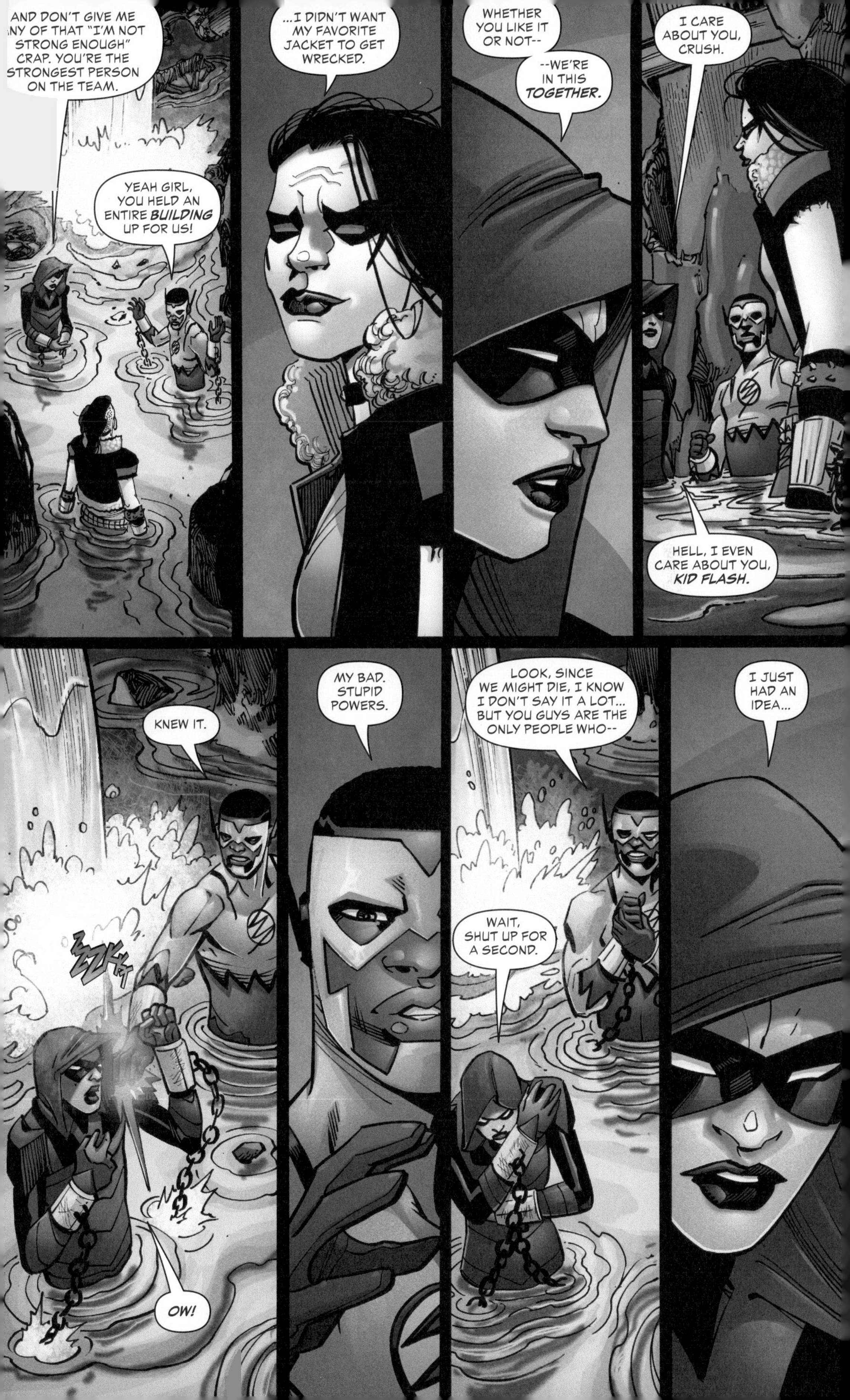
AND DON'T GIVE ME ANY OF THAT "I'M NOT STRONG ENOUGH" CRAP. YOU'RE THE STRONGEST PERSON ON THE TEAM.
YEAH GIRL, YOU HELD AN ENTIRE BUILDING UP FOR US!
...I DIDN'T WANT MY FAVORITE JACKET TO GET WRECKED.
WHETHER YOU LIKE IT OR NOT--
--WE'RE IN THIS TOGETHER.
I CARE ABOUT YOU, CRUSH.
HELL, I EVEN CARE ABOUT YOU, KID FLASH.
KNEW IT.
ZZKT
OW!
MY BAD. STUPID POWERS.
LOOK, SINCE WE MIGHT DIE, I KNOW I DON'T SAY IT A LOT... BUT YOU GUYS ARE THE ONLY PEOPLE WHO--
WAIT, SHUT UP FOR A SECOND.
I JUST HAD AN IDEA...

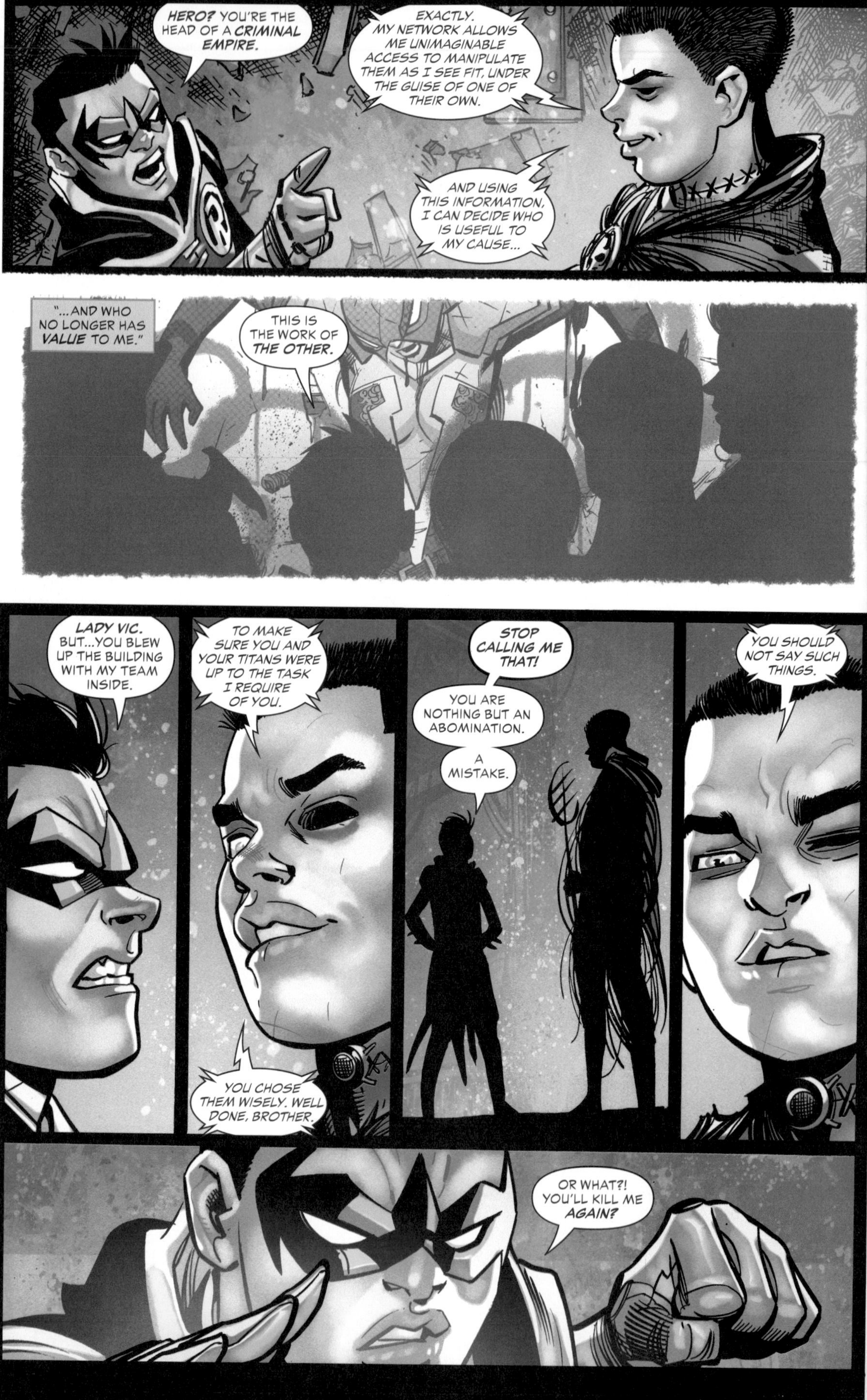

HERO? YOU'RE THE HEAD OF A CRIMINAL EMPIRE.
EXACTLY. MY NETWORK ALLOWS ME UNIMAGINABLE ACCESS TO MANIPULATE THEM AS I SEE FIT, UNDER THE GUISE OF ONE OF THEIR OWN.
AND USING THIS INFORMATION, I CAN DECIDE WHO IS USEFUL TO MY CAUSE...
"...AND WHO NO LONGER HAS VALUE TO ME."
THIS IS THE WORK OF THE OTHER.
LADY VIC. BUT...YOU BLEW UP THE BUILDING WITH MY TEAM INSIDE.
TO MAKE SURE YOU AND YOUR TITANS WERE UP TO THE TASK I REQUIRE OF YOU.
YOU CHOSE THEM WISELY. WELL DONE, BROTHER.
STOP CALLING ME THAT!
YOU ARE NOTHING BUT AN ABOMINATION.
A MISTAKE.
YOU SHOULD NOT SAY SUCH THINGS.
OR WHAT?! YOU'LL KILL ME AGAIN?

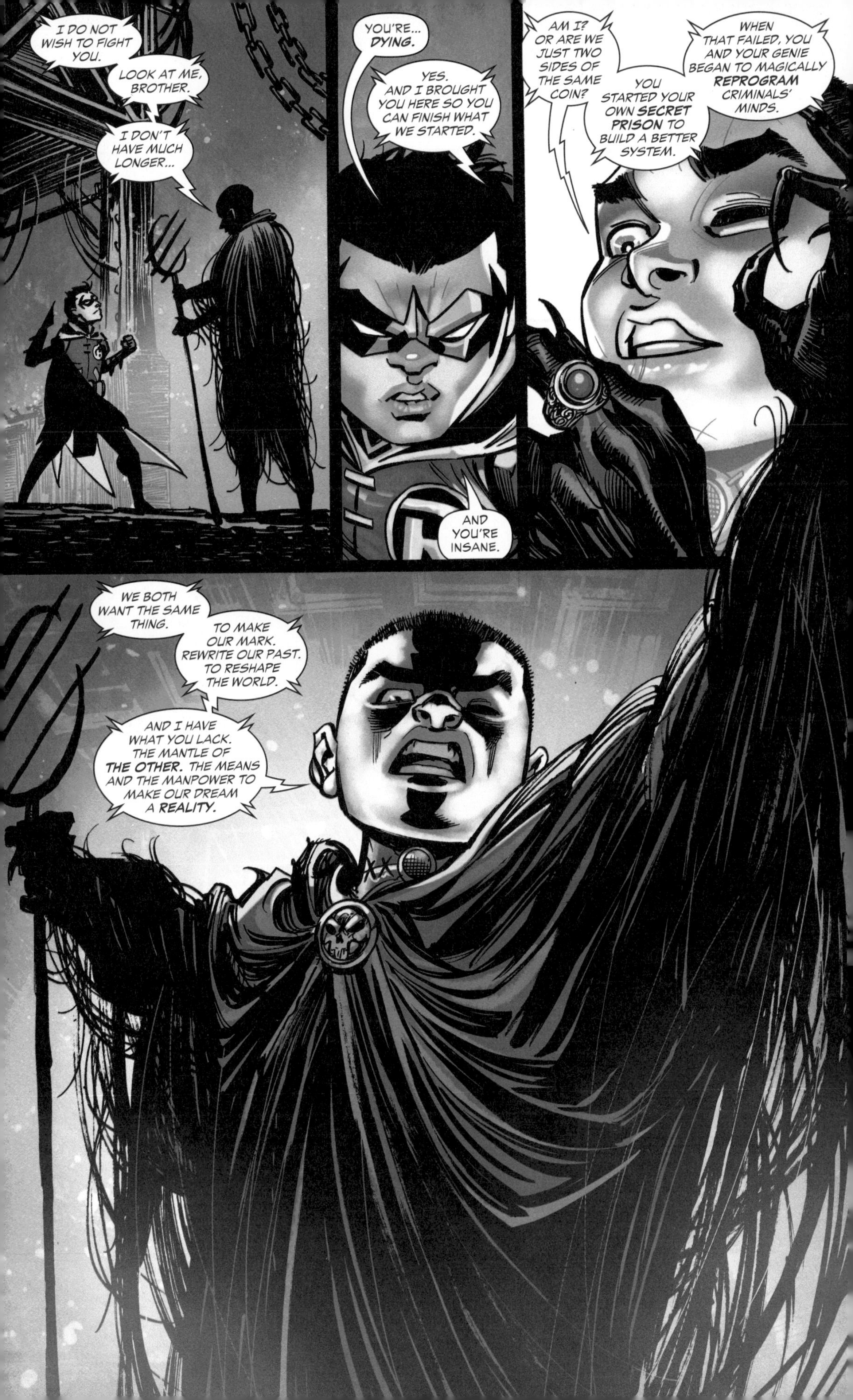
I DO NOT WISH TO FIGHT YOU.
LOOK AT ME, BROTHER.
I DON'T HAVE MUCH LONGER...
YOU'RE... DYING.
YES. AND I BROUGHT YOU HERE SO YOU CAN FINISH WHAT WE STARTED.
AND YOU'RE INSANE.
AM I? OR ARE WE JUST TWO SIDES OF THE SAME COIN?
YOU STARTED YOUR OWN SECRET PRISON TO BUILD A BETTER SYSTEM.
WHEN THAT FAILED, YOU AND YOUR GENIE BEGAN TO MAGICALLY REPROGRAM CRIMINALS' MINDS.
WE BOTH WANT THE SAME THING.
TO MAKE OUR MARK. REWRITE OUR PAST. TO RESHAPE THE WORLD.
AND I HAVE WHAT YOU LACK. THE MANTLE OF THE OTHER. THE MEANS AND THE MANPOWER TO MAKE OUR DREAM A REALITY.

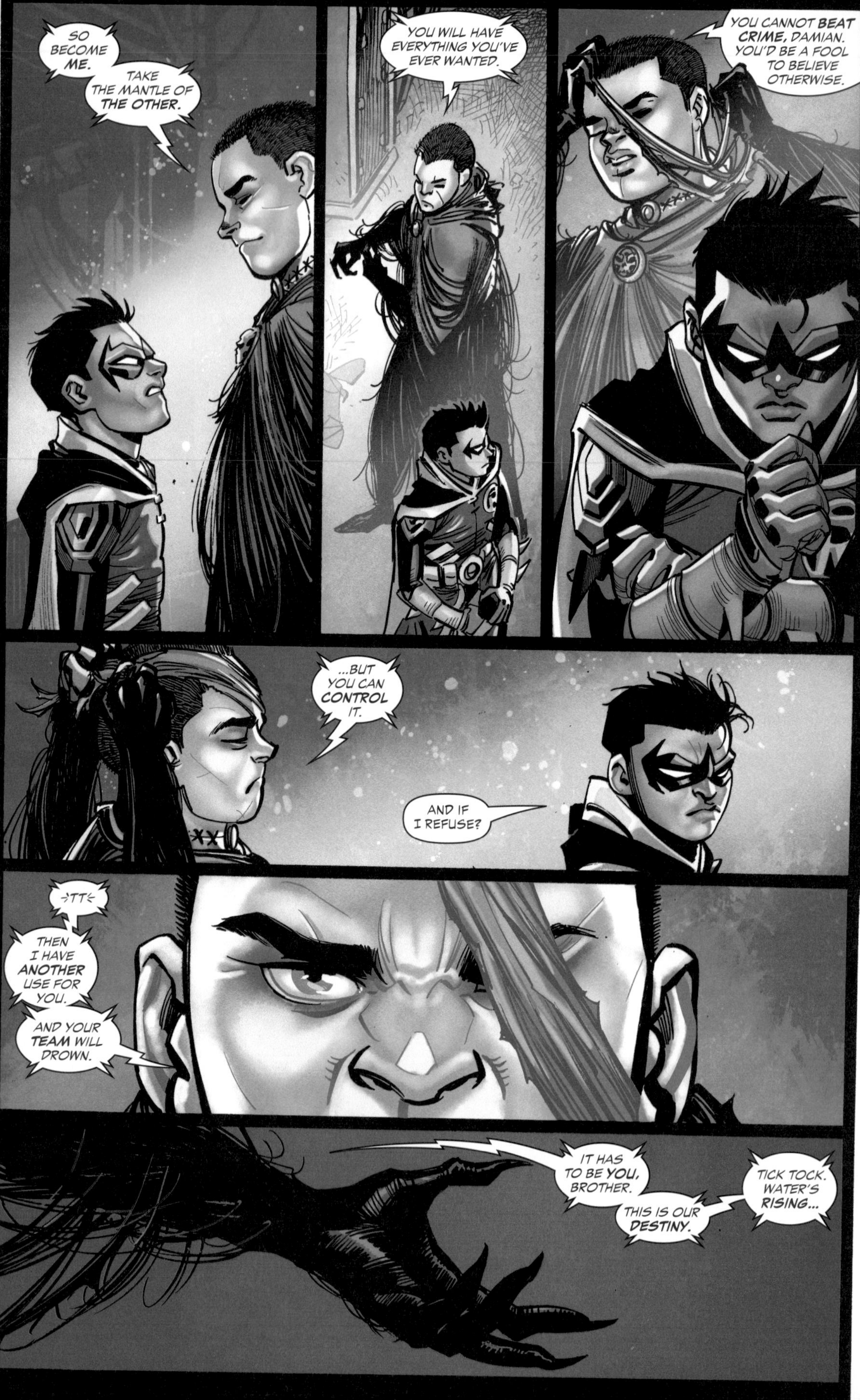
SO BECOME ME.
TAKE THE MANTLE OF THE OTHER.
YOU WILL HAVE EVERYTHING YOU'VE EVER WANTED.
YOU CANNOT BEAT CRIME, DAMIAN. YOU'D BE A FOOL TO BELIEVE OTHERWISE.
...BUT YOU CAN CONTROL IT.
AND IF I REFUSE?
TT
THEN I HAVE ANOTHER USE FOR YOU.
AND YOUR TEAM WILL DROWN.
IT HAS TO BE YOU, BROTHER.
THIS IS OUR DESTINY.
TICK TOCK. WATER'S RISING...

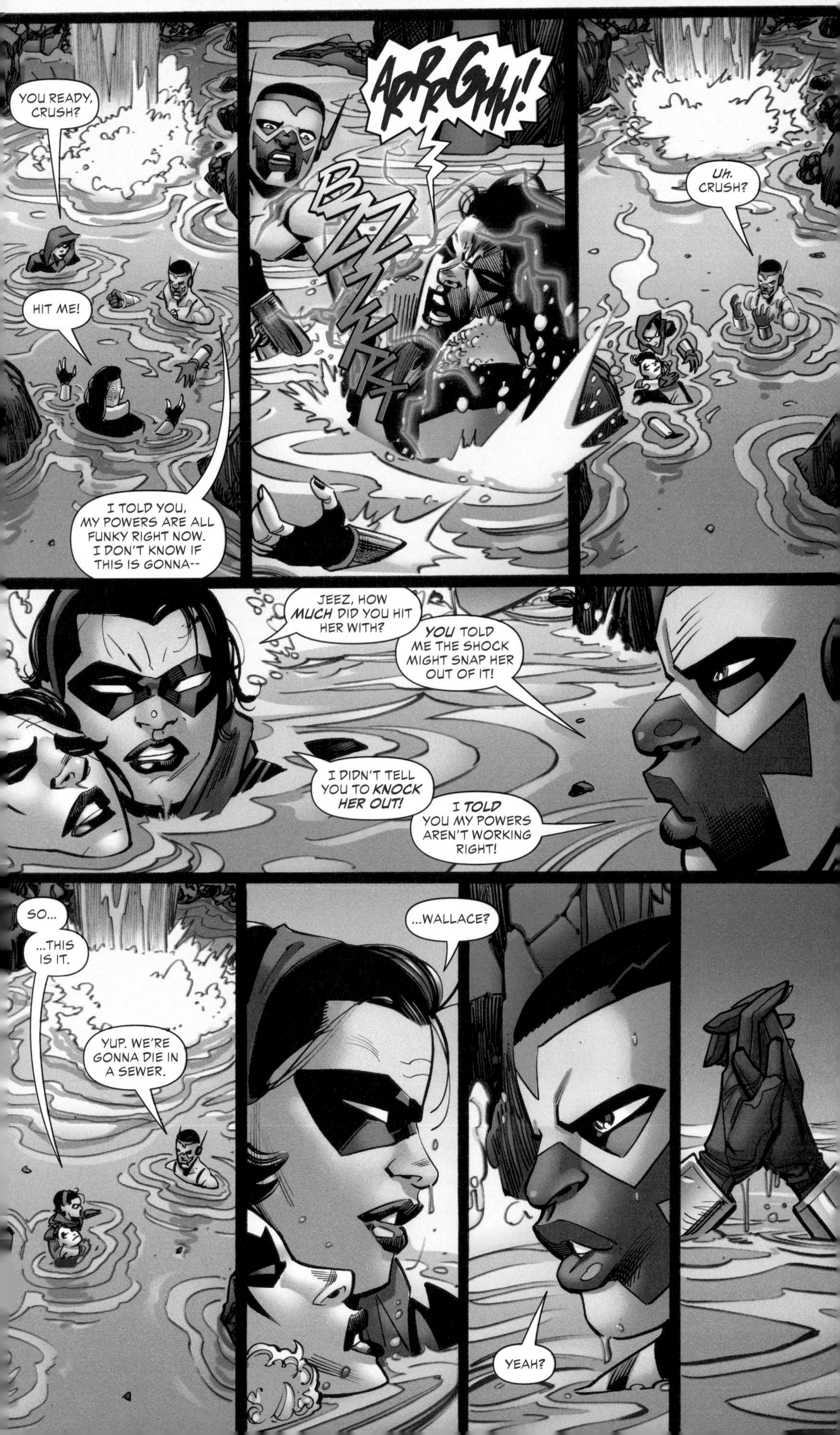
YOU READY, CRUSH?
HIT ME!
I TOLD YOU, MY POWERS ARE ALL FUNKY RIGHT NOW. I DON'T KNOW IF THIS IS GONNA--
ARRRGHH!
BZZWKRK
Uh. CRUSH?
JEEZ, HOW MUCH DID YOU HIT HER WITH?
YOU TOLD ME THE SHOCK MIGHT SNAP HER OUT OF IT!
I DIDN'T TELL YOU TO KNOCK HER OUT!
I TOLD YOU MY POWERS AREN'T WORKING RIGHT!
SO...
...THIS IS IT.
YUP. WE'RE GONNA DIE IN A SEWER.
...WALLACE?
YEAH?

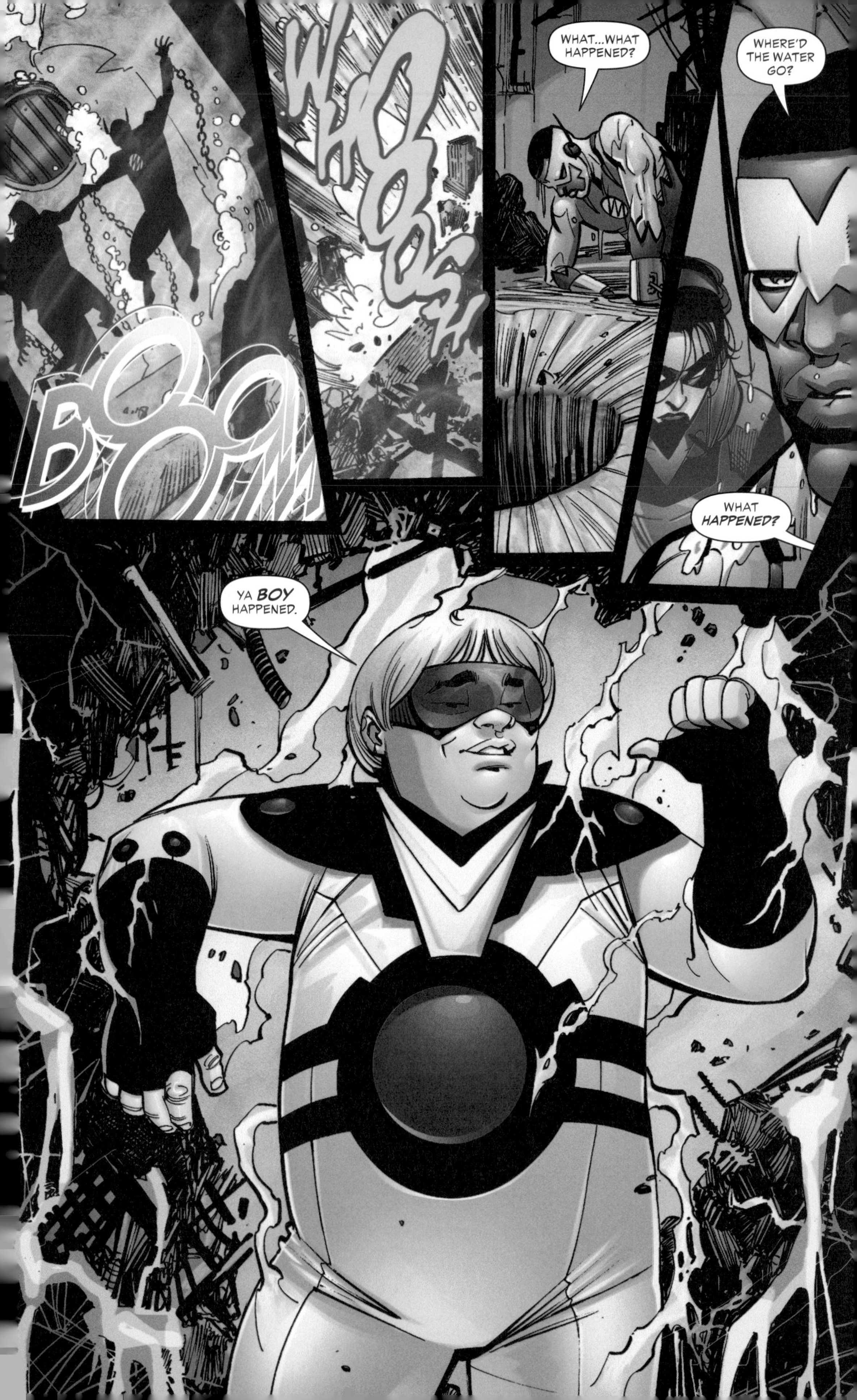
BOOOM
WHOOSH
WHAT...WHAT HAPPENED?
WHERE'D THE WATER GO?
WHAT HAPPENED?
YA BOY HAPPENED.

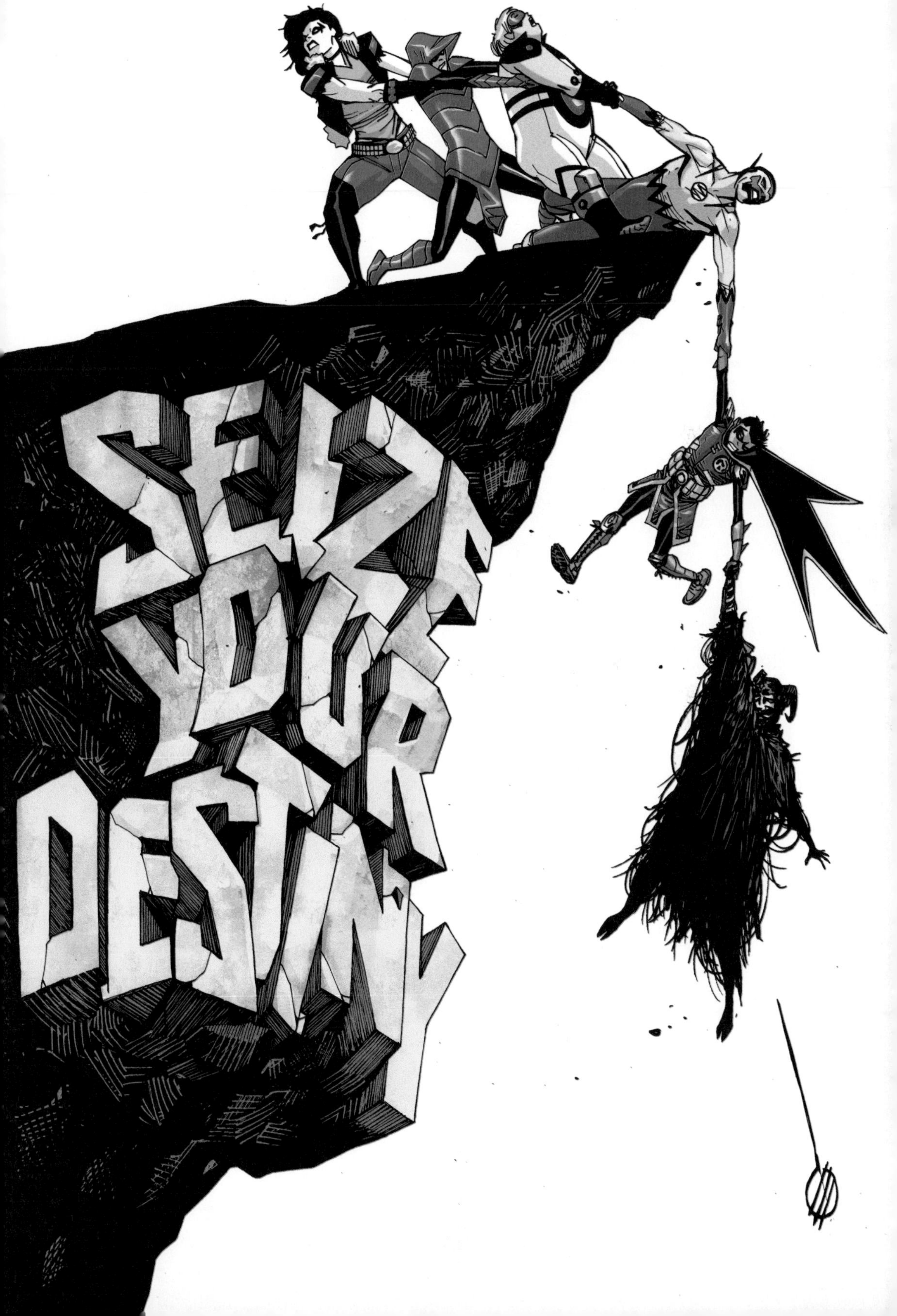
SEIZE YOUR DESTINY

SEIZE YOUR DESTINY

TEEN TITANS

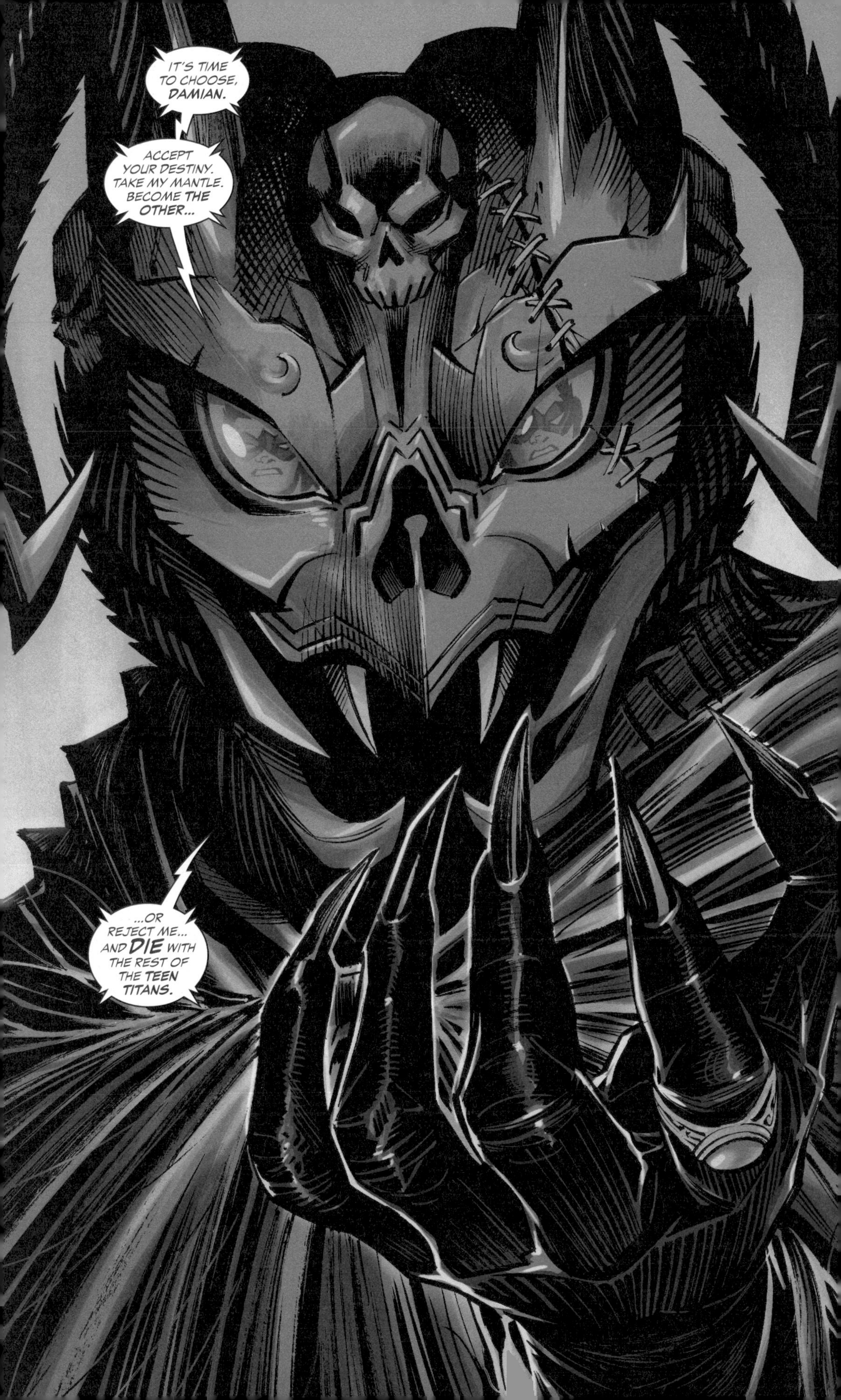
IT'S TIME TO CHOOSE, DAMIAN.
ACCEPT YOUR DESTINY. TAKE MY MANTLE. BECOME THE OTHER...
...OR REJECT ME... AND DIE WITH THE REST OF THE TEEN TITANS.

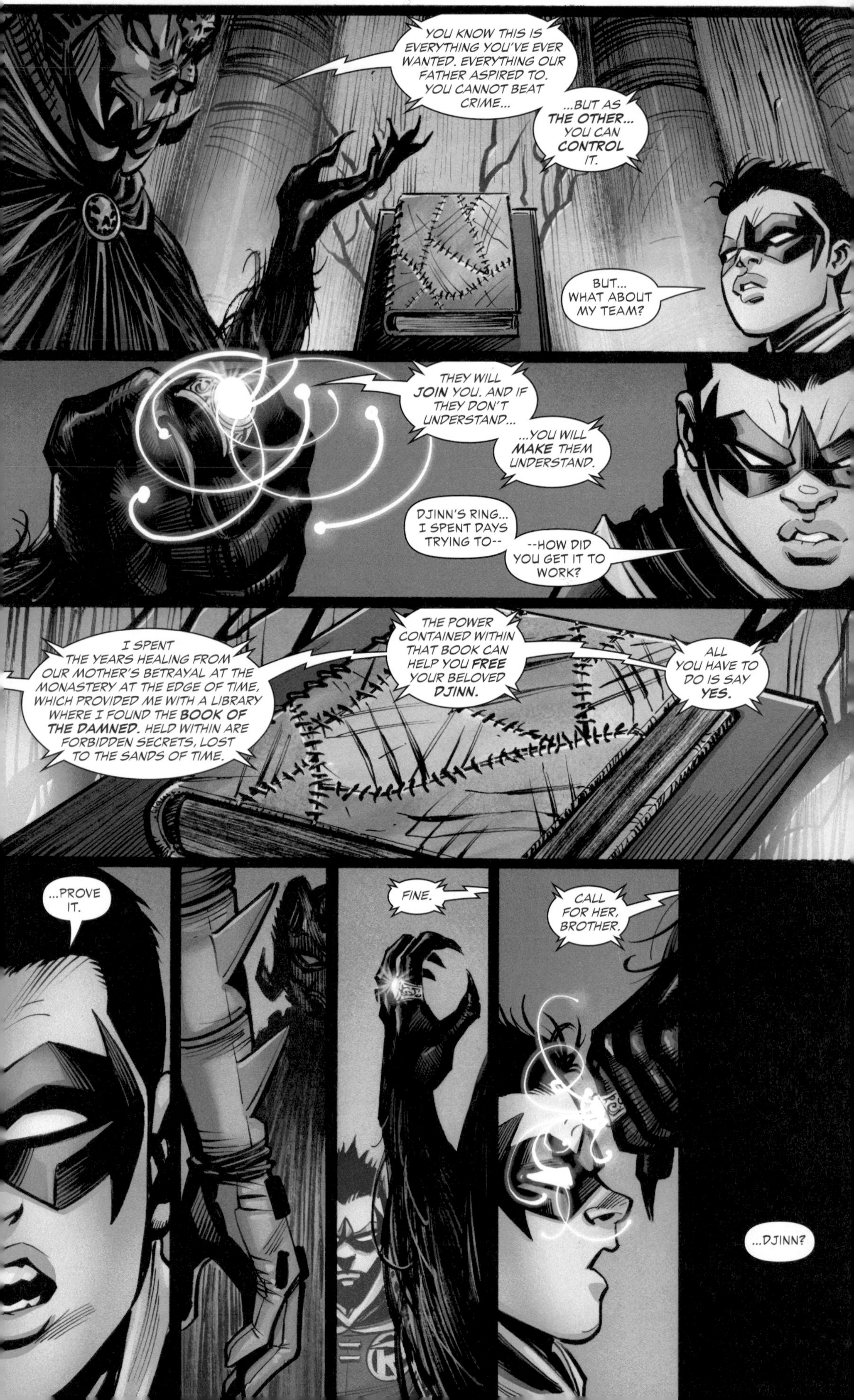
YOU KNOW THIS IS EVERYTHING YOU'VE EVER WANTED. EVERYTHING OUR FATHER ASPIRED TO. YOU CANNOT BEAT CRIME...
...BUT AS THE OTHER... YOU CAN CONTROL IT.
BUT... WHAT ABOUT MY TEAM?
THEY WILL JOIN YOU. AND IF THEY DON'T UNDERSTAND...
...YOU WILL MAKE THEM UNDERSTAND.
DJINN'S RING... I SPENT DAYS TRYING TO--
--HOW DID YOU GET IT TO WORK?
I SPENT THE YEARS HEALING FROM OUR MOTHER'S BETRAYAL AT THE MONASTERY AT THE EDGE OF TIME, WHICH PROVIDED ME WITH A LIBRARY WHERE I FOUND THE BOOK OF THE DAMNED. HELD WITHIN ARE FORBIDDEN SECRETS, LOST TO THE SANDS OF TIME.
THE POWER CONTAINED WITHIN THAT BOOK CAN HELP YOU FREE YOUR BELOVED DJINN.
ALL YOU HAVE TO DO IS SAY YES.
...PROVE IT.
FINE.
CALL FOR HER, BROTHER.
...DJINN?

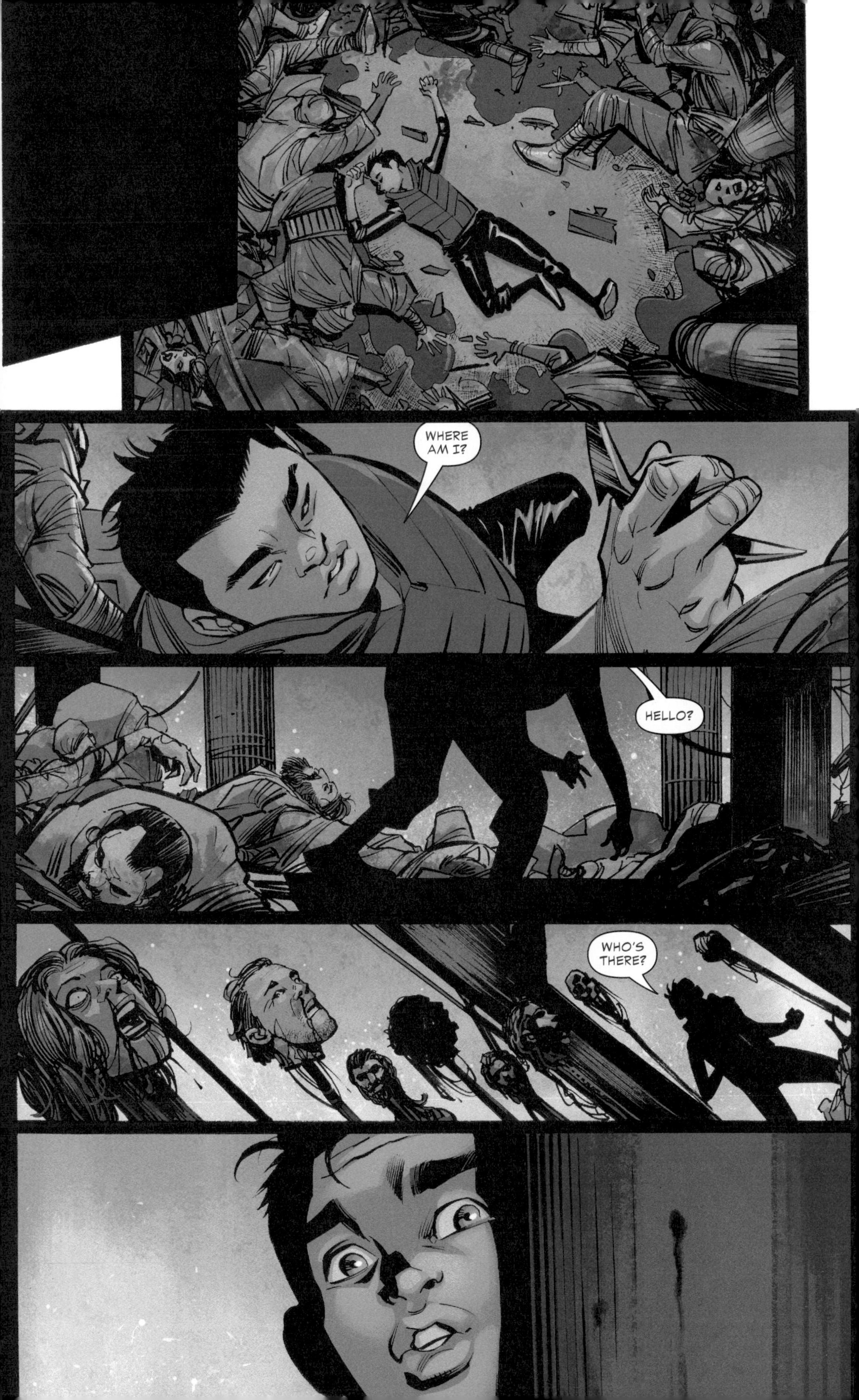
WHERE AM I?
HELLO?
WHO'S THERE?

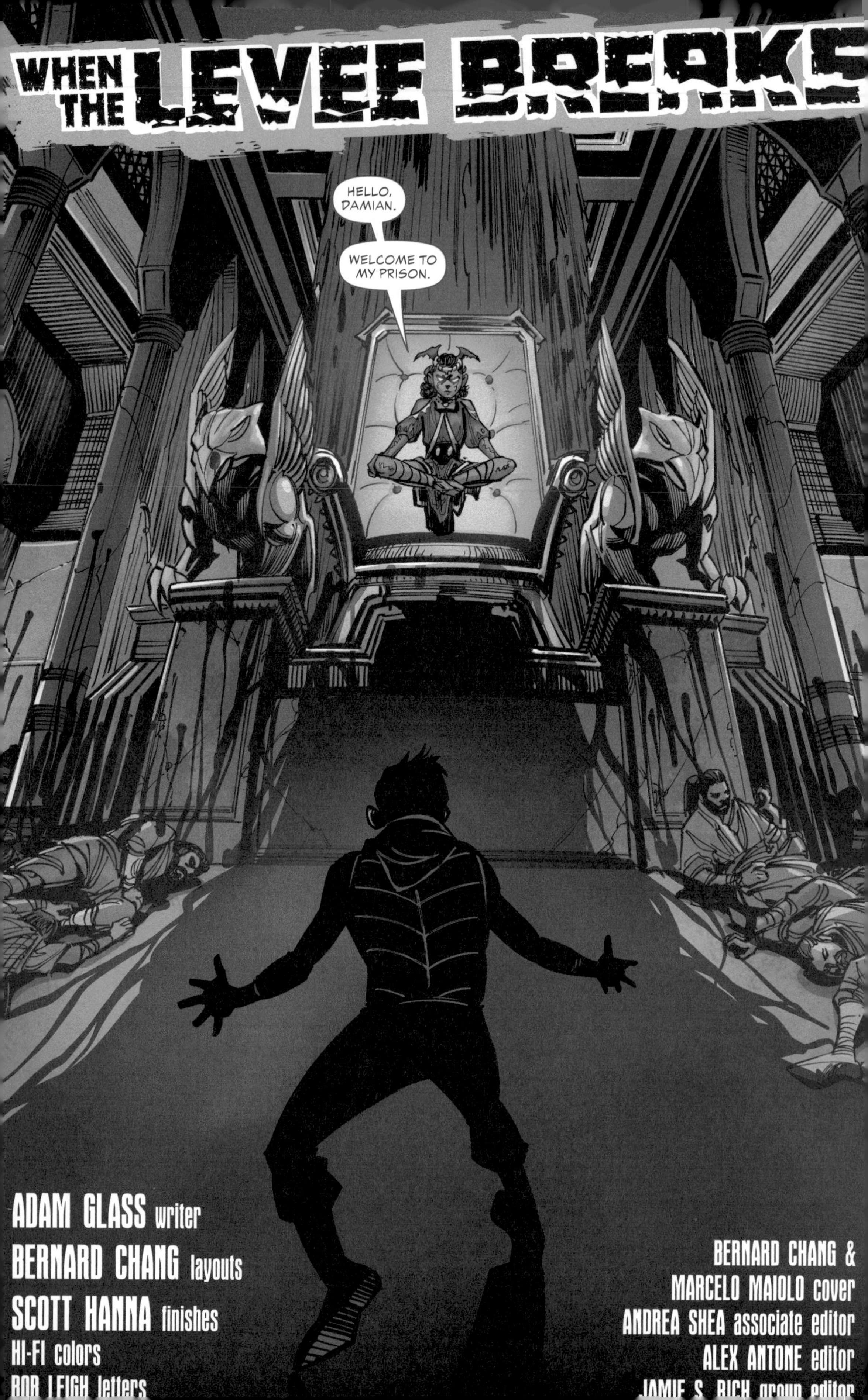
WHEN THE LEVEE BREAKS
HELLO, DAMIAN.
WELCOME TO MY PRISON.
ADAM GLASS writer
BERNARD CHANG layouts
SCOTT HANNA finishes
HI-FI colors
BOB LEIGH letters
BERNARD CHANG & MARCELO MAIOLO cover
ANDREA SHEA associate editor
ALEX ANTONE editor
JAMIE S. RICH group editor

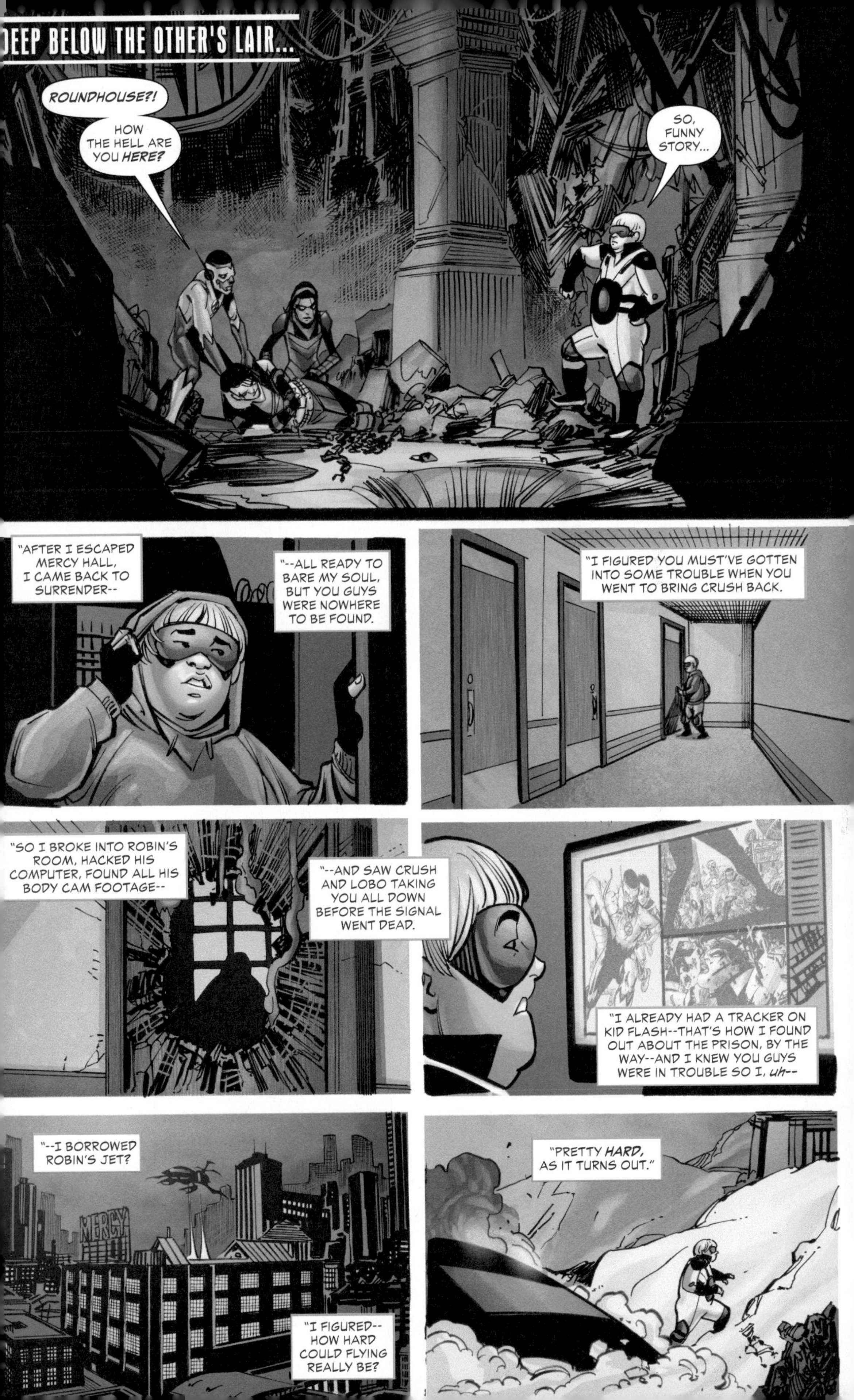
DEEP BELOW THE OTHER'S LAIR...
ROUNDHOUSE?!
HOW THE HELL ARE YOU HERE?
SO, FUNNY STORY...
"AFTER I ESCAPED MERCY HALL, I CAME BACK TO SURRENDER--
"--ALL READY TO BARE MY SOUL, BUT YOU GUYS WERE NOWHERE TO BE FOUND.
"I FIGURED YOU MUST'VE GOTTEN INTO SOME TROUBLE WHEN YOU WENT TO BRING CRUSH BACK.
"SO I BROKE INTO ROBIN'S ROOM, HACKED HIS COMPUTER, FOUND ALL HIS BODY CAM FOOTAGE--
"--AND SAW CRUSH AND LOBO TAKING YOU ALL DOWN BEFORE THE SIGNAL WENT DEAD.
"I ALREADY HAD A TRACKER ON KID FLASH--THAT'S HOW I FOUND OUT ABOUT THE PRISON, BY THE WAY--AND I KNEW YOU GUYS WERE IN TROUBLE SO I, uh--
"--I BORROWED ROBIN'S JET?
MERCY
"I FIGURED--HOW HARD COULD FLYING REALLY BE?
"PRETTY HARD, AS IT TURNS OUT."

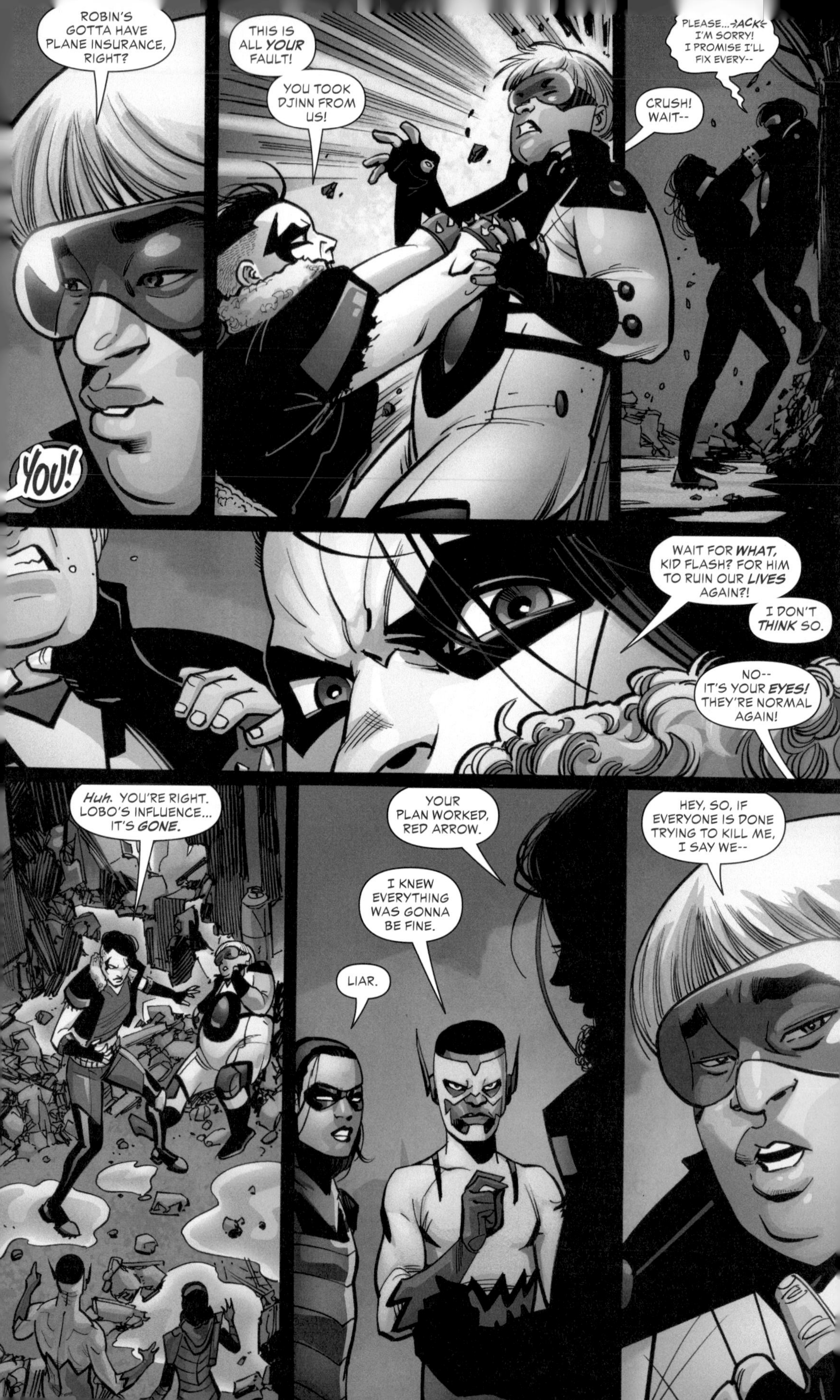
ROBIN'S GOTTA HAVE PLANE INSURANCE, RIGHT?
YOU!
THIS IS ALL YOUR FAULT!
YOU TOOK DJINN FROM US!
PLEASE... ACK I'M SORRY! I PROMISE I'LL FIX EVERY--
CRUSH! WAIT--
WAIT FOR WHAT, KID FLASH? FOR HIM TO RUIN OUR LIVES AGAIN?!
I DON'T THINK SO.
NO-- IT'S YOUR EYES! THEY'RE NORMAL AGAIN!
Huh. YOU'RE RIGHT. LOBO'S INFLUENCE... IT'S GONE.
YOUR PLAN WORKED, RED ARROW.
I KNEW EVERYTHING WAS GONNA BE FINE.
LIAR.
HEY, SO, IF EVERYONE IS DONE TRYING TO KILL ME, I SAY WE--

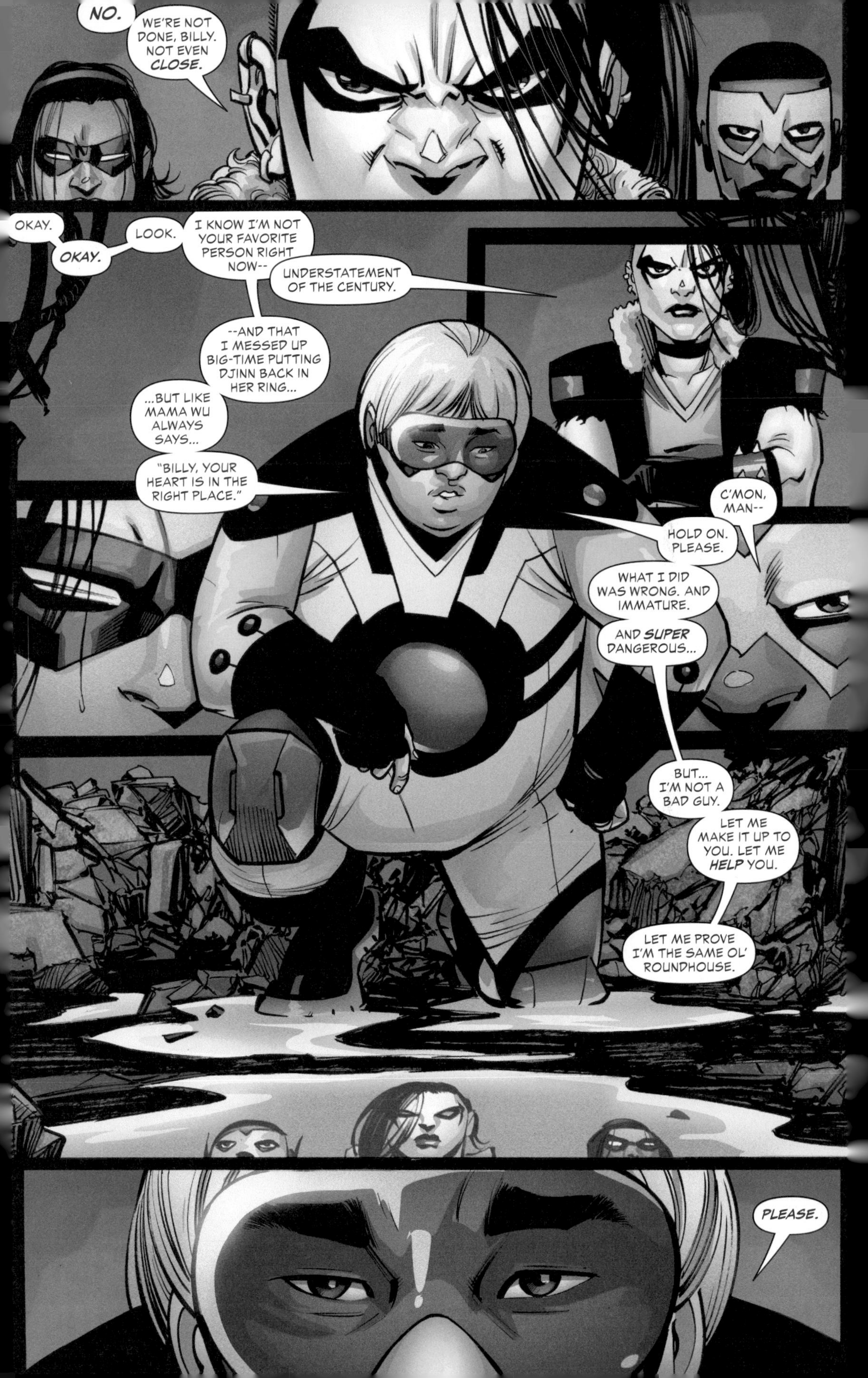
NO.
WE'RE NOT DONE, BILLY. NOT EVEN CLOSE.
OKAY.
OKAY.
LOOK.
I KNOW I'M NOT YOUR FAVORITE PERSON RIGHT NOW--
UNDERSTATEMENT OF THE CENTURY.
--AND THAT I MESSED UP BIG-TIME PUTTING DJINN BACK IN HER RING...
...BUT LIKE MAMA WU ALWAYS SAYS...
"BILLY, YOUR HEART IS IN THE RIGHT PLACE."
C'MON, MAN--
HOLD ON. PLEASE.
WHAT I DID WAS WRONG. AND IMMATURE.
AND SUPER DANGEROUS...
BUT... I'M NOT A BAD GUY.
LET ME MAKE IT UP TO YOU. LET ME HELP YOU.
LET ME PROVE I'M THE SAME OL' ROUNDHOUSE.
PLEASE.

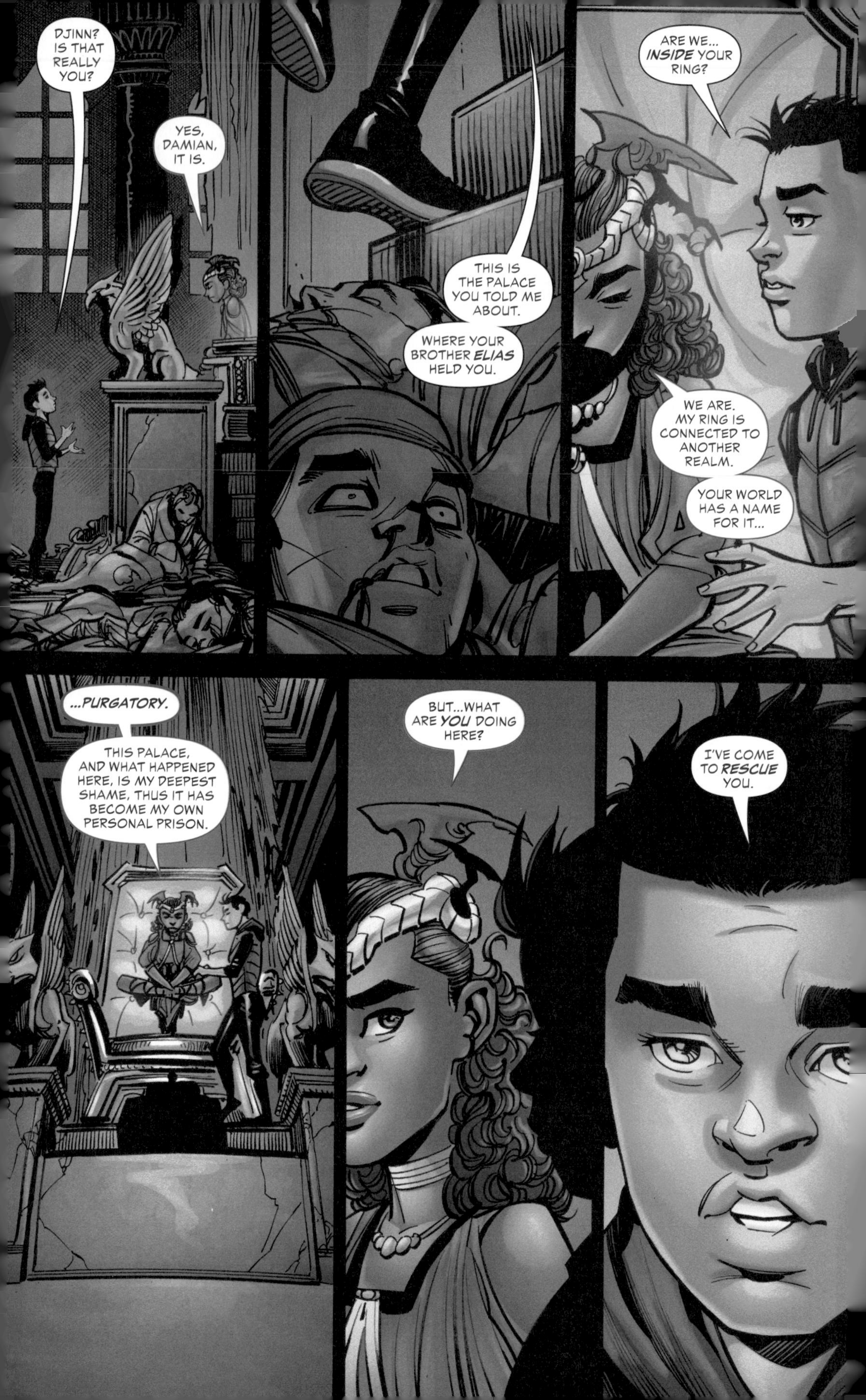
DJINN? IS THAT REALLY YOU?
YES, DAMIAN, IT IS.
THIS IS THE PALACE YOU TOLD ME ABOUT.
WHERE YOUR BROTHER ELIAS HELD YOU.
ARE WE... INSIDE YOUR RING?
WE ARE. MY RING IS CONNECTED TO ANOTHER REALM.
YOUR WORLD HAS A NAME FOR IT...
...PURGATORY.
THIS PALACE, AND WHAT HAPPENED HERE, IS MY DEEPEST SHAME, THUS IT HAS BECOME MY OWN PERSONAL PRISON.
BUT...WHAT ARE YOU DOING HERE?
I'VE COME TO RESCUE YOU.

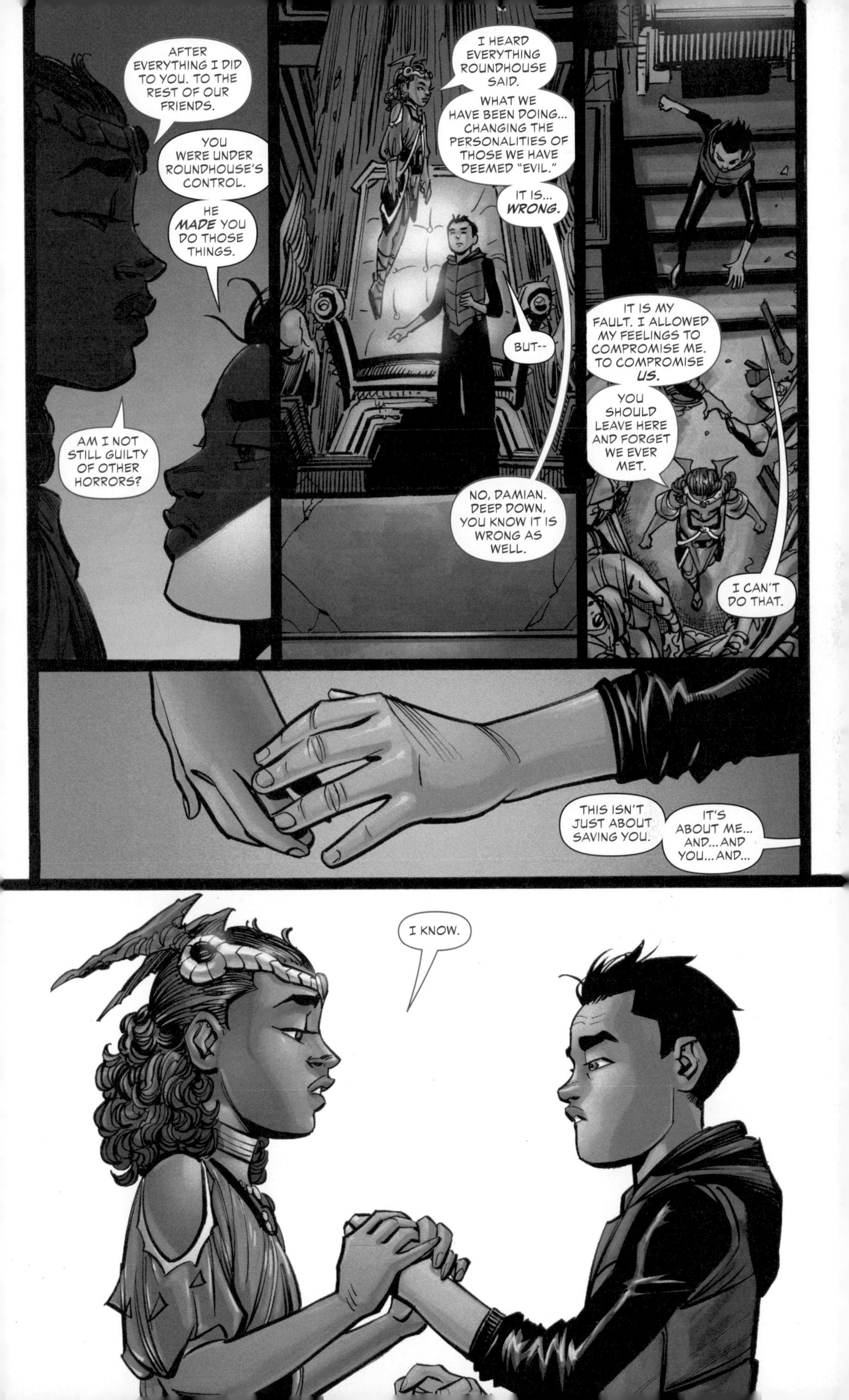
AFTER EVERYTHING I DID TO YOU. TO THE REST OF OUR FRIENDS.
YOU WERE UNDER ROUNDHOUSE'S CONTROL.
HE MADE YOU DO THOSE THINGS.
AM I NOT STILL GUILTY OF OTHER HORRORS?
I HEARD EVERYTHING ROUNDHOUSE SAID.
WHAT WE HAVE BEEN DOING... CHANGING THE PERSONALITIES OF THOSE WE HAVE DEEMED "EVIL."
IT IS... WRONG.
BUT--
NO, DAMIAN. DEEP DOWN, YOU KNOW IT IS WRONG AS WELL.
IT IS MY FAULT. I ALLOWED MY FEELINGS TO COMPROMISE ME. TO COMPROMISE US.
YOU SHOULD LEAVE HERE AND FORGET WE EVER MET.
I CAN'T DO THAT.
THIS ISN'T JUST ABOUT SAVING YOU.
IT'S ABOUT ME... AND... AND YOU... AND...
I KNOW.

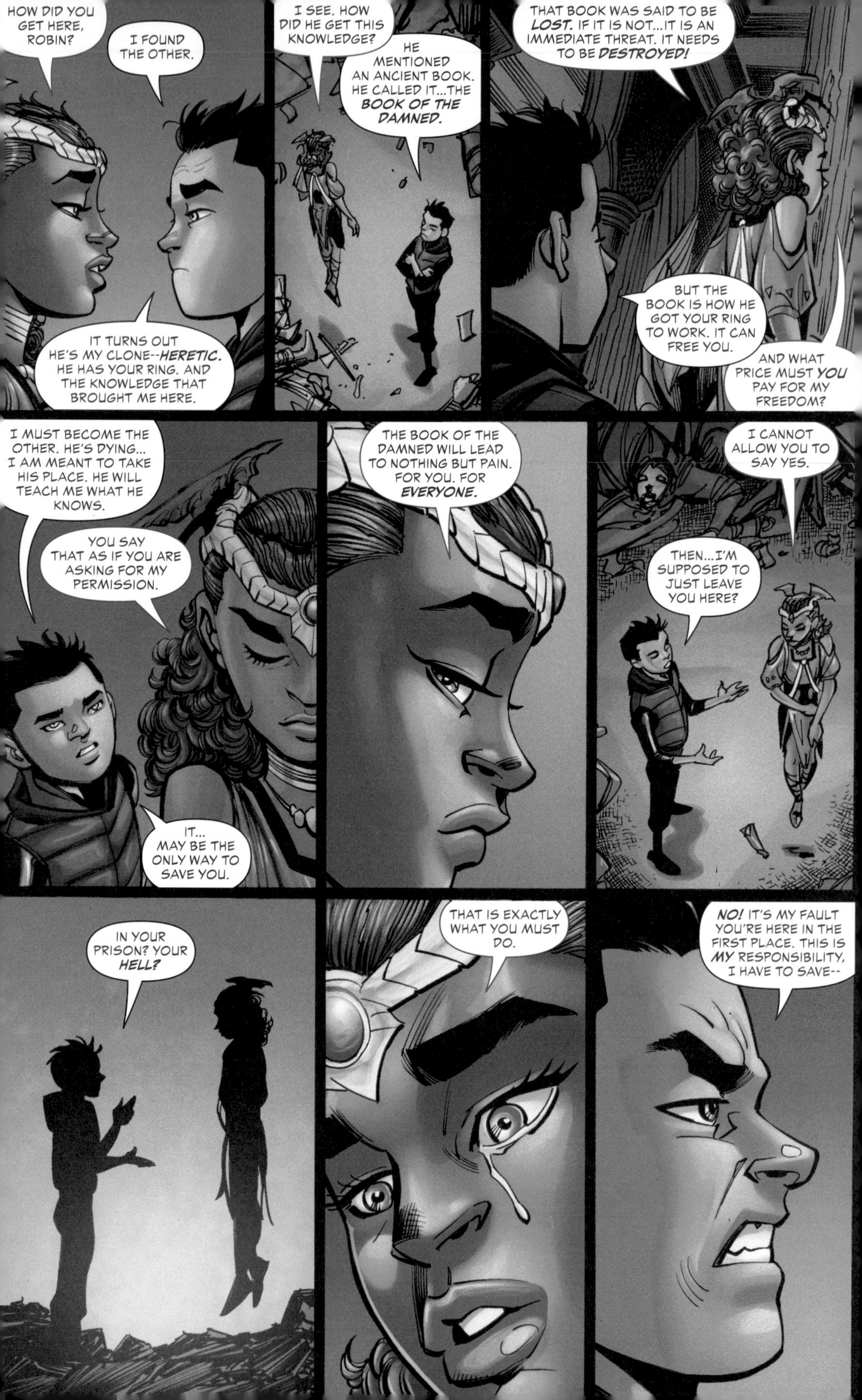
HOW DID YOU GET HERE, ROBIN?
I FOUND THE OTHER.
IT TURNS OUT HE'S MY CLONE--*HERETIC.* HE HAS YOUR RING. AND THE KNOWLEDGE THAT BROUGHT ME HERE.
I SEE. HOW DID HE GET THIS KNOWLEDGE?
HE MENTIONED AN ANCIENT BOOK. HE CALLED IT...THE *BOOK OF THE DAMNED.*
THAT BOOK WAS SAID TO BE *LOST.* IF IT IS NOT...IT IS AN IMMEDIATE THREAT. IT NEEDS TO BE *DESTROYED!*
BUT THE BOOK IS HOW HE GOT YOUR RING TO WORK. IT CAN FREE YOU.
AND WHAT PRICE MUST *YOU* PAY FOR MY FREEDOM?
I MUST BECOME THE OTHER. HE'S DYING... I AM MEANT TO TAKE HIS PLACE. HE WILL TEACH ME WHAT HE KNOWS.
YOU SAY THAT AS IF YOU ARE ASKING FOR MY PERMISSION.
IT... MAY BE THE ONLY WAY TO SAVE YOU.
THE BOOK OF THE DAMNED WILL LEAD TO NOTHING BUT PAIN. FOR YOU. FOR *EVERYONE.*
I CANNOT ALLOW YOU TO SAY YES.
THEN...I'M SUPPOSED TO JUST LEAVE YOU HERE?
IN YOUR PRISON? YOUR *HELL?*
THAT IS EXACTLY WHAT YOU MUST DO.
NO! IT'S MY FAULT YOU'RE HERE IN THE FIRST PLACE. THIS IS *MY* RESPONSIBILITY. I HAVE TO SAVE--

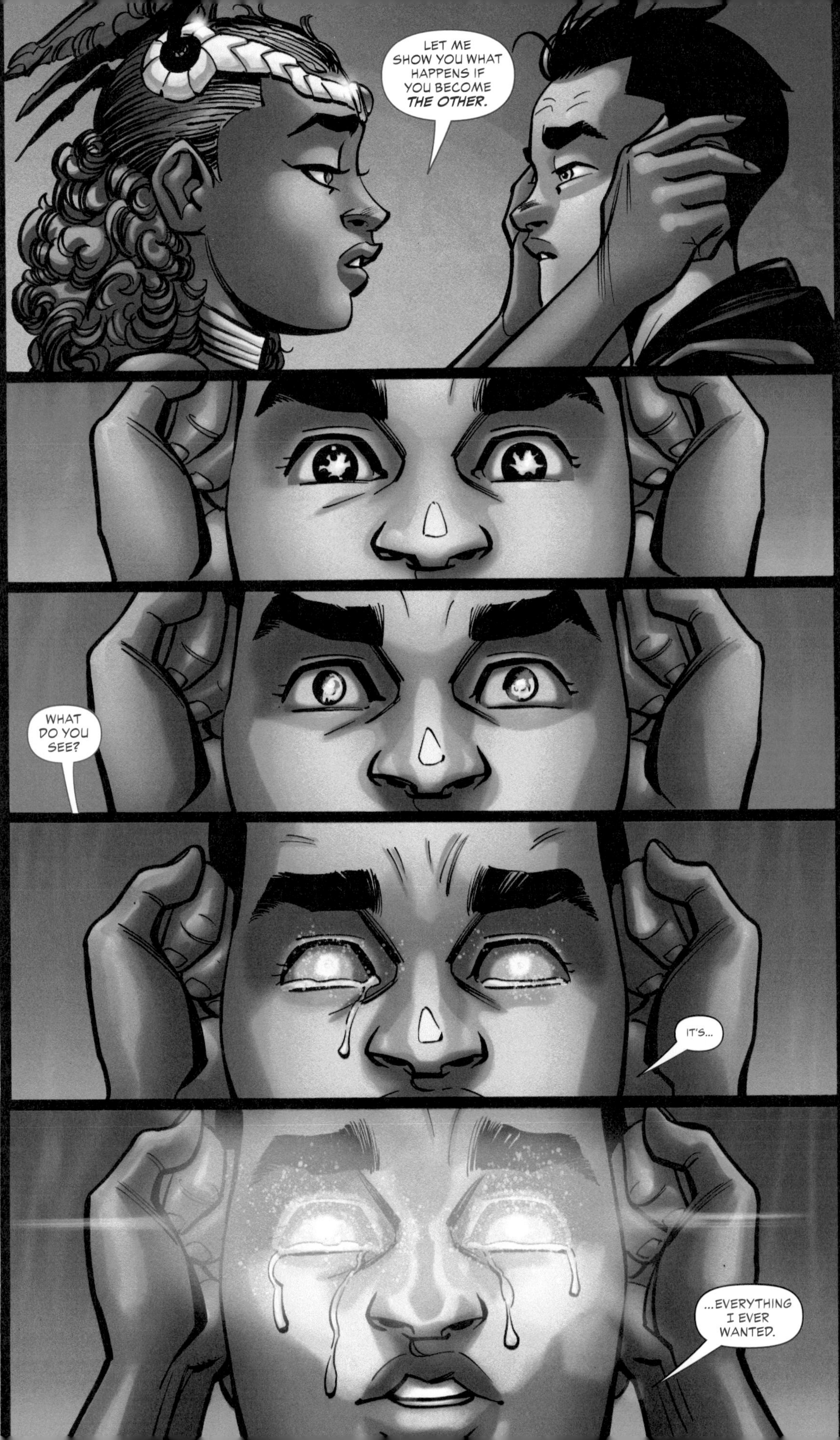
LET ME SHOW YOU WHAT HAPPENS IF YOU BECOME *THE OTHER.*
WHAT DO YOU SEE?
IT'S...
...EVERYTHING I EVER WANTED.

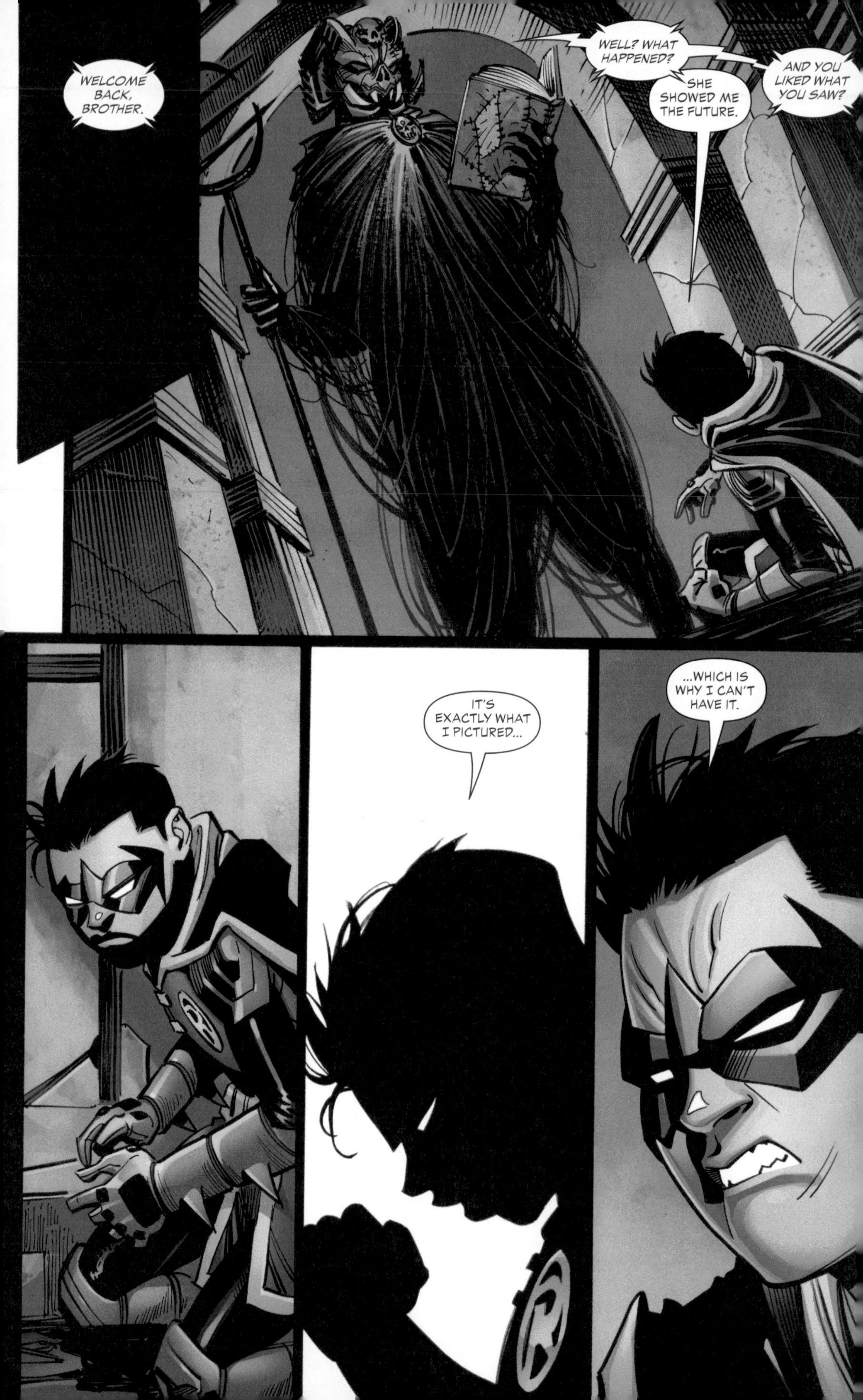
WELCOME BACK, BROTHER.
WELL? WHAT HAPPENED?
SHE SHOWED ME THE FUTURE.
AND YOU LIKED WHAT YOU SAW?
IT'S EXACTLY WHAT I PICTURED...
...WHICH IS WHY I CAN'T HAVE IT.

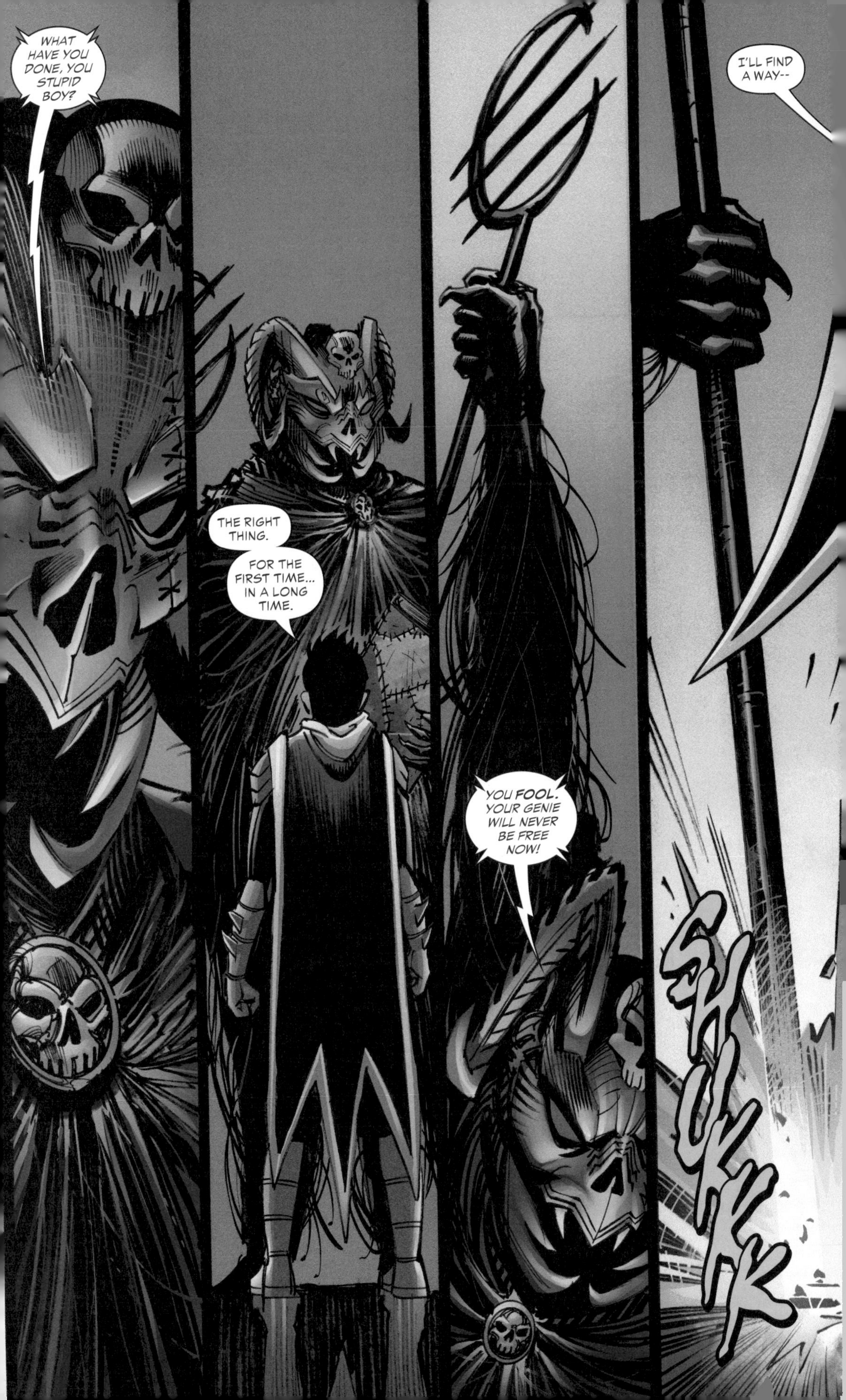
WHAT HAVE YOU DONE, YOU STUPID BOY?
THE RIGHT THING.
FOR THE FIRST TIME... IN A LONG TIME.
YOU **FOOL**. YOUR GENIE WILL NEVER BE FREE NOW!
I'LL FIND A WAY--
SHUKK

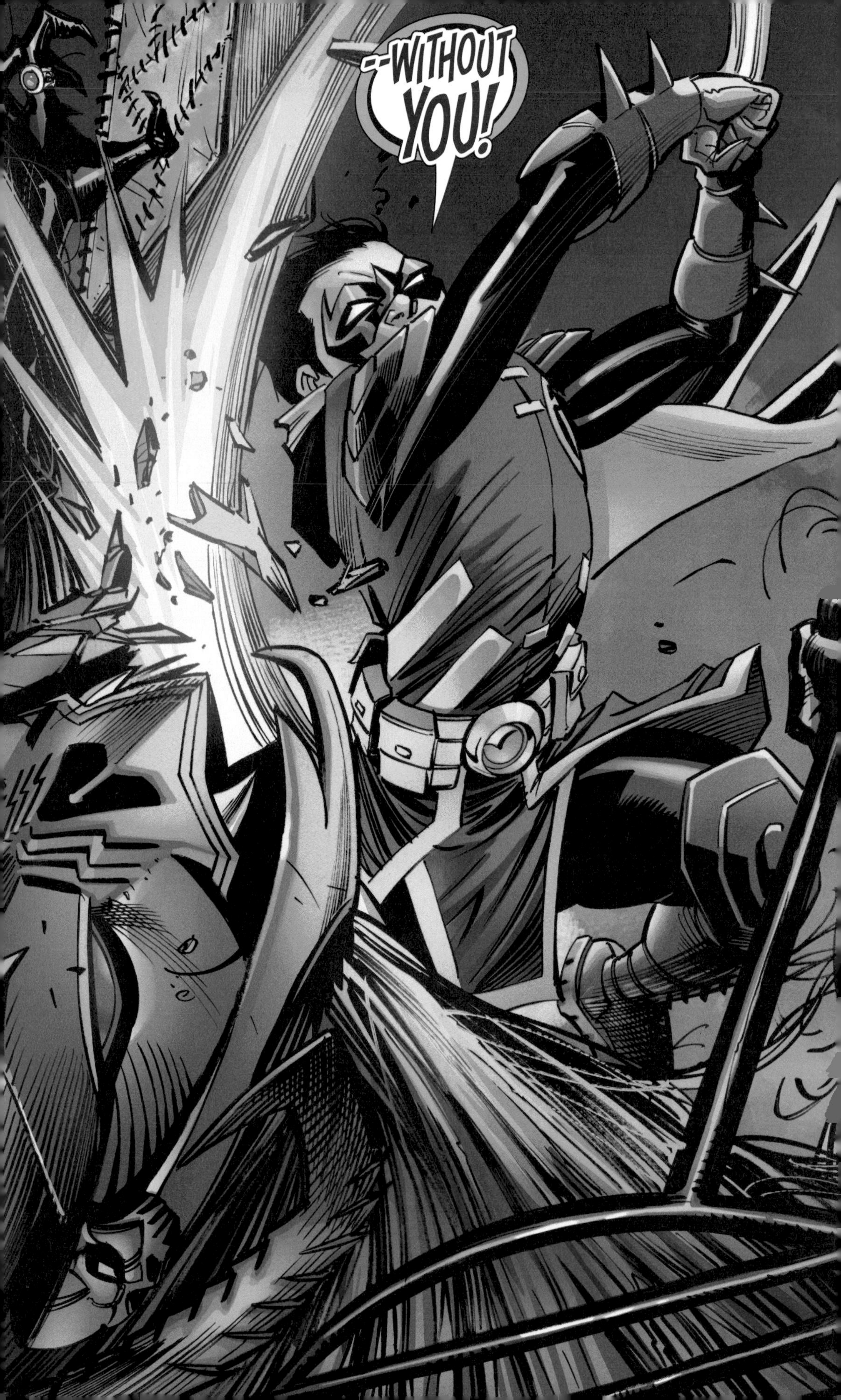
--WITHOUT YOU!

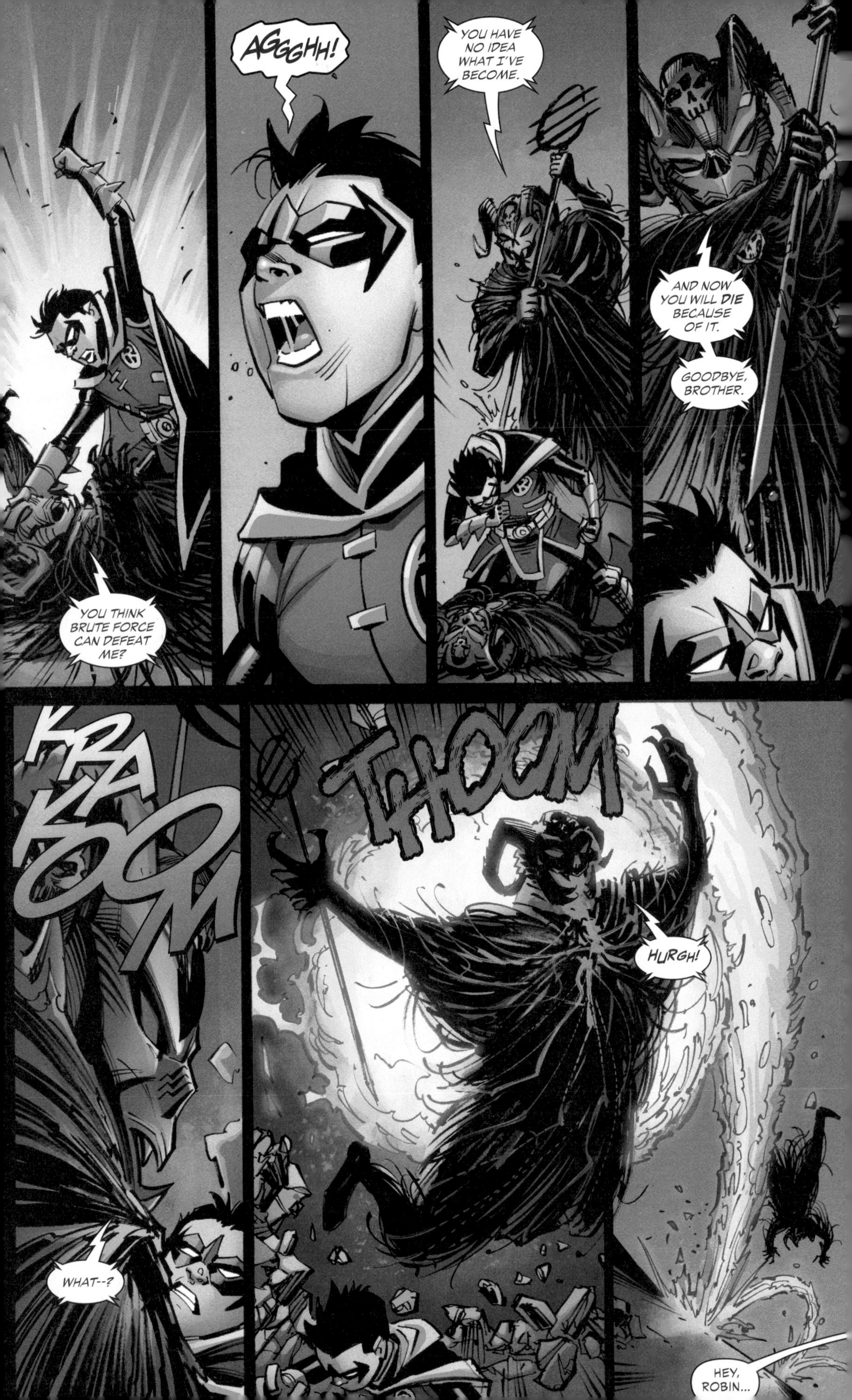
AGGGHH!
YOU THINK BRUTE FORCE CAN DEFEAT ME?
YOU HAVE NO IDEA WHAT I'VE BECOME.
AND NOW YOU WILL **DIE** BECAUSE OF IT.
GOODBYE, BROTHER.
KRA-BOOM
WHAT--?
THOOM
HURGH!
HEY, ROBIN...

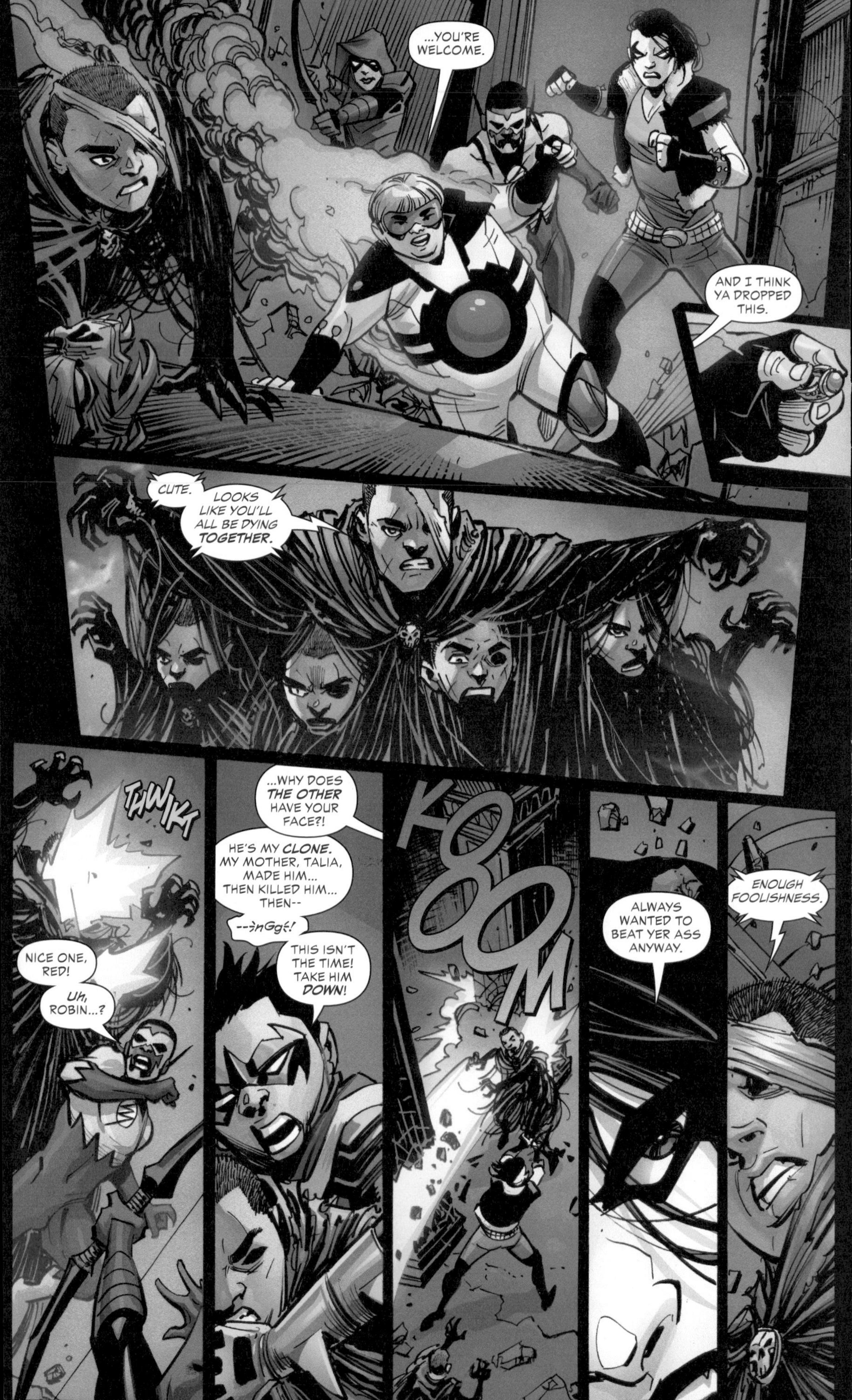
...YOU'RE WELCOME.
AND I THINK YA DROPPED THIS.
CUTE.
LOOKS LIKE YOU'LL ALL BE DYING TOGETHER.
THWIKT
NICE ONE, RED!
Uh, ROBIN...?
...WHY DOES THE OTHER HAVE YOUR FACE?!
HE'S MY CLONE. MY MOTHER, TALIA, MADE HIM... THEN KILLED HIM... THEN--
--nGg!
THIS ISN'T THE TIME! TAKE HIM DOWN!
KOOOM
ALWAYS WANTED TO BEAT YER ASS ANYWAY.
ENOUGH FOOLISHNESS.

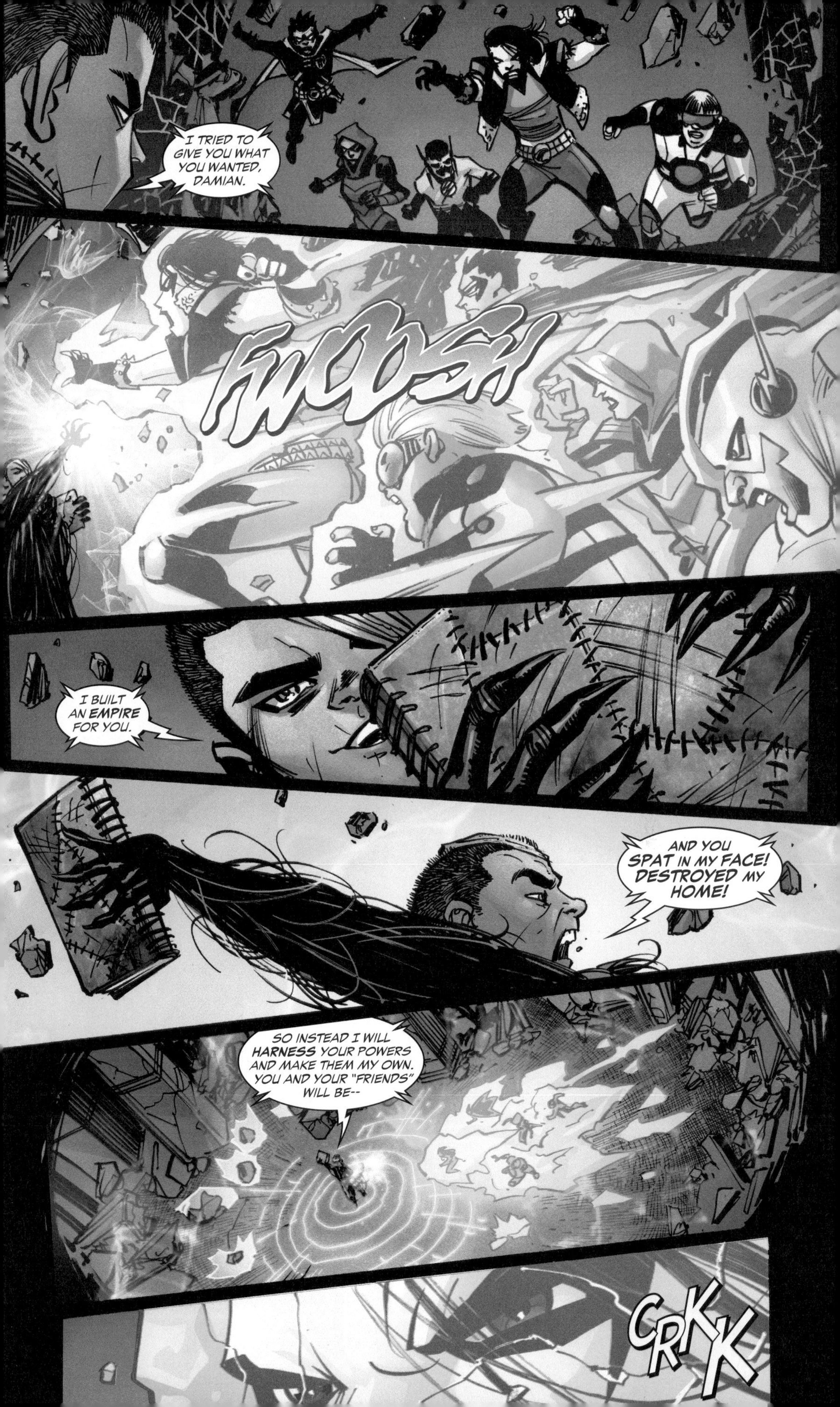

I TRIED TO GIVE YOU WHAT YOU WANTED, DAMIAN.
FWOOSH
I BUILT AN EMPIRE FOR YOU.
AND YOU SPAT IN MY FACE! DESTROYED MY HOME!
SO INSTEAD I WILL HARNESS YOUR POWERS AND MAKE THEM MY OWN. YOU AND YOUR "FRIENDS" WILL BE--
CRKK

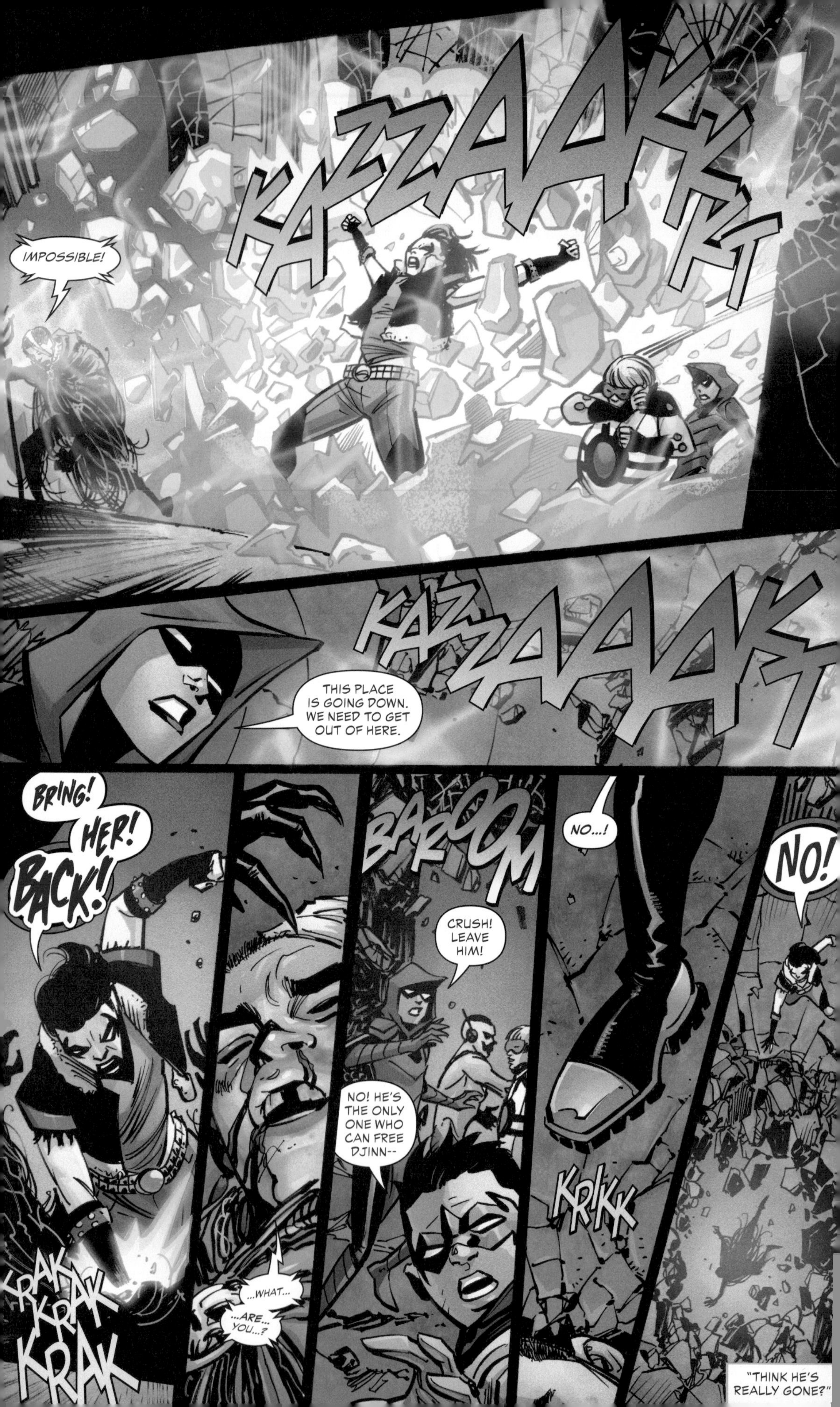
KAZZAAK-KRT
IMPOSSIBLE!
KAZZAAAK-KT
THIS PLACE IS GOING DOWN. WE NEED TO GET OUT OF HERE.
BRING! HER! BACK!
KRAK KRAK KRAK
...WHAT... ...ARE... YOU...?
BAROOM
CRUSH! LEAVE HIM!
NO! HE'S THE ONLY ONE WHO CAN FREE DJINN--
NO...!
KRIKK
NO!
"THINK HE'S REALLY GONE?"

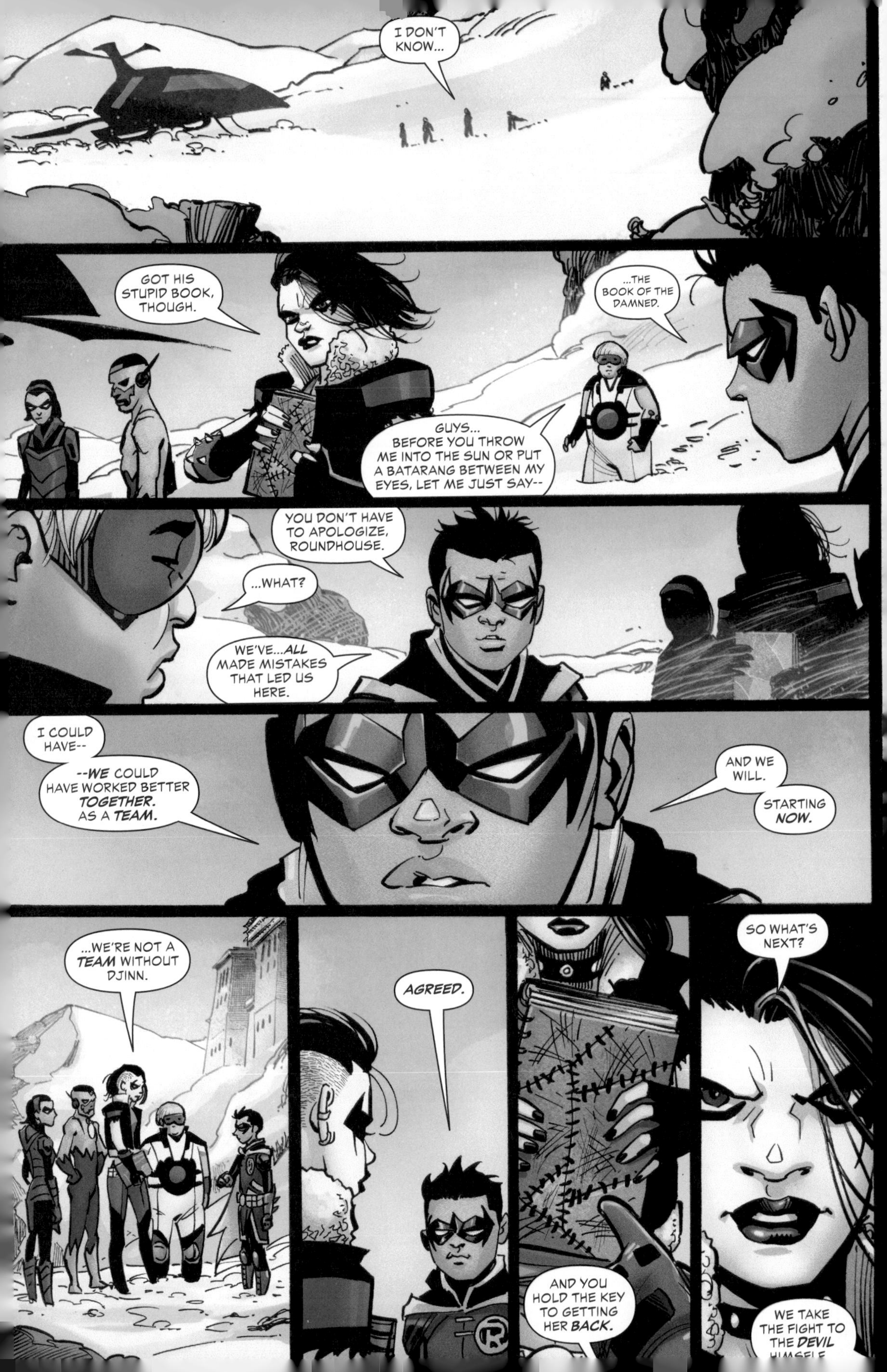

I DON'T KNOW...
GOT HIS STUPID BOOK, THOUGH.
...THE BOOK OF THE DAMNED.
GUYS... BEFORE YOU THROW ME INTO THE SUN OR PUT A BATARANG BETWEEN MY EYES, LET ME JUST SAY--
YOU DON'T HAVE TO APOLOGIZE, ROUNDHOUSE.
...WHAT?
WE'VE...ALL MADE MISTAKES THAT LED US HERE.
I COULD HAVE--
--WE COULD HAVE WORKED BETTER TOGETHER. AS A TEAM.
AND WE WILL.
STARTING NOW.
...WE'RE NOT A TEAM WITHOUT DJINN.
AGREED.
AND YOU HOLD THE KEY TO GETTING HER BACK.
SO WHAT'S NEXT?
WE TAKE THE FIGHT TO THE DEVIL

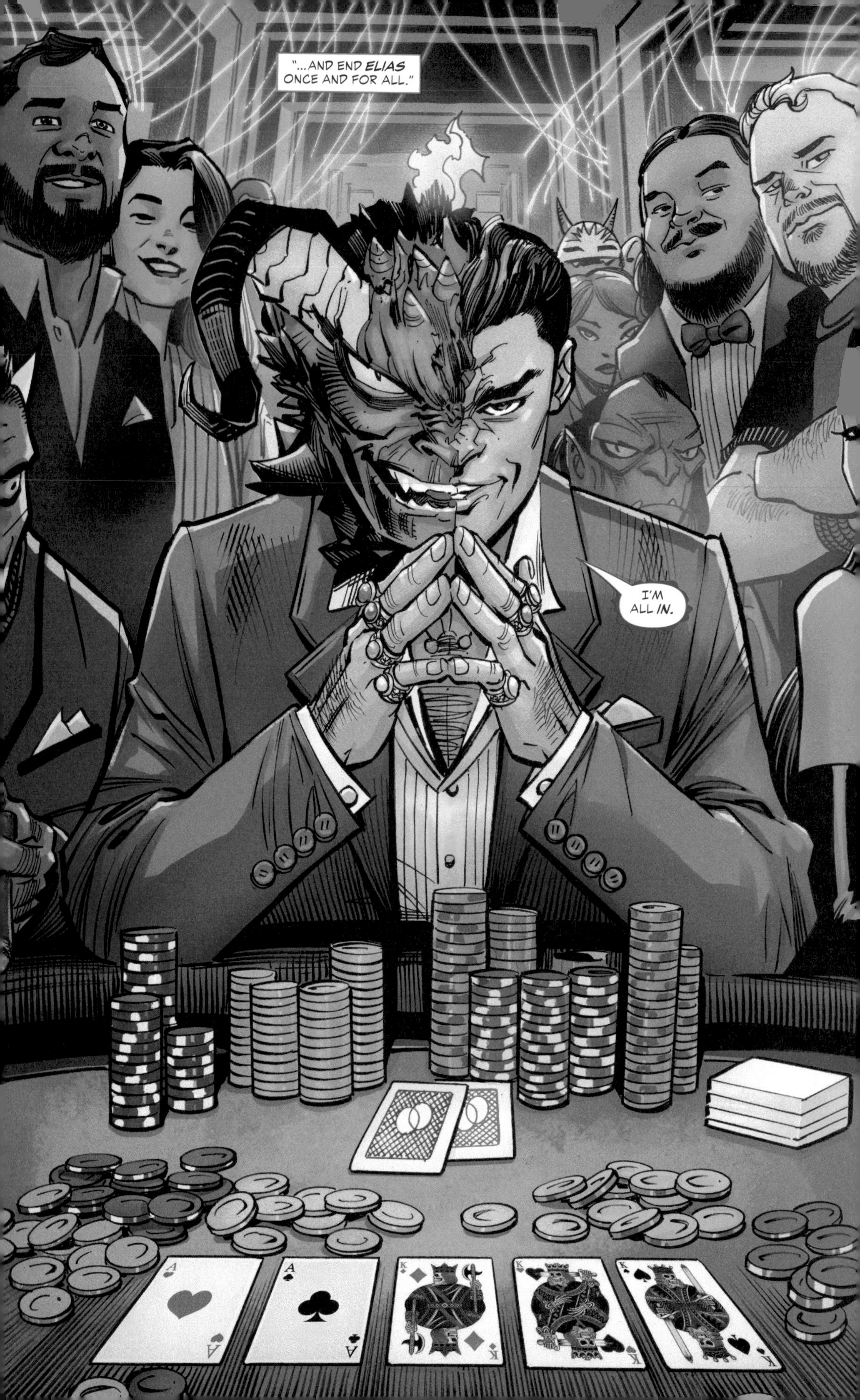
"...AND END ELIAS ONCE AND FOR ALL."
I'M ALL IN.

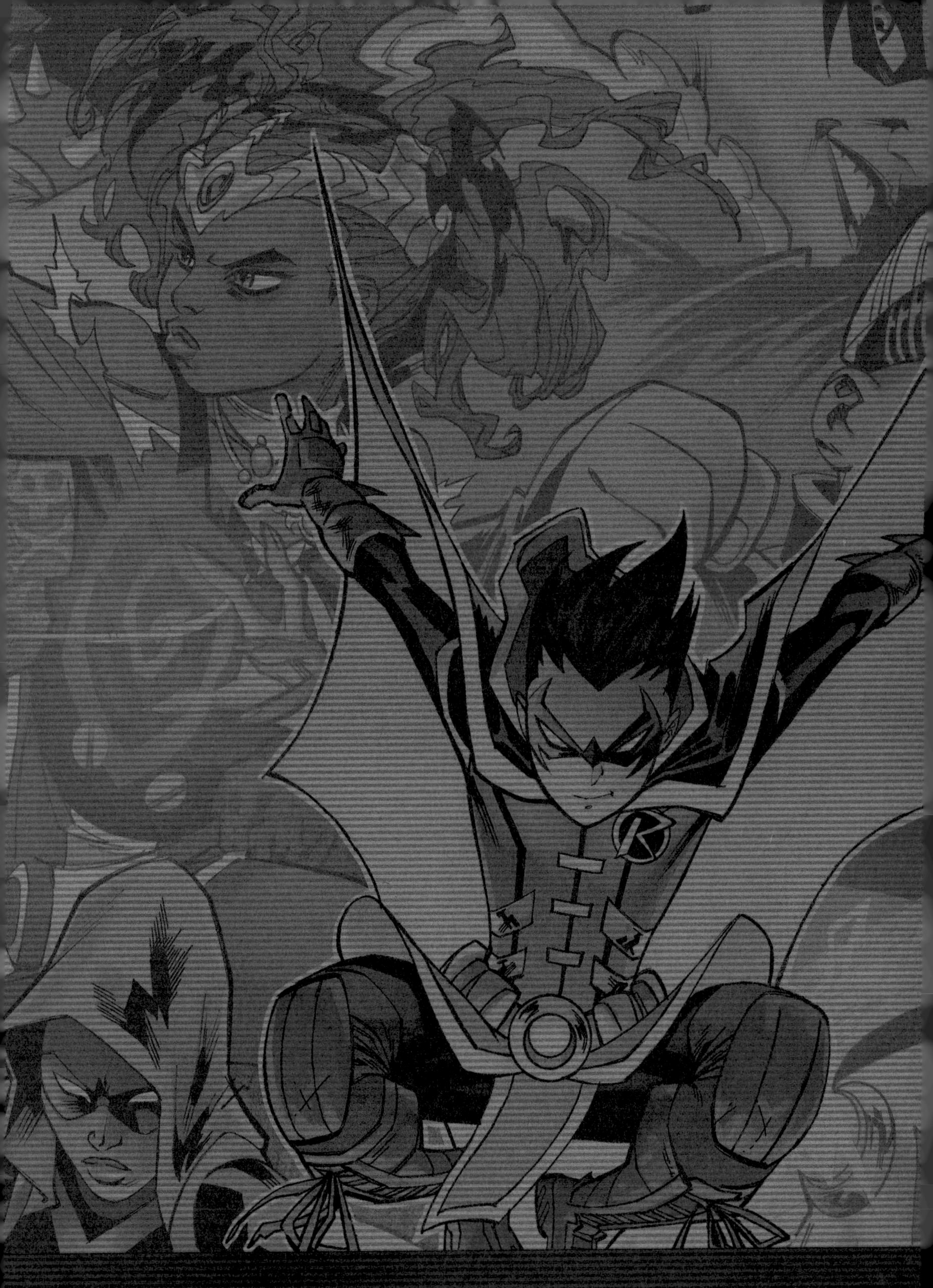

VARIANT COVER GALLERY

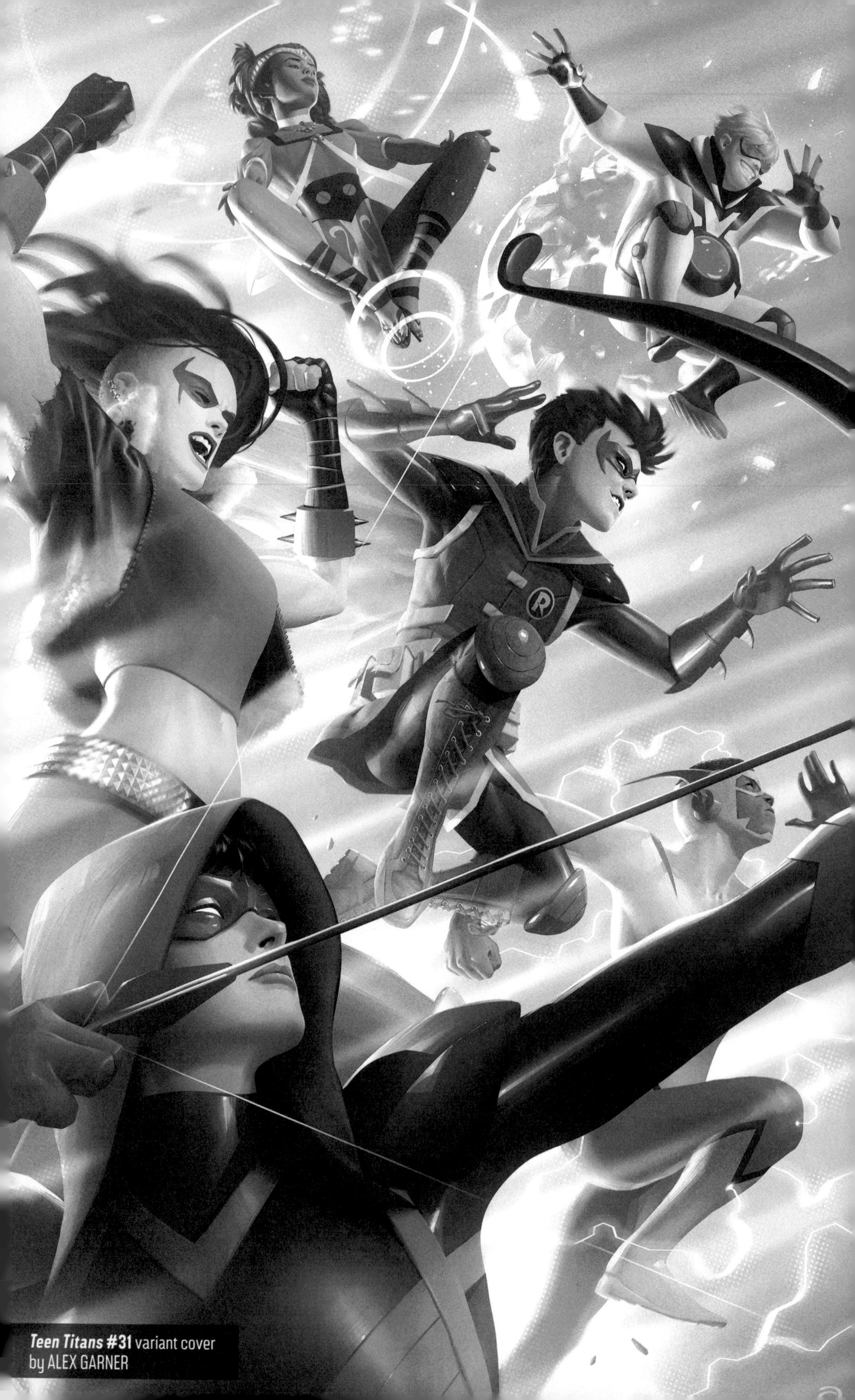

***Teen Titans* #31** variant cover
by ALEX GARNER

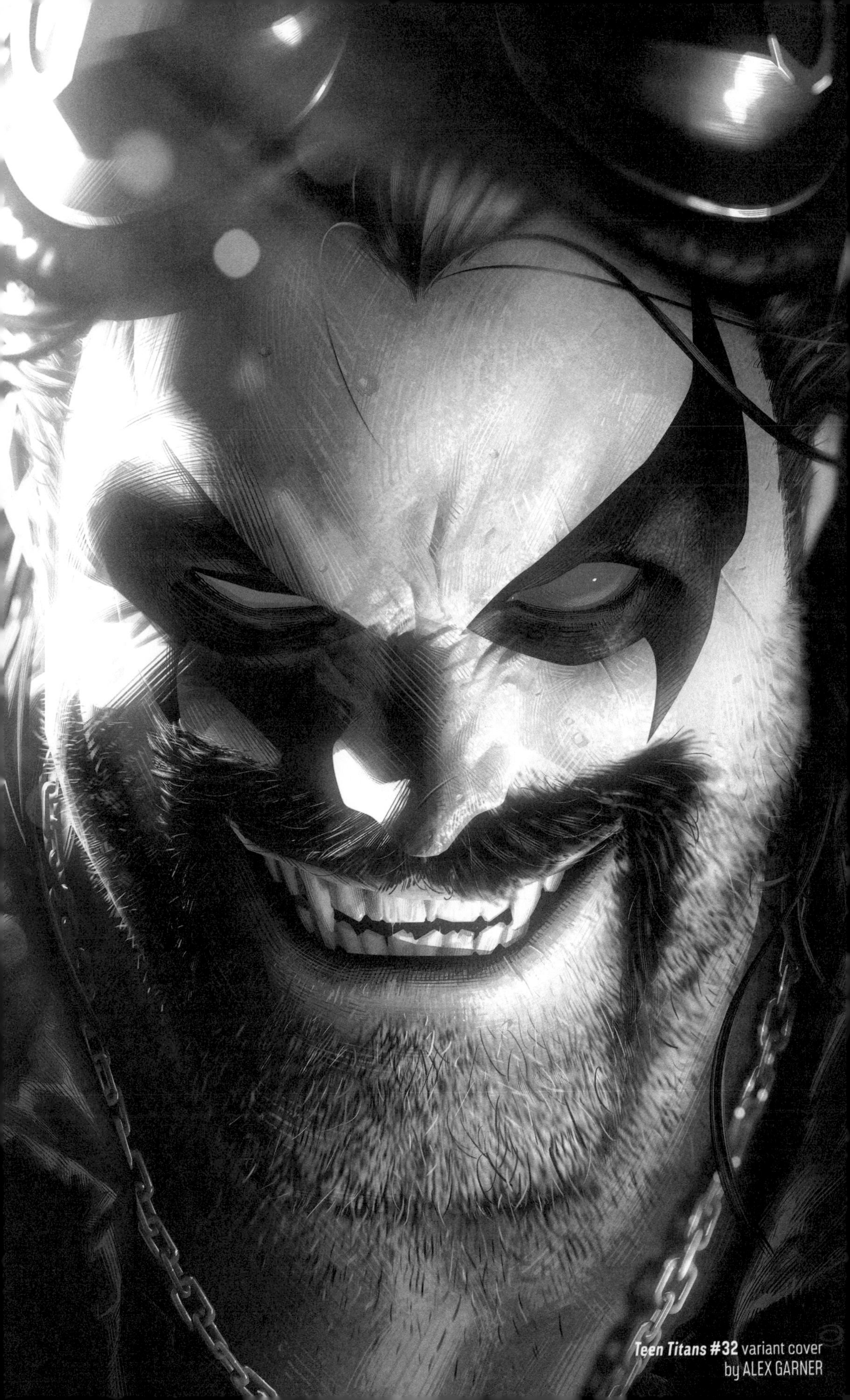

Teen Titans **#32** variant cover
by ALEX GARNER

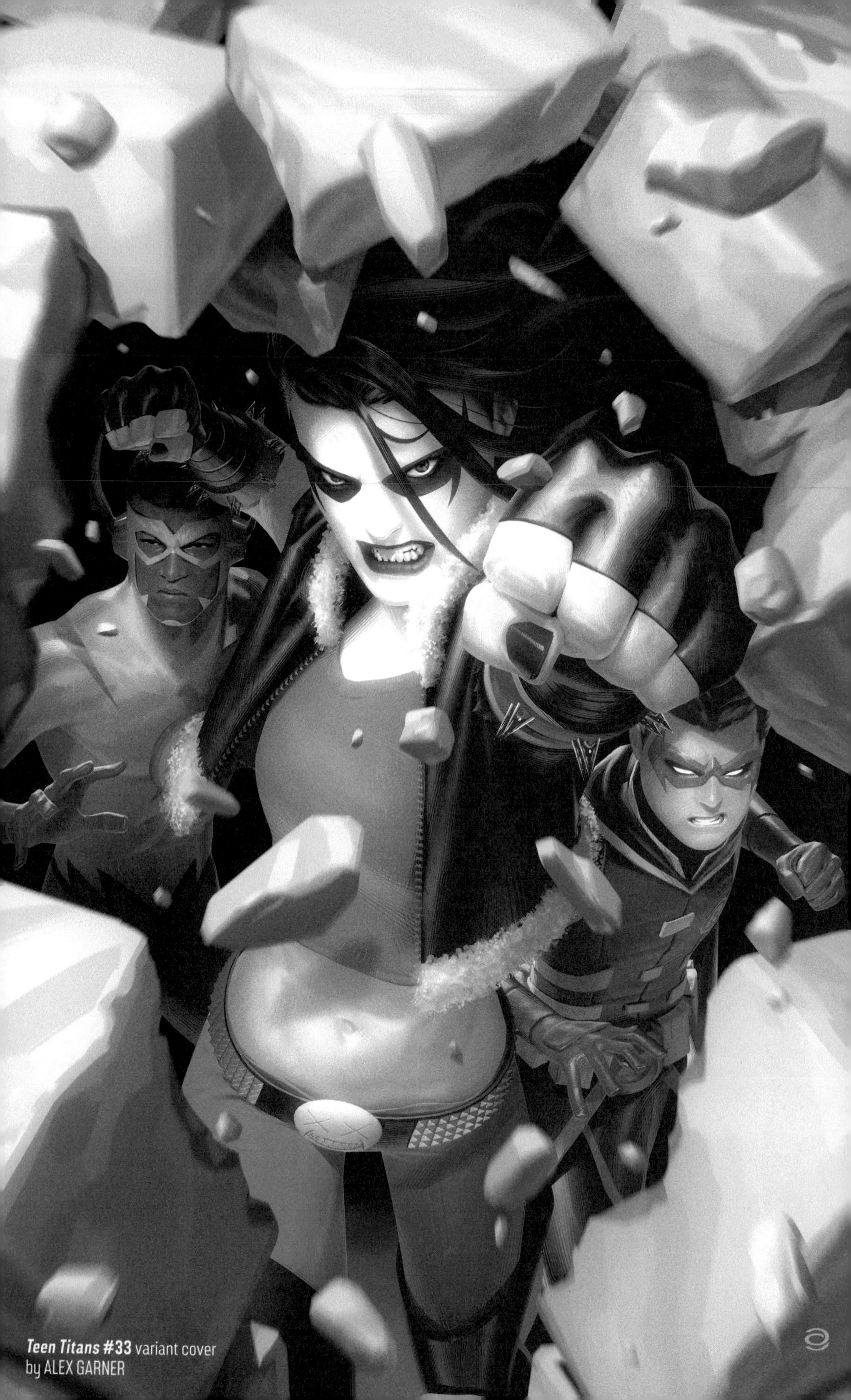

Teen Titans #33 variant cover
by ALEX GARNER

Teen Titans **#34** variant cover
by ALEX GARNER

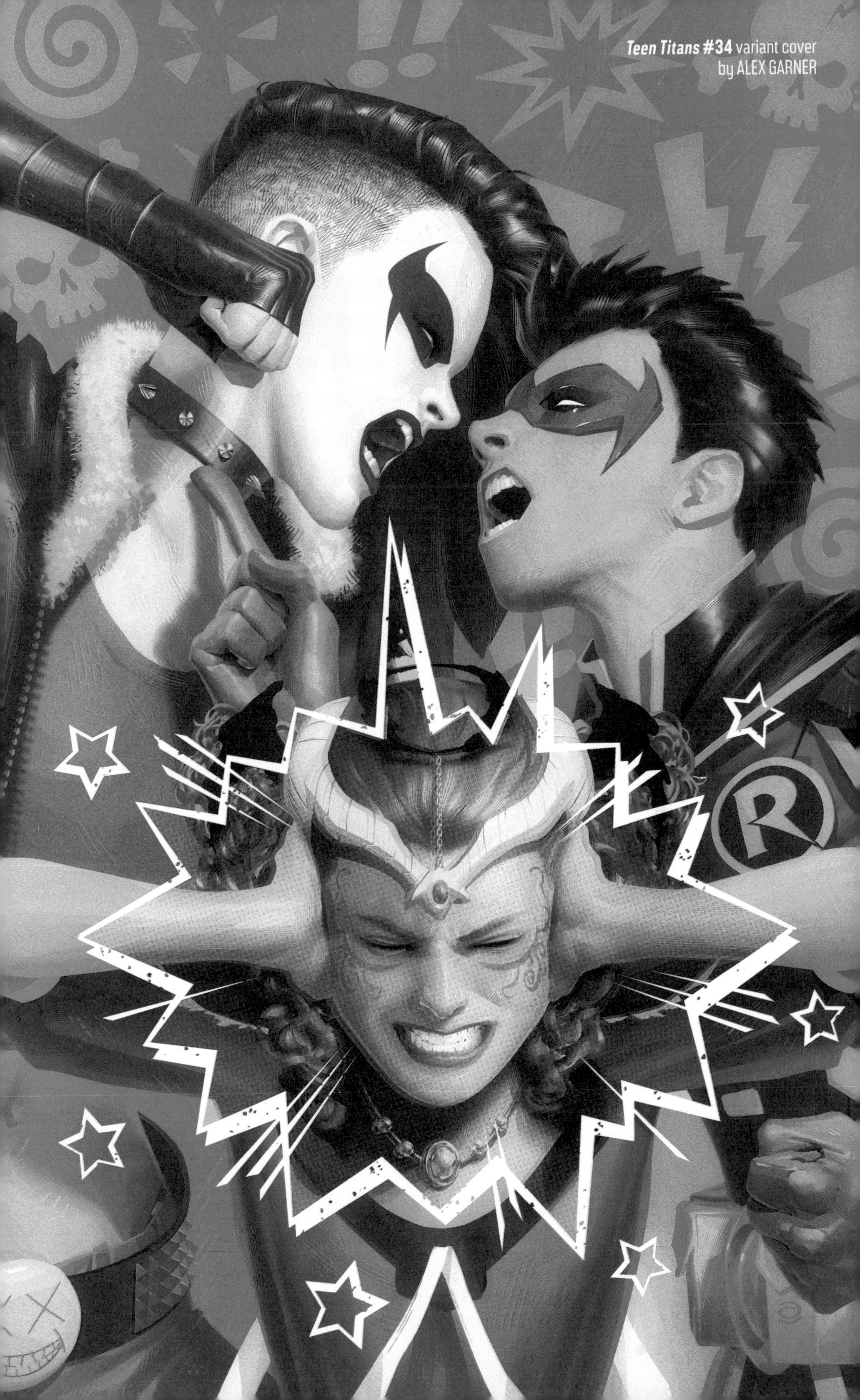

Teen Titans **#35** variant cover
by LEE GARBETT and DAVID CALDERON

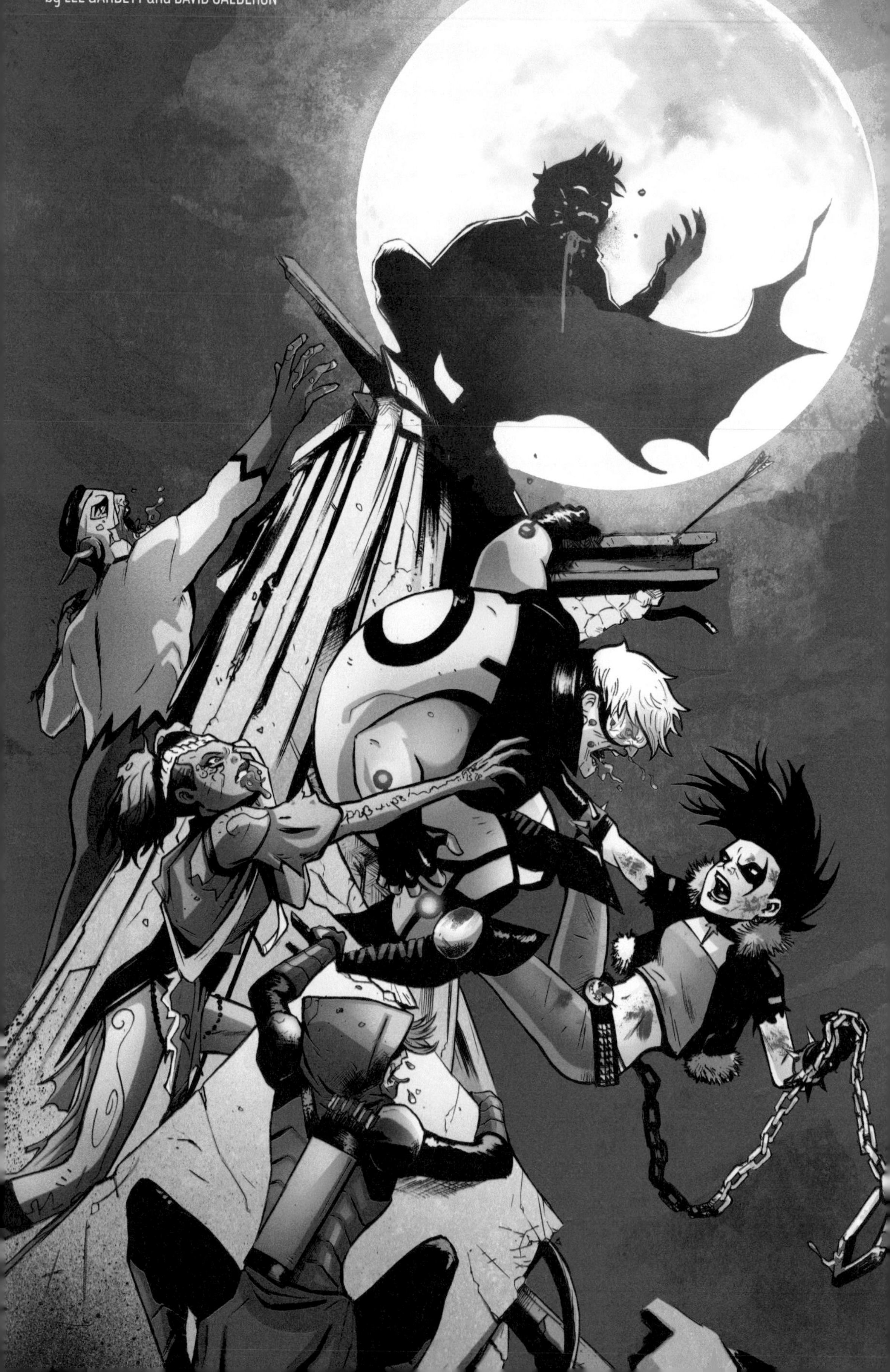

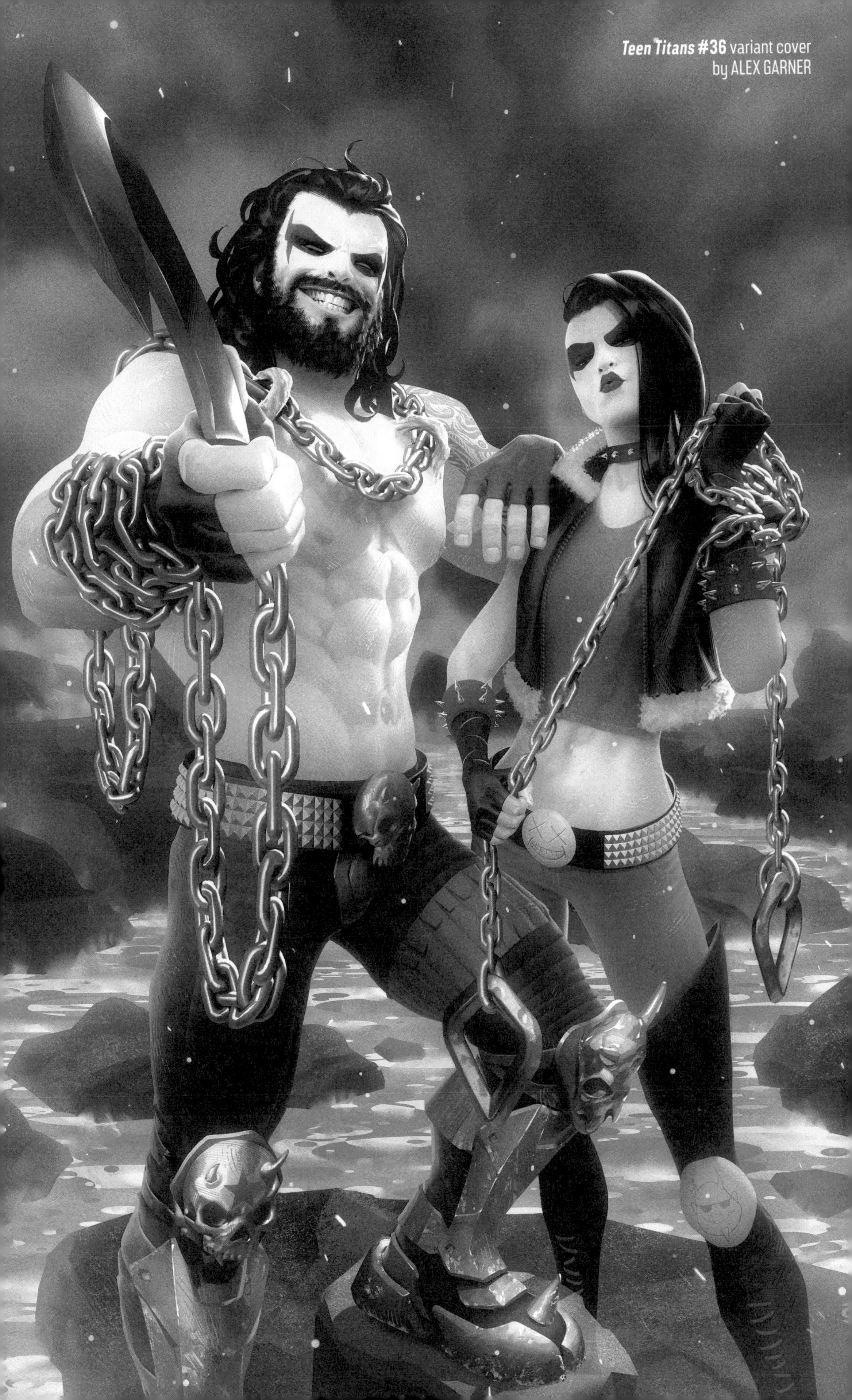

***Teen Titans* #36** variant cover
by ALEX GARNER

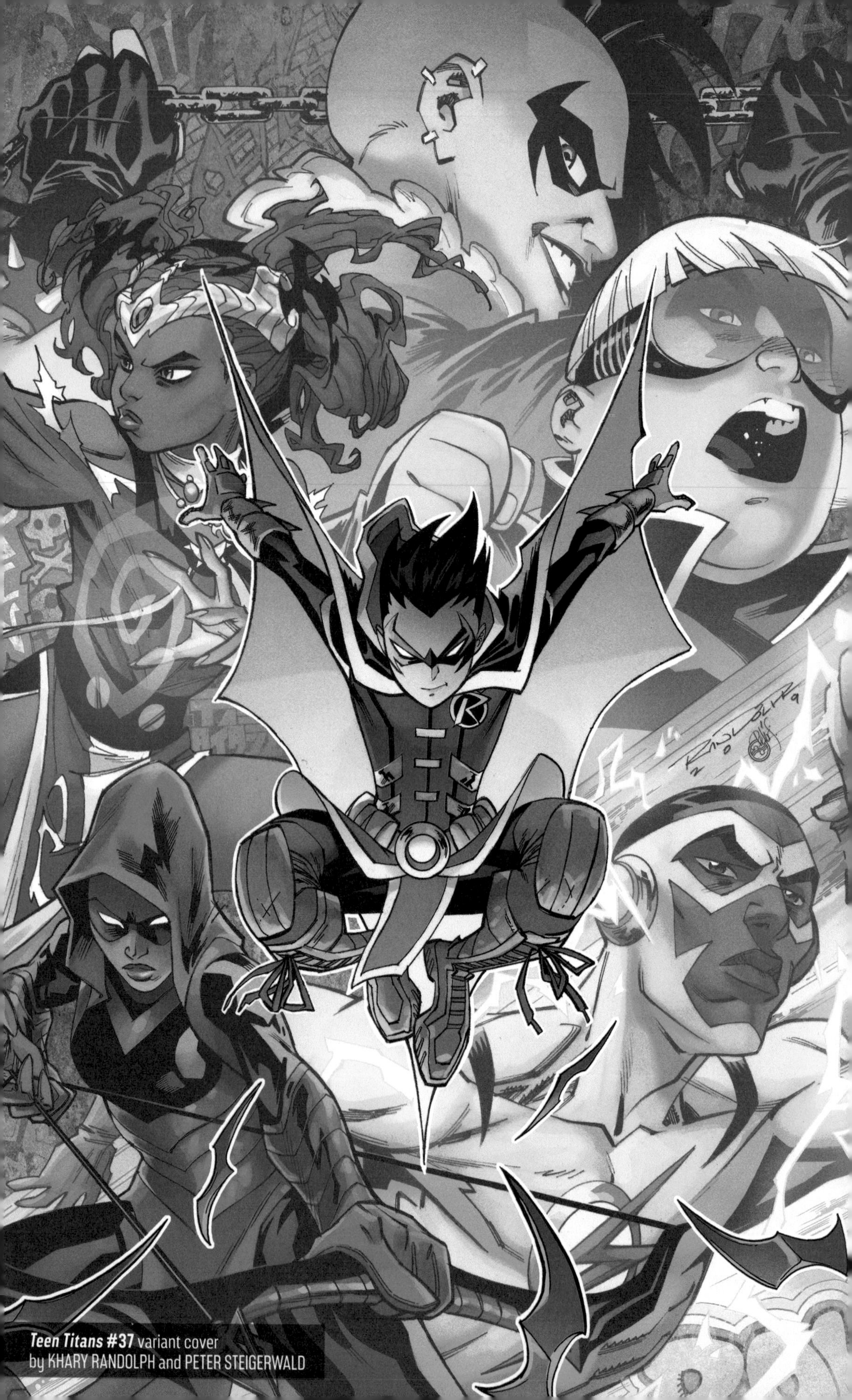

***Teen Titans* #37** variant cover
by KHARY RANDOLPH and PETER STEIGERWALD

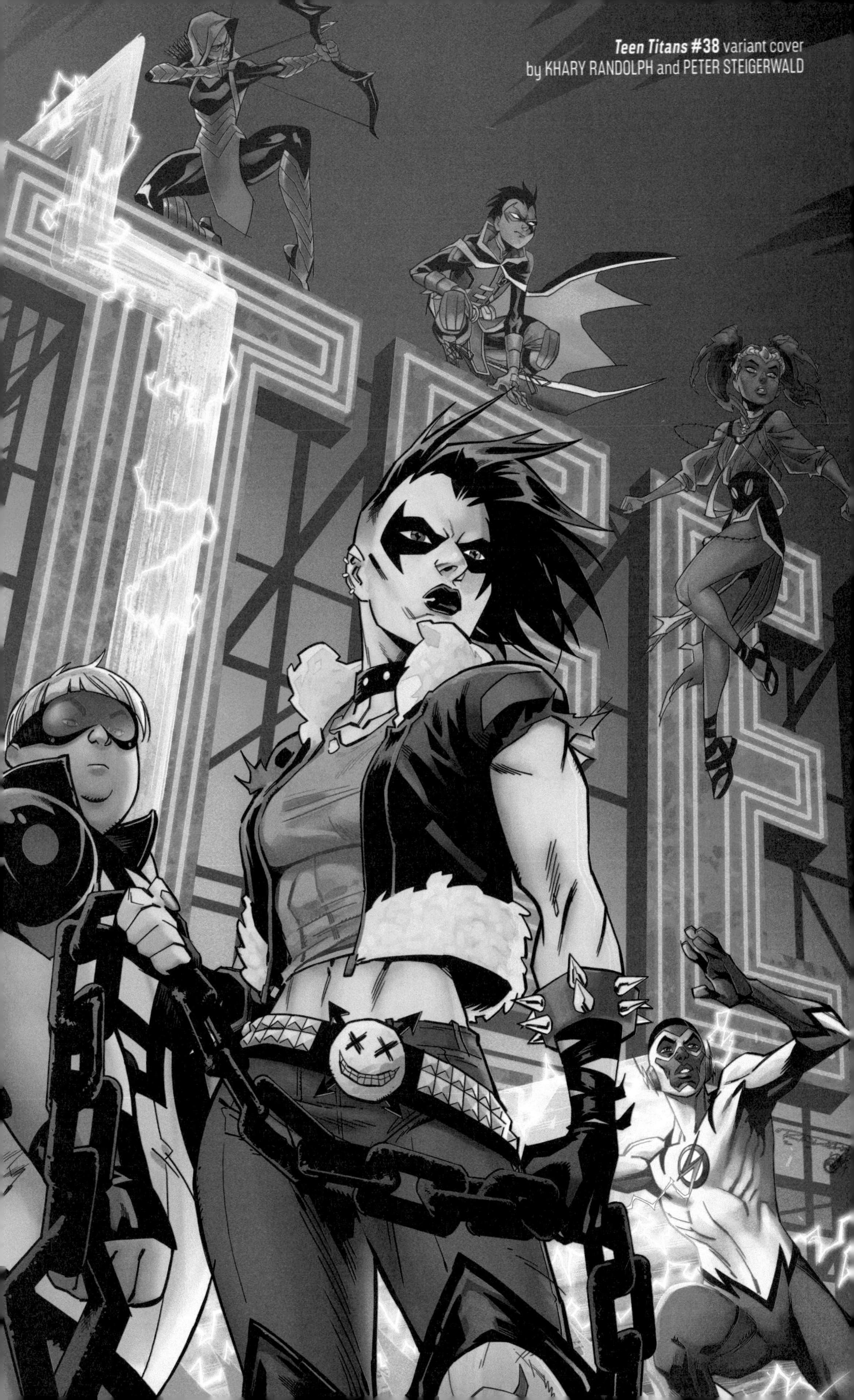

Teen Titans **#38** variant cover
by KHARY RANDOLPH and PETER STEIGERWALD

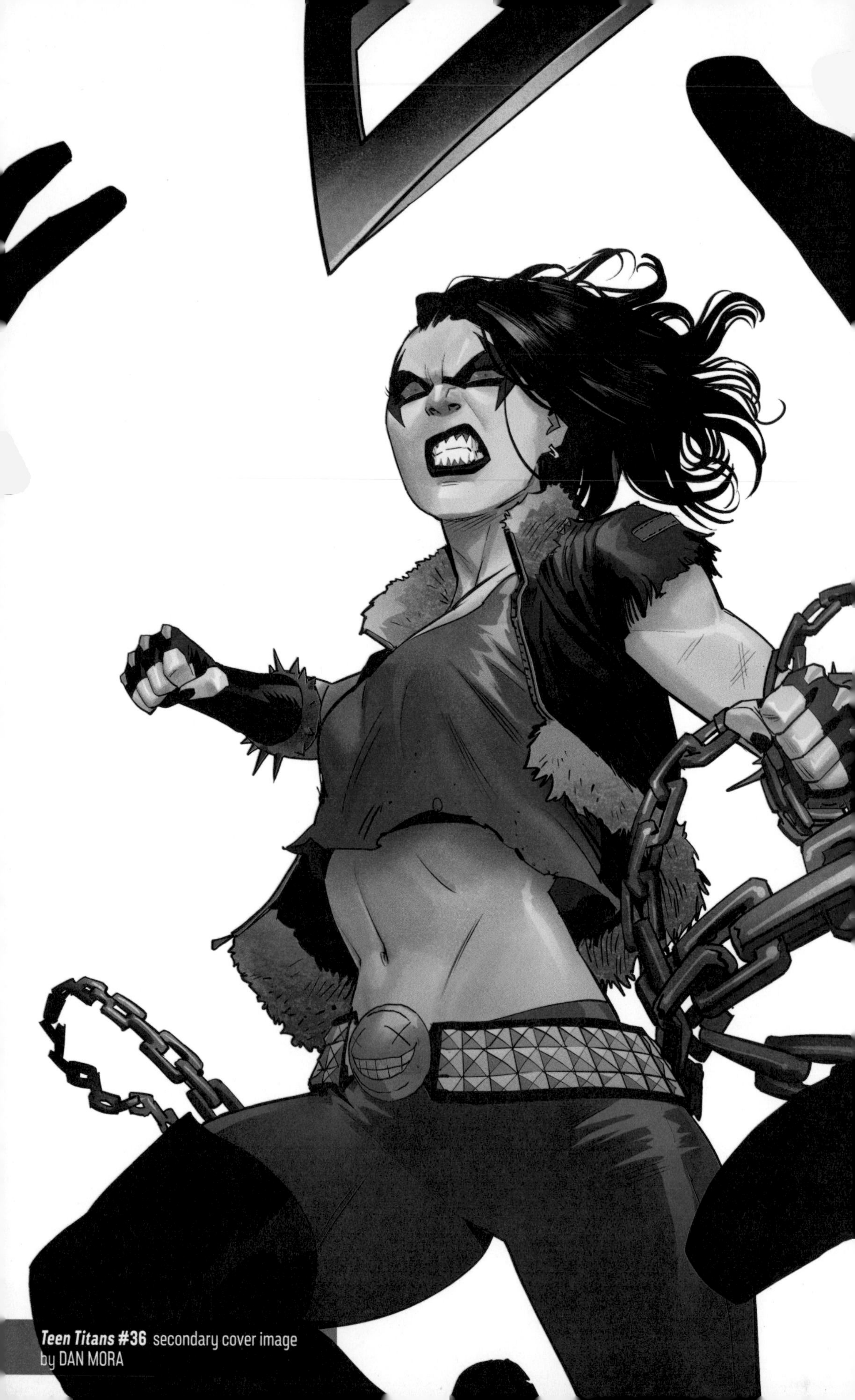

Teen Titans #36 secondary cover image
by DAN MORA

"Brilliantly executed."
–IGN

"Morrison and Quitely have the magic touch that makes any book they collaborate on stand out from the rest."
–MTV's Splash Page

GRANT MORRISON
with FRANK QUITELY & PHILIP TAN

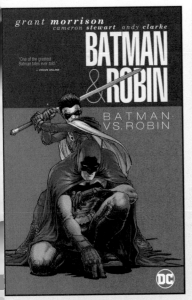

**VOL. 2:
BATMAN VS. ROBIN**

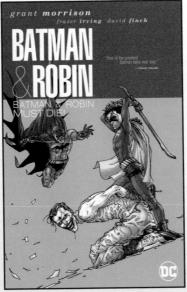

"Thrilling and invigorating... Gotham City that has never looked this good, felt this strange, or been this deadly."
–Comic Book Resources

**VOL. 3:
BATMAN & ROBIN MUST DIE!**

YOUNG JUSTICE
VOL. 1: GEMWORLD
BRIAN MICHAEL BENDIS, PATRICK GLEASON and JOHN TIMMS

GEMWORLD
BRIAN MICHAEL BENDIS
PATRICK GLEASON
JOHN TIMMS

NAOMI
VOL. 1: SEASON ONE

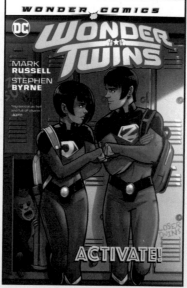

WONDER TWINS
VOL. 1: ACTIVATE!

DIAL H FOR HERO
VOL. 1: ENTER THE HEROVERSE